INDIE BUSINESS POWER

A Step-By-Step Guide for 21st Century Music Entrepreneurs, 2nd Edition

by Peter Spellman

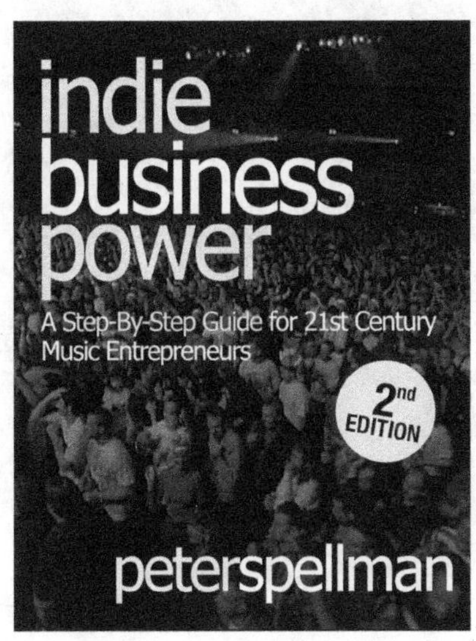

Turning music business data into useful knowledge
ISBN: 978-0-9978723-0-9
Cover design by Mike Roberts

indie business power

A Step-By-Step Guide for 21st Century Music Entrepreneurs

2nd EDITION

peterspellman

Training Resources for 21st Century Music Entrepreneurs

***"Blessed is he who has found his work.
Let him ask no other blessing." – Thomas Carlyle***

INDIE BUSINESS POWER

A Step-By-Step Guide for 21st Century Music Entrepreneurs

TABLE OF CONTENTS – Quick View

INDIE BUSINESS POWER
A Step-By-Step Guide for 21st Century Music Entrepreneurs

TABLE OF CONTENTS – Expanded

BUSINESS CONDUCTING

ACKNOWLEDGEMENTS

Thanks first to those who have helped me see further: The Creator, Linda Sullivan, John Donne, Thomas Carlyle, George Herbert, C.S. Lewis, Herbert Marcuse, Thomas Howard, Paul Saffo, Alvin Toffler, J.R.R. Tolkien, and Lyall Watson.

For their contributions to independent music (and to this book) I wish to thank Jay Andreozzi, John Braheny, Claire Chase, Jandro Cisneros, Dave Cool, Wendy Day, Jeannie Deva, Serona Elton, Kyler England, Patrick Faucher, Eric de Fontenay, Kerry Fiero, Sean Hagon, Norihiko Hibino, Chris Hicks, Keith Holzman, Ariel Hyatt, Ralph Jaccodine, Andreas Katsambas, Steve Kercher, Dan Kimpel, Gerd Leonard, Steve Lurie, Matt McArthur, Bridget McDaniel, Gilli Moon, Panos Panay, Sergio Peramo, Jess Perry, Shea Rose, Clay Shirky, Derek Sivers, Tess Taylor, Randy Tobin, Jenny Toomey, and Sara Wheeler.

Thanks also to Berklee College of Music/Boston Conservatory for continuing to provide a lab in which contemporary music can thrive and from which music entrepreneurs can launch. For their support at different stages of the project, I wish to thank: Julia Bingham, Robert Bloodworth, Ingrid Bock, Scott Canney, Gian Santos, Ky Choi, Dwight Heckelman, Zoe Hillengas, Erin Lyder, Elise MacDonald, Phil Ruokis, Bernise Salim and Michael Silvey.

You all rock!

> **"Perfect freedom is reserved for the man who lives by his own work and in that work does what he wants to do."**
>
> ***– R. G. Collingwood***

INTRODUCTION – THE POWER & CHALLENGE OF ENTREPRENEURSHIP TODAY

"The Industrial Revolution put us to sleep in the name of the efficiencies of functional specialization. It forced us to master very narrow tasks and to blindly follow standard procedures. In many of us, it diminished the capacity to innovate. It's time to reclaim our most creative, most fulfilling, most human functions." – Harry Dent, Job Shock

Indie Business Power is written for artists, songwriters and musical entrepreneurs who want to control their own destinies. Never before have you had such power at your disposal to actually achieve this goal. Technological tools, combined with a rapidly segmenting music marketplace and ever-increasing musical appetites among consumers, have combined to create almost ideal conditions for independent music companies to thrive and prosper in the 21st century.

Independent companies, by their very nature, are better positioned to develop businesses today than corporate ones. In this mercurial music market it is the small and nimble company that has the advantage. Smart micro-businesses can instantly respond to shifts in the marketplace, make quick decisions, and generally turn themselves on a dime.
This is a reflection of the "global paradox" trend-analyst John Naisbett predicted in his book by that title. The subtitle to Naisbett's book says it all: "The larger the world economy, *the more powerful its smallest players".*

The Role of the Entrepreneur in Business

Something huge is happening and it affects us all. A global revolution is changing business, and business is changing the world. With unsettling speed, two forces are converging: a new generation of business leaders rewriting the rules of business, and a new breed of fast companies challenging the corporate status quo.
That convergence overturns 100 years of received wisdom on the fundamentals of work and competition. No part of business is immune. The structure of the company is changing; relationships between companies are changing; the nature of work is changing; the definition of "success" is changing. The result is a revolution as far-reaching as the Industrial Revolution.

It is commonplace to say that we live in the Information Age. But also true is the fact that we live in an *Entrepreneurial* Age.

The twin engines of entrepreneurship and the information economy have ushered in many radical innovations: new forms of technology—from IT to biotech—new patterns in society, new demands on the workplace, even new modes of living we only now are beginning to perceive and appreciate.

Interest in entrepreneurship has never been higher than it is today. A study by Ernst & Young found that 78 percent of influential Americans believe that entrepreneurship will be *the* defining trend of this century. The reasons are not that difficult to see.

Many of the world's largest companies continue to engage in massive downsizing campaigns, drastically cutting the number of managers and workers on their payrolls. This downsizing has all but destroyed the long-standing notion of *job security* in large corporations. As a result, members of Generation X (those born between 1965 and 1976)

and Generation Y (those born between 1977 and 1994) no longer see launching a business as being a risky career path. Having watched large companies lay off their parents after many years of service, these young people see entrepreneurship as the ideal way to create their own job security and success. They are eager to control their own destinies.
We're seeing more and more young, tech-savvy entrepreneurs entering an environment once dominated by adults in suits and ties. This frenzy of teen-driven start-ups is evident in everything from conferences like "Teens in Tech" to highly-trafficked web sites like Ypulse.com. Teens like Fraser Doherty (Superjams), Nick D'Aloisio (Summly), Catherine Cook (Meetme.com formerly Myyearbook.com) are finding news-worthy opportunities to express their entrepreneurial passions.

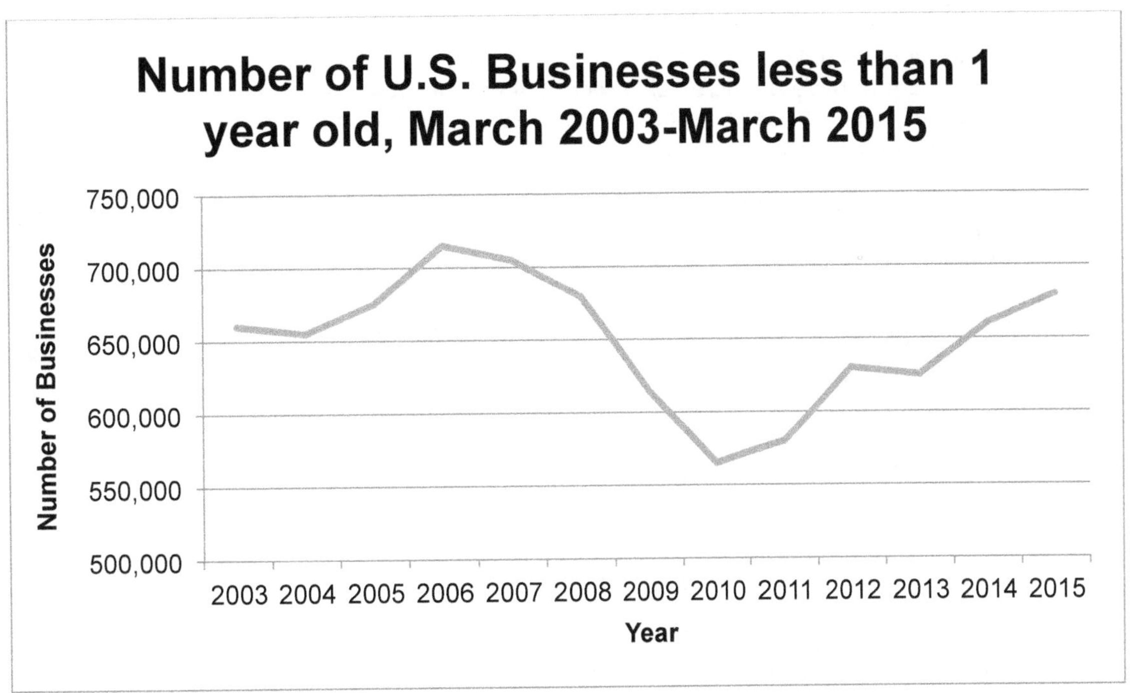

A NEW SURGE IN ENTREPRENEURIAL ACTIVITY

The United States and many other nations are benefiting from this surge in global entrepreneurial activity too. Eastern European countries, China, Vietnam, and many others whose economies were state controlled and centrally planned are now fertile ground for growing small businesses.

One of the most comprehensive studies of global entrepreneurship shows the rate of entrepreneurial activity in different countries around the world. The study found that 13.8 percent of the adult population in the United States is working to start a business. Cameroon and Uganda led the world in entrepreneurial activity with 37.4 and 35.5 percent respectively, whereas only 5.3 percent of adults in Germany were trying to launch companies. Even in stately Great Britain, where total entrepreneurial activity index is a meager 10.7 percent, entrepreneurship is becoming more popular yearly (Source: GEM Population Survey, 2015).

WHY EVERY STUDENT SHOULD START A BUSINESS

Young company founders, like Facebook's Mark Zuckerberg, rid the word *entrepreneur* of its misconceptions – you don't have to hold an MBA to strike it big with a start up. Quite the contrary, young people have a vast number of important entrepreneurial qualities; they tend to be more innovative and more likely to take risks. So here are...

9 Reasons to Abandon Your Fear of Start-Up and Launch a Business Today

1. You gain experience. Owning and running your own business is an incredible way to gain experience and credentials regardless of whether you decide to stay in business once you graduate

2. You have nothing to lose. The worst thing that could happen if your business fails is that you get a job, have an incredible credential on your resume, and have experience that will increase your chances of success in the future. The best thing that can happen is that you'll become the next Microsoft.

3. Two-thirds of millionaires are entrepreneurs, according to Thomas Stanley and William Dank, authors of *The Millionaire Mind*. Michael Furdyk, a successful young entrepreneur, was able to sell his business, MyDesktop.com, for $1 million when he was 16 years old!

4. You develop networking skills. You've likely heard that your network increases your net worth. Consider the fact that by running a business and constantly being in a business community, you will develop excellent contacts.

5. You increase your value. Put simply, starting a business in college increases the value of "the brand called you" and gives you more options.

6. Operating a profitable business in the long term is less risky than being an employee in the long term. I can guarantee the owners of profitable businesses are still with the business. They will be the last people to go down with a ship.

7. You will learn more about yourself and what they don't teach or prepare you for in school. Already having knowledge of these topics before you take classes on them allows you to see more clearly how everything applies.

8. It is yours. You make the rules, create your own hours, work from wherever you want and choose who you want to work with.

9. You'll grow. You'll do things you never thought you could because you have to – and that makes you grow!

Before launching into the nuts & bolts of entrepreneurship, let's first get a sense of the role of small business in American economic life.

First, some telling statistics from the Small Business Administration (sba.gov):

- The 28 million small businesses in America account for 54% of all U.S. sales;
- Small businesses provide 55% of all jobs and 66% of all net new jobs since the 1970s;
- The number of small businesses in the United States has increased 49% since 1982;
- Since 1990, as big business eliminated 4 million jobs, small businesses added 8 million new jobs.
- Research conducted by the NSF (National Science Foundation) concluded that small

- businesses create *four times* more innovations per research & development (R&D) dollar than medium-size firms and *24 times* as many as large companies. Hundreds of important inventions trace their roots to an entrepreneur including the zipper, FM radio, lasers, air conditioning, the escalator, the light bulb, the automatic transmission, and the personal computer.

> **Thomas Edison** discovered over 1800 ways how *not* to make a light bulb before hitting on a design that worked!
>
> 'Failure' means *Forward!*

In the same way that independent record labels have been the R&D (research and development) labs for larger record companies (taking the risk, discovering talent, developing product and pre-testing the market), so have small businesses been the life blood of the larger economy. They are the creative "labs" in which innovative products and services are born.

In the marketplace, new small businesses often have advantages over the larger, well-established corporate institutions. Think of the difference between a fleet of luxury liners and a speedboat. When it comes to making a change, the smaller, more maneuverable speedboat has the edge. Like a speedboat, a small business can easily maneuver around the huge corporate boats. It doesn't require the deep waters of enormous capital investment necessary to launch the giant corporate fleets. It can play in the shallow waters of innovation. Consequently, small businesses often discover and develop ideas that larger corporations won't even touch until there is a "proven market".

And while the economic downturn is forcing entrepreneurs to handle their operations more efficiently, either by sharing office space or by honing their sales efforts through deeper market research, there continues to be an unabated explosion of business startups.
The Trendwatching Institute dubs this trend the Rise of the "Minipreneurs": a vast army of consumers turning entrepreneurs, including small and micro businesses, freelancers, side-businesses, weekend entrepreneurs, web-driven entrepreneurs, part-timers, free agents, cottage businesses, seniorpreneurs, co-creators, mompreneurs, crowdpreneurs, pro-ams [professional-amateurs], solopreneurs, eBay traders, advertising-sponsored bloggers and so on.
Some statistics on this vast group are something of a surprise:

- According to Bloomberg, Amazon's pool of merchants doubled to about 2 million in 2014, and eBay merchants increased to 25 million that same year;
- Over 50,000 people in the UK draw a significant portion of their income from selling goods online. A study by the Centre for Economics and Business Research (CEBR) shows that the average household boosts its earnings by GBP 3,000 through online trading.
- And MasterCard and Warillow International published a research study on a new class of small business: the 'Web-Driven Entrepreneur', estimating that there are 5 million of these businesses in the United States, representing 25% of all small businesses.

Source: trendwatching.com

Most of these mini-businesses are run by solo entrepreneurs – another trend that seems to be on the rise, as the chart below indicates.

Top 10 Entrepreneurial Countries

1. United States
2. Canada
3. Australia
4. Denmark
5. Sweden
6. Taiwan
7. Iceland
8. Switzerland
9. United Kingdom
10. France

Source: *2016 Global Entrepreneurship Index*

The Entrepreneurial Mindset

Even a casual glance at history suggests that entrepreneurs have always existed and always "made waves" in their societies. Vast fortunes were certainly amassed by entrepreneurs of the past such as John D. Rockefeller, Andrew Carnegie, and Cornelius Vanderbilt. However, considerable evidence suggests that more people than ever are pursuing, or considering, this role today.

While it's easy to see this flurry of entrepreneurial activity, it's less easy to define it. At its roots, the word "entrepreneurship" derives from the French word meaning "to undertake". Many definitions of "entrepreneur" and "entrepreneurship" have been put forth over the years. Here are several of the more popular ones:

- "Entrepreneurship is the process of bearing the risk of buying at certain prices and selling at uncertain prices," (Richard Cantillon, 18th century);

- An entrepreneur is the agent "who unites all means of production and who finds in the value of the products...the reestablishment of the entire capital he employs, and the value of the wages, the interest, and rent which he pays, as well as profits belonging to himself," (Jean Baptiste, 19th century);

- "Entrepreneurs attempt to predict and act upon change within markets, taking the role in bearing the uncertainty of market dynamics. Entrepreneurs are required to perform such fundamental managerial functions as direction and control," (Frank Knight, 1921);

- "The entrepreneur is the innovator who implements change within markets through the carrying out of new combinations. The role of entrepreneurship is to assemble and deploy resources in new combinations that disrupt the otherwise static nature of the market," (Joseph Schumpter, 1934);

- "Entrepreneurs innovate. Innovation is the specific instrument of entrepreneurship. It is the act that endows resources with a new capacity to create wealth. Innovation, indeed, creates a resource," (Peter Drucker, 1985).

These classic definitions give us a sense of the attitudes and skills of the entrepreneur: risk-taker, opportunity-discoverer, manager, value-creator, innovator, market disruptor, creative coordinator.

The Entrepreneurship Center at Miami University, Ohio has one of the better formal definitions of entrepreneurship I've come across: "Entrepreneurship is the process of identifying, developing, and bringing a vision to life. The vision may be an innovative idea, an opportunity, or simply a better way to do something. The end result of this process is the creation of a new venture, formed under conditions of risk and considerable uncertainty." Artist Shea Rose offers some different language to describe what she does as a creative entrepreneur: "Transforming intuitive visions into tangible experiences through collaboration, partnerships and enterprise." I think that's pretty good.

The Artist-Entrepreneur

Lately, we've seen a number of people latching onto the phrase "artist-entrepreneur", an idea that expresses the emotional and creative sides of entrepreneurship. It's suggested that all entrepreneurs should approach their business ideas with the same passion and creativity that an artist might approach her canvas, or cello or potter's wheel. This idea is reflective of a larger trend I've noticed where business literature is employing arts and music-related metaphors to describe how business should be conducted today. For example, Harvard Business School instructor John Kao wrote a book in 1997 called *Jamming.* In it he suggested the improvisational jazz ensemble as an instructive model for conducting business in a fast-changing environment.

Workplace analyst Daniel Pink proposed *A Whole New Mind: Why Right-Brainers Will Rule the Future.* In this book he explores different dimensions of artistic creativity (Design, Story, Symphony, Empathy, Play and Meaning) and how they will help us engage with the world of careers and business. He senses a new valuing of "right-brain" thinkers in our societies where creativity and intuition are perceived to contribute as much as formal analysis and traditional logic have in the past.

Artist-entrepreneurs may not necessarily even have set out to start a business. Their main focus may be on developing their own craft, but they soon face a need to come to terms with a commercial environment in order to be able to make enough money to continue their artistic work, or they see the commercial market as a means of communicating with a larger audience. From this then evolves developing the necessary management and organizational skills to facilitate the performance and promotion of their work (e.g. organizing touring productions/companies, writing business plans and understanding of copyright and contractual issues).

Of course, this is quite familiar to musicians. Most music-related work is of a freelance nature requiring personal success skills like organization, self-promotion and management. This has along history. Even Beethoven worked hard securing gigs, hanging fliers and negotiating his fees. "I don't feel 'business' puts a damper on the pleasure of making music," says Sean Hagon, owner of Music Media Solutions. "The business side of things creates the music making opportunities. When one is feeding the creative soul at any level and consistently, then one can feel fulfilled."

Freelancing and self-employment are perhaps the most familiar types of employment in the creative sector. There are large concentrations of small enterprises and sole proprietors in music and the performing arts, film, TV and radio. Enterprises of this nature tend to remain small-scale because of the creative nature of the activities involved; 'artist-entrepreneurs' need to have control over their creativity and the integration of innovation into their practice.

The Path Within: "Intrapreneuring"

Find the biggest problem your employer faces for which you and your skills are the solution.

– Robert Horton, Executive Recruiter

Anyone who has worked for a company for any length of time knows who the intrapreneurs are. They are the staff members who are always sparking new ideas, finding solutions, taking on new initiatives and coming up with creative strategies for furthering the company's mission.

We can define *intrapreneuring* as creating and maintaining the innovation and flexibility of a small business environment within the confines of a larger bureaucratic structure. While the focus will be on entrepreneurship throughout this book, it's important to note that individuals can act entrepreneurially in many different contexts, including large corporations.

Dave Cool (yes, that's his real name) is Director of Artistry & Industry Outreach at Bandzoogle, a service that empowers artists to create a web presence. "I'm fortunate to be given a lot of freedom within the departments at the company that I help to oversee, mainly Communications and Partnerships," says Cool. "Some of that involves budgetary decisions, especially when it comes to sponsorships and events. But it also includes the freedom to make strategic decisions, which can be as simple as which articles to run on our blog, to which events we'll sponsor and attend, as well as which companies we will or won't work with." At the end of the day, Cool feels a personal sense of accomplishment. "If I feel that I can take ownership over the work I'm doing and that it's having an impact, it motivates me to succeed."

Since most innovations have come from people in small businesses (entrepreneurs), it's logical that many companies encourage a corporate culture receptive to new ideas. The good news is, intrapreneurship is catching on. Google has long been an advocate. Products like Gmail, Google News, and Adsense resulted from its Innovation Time Off program, in which employees are able to devote 20% of their work day to independent endeavors. Other organizations, including marketing and engineering firms, are eager to follow Google's lead.

With today's ever-changing workplace, we are all expected to be entrepreneurs to stay competitive and promote our value to employers. It is recommended that you work to promote yourself within whatever company you find yourself in. Try to position yourself as the go-to person, and keep an eye out for ways you can save your employer money or increase profits in tough times. Volunteer for assignments, be cheerful, maintain high visibility, and follow up with your boss to keep him or her abreast of your accomplishments – in other words, act like an entrepreneur.

If you do plan on working for a company, even temporarily, try seeing yourself as "self employed" and your company as your "client". This has to do with *mind set.* The following chart compares and contrasts the two different mindsets.

THE EMPLOYEE VS. INTRAPRENEUR MIND-SET	
The Employee Mind-Set	**The Intrapreneur Mind-Set**
Blending in	Having a distinct personal identity
Seeking job security	Seeking employability security (the ability to find work)
Sticking to a linear, predictable career path	Looking for the next career opportunity; being open to alternate paths
Emphasizing company loyalty	Focusing on loyalty to a project, to your profession, to your coworkers, and to yourself
Striving for career success	Aiming for work/life blending (holistic life success)
Being a "company person" (merging your identity with your company values)	Understanding how you and your personal brand fir in with your company's work culture
Relying on academic degrees to open doors	Building on lifelong learning

Seeking a particular position or title	Showcasing your competencies
Depending on full-time employment	Embracing fluid, "gig" employment – Hollywood style
Hoping for a single job to carry you through your career	Knowing you'll have multiple positions in your work life
Creating an externally driven career	Creating a self-driven career

The Power In Your Corner

The real social revolution of the last 30 years, one we are still living through, is the switch from a life that is largely organized for us to a world in which we are all forced to be in charge of our own destiny. *– Charles Handy*

In recent years, the allure of entrepreneurship has increased, with the result that more people than ever are choosing this path as a career. What are some of the forces driving this trend?

• ***The rapid growth of networked business*** - Internet and intranets (networks within companies) are allowing for a greater flow of information and quicker decision-making. The Internet alone is responsible for enabling thousands of companies to affordably transact commerce on a global scale, no matter what their size.

• ***A rapidly segmenting marketplace*** - Mass markets are giving way to "micro markets" as customers demand to have it *their way*. Small companies can focus on these niche markets; those that can meet these markets' demands most effectively will be the winners.

• ***Plug and play technology infrastructures*** - Smart phones, affordable laptops, fax machines, copiers, scanners, and wireless technology have brought the look and efficiencies of larger companies to the fingertips of micro business owners worldwide. Digital recording technology has literally revolutionized the music business and sparked the emergence of whole new genres of music, most notably hip-hop, dance/electronica and new age.

• ***Opportunities for minorities and women*** – The number of businesses owned by African-Americans, Hispanic people and Asian-Americans has seen double-digit growth in recent years. Over the last 15 years, women-owned firms have grown by one and a half times the rate of other small enterprises and now account for almost 30 percent of all businesses. Additionally, one in five firms with revenue of $1 million or more is woman-owned as of 2014, according to the Center for Women's Business Research.

To repeat, these enormous developments overturn 100 years of received wisdom about the fundamentals of work, markets and competition. The structure of the company is changing; relationships between companies are changing; the nature of work is changing; the definition of success is changing. The result is a revolution as far-reaching as the Industrial Revolution was in its own day.

We are just beginning to comprehend this new world even as we create it. This much we know: we live and work in a time of unparalleled opportunity and unprecedented uncertainty. An economy driven by technology and innovation makes old borders obsolete. We also should not forget the words of Peter Parker's Uncle Ben as he lay dying on a NY street: "Remember, with great power comes great responsibility".

We are at a turning point in the history of business practice and its accelerant is the Internet. Because the internet is still so new and dynamic, there are few set rules about how to use it to build and market a business. Non-conventional, small business tactics are capturing market share from large established corporations. And this trend will continue in most industries, especially those that trade in "information" (e.g., music, software, video, film, etc.).

We've seen a shift from an industrial-based society to an information-based society: from brawn to brainpower, from manufacturing to services, from mainframe to microprocessor, and from big, smokestack-belching heavy industries vertically integrated under hierarchical management structures to the lighter, cleaner, more decentralized technology industries horizontally networked into matrices of "virtual" organizations. Welcome to the Entrepreneurial Age.

What's Inside?...Chapter-By-Chapter

The first ten chapters of ***INDIE BUSINESS POWER*** cover the ***ARRANGEMENT*** of a successful start up business. Beginning with chapter 11 we move into the ***CONDUCTING*** of the business – that is, the managing and growing of a successful music-related company today.

Throughout we'll meet various music entrepreneurs who will tell us in their own words what it means to be and live the entrepreneurial life. What makes them tick? How did they make their mark? And, most importantly, what can we learn form them for our own ideas and projects today?

BUSINESS ARRANGEMENT

In **Chapter 1** the focus is on *you*, the independent music entrepreneur. Are you ready to undertake this task? Do you have the state of mind needed for an entrepreneurial venture? Better find out now before you flush your hard-earned money down the toilet. Starting and running a business will require a good measure of skill, personality and stamina. We'll look at these dimensions, as well as a number of crucial questions you must answer before jumping into your venture.

Chapter 2 explores the players and dynamics of *today's transforming music business*. The immense shift from the traditional music biz paradigms to "new economy" paradigms is creating unprecedented opportunities for music entrepreneurs of all stripes. We'll look at how the money flows in this industry and where some of the key areas for profit lie for those starting companies today.

Chapter 3 puts the focus on *discovering opportunity* in the transforming business world described in the previous chapter, and then developing an effective marketing mindset that understands the customer you will be targeting with your product or service.

Chapter 4 introduces the *key business information resources* you will need to run your fledgling company creatively and intelligently. Throughout history it has been those with the best information and contacts who have had the power to steer the course of their times, no matter their size. Today the right information often makes the difference between success and failure in business. Fortunately, business information is hyper-abundant today and this chapter filters out the best information and support resources for operating a music-related company today. Pay close attention; these may someday save your life.

Existing evidence suggests that new ventures that draw a careful bead on specific markets or specific geographic areas are more successful than ones that do not focus their efforts in this way. So **Chapter 5** applies the preceding chapter's vast information resources to the market research necessary to put an *effective communication strategy* together for taking your product of service out to the world.

Chapter 6 gets into the nitty-gritty of *planning for success* – outlining your business plan. What is your company's mission? What are its short- and long-range goals? How will you legally structure your business? Should you incorporate now, wait, or not incorporate at all? What kind of budget will you need and how will you raise the necessary funds? How do you write a formal business plan and how do you prepare it for investor formation? These and many other related questions are tackled in this chapter.

Chapter 7 explores *the power of the Internet* and how to put its power to work for your business through the use of a full-spectrum web presence, the integration of ecommerce and the implementation of a dynamic web marketing plan.

Chapter 8 addresses ways you can *finance your business.* Everything from traditional approaches like bank loans and self-financing, to special micro-loan programs "angel" investments, and crowdfunding are covered. The age-old arrangement called bartering is also explored and realistic guidelines for giving yourself the money-hunting edge when appealing to the investor community are exposed.

Chapter 9 goes over all your *paperwork checklists*: required business licenses, tax obligations, insurance coverage, music copyrights, business trademarks and servicemarks, barcodes, union agreements and, of course, contracts. These documents will provide definition and description to your many business transactions. Keeping all this paperwork well-managed and current will save you countless headaches in the long run. We'll look at some practical ways to make this as painless as possible.

Chapter 10 looks at the *essential equipment* you will need to run your business smoothly and efficiently. From creating the right physical space to the best kinds of software to run your business; from guidelines for setting up a project studio to ergonomically correct chairs – this section provides you with all you need to know for setting up the optimal music business office for your specific needs.

With Chapter 11 we move into the strategic management or ***Conducting*** of your start up company. Management is essentially orchestrating the flow of energies, whether it's your energy or that of others, the energies of time, information, money and marketing. Strategic management *focuses* you, your team, your time, your money and your marketing efforts.

BUSINESS CONDUCTING

If it's true that management incompetence is the #1 reason for most business failures, then it is crucial for the music executive to learn and practice good management skills. Like a conductor, the business owner-manager coordinates the work, times its execution, and prompts its workers to bring out their best. This is why we explore tried-and-true ways for *managing your company* and its processes in five chapters (11-15). These chapters will take you out of "crisis mode" (always reacting to your business) and put you into "creative mode" (consistently pro-acting on behalf of your business).

Chapter 11 digs into the elements of *successfully building your team*. Discussed are ways to define your talent requirements, create effective job descriptions, build your advisory board, make the most of meetings, and develop your company internship program.

In **Chapter 12** we'll look at management in two of its many expressions: *management of self, and of your team*.

Chapter 13 covers *management of time and information*. These form the nervous system of your business success.

Chapter 14 digs into the elements of *smart money management* and how to put financial strategies in place that will help you maximize your revenue.

Chapter 15 highlights all the *marketing and branding tactics* that will help boost your profile in the marketplace and increase profits.

Chapter 16 provides guidance for *future company growth*, primarily through "diversification" – conceiving and developing different expressions of your business and their possible revenue streams. We'll look at these, as well as explore joint ventures with larger companies and other creative alliances. Also included are some key tips to follow when planning to expand internationally.

At the end of each chapter you will find **Resource Directories** containing all the important contact info and resources discussed in that chapter.

Indie Business Power is designed to give you all the "best practices" for starting, operating and succeeding in a music business of your own. It's a manual you can refer to again and again to help keep you on track toward your goals.

Entrepreneurs *Are* the Economic Stimulus!

In August 2008, the United States economy lost 259,000 jobs, and the unemployment rate rose to 6.1 percent. The country was in the midst of a stretch of twenty-three consecutive months of job losses. That same month, the startup Airbnb was officially formed. Seven months later, in March 2009, the U.S. economy lost 824,000 jobs, and the unemployment rate rose to 8.7 percent, on its way to peaking at 10 percent shortly after. That same month, the startup Uber launched a prototype, and Airbnb was admitted to startup accelerator Y Combinator.

Today, Uber is valued at $51 billion, and Airbnb is valued at $25.5 billion. The two companies represent the vanguard of both the "unicorn club" and what is variously known as the "sharing," "peer-to-peer," or "on-demand" economy. They also have come to represent modern American entrepreneurship, the phenomenon that fuels our economy and ensures job creation and growth.

In fact, in any given year, new and young businesses create nearly all net new jobs in the U.S. economy. Put more starkly: if you want new jobs, then you want new and young firms. Older, established companies tend, on balance, to be net destroyers of jobs.
This apparently straightforward conclusion, however, becomes more complicated when we examine new and young businesses more closely. Each year, tens of thousands of new companies are formed in the United States. Many of these companies don't survive. On average, 20 percent will fail within two years, and half won't make it past the five-year mark. Most of those that do survive will not grow significantly in terms of revenue or employment; the vast majority of new and young companies will remain small businesses. Only a handful of young firms grow much more rapidly than most others.

Indeed, much of the net job creation and productivity attributed to startups comes from this small group of fast-growing firms like Airbnb and Uber and those on the Inc. 5000 list of new, young, and fast-growing firms. At the ninetieth percentile, some of these young companies enjoy employment growth rates of between 60 and 100 percent each year. Some of them grow rapidly to fifty employees and then remain there; others grow to employ a few thousand people.

And, importantly for the economy, these young, high-growth firms can be found in every sector, not just high tech. In this respect, the United States is not unique—many developed and emerging economies have similar patterns wherein new companies and high-growth young companies account for nearly all net job creation. Economists describe this distribution by saying that there is a lot of "skewness" among young firms. This skewness, or dispersion, is a feature of entrepreneurial growth and is the heart of dynamism and job creation.

– The Looming Entrepreneurial Boom, http://www.kauffman.org

BUSINESS

'ARRANGEMENT'

A piece of music that has been adapted for performance by a particular set of voices or instruments;

The pattern into which a group of things is organized;

Plans and preparations that you must make so that something can happen;

An orderly grouping (of things or persons) considered as a unit.

1

CHARACTERISTICS OF A SUCCESSFUL MUSIC ENTREPRENEUR

"If we did all we were capable of doing, we would literally astonish ourselves."
– Thomas Edison

A true definition of an entrepreneur comes closer to: A poet, visionary, or packager of social change.
– Robert Schwartz

Many successful entrepreneurs share characteristics that set them apart from most other business owners – for example, creative resourcefulness and a relentless concern for customer service. Most of them also have a strong desire to be their own bosses. Many express a need to "gain control over my life" or "build for the family" and believe that creating successful businesses will help them do it. They also have a knack for dealing well with uncertainty, risk and ambiguity.

We'll explore the inner regions of the entrepreneurial mind in this chapter.

Entrepreneurial Traits

If you are going to risk your time, money and energy in your own business you must have a strong feeling that you will be successful. Entrepreneurs typically have an abundance of confidence in their ability to succeed. This high level of optimism may explain why some of the most successful entrepreneurs have failed in business – often more than once – before finally succeeding.

Some have suggested that just being a small business *owner* doesn't necessarily mean that person is an *entrepreneur*. Entrepreneurs are people who assume the risk of business ownership with a primary goal of growth and expansion. Many small business owners have no plans for dramatic growth, seeking only a secure and comfortable income. Entrepreneurs, on the other hand, tend to be motivated to grow, expand, and build – that is, to risk.

The following chart illustrates the different kinds of traits and competencies arts entrepreneurs often display.

Traits and Competences of Arts Entrepreneurs

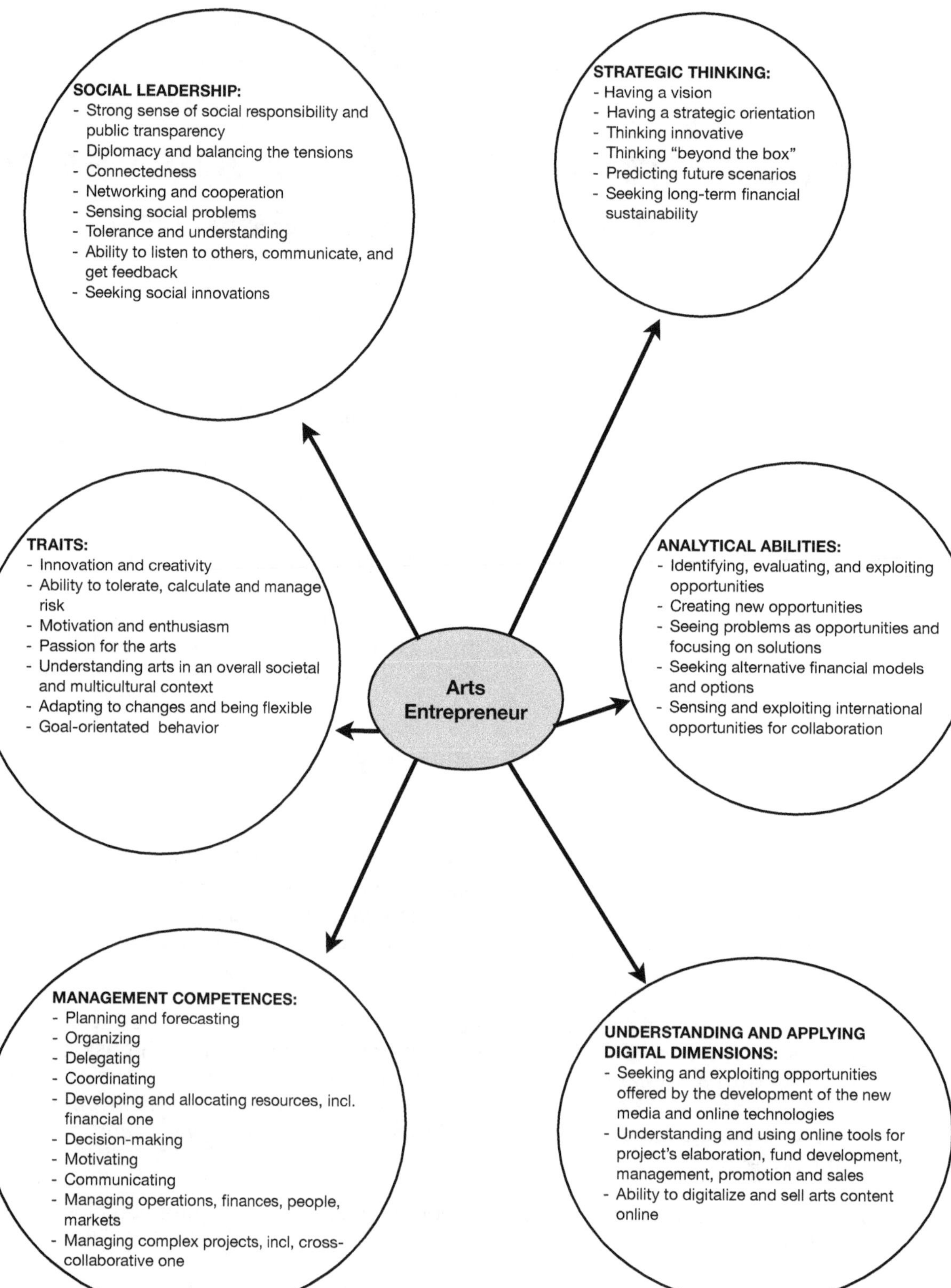

Besides risk, entrepreneurs often share the following attitudes as well.

If you want to start your own business you may have *mixed feelings about authority*. You know a manager must have authority to get things done, but you're not comfortable working under someone. This may also have been your attitude in an academic, family or other authority structure. You like to be your own boss, prefer to be in control of your own resources, and use those resources to achieve self-determined goals.

This doesn't necessarily mean going at it alone. Today's entrepreneur is seen more often as an open-minded leader who relies on networks of relationships, collaboration, and consensus to get things done.

Entrepreneurs also are likely to have *a strong need for achievement*. One of the most common misconceptions about entrepreneurs is that they are driven wholly by the desire to make money. On the contrary, *achievement* seems to be entrepreneurs' primary motivating force; money is simply a way of "keeping score" of accomplishments – a symbol of achievement. "Successful entrepreneurship requires an 'all in' way of executing," says artist manager Ralph Jaccodine. "Success comes to those who work harder, have the talent, vision, focus to execute a plan, and wrap that in a blanket of Karma/luck."

This need for achievement is a psychologist's term for motivation and is usually measured by tests. It can be an important factor in success. The person who wouldn't think of starting a business, might call an entrepreneur a maverick, a gambler, a high risk taker. Yet entrepreneurs tend not to feel that about themselves. They sense an opportunity and are driven to pursue it.

Studies have shown that very often the small business owner doesn't differ from anyone else in risk avoidance or aversion when measured on tests. At first thought this may seem wrong since logic tells us that it *is* risky to open your own business. A management expert once explained this apparent contradiction very simply. "When a person starts and manages his own business he doesn't see risks; he sees only factors that he can control to his advantage."

Successful entrepreneurs find a way to *balance their passions with business smarts*. After being laid off from her job at a concert promotion company, Ariel Hyatt (Cyber PR Music) started her music publicity service at the start of the new millennium. She quickly learned, however, that passion alone won't make a business succeed and she adapted as best she could by putting herself through a crash course she calls "Business 101". "Understand that music is a passion but business is learnable," she advises. "When you lead only with your heart, you can get yourself into a lot of trouble. No matter how much you like the music, at the end of the day, you still need to have basic business skills too."

Entrepreneurs also tend to have *a high tolerance for ambiguous, ever-changing situations*. This is the environment in which they most often operate. The ability to handle uncertainty is critical because these business builders constantly make decisions using new, incomplete, or even conflicting information gleaned from a variety of unfamiliar sources. "Entrepreneurship is also getting out of your comfort zone and pushing the boundaries," says Sean Hagon of Music Media Solutions. "Life begins at the end of that comfort zone."

Related to a tolerance for ambiguity is the entrepreneur's *ability to adapt to the changing demands* of their customers and their businesses. They must be willing to change plans and go in a different direction when needed. Co-founder of Apple Computer, Steve Wozniak said: "Entrepreneurs have to keep adjusting...everything's changing, everything's dynamic, and you get this idea and you get another idea and this doesn't work out and you have to replace it with something else. Time is always critical because somebody might beat you to the punch."

Today's music entrepreneur is often a composite of various skill sets and these allow one to take on a great variety of work on the front end of one's career. "For example, being a video producer, a photographer and graphic designer next to Berklee musicians made me a very helpful resource for professors, staff and students," writes Jandro Cisneros. "And combining those skills with also being an expert musician, film composer and audio engineer, brought our company [The Pillar Productions] to where we are today."

Entrepreneurs are not of one mold – no one set of characteristics can predict who will become entrepreneurs and whether of not they will succeed. Entrepreneurship is not a mystery; it is a practical discipline. Entrepreneurship is not a genetic trait; it is a skill that most people can learn. The editors of small business magazine, *Inc.* confess, "Entrepreneurship is more mundane than it's sometimes portrayed...You don't' need to be a person of mythical proportions to be very, very successful in building a company."

Behaviors	**Attitudes**	**Skills**
Taking the initiative	Achievement orientation and ambition	Creative problem solving
Solving problems creatively	Self-confidence and self-esteem	Negotiating
Managing autonomously	Tolerance for ambiguity	Management
Networking effectively to manage independence	Preference for learning by doing	Strategic thinking
Putting things together creatively	Adaptability / Flexibility	Intuitive decision making in uncertainty
Using judgment to take calculated risk	Creativity / Innovation	Social networking

ENTREPRENEURIAL BEHAVIORS, ATTITUDES & SKILLS

The Innovation Attitude

"Thus, the task is not so much to see what no one yet has seen, but to think what nobody yet has thought about that which everybody sees." –Schopenhauer

That Schopenhauer quote underlines a key aspect of creativity – the ability to see something new within the familiar – and sometimes the not-so-familiar. Remember:

- Light bulbs weren't invented by exploring candles
- Iron ships weren't made by exploring wood boats
- Skyscrapers weren't designed by exploring bungalows
- Walkmans weren't invented by exploring turntables
- Cell phones weren't conceived by exploring land lines

A recent study by the Small Business Administration found that small firms produce more economically and technically important innovations than larger firms. Small firms and individuals invented the Mac and the PC, the stainless-steel razor, the transistor radio, the jet engine, and the self-developing photograph (remember those Polaroids?).

One individual came up with the graphical interface that launched the World Wide Web.

What is the entrepreneurial "secret" for creating innovative value in the marketplace? In reality, the "secret" is no secret at all: it is applying creativity and innovation to solve problems and to exploit opportunities that people face every day. ***Creativity*** is the ability to develop new ideas and to discover new ways of looking at problems and opportunities. ***Innovation*** is the ability to *apply* creative solutions to those problems and opportunities to enhance or enrich peoples' lives.

There's definitely an idea out there. Maybe you'll spot it by seeing how others tackle problems and find solutions. In the 1950s, fast-food restaurants added drive-through lanes to serve car-loving customers. Banks and dry-cleaners soon borrowed the same idea. Today, all types of businesses use drive-throughs. The Little White Wedding Chapel in Las Vegas offers drive-through ceremonies. Loma Linda Medical Center gives flu shots while patients sit in cars. Seigl's Lumber Yard has drive-through lanes for tools and materials.

The hypercarbon now used in tennis rackets was first developed to stabilize satellites. Home smoke detectors and scratch-resistant lenses also stemmed from space-industry applications.

In his book *Get Back in the Box,* Douglas Rushkoff views *open collaboration* as an important strategy that creates a tie to innovation. He believes this approach will lead to revolutionizing industries worldwide. It "requires willingness to challenge and even rewrite the most accepted tenets underlying our industries, and to invite our employees and even our customers to engage in that process with us. This is the real meaning of open source and the surest path to a sustained 'culture of innovation'."

Often, a genuinely successful solution can be discovered by entertaining non-traditional ideas. But not just because the idea was non-traditional. When Linux group was considering how to keep from being swallowed up in the Microsoft world, someone suggested, "Let's make it free." A crazy idea, but they did it. 3M made a new adhesive that didn't stick very well. Instead of discarding it, they built a whole industry on it. And the Post-it Note was born.

Shawn Fanning saw the Internet and his vast music collection and figured out a way to share his music with others around the world (Napster); Panos Panay sought for a way to bring music performers together with talent buyers and Sonic Bids was born; Derek Sivers needed a way to distribute his band's CD when every major distribution company refused to do it, and CDBaby was launched.

So why does one creative person succeeds while another struggles? Some reasons favoring success include:

- A keen understanding of the marketplace
- Abundant self-knowledge
- The right combination of integrity and cooperation
- Willingness of others to work with you (based on track record industry reputation, personality, quality of the opportunity)
- The ability to raise necessary resources and /or support

Some think you have to be a maverick in order to innovate. After all, there have been geniuses that have not gone the standard educational route and not only succeeded, but turned their respective disciplines on their ears, right?

Take Albert Einstein. Didn't he fail mathematics in high school? Actually, no – that 's a myth. Albert not only did well in math, but taught himself Euclidean plane geometry by using a booklet from school. He also taught himself calculus. The myth about his having failed math or algebra in high school is a misinterpretation of grading system numbers from his school records. This Einstein myth is perpetuated because it supports our desire to believe that "gifted" individuals don't have to learn the rules, much less follow them.

What about Mozart? Didn't he write his first concerto at four, a symphony at seven and an opera at twelve? Yes, but that didn't mean he did it without learning the basics of music. He was born into a family of musicians; his father tutored him relentlessly from the age of three and trained him in organ, harpsichord and violin. And he still wasn't "successful" during his lifetime, by most professional, financial or personal standards. But he didn't do his great music just from his personal genius without education; he simply didn't get musical education in school.

What about Leonard da Vinci? He was the original Renaissance man, a multi-faceted genius: painter, inventor, engineer and scientist. Many of those pursuits were self-taught, to be sure. But to become a painter he was apprenticed to Verrocchio, a prominent master painter of Florence. You had better believe that he was not exempted from doing all the drudgery and work that apprentices normally did.

Too bad! Three perfectly good myths gone up in a puff of facts! One of the sad truths of life that any aspiring artist must face is that EVERY creative field requires learning. Masters of the arts often make them look easy, but they aren't. These achievers are often ten year "overnight success stories." Everyone has to learn the basics thoroughly. Quite often that fundamental learning is not fun or exciting. But it is a necessary foundation on which any creative career must be built.

Related to this is the need to "pay your dues". "Get competent on your own projects, well before you start charging others for your services," advises Randy Tobin, owner of Theta Media Group. "I spent hundreds of hours writing, playing, recording, mixing, reading, listening, playing live, etc., before ever charging a cent!" Preparation precedes paycheck.

Entrepreneurial Self-Quiz

Entrepreneurship isn't for everyone, but is it for you? Here's a "Would-Be Entrepreneur" Self Quiz to help you discern your own entrepreneurial readiness. See how you do. Under each question, check the answer that says what you feel, or comes closest to it. There are no right or wrong answers, but honesty is key.

Circle the answer that best represents how you feel. Here we go –

1. *You are at a party and a friend tells you that the guy in the expensive-looking suit recently invested in another friend's business. What do you do?*

    a. Race over to him, introduce yourself, and tell him every detail of your business idea while asking if he would be interested in investing in it.

b. Ask your friend to introduce you. Once introduced, you hand the potential investor your business card and politely as whether you might be able to call on him sometime to present your business plan.

c. Decided that it is probably not a good idea to bother the man at a party. After all, he is here to relax. Maybe you will run into him again somewhere else.

2. *Your boss asks you to take charge of researching office supply stores and choosing the one that you think would be best for the company to use. What is your response?*

    a. Yes! Finally, a chance to show the boss what you are made of-plus, you will be able to spirit a few of the supplies away for your own business.

    b. You are terrified; this is more responsibility than you really want. What if you make a mistake and cost the company money? You do not want to look bad.

    c. You are excited. This is a good opportunity to impress your boss and also learn how to compare and negotiate suppliers...something you will need to do for your own business.

3. *You are already going to school full time when you are offered a part-time job that is in the same field as the business you want to start when you graduate next year. What do you do?*

    a. Take the job, after talking with your student advisor about how to juggle your schedule so it will fit, because you believe the experience and the contacts you will develop will be invaluable when you start your business.

    b. Take the job. In fact, you ask for extra hours so you can finally start making some real money. Who needs sleep?

    c. Turn down the job. School is hard enough without working, too. You don't want your grades to suffer.

4. *You are offered a job as a survey-taker for a marketing firm. The job pays really well but will require you to talk to a great many people. What do you do?*

    a. Take the job. You like people and the job will be a good way to practice getting to know what consumers want.

    b. Turn down the job. Just the thought of approaching strangers makes you queasy.

    c. Take the job so you can conduct some market research of your own by also asking the people you survey what they think about your business idea.

5. *Your last job paid well and was interesting, but it required you to put in long hours and sometimes work on the weekends. What was your response?*

    a. You put in the extra hours without complaint, but mainly because you felt that the rewards were worth it.

   b. You went a little overboard and worked yourself into a state of exhaustion: moderation is not your strong suit.
   c. You quit. You are strictly a nine-to-five person. Work is definitely not your life!

6. *You are such a good guitar player that friends keep offering to pay for you to give them lessons. What is your response?*

   a. You spend some money to run a six-week advertisement tin the local paper, announcing that you are now available to teach at the same rate that established teachers in the area charge.

   b. You start teaching a few friends to see how it goes. You ask them what they are willing to pay and what they want to learn.

   c. You give a few friends some lessons but refuse to take any money.

7. *Your best friend has started a business designing Web sites. He needs help because the business is really growing. He offers to make you a partner in the business even though you are computer-illiterate. What is your response?*

   a. You jump in, figuring that you will learn the ropes soon enough.

   b. You ask your friend to keep the partnership offer open but first to recommend a class you can take to get your skills up to speed.

   c. You pass. You do not see how you can work in a business you know nothing about.

Analysis of the "Do You Have What It Takes?" Quiz
Scoring

1. a = 2 b = 1 c = 0
2. a = 2 b = 0 c = 1
3. a = 1 b = 2 c = 0
4. a = 1 b = 0 c = 2
5. a = 1 b = 2 c = 0
6. a = 2 b = 1 c = 0
7. a = 2 b = 1 c = 0

12 Points or More: You are a natural risk-taker and can handle a lot of stress. These are important characteristics for an entrepreneur to have to be successful. You are willing to work hard but have a tendency to throw caution to the wind a little too easily. In your enthusiasm, do not forget to look at the opportunity costs of any decision you make.

6 to 12 Points: You strike an excellent balance between being a risk-taker and someone who carefully evaluates decisions. An entrepreneur needs to be both. You are also not overly motivated by the desire to make money. You understand that a successful business requires hard work and sacrifice before you can reap the rewards.

6 Points or Fewer: You are a little too cautious for an entrepreneur, but that will probably change as you learn more about how to run a business. You are concerned with financial security and may not be eager to put in the long hours required to get a business off the ground. This does not mean that you cannot succeed as an entrepreneur; just make sure that whatever business you decide to start is the business of your dreams, so that you will be motivated to make it a success. Choose a business that you believe has the best shot at providing you with both financial security and the motivation you require.

By the way, don't think you have to jump into an entrepreneurial venture 100% from the start. In his book *Originals: How Non-Conformists Move the World,* Adam Grant relates a fascinating study by management researchers Joseph Raffie and Jie Feng, who asked a simple question: *When people start a business, are they better off keeping or quitting their day jobs?* From 1994 until 2008, they tracked a nationally representative group of over five thousand Americans in their twenties, thirties, forties, and fifties who became entrepreneurs. Whether these founders kept or left their day jobs wasn't influenced by financial need; individuals with high family income or high salaries weren't any more less likely to quit and become full-time entrepreneurs. A survey showed that the ones who took the full plunge were risk takers and spades of confidence. The entrepreneurs who hedged their bets by starting their companies while still working were far more risk averse and unsure of themselves.

If you think like most people, you'll predict a clear advantage for the risk takers. Yet the study showed the exact opposite: Entrepreneurs who kept their day jobs had 33 percent lower odds of failure than those who quit. Grant shares the lesson in all this: " If you're risk averse and have some doubts about the feasibility of your ideas, it's likely that your business will be built to last. If you're a freewheeling gambler, your startup is far more fragile."

The 21st-Century Skill Set

You are...

- A critical thinker
- An innovator
- An effective collaborator
- Globally aware
- Civically engaged
- A problem-solver
- An effective communicator
- A self-directed learner
- Information and media literate
- Financially and economically literate

Clearing Obstacles

I often run into entrepreneurs who suffer from insecurities of various kinds. They reach plateaus in their work life because they don't believe they can accomplish the tasks necessary to move forward. Usually, it is not a real barrier that holds a person back, but a *psychological* one. The poet Robert Frost once observed: "Something we were withholding made us weak, until we found out that it was ourselves."

Common insecurities I hear about from people who run their own music businesses include: 'I can't sell', 'I'm not a good promoter', 'I am not technically oriented', 'I can't "schmooze",' and 'I'm a lousy organizer'.

Most of these worries can be reduced to common anxieties such as:

- *Fear of rejection*
- *Fear of being laughed at*
- *Fear of the unfamiliar*

Working for yourself demands expanding your breadth of skills so that you can wear many hats. This doesn't mean that you should master *everything* and avoid relying on experts or staff to complement your skills. It does mean you should hone skills in core areas, rather than allowing a lack of confidence to hold you back. The following steps can help you clear real or imagined barriers that are keeping your skills or business from moving forward.

HOW TO BURN OUT AND STAY STRESSED

- Set impossibly high personal standards
- Don't exercise
- Eat anything, anytime you want
- Stay over weight
- Take plenty of stimulants
- Avoid all meditation, yoga, relaxation
- Eliminate your support systems
- Get rid of your sense of humor
- Take all criticism personally
- Never ask for help
- Become a workaholic
- Eliminate all time management practices
- Avoid fun
- Worry about things you cannot control

❑ **Act.** When fear or doubt hits, take action. Doing something is better than doing nothing. Even if the action isn't the right one, it moves you away from a state of immobility. Also, action changes the circumstances and, therefore, presents an opportunity to attack from a new position. This new perspective may help you find a different approach toward something that makes you ill at ease.

❑ **Prepare for the worst.** Mentally rehearse the worst possible outcomes that might result from attempting the thing that you dread. Chances are, you will be left with a better scenario. Knowing that you'll be able to control the situation – no matter what the outcome – will reduce the fear factor.

❑ **Get inspired by reading books about successful people.** One of the benefits of reading biographies and autobiographies about successful people is learning about their fears and how they overcame them. The benefit: You learn that fears do not have to squash success.

❑ **Speak positively.** Surround yourself with positive people, those who see the glass as half full. Speaking positively about yourself aloud will strengthen it too.

❑ **Mark your course.** When you're in the middle of climbing a mountain, it's hard to determine how far you are from the top or the bottom. Keep track of your progress toward overcoming fears. Claire Chase, creative director of the International Contemporary Ensemble, relates the importance of marking your course: "My first year, I wrote 13 proposals to private foundations; 13 were rejected. The second year, I wrote 15; 2 were funded. The third year, I wrote 17; and 5 were funded. Now I write around 35-40 a year, and around 20 of them are funded. You just keep keeping on, and you remind yourself that you learn much more from failures than you do from successes".

❑ **Reduce risk.** Contrary to what most people think, successful business people aren't risk-takers. They're bet-hedgers. They risk new trails, but not without the right insights and supplies. Reduce the risk of trying the unknown or the unpleasant by setting up a scenario for success along with "what-if?" scenarios. Mentally anticipating your obstacles and opportunities provides advanced preparation. This is what writing out a plan for your business does and we'll look at this process more closely in chapter 6, "Plan to Succeed".

Improving the Creative Process

"Companies are increasingly falling into two categories - those that are innovative and those who go out of business." – *Dan Branda, CEO HP Canada*

Nothing speaks louder than something creative. While no one can adequately define "creative", we all know it when it's present. Unfortunately, most of us traffic with societies demanding little in the way of creativity. We can get by, and even be very "successful" with partial participation, recycling culture and conversation *ad nauseum*. Studies show that a child's creativity plummets at around age 5. What activity usually begins at that age? Correct – formal education.

Though the word "education" comes from the Latin 'educare' (meaning, 'to draw out'), our systems betray a fear of human nature and instead *pour in* reams of information that a committee somewhere decided we should know.

In the process, the multidimensional child-artist is flattened and "de-programmed". To make room for all this "formal education" art, music and drama are pushed to the margins of and are often the first casualties during budget reviews.
Few of us, therefore, get any training in how to tap our inner creative. The last few centuries were outward-oriented to the extreme and much of the ancient knowledge about human power went underground. As a result, we hear that humans use only 10% of their inner potential.

There are two responses to this: accept it as the "expert opinion," or *push on to the other 90%!*

Beginning in the 1950s a more inclusive consciousness began to spread, and people experimented more readily with new ways of thinking and acting. These "new ways" were, of course, often old ways rediscovered and renamed. They included a more appreciative attitude about the body, the environment, and different lifestyles and cultures. Another was a "turning inward" and a renewed emphasis on the power of thinking to affect reality. In its most basic form, it says, 'you are what you think you are' – a powerful idea we'll explore more deeply in chapter 12.

Today we all have the chance to compose our own lives. It's a liberating prospect, but also daunting, because it requires a high degree of self-knowledge. If we don't start at the core – if we instead accept reflexive, inherited, or half-thought-out definitions of who we are and what we have to contribute – we run the risk of being overwhelmed by the possibilities that we face.

To break through to those other parts of ourselves that sit submerged beneath our everyday consciousness demands courage. In the words of psychologist Rollo May, it is the "courage to create."

There is nothing more brave than filtering out the chatter that tells you to be someone you're not. There is nothing more genuine than breaking away from the chorus to learn the sound of your own voice.

A creative world might not look much different from what came before. But as with the skateboarders who took the architecture of the city and saw in its shaped the potential for speed and style, *creativity is about repurposing, subverting, and improving what is already there.*

While there are many tools available for helping us think "outside the box", here is a simple technique I find helpful for boosting creativity. It was developed by George Torok and is helpful for discovering unusual solutions to common problems. Called SCAMPER, each letter stands for a creative activity that can be applied to any business idea:

❑ **Substitute:** Substitute one of the components for some other material or value. For example, auto manufacturers substituted plastic for metal to reduce weight to improve mileage. They are now substituting with lighter stronger steel. Look at the construction industry where materials have been substituted for cement, metal, wood and plastic.

❑ **Combine:** Combine two or more concepts that do not normally go together. The Earl of Sandwich slapped a piece of meat on a slice of bread centuries ago and created the sandwich. Gutenberg changed the world when he combined a wine press with a coin stamp creating the first printing press which spawned the first information age. Walk down the soup aisle at the grocery store to see some unusual combinations.

❑ **Adapt:** Zenon Environmental adapted nature's principle of osmosis to create a water purification system which is sold around the world. A Swiss inventor discovered the principle of hooks and loops by observing how burs clung to clothing, then adapted that to create Velcro.

❑ **Modify** - Minimize/Maximize: Chrysler launched the successful mini-van by making vans a little smaller. Retail was revitalized by making stores bigger with the big box store (Best Buy, Staples). Radio maximizes news content to become a 24/7 news station.

❑ **Put to another use**: After SPAR Aerospace sold NASA all the Canadarms that were needed, they looked around for another market. They put their robotic arm to another use by selling it as a backhoe for use by the US military in cleaning up old missile silo sites. I remember watching the TV show McIver to see what new use he would create for duct tape.

❑ **Erase** - Eliminate: Take out the parts that don't add value. Food companies do this with Caffeine-free, no-salt, and sugarless product. Eliminate excess packing to reduce costs and environmental waste. Remove steps in the process that annoys customers. A buyer for a medium sized institution told me they achieved a better price than a much larger buyer because they eliminated unnecessary paperwork in the transaction.

❑ **Reverse** - Rearrange: Which came first - the microscope or the telescope? One is just the reverse of the other. Try reversing perceptions. If people hate going to the dentist, then reverse the perception by making it an enjoyable experience. My dentist introduced himself by his first name and showed me the underwater photos he took scuba diving.

We humans are not godlike; we cannot create out of nothing. Creativity for us is an act of synthesis, and in order to create and synthesize, we need to stimuli – bits and pieces to put together in new and unfamiliar ways, existing frameworks to deconstruct and transcend. I also feels it is inherent to the creative mindset to want to maximize choices and options, to always be looking for new ones, because in the game that Einstein called combinatory play, this increases your chances of coming up with novel combinations.

If you recognize some of these traits in yourself and desire to tap your deeper potential, then welcome to the brave new world of 21st century music entrepreneurship.

Social Entrepreneurship

For the first two thirds of the 20th century, a powerful tide bore Americans into ever-deeper engagement in the life of their communities, but a few decades ago – silently, without warning – that tide reversed and we were overtaken by a treacherous rip current. Without at first noticing, we have been pulled apart from one another and from our communities over the last third of the century. American corporate business has certainly played its part in this fissure.

The spate of corporate scandals and incredible revelations in the last few years may revive negative attitudes and skepticism toward business, the same attitudes that marked U.S. society during the 1930s when the "robber barons" were finally brought down. In Washington, critics and government officials alike are already calling for tighter standards for business practices and increased control on accounting procedures. And to the extent that society begins to see economic problems as stemming from irresponsible business activities and unethical executive conduct, there may indeed be a return to the mind-set of the 1930s. Such a shift could result in business being seen as less capable of controlling itself and thus requiring increased control and constraint by government.

This is all the more reason to explore what kind of "social" dimension your business idea may have in the world. Entrepreneurs can use their abilities and opportunities to be self-serving, or they can use their skills and good fortune to improve their communities and help others achieve their goals. Entrepreneurs are, therefore, in a great position to impact society on so many levels and "social entrepreneurship" is a term that has developed to describe this business/society dynamic. "A social entrepreneur," according to Wikipedia, "is someone who recognizes a social problem and uses entrepreneurial principles to organize, create, and manage a venture to make social change".

Social entrepreneurship has traditionally been associated with the non-profit sector but this is changing today. Nonprofits are realizing that they are businesses as well as causes, and for-profits are realizing they can play powerful roles in causes as well as in traditional business. Some see this hybrid as the wave of the future for both profit and nonprofit companies.

The following chart is designed to help you explore what role you would ideally have your own company (and, by extension, your career) play as you consider the social dimensions of business ideas.

Social Responsibility Activities/Projects for Entrepreneurs

What are your business goals?

❑ Visibility in community ❑ Visibility in industry ❑ Aid in recruiting employees	❑ Enhancing employee morale/employee involvement ❑ Developing contacts with other companies ❑ Other: ______________________

In what ways will you participate?

❑ Donate money from operating budget ❑ Donate a set percentage of profits/sales ❑ Allow employees to be active in projects on paid time ❑ Encourage employees to be active on a volunteer basis/after-hours ❑ Donate company facilities for use by community groups ❑ Donate product overruns	❑ Participate as a company in community events ❑ Donate in kind products or services ❑ Formulate socially responsible operations practices (e.g. waste disposal management) ❑ Encourage company personnel/mngmt. to serve on agency boards ❑ Formulate socially responsible purchasing practices (e.g., environ-friendly only products or type of vendor) ❑ Other:______________________

What types of concerns do you want to be involved with?

❑ Animal Welfare ❑ The Arts ❑ Children ❑ Community Enhance. & Improvement ❑ Economic empowerment ❑ Education	❑ Environment ❑ Gender Equality/Issues ❑ Health Issues ❑ Recreation/Athletics ❑ Safety ❑ Other:______________________

Lifelong Learning & The Entrepreneur

Teachers go to college for four years to train for their profession. Doctors go to university, then medical school for an additional four years. But there has never been such a tidy map to becoming an entrepreneur.

There is no one school, no one skill, no one way into entrepreneurship – just ask the millions of business owners out there. Some people start with no formal training, while others spend years in prestigious MBA programs. But is a formal entrepreneurial education

the inside track to business success? Can you learn to be an entrepreneur? Or are you better off jumping in feet-first and learning as you go?
Or is it even possible to answer that question?

The consensus seems to be, yes, you *can* learn the art and science of entrepreneurship. In fact, it would almost seem necessary, as hardly anyone knows instinctively what to do from the start.

Education of a practical nature is most helpful in this line of work - supervising workers, working with spreadsheets, organizing a work project, producing events, delegating tasks, building databases. The majority of music entrepreneurs often have one or more college degrees in areas like business, music or music production. If you're fortunate enough to go to college you will have rich resources available to you as well as time to conceive and develop your business idea. Of course, writing and communication skills are a must today. Clear and effective communication can make the difference between success and failure in the unforgiving world of business.

The last decade has certainly seen a rapid growth of university-level entrepreneurial training, as the above chart illustrates. The next decade will see the continuation of this trend, but also see the growth of entrepreneurial training aimed at youth, mid-career professionals, artists and musicians, as well as trades people of all kinds. These training programs will, hopefully, lead to an increase in the formation and success of small businesses around the world - the true source of innovation and employment.
But entrepreneurship education doesn't have to come only from a schoolhouse. Online resources continue to improve daily, both online and offline. The best of these are included in this book's Resource Directory. Drink deeply and thrive.

CHAPTER SUMMARY

CHARACTERISTICS OF SUCCESSFUL MUSIC ENTREPRENEURS

- **Entrepreneurial Traits**
  Entrepreneurs typically have an abundance of confidence in their ability to succeed. Entrepreneurship is not a mystery, it is a skill that most people can learn. Some of the traits that most entrepreneurship should have are confidence, a comfort level with uncertainty, a strong need of achievement, adaptability and creativity.

- **The Innovation Attitude**
  The secret for creating innovative value in the marketplace is applying creativity and innovation to solve problems and to exploit opportunities that people face every day. Creativity is the ability to develop new ideas and to discover new ways of looking at problems and opportunities. Innovation is the ability to apply creative solutions to those problems and opportunities to enhance or enrich people's lives. Some reasons favoring success include a keen understanding of the marketplace, abundant self-knowledge, the right combination of integrity and cooperation, willingness of others to work with you, the ability to find and use necessary resources and/or support.

- **Entrepreneurial Self-Quiz**
  Some questions that is useful for discerning your own entrepreneurial instincts; Are you a self starter? How do you feel about other people? Can you lead others? Can you take responsibility? How good of an organizer are you? How good of a worker are you? Can you

make a decisions? Can people trust what you say? Can you stick with it? How good is your health? Should you jump in 100% right form the get-go, or maintain a "day job" and build your business on the side?

- **Clearing Obstacles**

  Working for yourself demands expanding your breadth of skills so you can "wear many hats." You should hone skills in core areas, rather than allowing a lack of confidence to hold you back. These steps can help your skills or business moving forward:

  - Act; When fear or doubt hits, take action. Doing something is better than doing nothing.
  - Plan for the best; prepare for the worst.
  - Get inspired by reading books about successful people.
  - Speak positively. Surround yourself with positive people, those who see the glass as half full.
  - Mark your course; keep track of your progress toward overcoming fears.
  - Reduce Risks by setting up scenarios for success along with "what-if?" scenarios.

- **Improving the Creative Process**

  While there are many tools available for helping us think "outside the box", here is a simple technique for discovering unusual solutions to common problems. Called SCAMPER, each letter stands for a creative activity that can be applied to any business idea:

  - Substitute: Substitute one of the components for some other material or value.
  - Combine: Combine two or more concepts that do not normally go together.
  - Adapt
  - Modify: Minimize/Maximize.
  - Put to another use
  - Erase: Take out the parts that don't add value.
  - Reverse: Try reversing perceptions by turning your idea inside out.

- **Social Entrepreneurship**

  Entrepreneurs can use their abilities and opportunities to be self-serving, or they can use their skills and good fortune to improve their communities and help others achieve their goals. Entrepreneurs are, therefore, in a great position to impact society on so many levels and "social entrepreneurship" is a term that has developed to describe this business/society dynamic. "A social entrepreneur," according to Wikipedia, "is someone who recognizes a social problem and uses entrepreneurial principles to organize, create, and manage a venture to make social change".

- **Lifelong Learning & the Entrepreneur**

  Education of a practical nature is most helpful in this line of work supervising workers, working with spreadsheets, organizing a work project, producing events, delegating tasks, building databases. The majority of music entrepreneurs often have one or more college degrees in areas like business, music or music production. If you're fortunate enough to go to college you will have rich resources available to you as well as time to conceive and develop your business idea.

FURTHER RESOURCES

ONLINE RESOURCES

Business Owner's Toolkit
www.toolkit.cch.com
From business, legal an tax information publisher and software provider CCH Inc., this is an essential bookmark for entrepreneurs. Get templates, advice, business credit reports and more.

CEO Express
www.ceoexpress.com
A "Grand Central Station" of business information.

Entrepreneur
http://entrepreneur.com
The online home of Entrepreneur magazine is an invaluable resource for growing a business.

The Global Entrepreneurship Monitor
http://www.gemconsortium.org
Research program that annually assesses the national level of entrepreneurial activity.

Idea Café
www.businessownersideacafe.com
The lighter side of running small and home-based businesses.

National Federation of Independent Business
http://nfib.org
The National Federation of Independent Business is an advocacy organization that also offers its members business insurance coverage and health plans. Visit their site to find out about affordable coverage for you and your employees.

Springwise
http://www.springwise.com
Scans the globe for smart new business ideas, delivering instant inspiration to entrepreneurial minds from San Francisco to Singapore.

Zero Million
www.zeromillion.com
A rich and resourceful site for entrepreneurs.

BOOKS

Courage to Create by Rollo May (W.W. Norton). *A classic meditation on creativity and its constriction in Western civilization.*

Creativity, Inc.: Overcoming the Unseen Forces That Stand in the Way of True Inspiration by Ed Catmull (2014, Random House).

The E-Myth Revisited: Why Most Small Business Don't Work and What to Do About It by Michael E. Gerber (2004, HarperCollins).

Grit: The Power of Passion and Perseverance by Angela Duckworth (2016, Scribner).

The Illusions of Entrepreneurship by Scott Shane (2008, Yale University Press).

Jamming: The Art & Discipline of Business Creativity by John Kao (Harper/Business). *Designed to give business people the precision of the artist and the artist the passion of the business-minded entrepreneur. Modern business as jazz.*

The Knack: How Street-Smart Entrepreneurs Learn to Handle Whatever Comes Up *by Norm Brodsky & Bo Burlingham (2008, Portfolio).*

Outliers: The Story of Success by Malcolm Gladwell (2011, Back Bay Books).

Reality Check: The Irreverent Guide to Outsmarting, Outmanaging, and Outmarketing Your Competition by Guy Kawasaki (2008, Portfolio).

Re-imagine! Business Excellence in a Disruptive Age by Tom Peters (2003).

Small Business, Big Life: Five Steps to Creating a Great Life with Your Own Small Business by Louis Barajas (2007, Thomas Nelson).

The Creator's Code by Amy Wilkinson (2015, Simon & Schuster).

Originals: How Non-Conformists Move the World by Adam Grant (2016, Viking).

Zen & the Art of Making a Living: A Practical Guide to Creative Career Design
by Laurence Boldt (2009, Penguin Books).

MAGAZINES

Entrepreneur, www.entrepreneur.com
Fast Company, www.fastcompany.com
Fortune, www.fortune.com
Forbes, www.forbes.com
Wired, www.wired.com

ASSOCIATIONS

The Edward Lowe Foundation
(800) 232-LOWE
www.lowe.org

Ewing Marion Kauffman Foundation
For Entrepreneurship and Education
(816) 932-1000
www.kauffman.com

2

DISCERNING TODAY'S MUSIC OPPORTUNITIES

"When old words die out on the tongue, new melodies break forth from the heart; and where the old tracks are lost, new country is revealed with its wonders."
– Rabindranath Tagore

"For the first time in history the artist is realizing financial success in his lifetime."
– Joe Walsh, rock musician

Unless you've buried yourself in the world of game-show television, we've all been seeing symptoms of fundamental change in American business – layoffs, plant closings, cost cutting, and benefit slashing. You've seen companies shift alliances with more vigor than usual. And you've seen the emergence of a new business phrases: *downsizing, de-siloing, re-engineering the corporation, de-layering*, etc.

You've seen all this, but have you figured out what's happening? And what does it all have to do with music and musicians? Don't be fooled into thinking we're just experiencing a brief shudder in the economy and things will return to "normalcy" soon. Uh-uh. *We today are living through nothing less than a global restructuring of the economy and this restructuring has vast implications for both musicians and the music industry.*

Like a breeder reactor, change feeds on change. It's become clear that we should accept the fact that our careers will be lived out in a state of constant transition. We must prepare for a work environment that is fluid, fuzzy and fast. We will constantly be confronted by the "new", and often the unexpected.

We are just beginning to comprehend this new world even as we create it. This much we know: we live and work in a time of unparalleled opportunity and unprecedented uncertainty. An economy driven by technology and innovation makes old borders obsolete. Smart people working in smart companies have the ability to create their own futures – and also hold the responsibility for the consequences. The possibilities are unlimited – and unlimited possibilities carry equal measures of hope and fear.

The New Opportunity

While devastating to large corporations, small companies are the true beneficiaries of this global restructuring of the economy. With lower barriers to reaching new customers and markets, and a global market open of business, small businesses are poised to compete in any industry, anywhere in the world.

The Institute for the Future (iftf.org) laid out this multi-dimensional opportunity for the small business sector in a report titled, "The New Entrepreneurial Economy":

• Entrepreneurial firms will see their ideas come to life, as large companies increasingly tap small businesses for innovation. The rising cost of benefits, especially health insurance, is part of what's driving this trend. Other factors include the difficulty and expense of terminating employees in our litigious society, and the lack of flexibility to reduce costs during lean times. And then there is the increasing complexity of business, requiring pockets of expertise that would be difficult or inefficient to staff internally. In turn, small companies gain access to big business scale and reach as freelance providers.

• Niche knowledge: Small businesses' agility, flexibility and deep customer knowledge will make them ideal partners for big business looking to serve niche markets with highly customized products and services.

• Although most corporations historically paid little attention to small business, large companies have begun to recognize the small business sector as a fundamental supplier, partner and customer base. It is no accident that professors of business management in prestigious business schools are noticing that global companies are beginning to operate in precisely the same way that microbusinesses do. In both instances, the lure is obvious; by opting to use contracting and partnering to manage the value chain, firms are able to produce output less expensively than they could if they were to own and control all aspects of production. The trend toward this kind of lean operation is a matter of improving corporate profits for the big boys, but it is a matter of survival for the small business. Today's entrepreneurs have the additional advantages of lightweight technologies and "plug-and-play" infrastructures, such as Amazon's e-commerce storefronts and UPS' distribution and supply chain logistics. Technology allows small businesses to enter and compete in industries formerly served only by big business. New production methods, which have automated some processes, customized others, and reduced the cost of still others, have combined to allow many owner-operators to produce more without staff.

In addition, small business owners find that they can cost-effectively outsource production (usually using domestic manufacturers), removing the need to build their own production facilities and hire their own employees. And, because so much of the U.S. economy is now in the services sector, in which people sell what they know or know how to do, production costs in many businesses can be kept extremely low.

"Borderless business" is another opportunity advantage for new entrepreneurs. U.S. small businesses will serve international markets almost as easily as their local customers. Similarly, foreign entrepreneurs will increasingly enter the U.S. market.

Meanwhile, professional and social networks, both online and offline, are muting soft trade barriers, such as language and cultural differences, and fueling cross-border trade.

Keep in mind, the "music business" is part of a larger entity known as the "entertainment and leisure industry" and, as such, touches on every area within it.

Entertainment and Leisure Industry Branches

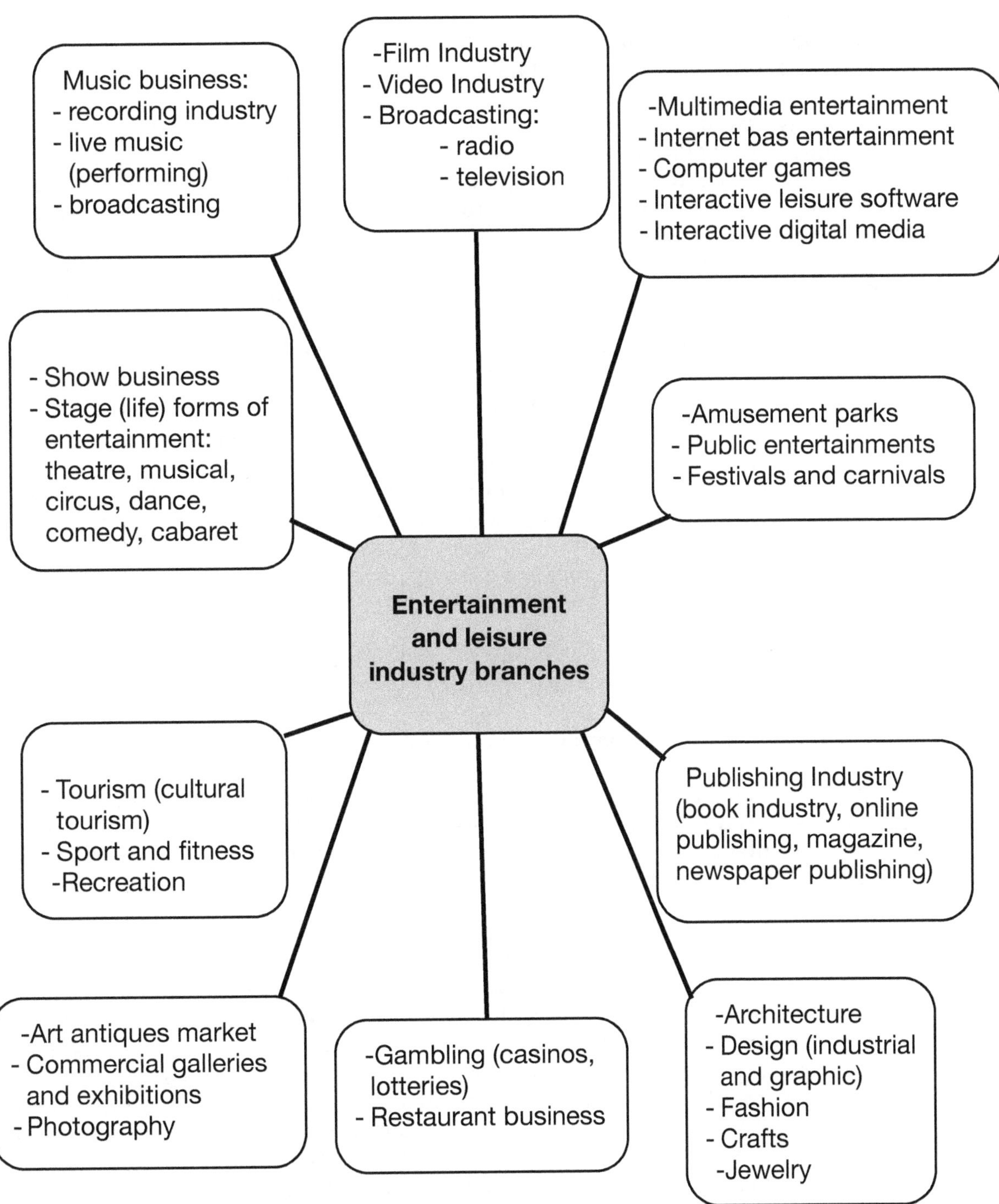

Music Business Trends Impacting Opportunity

Progress keeps picking up speed. The complexity of our world keeps increasing. The rate of change keeps accelerating. In fact, change is like a giant pinball machine where we keep adding several more steel balls every few minutes. They ricochet faster and faster. The game constantly grows more complex, the challenges multiplying moment by moment. Dr. Peter Vaill, a leading organizational theorist, coined the phrase "permanent whitewater" to describe the rapidly changing and highly competitive business environment. Small businesses are under continuous 24/7, "always-on" customer and market pressures.

No company operates in a vacuum. Every business is part of a larger, overall industry; the forces that affect your industry as a whole will inevitably affect your business as well. That's why it's a good idea to pause and take a long look at the landscape. One of the first things you do in business planning is an "environmental analysis." So let's take a look at the music and entertainment environment. In this chapter we'll explore the current "lay of the land" in the music marketplace. An important part of this includes exploring trends that are impacting the way people view and use entertainment products and services.

First, some noise from the trenches. Here are some revolutionary developments from the past few years among artists:

- Letting fans choose how much to pay for your album...
- Leaving the label you've called home for your entire career to hook up with a concert-promotions giant for a $100 million-plus deal...
- Recording iTunes-only one-off singles not slated for inclusion on an album...
- Offering "artist subscriptions" to fans, who pay a flat annual fee for more intimate access to their favorite acts...
- Serving up the millions of songs in your label's catalog to MP3 players and cellphones for one all-you-can-listen-to price per month....

All of the above are straws blowing in the wind, indicators of development, barometers registering the sea change in music industry dynamics.

Let's now delve a little deeper into this "creative destruction".

When I talk about "trends" I don't mean the common definition of "trendy, faddish or fashionable". Those are usually short-lived, "flavor-of-the-week" happenings that grip the market's attention for a time and then quickly fade into oblivion. Beanie Babies, pet rocks and 8-track tapes all fall into this category.

What I'm referring to when I say "trends" are emerging meta-currents in our social and cultural lives that herald new ways of living and thinking. These unfoldings have been gradual and sometimes difficult to arrest and analyze. Nevertheless, they are very real and they are changing the world, especially the world of the independent music provider. It wouldn't be extreme to say that for the past 50 years the world has been experiencing a comprehensive global restructuring of economic and social life. Massachusetts-based Amalgam Digital CEO Jay Andreozzi sees only opportunity in this picture: "Many believe it's an awful time to get into the music business. But with so many problems in the traditional music industry, and lack of solutions, now is the best time to get into the music business." As long as people value music enjoyment, music learning, music consumption, and music making, opportunities will continue to arise.

The 50,000-Foot View in Entertainment Marketing

Entertainment marketing left second-class status in its rear-view mirror decades ago, and as a result, created a heavily trafficked marketplace, constantly faced with the collision of time, money, and changing trends.

There are enormous trends unfolding throughout entertainment marketing. You may not have to dance directly with these trends, but you should be aware of them as you develop your own business idea. Consider these factors:

Entertainment marketing is consumed with *speed* – there is little or no time to test-market before release, before one source or another gets word of the buzz on a project and broadcasts it to the world at large.

Every film and CD is a new product, and each one is different: different content, different audiences, different deal structures. There may be two or three – or a thousand - of these products released every week, yet every campaign must hit the target on the money, on time.

With film, any misfire – any hint of bad box office- must be counteracted immediately, since the window of first-run distribution is only three to four weeks, at best.

Budgets for entertainment marketing can be huge - the average marketing budget for a film that costs between $50 and $100 million to produce is between $25 and $40 million - but the burn rate is extremely high, with much of the budget being spent during the six to eight-week period just before and during the film's theatrical release dates.

The product of entertainment content is based totally on creativity; therefore, it is fraught with the possibilities of human frailties. Production and release dates can change with the sneeze of a star. Bringing a product to the market often combines a fine balance of crossed fingers and creative finagling.

Entertainment marketing first focuses on selling an experience rather than an object. The audiences must first buy into the event, before the sale of objects associated with that encounter – a high desirable outcome, not to mention revenues streams – can occur.

Entertainment is subject to the same whims and vagaries as fashion. Trends and styles change; with the pre-production planning and strategizing stretching out years before actual release, entertainment producers must strive to catch the wave before it crashes into the cliffs of consumer apathy.

Award shows - not within the control of the marketer - can make or break entertainment products. Very few consumers may care what seal of approval a chair, a car, or a carton of eggs may carry, but the profitability – or failure – of a film, or an album, can rest on the opening of an envelope one evening each spring.

JOB TITLES IN THE NEW ECONOMY

Animation Skeptic
Jeff Pidgeon, Pixar

Director, Ethical Hacking
Chris O'Farrell, Predictive Systems

Chief Inspiration Officer
Han Ruinemans, Glo Corp.

Minister of Progress
Scott Eriksson, Aspen Tree Software

Knowledge Sorceress
Margot Silva, Business Innovation Consortium

Data Storyteller
Eliot Van Buskirk, Spotify

Intangible Asset Appraiser
Sam Khoury, Dow Chemical

Source: *Fast Company* Magazine

The changing face of technology carries with it ever-expanding channels of distribution for entertainment products, many of which have their own particular following. Each of these channels must be addressed, and marketers must be constantly aware of the demographics involved in every new format.

The marketing of entertainment focuses not only on the initial product itself – the movie, the CD, the program, the sports spectacle – but also on all the associated products spun off through licensing and merchandizing. Each product can launch billions of dollars in revenue, if carefully handled and strategically managed across all channels.

The global desire for entertainment requires a universal understanding of the language needed to promote the product, both locally and internationally.

Keep in mind that every single one of these factors impacts every single entertainment product - above and beyond all of this is the single biggest challenge facing every release and every promotion: competition from all other forms of entertainment.

That's the 50,000 foot view. Now let's get a little closer to the music entertainment landscape and explore some of the "megatrends" within *it*.

MEGATREND #1:
Every Business is Becoming an Entertainment Business

Toyota has started a record label. So have Artois Brewery, Cracker Barrel, Mountain Dew and Levi's Jeans. Apple Computer, Red Bull and Nike, three companies outside the orbit of the traditional music business, have spearheaded successful initiatives in the music space that record companies themselves seem constitutionally incapable of carrying out.

Last year Ellie Goulding, who likes to run almost as much as she likes to sing, hooked up with Nike, and through her Facebook pages invited a small number of selected fans to run with her in seven different cities on her UK tour.

Her record label, a Universal subsidiary, Polydor, then released a remixed version of Lights, aimed at providing a running soundtrack, in an effort get Goulding's music taken up by the national running subculture. "It took us out of the traditional record promotional cycle, based on peaks of activity around a record release and meant that she was being marketed over the whole of last year," said Paul Smernicki, the director of digital for Universal Music.

Here's how the Toyota brand Scion describes its mission: "to the discovery, nurture, funding, and distribution of compelling music and arts programming." Since 2003—a year after the Toyota car brand was launched—it's record label Scion AV has worked with over 1,500 artists ranging from The Black Lips, Chromeo, A-Trak and A$AP Rocky. In all senses of the word, Scion AV is a real record label, similar to other brand-led initiatives like Red Bull Records and Mountain Dew's Green Label, powered by Complex Media. It releases albums, music videos, films and Web series, as well as produces live events and even hosts pop-up record shops.

It's no mere coincidence that other industries try to model the way the entertainment industry is organized. The cultural industries - including the recording industry, the arts, television, and radio - commodify, package, and market *experiences* as opposed to physical products or services. Their stock and trade is selling short-term access to simulated worlds and altered states of consciousness. The fact is, they are an ideal organizational model for a global economy that is metamorphosing from commodifying goods and services to commodifying cultural experience itself.

Companies way outside the orbit of the traditional music business are awakening to this all around the planet. In early 2008, Bacardi announced that it would help the English electronic duo Groove Armada pay for and promote its next release. Caress, the body-care line owned by Unilever, commissioned the Pussycat Dolls singer Nicole Scherzinger to record a version of Duran Duran's "Rio" that it gave away on its web site to promote its "Brazilian body wash" product. Every business is becoming an entertainment business. As a result, you are no longer beholden to traditional "music industry companies" to achieve music success.

We'd mostly agree that the major record companies served their purpose well: They made recorded music available to us on a vast scale for seventy-plus years, instilling an insatiable appetite for music in the process.

As a result, music "sells". Music has accompanied just about every product that's come to market since the 1930s. In fact, today some of the most interesting music is heard more readily on TV commercials than on the radio. Wherever we go we hear music. Why? Because we love it and we want it. We want it when we drive, eat breakfast, shower, work, make love, shop for stuff – it's the aural landscape of our lives.

We hear music on recordings, on our computers, at concerts, on commercials and at the airport; we listen to music over the phone and in our video games, iPods, cell phones and through streaming services like Spotify. The global demand for music is chronic and ever-expanding.

We're purchasing music just about everywhere too. 25 years ago you bought recordings at record stores; today you can get them at record stores, grocery stores, drug stores, book stores, consumer electronic stores, department stores, plant stores, tattoo parlors, bars, gyms, museum shops, thru the mail, over the Internet, at kiosks, at the airport, at MacDonald's, at Starbucks, at Victoria's Secret, thru 800#s, and hundreds of other places –

MUSIC IS EVERYWHERE! Why?

Because music is a *connector*, and companies across the board are looking to associate themselves with music and its fans.

The lesson: These trends require a new way of thinking about the "music business" and "industry careers." It's time to stretch our minds and get outside the box of traditional music business models. The "digital common" brings all kinds of non-music businesses into a space where creative partnerships can develop. Non-music partners are fresh and excited about associating with musical and entertainment arts as a way of adding value to what they're offering.

We should reflect on where musical products and services are *used* rather than on where they have traditionally been *sold*. For example, think of companies you personally resonate with and then focus on those that may have an affinity with the kind of music product you offer. Make an alliance and use that alliance to market your music. Consider Craig Dory and Brian Levine of Dorian Recordings who got their recordings played on all the new hardware at consumer electronics shows. Or, Sean Hagon's donation of musical freestyles for clients of the United States Dressage Federation. He donates a portion of his proceeds to the foundation for any clients that are referred to his company through that organization. Smart alliances.

Remember, the economic structures of the last century are being torn apart. The rules are being rewritten. Today's business world is looking for new alliances.

MEGATREND #2:
Rise of the Customer-Creator

Consumers can now get more information about products and companies from Internet sources than previously available through traditional marketing communications. The most productive response to this is to bring customers into the value chain through collaboration and dialogue that make them part of a brand's story – and vice versa. Examples abound throughout the market: L'Oreal's "You make the commercial", MasterCard's "Write a Priceless Ad", Jet Blue's "Travel Stories", the Nokia "Concept Lounge", and Electrolux "Design Lab" are just a few.

Much of this is based on 'Open Innovation', first practiced in the software industry. The open source model of operation and decision making allows concurrent input of different agendas, approaches and priorities, and differs from the more closed, centralized models of development. This is closely linked to the ideas of "collective intelligence," "mass collaboration," and "crowdpower" – all hot buzz words in business communities today. People's expectations of the customer-supplier relationship are changing. Suddenly the audience is up on stage and starting to take over, telling the actors where to go and what to say. Now audience members are becoming the directors, script-writers and set-designers, and they are making up plays of their own. The entire audience, on the stage, has started exercising control – and businesses have to obey at the risk of losing revenue. This, in simplified terms, is the root concept of "crowd power."

The Customer-Creator is nothing short of reinvention of the business of market communications, a fundamental transformation from an intrusion-based marketing economy to an invitation-based model (see further exploration of this shift in chapter 15). This switch from the push model to the pull, from intrusion to invitation is a fundamental transformation for everyone involved in the business of content, whether the content is a 2-hour film, a half-hour sitcom, a radio program, recorded music, an Internet site, or a 30-scond advertising message. The end users rather than the creators and distributors of content are in control. And that changes all the rules.

Not only is the customer king: now he is market-research head, R&D chief and product development manager, too. More and more innovation is being driven by customer feedback. Richard Gooseen discusses this trend in his book, *E-Preneur: From Wall St. to Wiki*: "E-preneurs stop seeing customers as audience members and start seeing them as collaborators – creative directors, commentators, critics, inventors". For example, the fan community has had a tremendous influence on game design and the games are better as a result. When Peter Jackson set out to film *The Lord of the Rings* trilogy, he tapped into the rich community of Tolkien enthusiasts around the world via Internet portal sites like theonering.net and listened to fans' concerns and expectations.

Researchers call such customers "lead users" and their importance to product and service development continues to grow.

The result? – a bounty for music consumers. Today may be the very best time to be a music fan, especially one looking for a connection to a favorite artist or guidance and access to the exotic or rare.

Be it the iPod, alluring satellite radio services such as XM, the fan-beloved minutiae posted on Web sites, the availability of live music performances on Concert Window, the esoteric music videos streaming off YouTube or the self-tailored satisfaction of burning a homemade mix on CD at home, there is singular zest to the modern fan experience today.

The public is now driving the market. The challenge to the music industry is to respond positively in such a way as to secure the future of music while satisfying customer demand and providing choice.

And so it has gone with the creative arts. From musicians to Hollywood studios, and from network executives to owners of newspapers, the creators and purveyors of arts are realizing that Americans increasingly are unwilling to sit down, shut up and consume their culture in the time-honored fashion of grateful passivity.

In other words, this is the age of arts consumer as an empowered co-generator. And it's revolutionary.

Revolutions are nothing new in culture. In the 1950s, the rebellion was in the sound of rock 'n' roll, in its swagger and raunchy swivel, and in the 1960s the lyrics reflected and shaped youth culture, fashion and politics. The 1970s had punk and disco skirmishing with big-money rock, while the 1980s saw the rise of hip-hop, music that waged (and won) a street fight against the music industry status quo.

But by the end of the 1990s the new revolution, for the first time, wasn't in the music itself but in the *medium* - and for the first time the consumer called the tune. They are increasingly in the driver's seat of all economic transactions.

Music consumer reward systems are also emerging. Today's consumers are no longer passive recipients of brand messages. They've become active participants in co-creating the brands (and bands) they love. For example, TastemakerX is a social music discovery game. It allows fans to "buy" shares of emerging artists that are growing in popularity and earn points for discovering them early. Over time, fans build a virtual portfolio of artists and compete to be recognized as influencers.

It's becoming increasingly more difficult for companies to treat us like "mass market" ciphers. The trend is towards "mass customization" where consumers' unique needs are front and center. Some marketing gurus call this trend "The 1-to-1 Future".

The online environment also allows fans to try before they buy and enables them to experiment with new artists and genres. For example, a middle-aged Kinks fan might discover Blur and then listen to Damon Albarn's Mall Music to discover indigenous Malian artists such as Salif Keita.

The positive benefit of all this to consumers and the industry alike is that consumers' musical horizons are expanding and there will be more sales of more formats from a wider selection of 'retailers'. To flip Paul Simon's words, "the *music business* suffers, while the *music* thrives."

MEGATREND #3: Music as Service

"I work in a department called 'music services'."
- Darren Stupak, EMI, on the shift in thinking happening within major labels.

KEY IDEA

The future isn't about a change in distribution, it's about the atrophy of distribution itself. Instead of distributing things, we'll get access. It's a critical difference. The future isn't about downloading songs and burning CDs. It's about just-in-time customized delivery.

Music as service, not product.

Today, the service industries employ 80 percent of the U.S. economy and more than half of the value added in the global economy. Percy Barnevik, the former CEO of Asea Brown Boveri Ltd., predicts that by the year 2020, services will make up more than 90 percents of the U.S. economy, and manufacturing activities less than 10 percent.

In a service economy, it is human time that is being commodified, not places or things. Services always invoke a relationship between human beings as opposed to a relationship between a human being and a thing.

The old broadcast model is being replaced by total customer access to, and interaction with, the marketplace. Marketing becomes a network of relationships and responsibilities throughout the value and information chain. "Old" marketing, operating as it does on the venerable model of trying to sell through a vague notion of brand, promotion, entertainment and consumer manipulation, is unprepared for this change.

In marketing circles, using technologies to commodify long-term commercial relationships is called "controlling the customer." Continuous cybernetic feedback allows firms to anticipate and service customer' needs on an ongoing open-ended basis.

By turning goods into services and advising clients on upgrades, innovations, and new applications, suppliers become an all-pervasive and indispensable part of the experiential routines of customers. To borrow a Hollywood term, companies serve as "agents," performing a range of services. The goal is to become so embedded in the life of the customer as to become a ubiquitous presence, an appendage of the customer's very being, operating on his behalf in the commercial sphere.

Consumers have spoken, and they demand access to content by any means necessary. Digital distribution of music to consumers, via the Internet, allows recording companies to do away with suppliers, warehouses, inventories, distributors, and shippers, saving on the costs of handling a physical version of the recording. The electronic transmission of music products is still another example of the new weightless capitalism that is emerging in the cyberspace economy.

Presenting music as a service, like radio or TV, would seem on the surface to be less profitable than selling millions of CDs, but actually, this change will be positive for the music industry. It will be able to sell more things associated with music. But the actual sale of music as a product will make less sense. It will be a move from transaction-based *push* to flat-fee *pull*. Just as AOL has gone from selling you five minutes of access to a take-whatever-you-want model, music too will move to a flat-fee model.

The reason the future is so bright is that soon we'll all plug into around-the-clock streaming Internet audio, happily paying a few extra dollars a month to our Internet service provider

(ISP) for the privilege.

We're almost there. The requisite technology is now in place. Most of us carry a wireless Internet uber-gadget wherever we go – a unified cellphone/personal digital assistant/Blackberry/camera/GPS locater/video recorder/co-pilot for life. This device receives wireless Internet audio, a loose term I use to describe the various forms of streaming audio. With streaming audio, you can hear the music you love any time, anywhere.

So how will musicians make a living in the new world? We'll simply expand existing compensation systems. The owners of restaurants, bars, health clubs and other music-playing public venues already pay fees to central clearing houses (the performing rights organizations, or PROs) that forward the money to composers and publishers based on how often their music is played. One simple option is to put a flat surcharge on Internet service providers of only $7 a month – about what the average household in Canada pays per month on CDs. This creates a pool of money that can be distributed fairly to composers (and their publishers), artists (and their agents or labels), ISPs and the music providers (perhaps like Kazaa, or son of Kazaa) – *all based on actual use*.

Artists will generate revenues primarily through un-copyable events (concerts, promotions, meet-ups, etc.), and goods (special editions, memorabilia, merchandise, etc.), which are supplemental to the music itself. Artists' fans become their top promoters, by passing on the music that they like to friends along with means to connect with the artists, such as Web or e-mail addresses. This kind of "viral marketing" or super-distribution of artists' music provides an unprecedented opportunity for independent artists around the world to pursue their passions. The challenge is now to the electronic pioneers to use these new tools to build new business models or new twists on the old ones that sustain and enhance artists' livelihood in a digital world.

We are already seeing a pronounced shift of record company income from primary sources (selling records) to secondary sources (collection of publishing rights). The old music business of selling packages of music to relatively passive consumers will remain a large business for quite some time. The point is that a very different sort of music business is growing up along side it, one where music is becoming a *service* rather than a *product*. The digital downloading revolution is transforming the music business into a service business. No longer will we see the music industry as the selling of goods, but rather, as the provision of a distribution service, not unlike TV. This is why it is important to ask, not so much, where music is *sold*, but where music is being *used*.

In general, labels are not looking to change the media. They're going from today's media to digital wireless delivery. Eventually, it will come down to the point where you don't need the hard medium. But the emphasis online today and for the next several years (to 2020-ish) is to drive consumer awareness and to drive album sales.

All the products out there are just derivative of the CD. The next revolution in prerecorded medium will be on a chip with no moving parts. The popularity of devices like Apple's IPod and Google's Android are indicative of this.

MEGATREND #4:
New Music Company Models

Organizations used to have stable industries, predictable customers, and five and ten year strategic plans. Today whole industries are being turned completely upside down within two years.

And now the musical industrial complex is losing control. Its members can sue file-traders all they want, but they will not be able to prevent individuals from making their own music and distributing it via new technologies.

The EMI/Robbie Williams' deal (aka, the "360 deal") represented a major cultural shift on the part of a major record company. What made it different was that the deal recognized that everything to do with the artist counts. Traditionally, record companies would spend money developing an artist's income stream through sales of T-shirts, screen savers, ring tones and so-on, only to see none of the revenue. Now they do. The EMI deal includes a percentage cut of everything to do with the sales of Robbie Williams's related products, for the label. More and more labels are jumping on the 360 bandwagon.

Perhaps the biggest example comes from Live Nation, the concert heavyweight that is now pursuing a massive, 360-degree music business model *a la* Madonna, Nickelback and Jay-Z. Even talent agencies, the powerbrokers of Hollywood, are slowly spreading their tentacles into different areas of the music industry. "Traditionally, agencies handled the booking of tours, because the labels wouldn't let them touch anything else," one top agent at Creative Artists Agency (CAA) confessed. "Now, all kinds of models are emerging, in terms of what agents are involved in."

That includes sponsorship and branding partnerships, digital deals, and of course, film-related tie-ins. The day-to-day is still the PA [personal appearances] business, but this is now becoming the primary source of income for many artists.

Artists are increasingly looking outside of album sales for revenue and trying to exploit all rights as a brand.

I mentioned the practice of "crowdfunding" under Megatrend #2 (The Customer Creator), a development offering an alternative business model from the typical top-down funding model characteristic of most artist and start up business financing for the past 150 years. Crowdfunding can also replace the need for specialized grant applications or other more formal and traditional fundraising techniques with that of a casual, yet powerful, approach based on *crowd participation*. This approach is used widely among music industry artists to bypass major recording companies and "go direct" to their fans who are now seen as much as investors as listeners. I like to call it "arts patronage by the masses," as the following chart illustrates.

FUNDING MODELS: FROM 'TOP DOWN' TO 'BOTTOM UP'

TRADITIONAL MODEL	CROWDFUNDING MODEL
Lawyers & Managers Negotiate a support deal with... **↓** **Record company which supplies...** **↓** **Artist Support Revenue so artist can build...** **↓** **Fans/ Audience**	**Fans & Audience respond to Artist request for...** **↓** **Support**

Perhaps the term *record company* itself is losing its relevance - "Music Company" is more apt, dealing as it does with a bundle of rights, and not just the master right in the sound recording.

"I think we'll mutate into a new type of company – a mixture of artist management, publisher, marketing consultant, agent and promoter." *Steve Becket – Warp Records.*
"We're a *communications* company and that's what we're becoming more everyday. I don't think the model for a traditional record label will exist in this environment anymore." *Marc Jones – Wall of Sound.*

While mega-media is consolidating, *micro*-media has exploded. A "mainstream artist" seeking CHR (contemporary hit radio) fame *has* to align with the mega-conglomerates who own record labels, magazines, TV networks, film studios, and toy companies because these media giants control what hits the mainstream. In that system the artist will be one of a few of several who may get a chance to shine before a hunger for quarterly profits, marketing mishaps or personnel changes derail the project.

On the other hand, micro-media targets the tributaries off the mainstream and if the artist occupies one of these "niche streams", they have an open and ready channel for exposure to their target audience. Each niche stream has its own burgeoning media culture and the smart combination of high-quality music, good stories, creative event-making and strategic alliances gets the market's attention.

Remember, every business is becoming a music business – actually an entertainment business. Entertainment is a much-coveted value businesses are seeking to add to their image all over the world.

We're also seeing new models emerging that are redefining the artist/label relationship. Equity Records out of Nashville, TN does just what its name suggests: rather than going with the standard a royalty-bearing deal, it opts for an equity-sharing model. Taking a cue from EMI's multi-revenue deal made with artist Robbie Williams in 2003, other labels and artist are creating similar agreements where labels get more access to income streams previously off-limits, and artists receive higher advances and larger marketing commitments from the company.

All of this, if properly executed, could lead to a more efficient method of marketing acts by putting power in a largely singular and unified marketing vision. The Artist Collaborative,

Concord Bicycle Music, Combustion Music, and Redlight are some of the companies who have made considerable ventures into these new models of operation.

The traditional music industry is transforming. Companies are morphing into new hybrid service businesses. We need to think outside the box of the musical industrial complex and explore fresh possibilities. What new shapes can your company take?

MEGATREND #5: Rapidly Segmenting Music Markets

I'd often hear musicians and industry critics alike complain about how the monopolization of radio by companies like Clear Channel threatens musical diversity, yet today I can hear and obtain more interesting music than I could ever have obtained in the 1970s or 80s.

It's myopic and selfish to think that some music "deserves" to be heard and some doesn't, as the old music industry preached. The listening public is conditioned to being told what they should like. But the wall has come down, and music fans are becoming overwhelmed with new choices.

The new plurality of music requires the listener to actively *listen* for what they like instead of just *hearing* what they are told to like. This means, among other things, there is an increasing need for people willing to guide others through the expanded choices, without dictating choice. To put it simply, the *patterns* that used to govern music sales no longer work. The industry's biggest successes are now small ones.

Industry insiders are just as confused by the good news as they are by the bad. Here are the kinds of questions they've been asking themselves: Why didn't Eminem break out on the order of the Beatles and sell 10 million copies of every release? Why can't Britney, Whitney, Madonna and Mariah make hits like they used to? Why can't the Strokes break through to the mainstream, stymied at 500,000 units shifted? Conversely, they wonder how a one-off Sub Pop release like the Postal Service's *Give Up* — a mash-up of the niche genres of bedroom electronica and emo-punk — has sold well over 250,000 copies. How could Matador sell a half-million copies of the debut by an unheralded New York band like Interpol? Why are bands like Modest Mouse, the Shins, the Yeah Yeah Yeahs and Wilco selling hundreds of thousands of records, where a few years ago they would have — optimistically — sold 50 thousand?

Even the pop charts, which have made room in recent years for Alt-J, Marian Hill, Arcade Fire, Diana Krall and The Lumineers, suggests there's an audience starving for something other than musical junk food.

It's a strange landscape. When the Grammys started in 1958 there were 28 categories of awards; in 2016 there were 83! Check out the "Music Styles" chart below and then look at the sub-genres of "Dance" on the following page.

COMMON MUSIC STYLES

A Cappella
Alternative
Ambient
Asian
Bluegrass
Blues
Celtic
Childrens'
Classical (pre-20th c.)
Classical (contemporary)
Christian
Country
Crunk
>> Dance <<
DJs
Dub
EarlyMusic
Electronica
Emo
Experimental
Film
Folk
Funk
Fusion
Gospel
Heavy Metal
Industrial World
Pop
Punk
Rap/Hip Hop
Reggae
R & B
Rock

DANCE SUB-STYLES

(A Select List)

Though some of these sub-styles overlap with others, each one has been singled out in the marketplace as distinct in its own way.

abstract beat
abstract drum-n-bass
acid house
acid jazz
acid rave
acid-beats
acid-funk
acid-techno
alchemic house
ambient dance
ambient drum-n--bass
amyl house
analogue electro-funk
aquatic techno-funk
aquatic-house
atomic breaks
avant-techno
bass
big beat
bleep-n-bass
blunted beats
breakbeat
chemical beats
Chicago garage
Chicago house
coldwave
cosmic dance
cyber hardcore
cybertech
dark ambient
dark core
deep house
downtempo
drill-n-bass
dronecore
drum-n-bass
dub
dub-funk
dubstep
dub-n-bass
electro
electro-acoustic
electro-breaks
electro-house
freestyle
future jazz
futuristic breakbeat
futuristic hardbeats
futuristic hardstep
gabber
garage
global house
global trance
goa-trance
grime
hard dance
hard chill ambient
intelligent drum-n-bass
intelligent jungle
intelligent techno
jackin house
jungle
minimal-abstract
minimal techno
minimal trance
moombahton
mutant techno
mutated minimal techno
mystic-step
neurofunk
noir-house
nu-dark jungle
old school
organic chill out
organic electro
organic electronica
progressive house
progressive jungle
progressive trance
ragga
rave
techno jungle
trance
tribal
trip-hop
two-step
underground
world-dance

The music market continues to segment and each segment has become a "world", a cultural/economic portal, through which niche companies can create value and success.

While good news for niche companies, this is bad news for the musical industrial complex. The major labels cannot justify going after these smaller markets because they are optimized instead for the larger, pop mainstream. These niche music cultures can't generate the sales required to float the major label boat. While 20,000 unit sales are a cause to celebrate at a micro-label, they hardly register a blip on big company radar screens.

Related to this niche trend is what has been termed "the Long Tail Market". This phrase was coined by editor of Wired Magazine Chris Anderson. Anderson argued that products that are in low demand or have low sales volume can collectively make up a market share that rivals or exceeds the relatively few current bestsellers and blockbusters, if the store or distribution channel is large enough. Thus, the primary value of the internet to consumers comes from releasing new sources of value by providing access to products in the long tail. Online book and music stores (like Amazon) are a perfect example because they can carry large collections of music just as easily as just a small selection.

THE LONG TAIL AT WORK

"We sold more books today that didn't sell at all yesterday than we sold today of all the books that did sell yesterday."

– Amazon employee

The times call for focus. Mass customization and a segmenting market encourage the development of products and services of a "niche" nature. Since few of us have the time, money or energy to mount national marketing campaigns, it is in our best interest to discover and concentrate on a niche, a segment, we can explore towards successful enterprise. Whether your specialty is house, trance, bluegrass or neo-soul, learn to work that niche and scope out relationships and opportunities within it.

The "cost-of-entry" bar has been lowered, and the average skill level of recording engineers with it. This is bittersweet.

My son never took a music lesson in his life, but with Apple's Garageband software, he 's whipping up cool tunes and arrangements that stand up to critical listening, and he's showing interest in becoming more musically literate.

Of course, just because you *can* record and release a CD doesn't mean you *should* record and release a CD. Musical clutter is increasing (John Doe has a great song called "Too Many Goddamn Bands"), and only promises to get worse, and it will always take serious bucks and muscle to rise above the noise. Or creativity.

This is part of what Clay Shirky calls "The Big Flip" – where the old notion of "filter then publish" is giving way to the new practice of "publish then filter." Thus, the growing need for *context*.

MEGATREND #6:
The Growing Need for Context

"Too much information running through my brain;
Too much information driving me insane." - The Police, 1982

Every spare moment of our time is being filled with some form of commercial connection, making time itself the scarcest of all resources. Our fax machines, e-mail, voice mail, and cell phones, our twenty-four hour trading markets, instant around the clock ATM and online banking services, all night e-commerce and research services, twenty-four hour television news and entertainment, twenty-four hour food services, pharmaceutical services, and maintenance services, all holler out for our attention. They worm their way into our consciousness, take up much of our waking time, and occupy much of our thoughts, leaving little respite.

They also *overfill* us with information. This has come to be known as *infoglut*.

Futurist Paul Saffo talks about the different "scarcities" the world has experienced over the past hundred and fifty years. First there was a scarcity of "conduit" (that is, pipeline). Then electric wires were strung coast to cost and conduit was hyper-abundant. We then had a scarcity of "content", that is, information and programming to fill the conduit. Eventually, content became hyper-abundant too until today we're drowning in information.

The new scarcity, according to Saffo, is *context*, that is, giving meaning to all this information. The increasing flood of information has now created an urgent need for "filters", "editors" and "portals". The need for context is so strong that Saffo sees a time when people like Oprah Winfrey and Peter Jennings will be licensing their "worldviews" to software companies to create products that screen vast amounts of information and present digestible info-bites in an acceptable framework for users!

A good example of providing context in the hyper-abundant field of music is the compilation. Once a mere afterthought of the recording industry, these variety packs of music have emerged as a vital force in the market.

Have you noticed all those compilations on the counters of lifestyle retailers Pottery Barn, Structure, Williams-Sonoma and others? One man - Rock River Communications' Jeffrey Daniel - usually chooses the music. If mixing tracks is an art, then Daniel is the most popular artist you've never heard of: his branded compilations have sold nearly 8 million copies. Rock River's annual wholesale revenue is about $1 million, on par with a midsize record label. Read some of its own case studies at rockrivermusic.com

How might you, in your area of expertise, be a meaning-giver in the world of music? Are you an expert in the use of ProTools or on 70s soul? Is bluegrass your passion or is it music education for kids? Are you highly informed about microphones, roots reggae, or lyric writing? How can you put that to use using channels like the Internet and other digital tools?

Provide significant meaning in your niche and people will shove money in your pockets.

MEGATREND #7:
Resurgent Indie Culture

Historically, "indie" has been shorthand for second hand quality, but it can't be looked at that way any longer. The gulf between indie and major artists has narrowed greatly. Major label philosophy used to be "spend the money" because at the end of the day it will be recoupable to the artist anyway, but today's world is all about what makes good business sense.

For several decades now financial people have been making all the decisions at the majors, so they can't invest long term in an artist's career. One or two shots and it's time to move on to the next flavor. That opens an opportunity for indies. Profit margins and staffing have shrunk at larger labels, so the human resources issues that were an advantage for major labels no longer exist. They are outsourcing almost as much as indies now.

According to *Billboard Magazine*, 2014's year-end Nielsen Music statistics (based on master ownership) reveal that Independent labels were 35.1% of the overall U.S. recorded music industry, up from 34.6% in 2013 and 30.2% in 2012.

In the past major labels kept their foot on the throat of indies just by using their financial resources to horde all the opportunities. They can't do that anymore. The majors themselves are in a state of flux. There are cutbacks, mergers and proposed mergers everywhere. All those gulfs have tightened. We are now (2016) looking at a historical crossroad. The state of affairs we now find ourselves in isn't so much an end of the recording industry as it is a new beginning. Today's indies like XL Recordings, Soulection, True Panther Sounds, Local Action, Bromance, Boy Better Know, Wedidit, R&S, Tri Angle Records, Young Turks, Friends of Friends, Domino, Mixpak, Warp, Crazylegs, BrainFeeder, are all making themselves felt in this shaky marketplace for recorded music.

Also, as major label dynamics change, and as management and artists get dropped by these labels, indie label upstarts are able to recruit new executive talent and sign acts looking for more nimble handlers. This is what Sanctuary Records did with formerly-signed artists who still have thriving fan bases.

As the worlds of distribution, retail and consumer preferences migrate to the digital space, indies will be at less of a disadvantage as compared to the majors. It will be artist and music direct to consumer and the roles of many traditional middlemen will be diminished. We used to talk about the CD being the hardcover and the cassette being the paperback. Now we say the digital single is the paperback and the CD is the hardcover edition. Down the road it will be even less important whether you are indie or major, because no one is going to care.

In a real sense, the next Big Thing is... *small*.

The analogy is television. Thirty-five years ago, the three broadcast networks (CBS, NBC and ABC) had a ninety percent plus share of the viewing audience. Today it's less than forty. Where's the other 60%? Watching cable. Though cable channels have miniscule ratings, they're profitable. Why? Because they've discovered and developed their niche.

And this is what indie labels do – the Americana sounds of New West Records, Red House Records' focus on singer/songwriters, the creative acid jazz of Instinct, and the roots reggae catalog of Trojan insures listeners they can expect quality discs from each company within their respective niche.

Other Music Business Trends Worth Watching

1. Streaming Goes Mainstream While Fairer Formats Ascend. While the iPod popularized digital music, and iTunes popularized one-dollar downloads, streaming is now the norm. The streaming option puts users in control of what they listen to and when, because streaming service libraries are nearly limitless, and music can be streamed anywhere there is an Internet connection. The technology obviously works well, but industry professionals still need to get artists to buy in to the hype and believe that they are not getting thoroughly screwed by practically giving their music away. In light of the boycott by Taylor Swift in 2014 (she pulled her catalogue off of Spotify) the company is now focusing its energy on educating artists on the benefits of the service. Spotify claims that wider exposure of an artist's music and opportunities to promote themselves, outweighs the low royalty rate.

Many artists have a different take. In fact, there is a strong push being made towards a "Fair Trade Music Format" using blockchain, which will incorporate metadata (the basic data to identify writers, performers, owners, producers etc. of the music) and a cryptocurrency (digital currency that uses encryption techniques to regulate the generation of units of currency and very transfer of funds, operating independently of a central bank) such as BitCoin. The metadata factor ensures a database of music rights, ownerships, copyrights, and usage rights that is easily available to anyone to use. Artists, songwriters, producers, performers, record labels, and everyone else involved can assign rights and usage in real time. The cryptocurrency factor ensures fair payment for all involved with the track. The goal: payments will be accurate and fairly quick.

US Music Revenues 2015
Source: RIAA

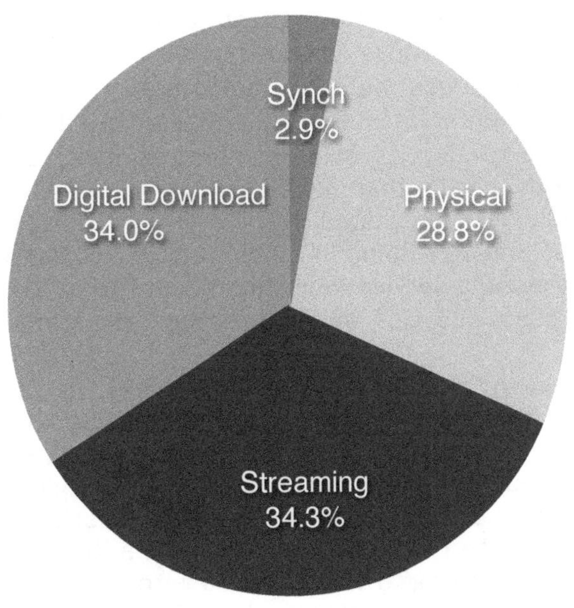

2. Dataming, Music and The Internet of Things. Advanced technology is now embedded in our daily lives. On the short horizon is mass connectivity of everyday objects via the "Internet of Things" (IoT) – with projections of anywhere between 50 and 250 billion net-connected objects over the next 20 years. The future of the Internet over the next two decades and beyond is most likely to see a whole new hyper-connected world of networked people, objects, and systems capable of transforming, reframing, and undermining the established norms of business and society. In automated systems today, the computer often takes on intellectual work – observing and sensing, analyzing and judging, even making decisions – that until recently was considered the preserve of humans. This is all part of the mega-trends of "Big Data", wearable tech and artificial intelligence. Music is going to play a huge role in the Virtual Reality and Augmented Reality industry. Soon, "seeing" Kurt Cobain or Janis Joplin live isn't going to be as impossible as it seems. 2Pac taking the stage at Coachella 2012 was one of the biggest steps forward in the commercialization of Augmented Reality, and that was about four years ago. Let your imagination run wild to what we can expect in the near future.

Of course, everyone is integrating their efforts with social media platforms since that is the new metric for success. It's pretty obvious that companies are jockeying to be your one-stop shop for music and while they have your attention they want to sell you some product. One example of this is Gimbal, a new developer platform, that enables the creation of context-aware apps for Android phones and tablets. Its standout capabilities are geofencing, image recognition, and interest sensing. Let's take one of these. *Geofencing* involves creating a virtual perimeter around a physical space. When a device crosses into one of these boundaries an automatic event is triggered — a push notification is sent, an app launches, or a check-in is recorded, etc. So, for example, Live Nation could geofence all of its venues, making it so walking through the doors would trigger a notification for a drink discount or upcoming concert promotion informed by your Facebook or Bandsintown profile. Expect more of these micro-targeting technologies to affect the music space in the near future.

3. Sizeable Music Spending Continues. While consumers purchase little physical content, music is still a big part of their budget, at $125 in 2015, according to consulting firm, Deloitte. It estimates that 80 percent of Millennials will attend a live event, and that most would like to spend more on live music than in prior years. This reflects the long-term trend across all age groups: between 1990 and 2010, spend on music concerts, performing arts and sporting events doubled from a quarter to a half of a percent of total consumer spending. It also estimates average spending on live music among 18-34 year-olds will be about $100, which is more than double the average $48 per capita in the US as of August 2014. Additionally, it is forecasted that Millennials will spend $25 on average on digital music downloads and streaming in 2015. Younger consumers represent a significant proportion of streaming service subscribers; an estimated 40 percent of Spotify's 50 million monthly active users and 12.5 million premium users are 18-24.

4. Achieving "Success" on Many Levels. The ability for an artist to achieve "success" in the music industry has less to do with being a Billboard chart topper and more to do with working smarter and more efficiently to create content that uniquely engages a fan base. For as much as Adele grows closer to 10 million albums sold, she represents one side of the paradigm of success. There are also artists like rappers Run The Jewels who engaged with their internet-based fan core with a Kickstarter campaign for a "Meow The Jewels" album featuring rap tracks remixed with cat sounds in 2015. More artists are likely to think totally outside, and just to the left of the box, than ever before. With so many unique points of engagement being created in the music industry, opportunities for growth are abound.

5. "Freemium" Business Models. What is the freemium model? In simple terms it's the delivery of Internet services that are free to the user because the marginal costs of manufacturing and distribution are zero, or close to it. This means that businesses can now experiment with giving away one thing to sell something else. In music, the model can be described as giving away your songs and then charging for a "premium service," like a concert appearance. Bands who use this model release free songs through their site or other sites and charge for additional content. This 'premium' content is only available to people who pay, so the band covers any overhead incurred in production. Can it work? Both Radiohead and Trent Reznor used this model with success. If you can figure out how to offer your fans a second tier of premium experience, then you can turn some of these into Super Fans.

6. A Yearning for the Authentic. We're seeing a strong return to basics throughout American life as we seek to bring our complicated and suddenly more dangerous world under control. In an "overcommunicated" society, it's harder to develop a message that penetrates and sticks. The new customer majority loathes artifice and is turned off by manipulative advertising. Powerful brands are simple messages that get through and provide comfort—an assurance of a company that has been and will be around. An increasingly high tech society will increasingly value high touch. Even in our "digital" age, the music industry has seen a surprising retro movement - vinyl records are back.

Some factors that suggest this return to "authenticity" include: 1) a reaction to "tech-produced" music and desire for less mediated sounds; 2) something more inward directed, looking at self improvement, and interactions among and within the groups and individuals that make up society; and, 3) a greater interest in sustainability, to include resources but also people, and more businesses and government are addressing issues that might be listed as sustainability, ethical or responsible behavior, and quality of life.

DJ artist (aka, Julius C.), Sergio Paramo, reveals a strong optimism when it comes to being authentic. "We are in a time where creative souls are rising to the front of every industry! The key is bringing the world something that is 100% you and organically prepared."

When reading and thinking about trends in the world and the market, it is also helpful to think about what career *implications* grow out of each trend, and then what career *application* may emerge from the implications.

For example, if we consider the Customer-Creator trend we may see the career implication as needing to be more collaborative with one's customers, clients or fans. A career application might be to develop a consulting service focused on helping businesses create programs and activities that enable this level of collaboration.

Of course, besides coming up with your own business there is also the franchise option, which we'll now look at briefly.

Music Franchising Opportunities

In just a few short decades, franchising has risen to become the most important new form of business organization since the advent of the modern corporation at the beginning of the twentieth century. Franchises currently account for more than 50 percent of all retail sales in the U.S., with gross revenues of $1.1 trillion. There are more than 780,000 franchised businesses employing more than 8.8 million people in sixty industries.

A new franchise opens its doors every eight minutes every business day, and the franchise industry itself is growing six times faster than the economy as a whole. There are more than 2000 franchised systems. Astonishingly, the majority of these franchise chains did not even exist twenty-five years ago. The most obvious franchises, of course, are the McDonalds, 7-Elevens and Subways. But there are hundreds of others you've probably never heard of, and several in the music category as well.

Franchising is a well-traveled road to entrepreneurship. A franchise typically enables you, the investor or "franchisee," to operate a "turnkey" business, that is, a business that is already set up and "ready to go". By paying a franchise fee, which may cost several thousand dollars, you are given a format or system developed by the company ("franchisor"), the right to use the franchisor's name for a limited time, and assistance. Think of franchising – or at least the costs of it – as paying for the work someone else has already done in developing a successful business model, marketing strategy, and superior operations efficiencies.

The popularity of the franchise business model has to do with its proven track record of success and ease in becoming a business owner; however, while the success rate for franchise-owned businesses is significantly higher than for independent businesses, no individual franchise is guaranteed to succeed.

❑ **Franchise Set Up.** Here is how the franchising process works. In exchange for obtaining the right to use the franchisor's name and its assistance, you may pay some or all of the following fees:

• *Initial Franchise Fee and Other Expenses.* Your initial franchise fee, which is often non-refundable, may cost several thousand to several hundred thousand dollars. Other start up costs include operating licenses and insurance. You also may be required to pay a "grand opening" fee to the franchisor to promote your new outlet.

• *Continuing Royalty Payments.* You may have to pay the franchisor royalties based on a percentage of your weekly or monthly gross income. You often must pay royalties even if your outlet has not earned significant income during that time.

• *Advertising Fees.* You may have to pay into a national or regional advertising fund.

❑ **Franchise Controls**. To help ensure uniformity, franchisors typically control how franchisees conduct business. The following are typical examples of such controls:

- *Site Approval.*
- *Design or Appearance Standards.* Depending on the franchise, periodic renovations or seasonal design changes will be required.
- *Restrictions on Goods and Services Offered for Sale.* Agreements with vendors will limit what you can sell on the premises.
- *Restrictions on Method of Operation.* These can include operating during only certain hours, using only pre-approved signs, employee uniforms, and advertisements.

NO NEED TO RE-INVENT THE WHEEL! - BORROWING BRINGS BOUNTY

- Mozart borrowed from Bach to compose concertos.
- Seventeenth-century French musicians borrowed from military music of ancient Greece and Turkey.
- Poussin's 'The Crossing of the Red Sea borrowed from Myron's 'Discus Thrower'.
- Paul Simon borrowed from South African musicians to create' Graceland'.
- The Rolling Stones borrowed from B.B. King, Muddy Waters and Solomon Burke.

Before buying into a franchise, spend some time speaking to franchise owners and take the following well-considered pros and cons to heart as you mull over your decision.

❑ **The Upside of Franchise Businesses**

- *Established Brand and Customer Base.* By far, the biggest advantage of buying into an established franchise is the strength and visibility of the brand.
- *Marketing Support.* Franchises often have the support of a national campaign, as well as prepared marketing materials for local outreach.
- *Reputable Suppliers*. Franchisors often have established relationships with suppliers for all the materials franchisees need.
- *Business Support*. There's a saying in franchising: "You're in business for yourself, but not by yourself" because you plug into a network of business owners facing the same daily challenges and problems.
- *Training*. Some of the better (and more expensive) franchise operations offer management, marketing and technical training.
- *Financial Assistance*. Some franchisors provide in-house loans as well as a "group rate" to reduce the costs of supplies, inventory, equipment and even medical, dental and eye care.
- *Access to Proprietary Methods*. There's no need to reinvent the wheel as franchisees get access to all the trade secrets.
- *Automatic R & D.* Franchisees can stick to improving their operations and let the franchisor spend the time and money researching and developing new products.
- *The Boss is You*. As with owning any business that you own, you are in control of your destiny.

THE WORST IDEAS THAT MADE A TON OF MONEY

• *Selling property on the moon:* Real estate on Earth might be undergoing a major price correction, but property on the moon still has many shelling out the dough.

• *The Million Dollar Homepage:* The idea of owning a piece of internet history convinced many to buy up Alex Tew's million-pixel homepage at $1 per pixel.

• *Pet Rock:* Never mind that consumers could find one on the ground for free. Paying $3.95 for a rock that came with eyes and a training manual was much more appealing-and transformed its creator into a millionaire.

• *Garbage Pail Kids:* Perhaps the grossest cards ever, they created quite a stir in the '80s.

• *Prairie Tumbleweed Farm:* Who knew the Kansas specialty, tumbleweeds, could be a hot commodity in other parts of the world?

• *Mood Ring:* Though wildly popular in the '70s, facial expressions served as a much better indicator of mood than the colors of this ring.

• *Chia Pets:* These animal-shaped clay figures grew popular by growing sprouts that closely resemble animal fur. While they're not nearly as popular now as they were in the '80s, the new Chia Obama might just bring about a rebirth.

Source: *Entrepreneur Magazine*

- *Reduced Risk*. Your risk is reduced as you are buying into a proven system for operating the business and generating profits.

❑ The Challenges of Franchise Businesses

- *Initial Payout (Franchise Fee and Start-up Costs).* Depending on the size of the franchise, operations can involve a very large initial costs, often more than what it would cost to start your own business.

- *Royalty Payments*. For as long as you are a franchisee, you will have to pay some percentage of the monthly gross back to the franchisor, reducing your profit margin.

- *Marketing/Advertising Fees*. To receive the wonderful marketing support from the franchisor, franchisees must sometimes pay a certain amount of marketing fees.

- *Limited Creativity/Flexibility*. Most franchise contracts have very explicit standards, allowing little or no alterations or additions to the brand, stifling any creativity on the part of the franchisee. If you use their system, you must follow their rules.

- *Cannibalization (profit eaters).* Franchisors sometimes get so eager to keep growing that they allow franchisees to locate so close to one another that they cut into one another's profits.

- *Locked into Operation by Long-Term Contract*. If for some reason you find yourself with the wrong franchise, you may be stuck for many years.

- *Dependent on Franchisor Success*. The reputation of your franchise is only as good as that of the franchisor, so any difficulties that the franchisor encounters will have a direct impact on you.

- *False Expectations*. Opening a franchise rather than starting your own business offers no guarantees of success. You still need to be a sharp businessperson to make it work.

- *Risk.* While it is certainly reduced with a franchise, there's always risk in starting any new business.

With such a long list of pros and cons, it’s clear that franchising isn’t for everyone. If you are fiercely independent, hate interference and want to design every aspect of your business, you may be better off starting your own company. On the other hand, the transition to entrepreneurship and doing everything for yourself can be jarring. Buying into a franchise could offer the support you need in making the switch to entrepreneurship. Again, speak to those who have done it before making any moves. Besides your own instincts, this is the best source for exploring business options.

The following chart provides an overview of the many different kinds of arts-related businesses currently in existence. Again, the musical arts have a close relationship to almost every one of them. Which area do you want to work in, and what role do you want to play? Any one of the following can be turned into an entrepreneurial venture.

TYPES OF ROLES AND BUSINESSES IN THE "CULTURE AND ENTERTAINMENT INDUSTRIES"

Role	Not-for-Profit Corporations	For-Profit Businesses	Government Agencies
PRODUCERS	• Theater company • Symphony orchestra • Community chorus • Summer theater • Dance Company	• Private galleries • Recording studios • Individual artists/bands • Broadway theater • Touring companies • Film industry	• School music, drama, art programs • Job programs with art focus
PRESENTERS	• Performing arts centers • Arts festivals • Arts and lecture series	• Arenas and stadiums • Movie theaters • Theme parks • Rock/country festivals	• Performing arts centers located at state universities or at high schools
CURATORS	• Museums • Historical sites • Public galleries • Botanical gardens	• Some touring art exhibits • Private collections • Private galleries • Record labels	• City/county museums • College art galleries • Zoos • Libraries • The Smithsonian Institutions
SERVICE PROVIDERS	• Local arts councils • State art service orgs • Discipline-specific organizations • Some arts-resource websites	• Some arts-resource websites • Some industry-specific groups • Booking agents	• NEA • State arts boards/councils • City/country arts agencies

Shaping Your Basic Business Concept

By now you're probably beginning to discern the outlines of a business idea. It may be a small entertainment company offering wedding and private party performances; or a service that helps artists organize and execute online social marketing campaigns; or perhaps it's an educational program that takes drumming and rhythm-making into the public schools. Sometimes your business idea is no more than a hunch with a dose of passion. After working in a marketing company designing reports, Andreas Katsambas decided he needed to do something more creative and passion-driven. "It wasn't a conscious decision," he says. "It [The End Records] started mostly as a hobby trying to help bands I liked. It was done after hours and the weekends and took three years to become a full time job".

The chart below shows the great variety of music-related businesses that can be developed today, most within your own home or apartment.

SOME MUSIC-RELATED BUSINESS OPPORTUNITIES TODAY

DJ Service	Private Music Instruction	Music & Brands Consultant
Booking Agent	Jingle writer	Acoustic Consultant
Film Scorer	Social Media Consultant	Game Music Supervisor
Music Copyist	Music Publisher	Music Journalist
Virtual Worlds Developer	Online Music Retailer	Music Widget Maker
Mobile Music Marketing	Music Supervisor	Online Editorial
Digital Marketing	Commercial Music Producer	Music Therapist
Project Studio Owner	Macro & Micro Blogging	Audio Forensic Specialist
Podcast Producer	Artist/Personal Manager	Music Publicist
New Media PR	Concert Promoter	Instrument Repair
Record Label	Music Web Portal	

Meeting needs is the basis of all business. You can devise a wonderful new software product, but if it doesn't address some real and important need or desire, people won't buy it, and your business will fail.

Typically, entrepreneurs get their original business inspiration from one of four sources: 1) previous work experience; 2) education or training; 3) hobbies, talents, or other personal interests; or 4) recognition of an unanswered need or market opportunity.

In her book, *The Successful Business Plan*, Rhonda Adams recommends incorporating at least one of the following elements into your thinking, as you refine your own business concept:

• **Something New**. This could be a new product, service, feature, or technology. The iPod is a good example of this.

• **Something Better.** This could be an improvement on an existing product or service encompassing more features, lower price, greater reliability, faster speed, or increased convenience. An online music instruction service, for instance, appeals to those looking for more convenience.

• **An Underserved or New Market**. This is a market for which there is greater demand than competitors can currently satisfy, an underserved location, or a small part of an overall market – a niche market – that hasn't yet been dominated by other competitors. Sometimes, markets become underserved when large companies abandon or neglect smaller portions of their current customer base. Digital marketing services are currently increasing in demand.

• **New Delivery System of Distribution Channel**. New technologies, particularly the internet, allow companies to reach customers more efficiently. Sonicbids is a prime example of this.

• **Increased Integration.** This occurs when a product is both manufactured and sold by the same company, or when a company offers more services or products in one location. A music school that includes dance and acting lessons will appeal to those with an interest in musical theater.

Your business should incorporate at least one of these factors – more than one, if possible. Evaluate the ways your business idea addresses the elements described above. Your concept should be strong in at least one area. If not, you should ask yourself how your company will be truly competitive.

Based on Adams' list we can now create a worksheet to help you clarify your basic business concept:

Basic Business Concept Worksheet

Using this worksheet as a guide, 'sketch' your business concept as you presently conceive it.

❑ Is yours a retail, service, manufacturing, distribution, or internet business?

❑ What industry does it belong to?

❑ What products or services do you sell?

❑ Who do you see as your potential customers?

❑ Describe your basic overall marketing and sales strategy:

❑ Which companies and types of companies do you consider to be your competitors?

List your competitive advantages, if any, in each area listed below.

❑ New Products/Services:

❑ Improved Features/Services and Added Value:

❑ New or Underserved Markets Reached:

❑ New/Improved Delivery or Distribution Method:

❑ Methods of Increased Integration:

Once an entrepreneur has gone through this business concept worksheet, she is able to proceed with the venture, with the opportunity, in an educated manner, feeling confident that her idea will have validation in the market place.

So how does your business idea stack up? Based on the preceding worksheet, do you consider it to be a true opportunity? Is there a demonstrated need, a ready market, and the ability to provide a solid return on investment? If you believe so, you deserve congratulations. If not, I encourage you to follow the tips earlier for generating and finding additional ideas and opportunities.

Those who feel they have a solid idea can now delve into the following chapter where we go into depth on the subjects of understanding your market and customer, and finding a unique market niche for your unique business idea.

CHAPTER SUMMARY

DISCERNING TODAY'S MUSIC OPPORTUNITIES

- **The New Opportunity**

  Technology allows small businesses to enter and compete in industries formerly served only by big business. New production methods, which have automated some processes, customized others, and reduced the cost of still others, have combined to allow many owner-operators to produce more with less. In addition, small business owners find that they can cost-effectively outsource production (usually using domestic manufacturers), removing the need to build their own production facilities and hire their own employees. And, because so much of the U.S. economy is now in the services sector, in which people sell what they know or know how to do, production costs in many businesses can be kept extremely low.

- **Music Business Trends Impacting Opportunity**

  One of the first things you do in business planning is an "environmental analysis." An important part of this includes exploring trends that are impacting the way people view and use entertainment products and services. What I'm referring to when I say "trends" are emerging meta-currents in our social and cultural lives that herald new ways of living and thinking. These currents have been gradual and sometimes difficult to arrest and analyze. Nevertheless, they are very real and they are changing the world, especially the world of the independent creative worker.

- **The 50,000 Foot View**

  Entertainment marketing is consumed with speed - there is little or no time to test-market before release, before one source or another gets word of the buzz on a project and broadcasts it to the world at large. The product of entertainment content is based totally on creativity; therefore, it is fraught with the possibilities of human frailties. Entertainment marketing first focuses on selling an experience rather than an object. The audiences must first buy into the event, before the sale of objects associated with that encounter can occur. Some of the "megatrends" within Music Entertainment:

  #1: Every Business is Becoming an Entertainment Business
  #2: Rise of the Customer-Creator
  #3: Music as "Service" (rather than "Product")
  #4: New Music Company Models
  #5: Rapidly Segmenting Music Markets
  #6: The Growing Need for Context
  #7: Resurgent Indie Culture

- **Other Music Market Micro-Trends**

  1. Streaming Goes Mainstream While Fairer Formats Ascend. The streaming option puts users in control of what they listen to and when, because streaming service libraries are nearly limitless, and music can be streamed anywhere there is an Internet connection. At the same time, there is a strong push being made towards a "Fair Trade Music Format" using blockchain, which will incorporate metadata and a cryptocurrency such as BitCoin.
  2. Dataming, Music and The Internet of Things. The future of the Internet over the next two decades and beyond is most likely to see a whole new hyper-connected world of networked people, objects, and systems capable of transforming, reframing, and undermining the established norms of business and society.
  3. Sizeable Music Spending Continues. While consumers purchase little physical content, music is still a big part of their annual budget, at $125 in 2015, according to Deloitte. It estimates that 80 percent of Millennials will attend a live event, and that most would like to spend more on live music than in prior years.
  4. Achieving "Success" on Many Levels. The ability for an artist to achieve "success" in the music industry has less to do with being a Billboard chart topper and more to do with working smarter and more efficiently to create content that uniquely engages a fan base.
  5. "Freemium Business Models." It's the delivery of Internet services that are free to the user because the marginal costs of manufacturing and distribution are zero, or close to it. This means that businesses can now experiment with giving away one thing to sell something else.
  6. A Yearning for the Authentic. Some factors that suggest this include: 1) a rise in the need

for interdisciplinary understanding 2) something more inward directed, looking at self improvement, and interactions among and within the groups and individuals that make up society; and, 3) a greater interest in sustainability, to include resources but also people, and more businesses and government are addressing issues that might be listed as sustainability, ethical or responsible behavior, and quality of life.

- **Music Franchising Opportunities**
  Franchising is a well-traveled road to entrepreneurship. A franchise typically enables you, the investor or "franchisee," to operate a "turnkey" business, that is, a business that is already set up and "ready to go".

- **Shaping Your Basic Business Concept**
  Meeting needs is the basis of all business. Typically, entrepreneurs get their original business inspiration from one of four sources: 1) previous work experience; 2) education or training; 3) hobbies, talents, or other personal interests; or 4) recognition of an unanswered need or market opportunity.

FURTHER RESOURCES

ONLINE RESOURCES

Franchiseknowhow.com

Franchising.com

Trendwatching.com

BOOKS

The Art of Immersion: How the Digital Generation Is Remaking Hollywood, Madison Avenue, and the Way We Tell Stories by Frank Rose *(2012, W.W. Norton).*

The Experience Economy: Work is Theater & Every Business a Stage by B. Joseph Pine and James Gilmore (2011, Harvard Business School).

Experience the Message: Experiential Marketing is Changing the Brand World by Max Lenderman (2006, Basic Books).

The Future of the Music Business, 2nd ed. by Steve Gordon (2005/2008, Backbeat Press).

In The Plex: How Google Thinks, Works, and Shapes Our Lives by Steven Levy (2011, Simon & Schuster).

The Long Tail: Why the Future of Business is Selling Less of More by Chris Anderson (2006, Hyperion).

Micro-Trends: The Small Forces Behind Tomorrow's Big Changes by Mark Penn (2007, Twelve Press).

Music 2.0: Essays by Gerd Leonard (2008, Media Futurist).

Smart Mobs: The Next Social Revolution by Howard Rheingold (2005, Basic Books).

The Startup Checklist: 25 Steps to a Scalable, High-Growth Business by David S. Rose (2016, Wiley).

The Third Wave by Alvin Toffler (1984, Wm. Morrow & Co.). Remarkably prescient.

Wikinomics: How Mass Collaboration Changes Everything by Don Tapscott (2010, Portfolio).

ASSOCIATIONS/ORGANIZATIONS

International Franchise Association
Franchise.org (202) 628-8000

Institute for the Future
iftf.org

3

FINDING YOUR NICHE IN TODAY'S MUSIC MARKET

There are myriad ways to distribute music, so the key question is how to acquire customers?
– Mark Cuban

The culmination of the first five chapters of this book will be the creation of a business plan, an important document that defines what an entrepreneur plans to accomplish and how she plans on accomplishing it.

Too often, business plans describe in great detail what the entrepreneur intends to accomplish (e.g. "the financials") and pay little, if any, attention to the strategies to achieve those targets. To be effective a solid business plan must, therefore, contain both a financial plan and a marketing plan. In fact, I would argue the marketing plan should be the first item to attend to because without a clear idea of your market (that is, your potential customers), everything else in your plan risks missing its intended target.

Most marketing experts agree the greatest marketing mistake small businesses make is failing to define clearly the target market to be served. In other words, most small businesses follow a "shotgun" approach to marketing, firing marketing blasts at every customer they see, hoping to capture just some of them. But most entrepreneurs simply cannot use shotgun marketing tactics and compete successfully with larger rivals and their bigger budgets.

Why, then, is the shotgun approach so popular? Because it is easy and does not require market research or a well thought-out marketing plan! The problem is that the shotgun approach is a *sales*-driven rather than a *customer*-driven strategy. Smart entrepreneurs know that they do not have the luxury of wasting resources: they must follow a more focused, "arrow" approach to marketing. This is DJ, Sergio Paramo's advice, "Every person has it in them to do something great but the secret is knowing your market well."

What is Marketing?

"Marketing" is one of those "putty" words that seems to have as many definitions as definers. According to the American Marketing Association, "marketing" is "the performance of business activities directed toward, and incident to, the flow of goods and services from producer to consumer or user." Um...sure; ok.

But let's get to the *essence* of marketing. When you boil down all the definitions to their essential core, you find that marketing is, quite simply, *communication.* Think of all the possible expressions of marketing: advertising, publicity, email, promotion, "tweets", phone calls, buttons, blimps, stickers, street teams, billboards, radio, brochures, networking, logos, displays, web sites, trade shows, packaging, sampling, public relations, performances, press kits, bios, photos – what do they all have in common? **Communication**. The effectiveness of your marketing will be a direct result of how well, how effective, how targeted, and how prepared your communication is.

Types Of Markets: Where Does Your Project Fit?

A "market" is simply any group of actual or potential buyers of a product or service. There are three major types of markets. Which one will be your focus?:

1. *The Consumer Market.* Individuals and households who buy goods for their own use or benefit are part of the consumer market. An example would be selling a CD to a buyer at a performance.

2. *The Business Market.* Represents individuals, groups or organizations that purchase your specific product or service for direct use in producing other products or for use in their day-to-day operations. This could be licensing a track to an advertising agency for the production of a TV commercial or contracting with the public schools to offer a special drum & rhythm workshop.

3. *The Reseller Market.* Represents middlemen or intermediaries, such as wholesalers and retailers who buy finished goods and resell them for the purpose of making a profit. An example would be selling a music video DVD to a distributor who then manufactures them and eventually ships them to retail chains.

Some music companies engage all three markets; others focus on just one. You will need to determine which of the three are appropriate for what you are selling and how you'd like to sell it. Part of figuring this out is coming to understand what your own particular market niche is.

The Challenge of Finding Your Market Niche

I always wanted to be somebody, but I should have been more specific. – Lily Tomlin

In study after study of successful individuals, one trait found to be common among them is this: they were all highly focused. At some point along the way, they had each realized that they had to make a committment to *one* business idea. And, in fact, many of them had to make difficult choices and let go of some possibilities that seemed appealing.

People don't focus for a number of reasons: Perhaps they fear that by focusing on one thing they risk not having enough business; or, maybe they don't want to miss an opportunity; or perhaps they just have multiple interests. Whatever the reason, you need to become attuned to the fact that the times call for focus. Mass customization and a segmenting

marketplace allow for the development of products and services of a "niche" nature. Since few of us have the time, money or energy to mount national marketing campaigns, it is in your best interest to discover and concentrate on a niche that you can develop towards successful enterprise.

What is a "niche"? *Niche* is an architectural term referring to a special place designed to display or show off an object of some kind, like an ornament, placed in a recess of a wall or an arched area of a room. And that's just what a niche can be for you. Finding your niche will set you off from others who offer something similar and draw the best possible attention to you and what you can offer. Another way of expressing the idea of a market niche is to call it a "strategic position."

"This is your distinguishing characeristic," says Jandro Cisneros, "something we call in Spanish, *ventaja diferencial competitiva*, which means the quality that makes you different from your competitors. In other words, having clarity about your mission, vision, and type of products/services that you can provide, and understanding why people should choose you among the competitors."

Examples of niche marketing abound in the world of music:

• Chris Silvers, a Dallas trumpeter, used to take out every Latin music recording from the Dallas Public Library and play along with them, until he mastered the horn lines. As a result, he became a first-call musician and horn arranger for all latin bands passing through the Dallas-Fort Worth area and beyond.

• Austin native Joycie Mennihan was always drawn to music's power to heal. She took this interest and turned it into "Sound Health", a company providing workshops, seminars and books about music therapy and its health benefits.

• Lee Jason Kibler (aka DJ Logic) turned an interest in sampling and a love of multiple music styles, into a unique production sound so that his chops are some of the most in-demand from top recording artists.

• Boston's Rosie Cohen, took a love of singer songwriters, a passion for adult literacy, and tireless devotion, and turned it into Big Girl Records' first release, "Can You Read This Boston?," a compilation album of singer-songwriters, with a portion of the proceeds going to the Boston Adult Literacy Fund.

• Nashville's Eric Stone took a love of music and boating and in 1999 turned it into boatsongs.com, music CDs and performances with a nautical theme. So far he's played in four continents and sold over 300,000 CDs, and his audience continues to grow.

Exercise - The niche you decide to focus on will be a reflection of your interests, values, personality and skills, as well as the times your living in. Your goal should be to define what you do by depth, not by breadth.

To help you decide on the one niche you want to become known for in music, or to just bring clearer focus to the music niche you already identify with, weigh your options by asking yourself:

- Which things do I do best in the world of music?
- Which activities do I enjoy most in the world of music?
- What do I do that people need and appreciate most?
- In what areas do I have the greatest expertise and experience?
- What am I already best known for?
- What do I have the best contacts to do?
- What will people most readily pay me for?
- What involves the least risk?

- What fits best with my lifestyle and personal goals?
- What am I most eager to promote?

If you notice the same activity showing up as an answer over and over again, you're getting close to understanding what your niche is.

Sometimes a niche appears out of necessity. That's what happened with the launch of online CD retailer CDBaby. Founder Derek Sivers couldn't get an online store to stock his band's recording so he started his own online store. "I had been a professional musician for 10 years at the time I started CD Baby as a hobby," says Sivers. "I deeply understood what musicians needed, because I really I just needed the same things myself."

Strategies for Finding Your Niche

"I often notice, when I'm talking with people involved in the arts, that their concept of what they want to do is to aim for the biggest, most obvious target, and hit it smack in the bull's eye. That's success, whatever the particular field is. Of course with everybody else aiming there as well, that makes it very hard to hit.... As Jon Hassell always says, I prefer to shoot the arrow, then paint the target around it. You make the niches in which you finally reside." —Brian Eno, Musician & Producer

Finding a niche means clearly identifying a group of people who need a particular product or service you're distinctly able to provide. Your niche needs to be small enough that you don't have much competition and can still reach most of your potential customers within the limits of your time and budget, yet large enough to include ample customers you can support yourself by serving.

Here is a samping of strategies for scoping out a niche that is right for you:

1) Select a growth area. When a market is growing, there is more room for everbody. Therefore, your chances of winning are highest when you pick a market that is on the upswing. This can apply to musical styles as well as to entire industries. For example, the technology explosion in media and entertainment is creating and will continue to create new jobs for musicians and all other digital content providers.

2) Don't automatically follow the crowd, and don't necessarily pick the obvious. It's always a good idea to select a market with as few competitors as possible. Do you want to be one of 400 bands trying out for the same gig? Me neither. Always look for opportunities that everyone else is overlooking.

3) Attempt to put a lock on a specific market niche. This is one of the most important competitive strategies. A market niche is a specialization within a market. For example, a studio musician in the L.A area who primarily plays piano on country sessions has created a personal niche as did the previously-mentioned Chris Silvers of Dallas. Select a market niche that is large enough to pay you well, one that you believe you can dominate.

Then take charge of it. Meet all the important people, develop an excellent reputation, and maintain the highest standards.

4) Be memorable. This is a stylistic version of items 2 and 3. If you want to go far in the music industry, you need to give others a reason to remember you. Whether you have a unique appearance, sound, stage presence, packaging or whatever, you must stand out from the crowd.

5) Excel at what you do. While technical skill and polish don't guarantee you success, there is *never* a penalty for being too good at what you do. And there are plenty of situations where the better player or the more confident performer wins.

Once you commit to focusing all your available time, money and effort on one endeavor, you'll be in a position to become known for that activity; and as your reputation grows, word of mouth will start bringing business to you.

If you're already doing or considering a multiplicity of things, you need to decide what you want your focus to be, what one thing you want to become known for. Making such a choice may not be easy. You may feel torn between pursuing what you enjoy doing and what people seem to be most willing to pay you to do. You may have to let go of some of your pet projects in order to pursue only one of them.

Choosing a focus will open certain doors for you while closing others. But just as you'll never get to see the world if you can't decide which destination to head for first, so it is with committing to one focus for your business marketing. The doors that will open to you once you fully commit to one endeavor will present new opportunities you may have never imagined.

Here are three additional ways to help define your focus:

1. Just pick one. In some cases the best decision is simply to pick one of the things you've been considering or pursuing and let the others fall by the wayside. That's essentially what I did when I started Music Business Solutions.

In order to commit to this focus I had to give up a lucrative performing schedule and booking agency gig. For me, time and family became extremely important when my first child was born. I could have kept on gigging four times a week but it would have meant little time with my growing family. Too, I could have kept the booking agency but it would have meant having less time to develop my consulting and writing pursuits.

2. Create an Umbrella Concept. Sometimes it's not possible to earn a full-time living doing a particular business. There may not be enough demand for what you want to offer, or you may live in an area where there aren't enough people to support such a business full-time. In this case, you can avoid the problems of being unfocused by providing a variety of closely related services under a unifying umbrella concept.

Singer/songwriter Ellen Bernfield and her composer friend Anne Bryant began singing lullabies to soothe and calm their new English springer spaniel puppies. Then their creative juices started flowing, and they decided to produce an entire album of music for dogs and the people who love them. Working out of Anne's home where Ellen has a recording studio, they produced a CD and fully illustrated book called *Songs for Dogs.* In order to expand their business, however, they've needed to add other CDs to their line, so they are now creating CDs under the umbrella concept music for pet owners. Their next album is *Songs for Cats and the People Who Love Them.*

As you can see, the secret to creating a successful umbrella concept is providing a cluster of products or services that are clearly related in the minds of those who need the service.

3. Develop a Hybrid. Some people don't want to chose among the various things they're doing, so instead of doing multiple things, they combine the activities they love most into one hybrid business. Marcy Hamm, for example, has three great loves: mathematics, music, and computers. But instead of trying to offer three different services like tutoring, composing, and computer programming, Hamm left her prestigious job as a software engineer to produce computer-generated music that reduces stress and speeds healing.

Matrixing: The Crossroads Where Niches Lie

There is a tool that is used in many businesses called "matrixing". It's a process developed by marketing analysts that provides a formula for finding a product's niche in the marketplace. The matrix idea was adapted by home office gurus, Paul & Sarah Edwards and applied to finding your own personal niche. It can be graphically illustrated as follows:

MATRIXING

Your ideal niche will lie at the crossroads where your ***INTERESTS*** and ***RESOURCES*** intersect with ***OPPORTUNITIES*** you have to meet ***REAL-LIFE NEEDS*** around you.

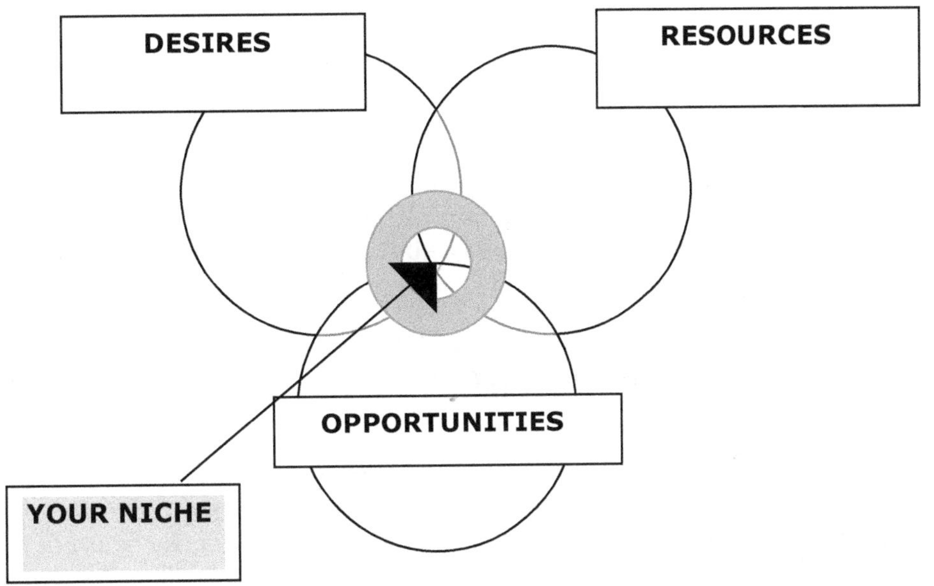

- ***Compelling Desires:*** the things in life you feel most passionate about, interested in, or concerned for.

- ***Personal Resources:*** your background, education, experiences, contacts, and other assets.

- ***Opportunities:*** problems, needs, and desires people are willing to pay you to address.

For me, it was a compelling combination of a passion for music, a desire to help people realize their potential, and a love for research and writing that led me to my present work. My background includes twenty-five years of music performing and recording experience, Sunday school teaching, a Masters degree in cultural history, management of a community center, youth-development work and a co-authored history book. The opportunity presented itself one night as I pondered all the information I had gathered over the years to help promote the bands I played with and the music I wrote. I knew there were many other musicians, like me, who needed practical guidance about how to create success for themselves in the unforgiving world of business. So, in 1991, Music Business Solutions was born, which led the following year to my being hired by Berklee College of Music to head its career development center.

The key is to find overlaps between your interests and passions, your background and experience, and the opportunities you see. Take one interest at a time and try different possibilities. You can do this by filling in the following statements:

"I could combine my interest in____

with my experience, background, and/or contacts in ___________________________

to meet the needs ______________________________(type of people, companies,

industries)____ have for

____.

To identify a niche, you must find good answers to the following:

- What can you offer they (your nearest competition) do not?
- Why will people come to you rather than going to them?
- What will you be able to say about yourself and your product or service that sets you apart from them?

Obviously there needs to be a market for what you settle on. But assuming there is one, can you see how much easier it is to answer the questions above about the need for a narrower focus?

In a narrow niche, it is much easier to set yourself apart from your competitors. Much easier to let your web site, for example, speak for itself and demonstrate your expertise. And it answers the question of why people should come to you, for you are now a specialist, soon to become an expert. This doesn't mean you can't "do it all." ***The point is to lead with what you do best.*** Once you attract customers to your business because of your specialty, you can introduce them to the other products or services you offer.

Testing Your Idea's Feasibility

Now that you have a business idea and a sense of your market niche, it is time to pass them through a test to determine if they truly are valid opportunities. This is known as testing the idea's *feasibility*. All of your ideas must have a demonstrated need, ready market, and ability to provide a solid return on investment.

Is your idea feasible in the marketplace? Is there a real demand? Can it be done? Are you able to pull together the people and resources to pull it off before the window of opportunity closes? The following questions must be considered and answered satisfactorily before launching your company. Answer them to the best of your ability. Your responses will, in turn, provide the "raw material" for your business plan.

Ten Questions to of Ask of Every Business Idea

1. What is the need you fill or problem you solve? (Value Proposition)
2. Who are you selling to? (Target Market)
3. How would you make money? (Revenue Model)
4. How will you differentiate your company from what is already out there? (Unique Selling Proposition or USP)
5. What are the barriers to entry? (Threats)
6. How many competitors do you have and of what quality are they? (Competitive Analysis)
7. How big is your market in dollars? (Market Size)
8. What type of company would this be? (Lifestyle or High Potential, Sole Proprietorship or Corporation)
9. How much would it cost to get started? (Start-up Costs)
10. Do you plan to use debt capital or raise investment? If so, how much and what type? (Investment needs)

You may not feel capable of answering all these questions right now. That's ok. This is why a business plan is written. It helps you do the necessary research to test your idea's feasibility and it allows you to mentally rehearse all aspects of your idea *beforehand*.

But before we get to the business and marketing planning, let's become acquainted with the vast resources you have available to help inform and support your efforts as a 21st century music entrepreneur. These will provide you with the right information to map your plan.

CHAPTER SUMMARY

ZEROING IN ON YOUR MARKET

- **What is Marketing?**
  According to the American Marketing Association, "marketing" is "the performance of business activities directed toward, and incident to, the flow of goods and services from producer to consumer or user. To make it even more simple: Marketing is communication. The effectiveness of your marketing will be a direct result of how well, how creative, how targeted, and how prepared your communication is.

- **Types of Markets: Where Does your Project Fit?**
  A Market is simply any group of actual or potential buyers of a product or service. There are three major types of markets: The Consumer Market, The Business Market and The Reseller Market. Some music companies engage all three markets; others focus on just one. You will need to determine which of the three are appropriate for what you are selling and how you'd like to sell it.

- **The Challenge of Finding Your Market Niche**
  In study after study of successful individuals, one trait found to be common among them is this: they were all highly focused. Finding your niche focus will set you off from others who offer something similar and draw the best possible attention to you and what you can offer. Another way of expressing the idea of a market niche is to call it a "strategic position."

- **Strategies for Finding Your Niche**
  Some strategies for scoping out a niche that is right for you include: Select a growth area; Don't automatically follow the crowd; and don't necessarily pick the obvious; Attempt to put a lock on a specific market niche; Be memorable; Excel at what you do.

- **Matrixing: The Crossroads Where Niches Lie**
  Matrixing is a process developed by marketing analysts that provides a formula for finding a product's niche in the marketplace. The matrix idea is adapted here and applied to finding your own personal niche distinction.

- **Testing Your Idea's Feasibility**
  Is your business idea feasible in the marketplace? Is there a real demand for it? Are you able to pull together the people and resources to pull it off before the window of opportunity closes? A certain group of questions must be considered and answered satisfactorily before launching your company.

FURTHER RESOURCES

BOOKS

Building Buzz to Beat the Big Boys by Steve O'Leary & Kim Sheehan (2008, Praeger Publishers).

Citizen Marketers: When People Are the Message by Ben McConnell & Jackie Huba (2012, Kaplan Business).

Contagious: Why Things Catch On by Jonah Berger (2016, Simon & Schuster).

Driving Demand: Transforming B2B Marketing to Meet the Needs of the Modern Buyer by Carlos Hidalgo (2015, Palgrave MacMillan).

Duct Tape Marketing by John Jantsch (2011, Thomas Nelson).

Growth Hacker Marketing: A Primer on the Future of PR, Marketing, and Advertising by Ryan Holiday (2014, Portfolio).

Mastering Niche Marketing: A Definitive Guide to Profiting From Ideas in a Competitive Market by Eric V. Van Der Hope (2008, Globalnet Publishing).

Stand Out: How to Find Your Breakthrough Idea and Build a Following Around It by Dorie Clark (2015, Portfolio).

The Tipping Point by Malcolm Gladwell (2000, Little, Brown & Company).

4

KNOWING YOUR RESOURCES

As a general rule, the most successful people in life are those who have the best information.
- Benjamin Disraeli

Info-Power is Yours

The most strategic factor in business today is knowledge. Most people think that large businesses (with their lawyers, accountants, engineers, etc.) have a major advantage over the small business owner in terms of knowledge. This may be true in some cases, but the situation isn't as bad as it seems.

The Internet and, equally important your local library, bring tons of useful information within the grasp of every entrepreneurial citizen. Information is *power* and don't forget it. Check this out: Historians trace the transformation of ancient Egyptian society to the invention of papyrus as a writing surface. Before this, precious and rare agricultural information was stored on expensive stone tablets *and* hoarded by the ruling elite. Once this information became available on a more portable (and cheaper) surface, it was diffused more easily throughout Egyptian society. Subsequently, lower economic classes began using this information to their own advantage and the control of wealth came into the hands of the many rather than just the few. This, of course, affected the authority of the traditional rulers and an incipient democracy began to emerge in ancient Egyptian society.

A similar development took place in 16th-century Europe. The written word was under the control of churches, kings and lawyers. Most people couldn't read and the ruling class liked it this way. Each parish had a single Bible, written by hand, and often chained to the altar of the local church building - an apt metaphor for how information was held captive. Then in 1524 Johannes Gutenberg changed the western world with his invention of printing by movable type. Whereas before his invention it took several weeks to produce a single volume by hand, Gutenberg's press could print out a book in less than a day.

So information certainly brings power and there is more of it is available to day than at any other time in recorded history. However, while information is hyper-abundant, the key is getting to the *right* information for your particular needs. As already discussed in chapter 2, what information needs is *context* so that is can be genuinely *useful*. Otherwise it's just data, like a bunch of beads with nothing to string them on.

What kinds of information do you need? You'll begin figuring this out as you ask and answer those questions at the end of last chapter. In general you'll need:

- Information about your industry
- Information about key players and influencers in that industry
- Information about a specific market
- Information about competitors in that market
- Information about legal requirements for your business idea
- Information about start up costs in your line of business
- Information about taxes and other financial requirements

The music industry is fairly complex and you really need as much industry knowledge as you can get. By that, I mean that you have some understanding of issues such as these, as they affect your business: Are there slow and busy times within the industry? What professional organizations are important to belong to? How is your profession or industry structured? What divisions exist for entry level, mid career, and advanced levels? What happens during the normal course of business? For instance, if your focus is recorded music, what happens in order for a song to be published? Can you name all the steps? Which steps would a customer expect you to perform, and which would be referred elsewhere? What is the jargon used in your industry or profession? What words will you need to know in order to communicate with people while doing your work? How is the industry segmented? Using publishing as an example again, do you know that the industry is segmented into small publishers, specialty publishers, large publishers with multiple sub-publishers, and so on? What rules govern your industrial profession? What licensing is required? Which government agencies regulate the industry/profession?

It's also important to look beyond your own industry for insights. "Try to garner as much outside help as you can and don't stop at one source," advises Jay Andreozzi of Amalgam Digital. "Get multiple perspectives. You may learn from other business owners even outside of the industry you are in."

Planning a business is like drawing a map. The map (in this case, your business plan) will ultimately be used to help you get to your destination. What you need, therefore, is the right information to help you construct your map. What does the market "terrain" look like? Where are the rivers, mountains, hills and valleys? How can you avoid the bogs and quicksand pits? Where can you take a paved road and where might you have to cut your own path through untried territory?

An understanding of your knowledge resources allows you to create a map that will get you to your destination in the most effective and efficient way possible. Having the right information always gives you the upper hand.

Information and knowledge also help us compensate for our own blind spots and myopia. It's tough to get a new slant on something when you're looking at it head-on.
A cube seen head-on is a square. Step left or right and you begin to see its full dimensions. That's often what happens when you acquire more knowledge. By seeing more of what you're looking at you have a better chance of noticing slants, angles and dimensions you may not have considered before. Again, information is *power*.

In this chapter we'll look at the various information resources you have at your disposal. In the following chapter ('Researching Your Market') we'll apply these resources to your specific target market.

Free Tools to Help Your Research

As your revenue grows, you may need to hire more specialists for your information needs. For now, however, there are plenty of places to go to get information costing very little, except for time. Here are a few:

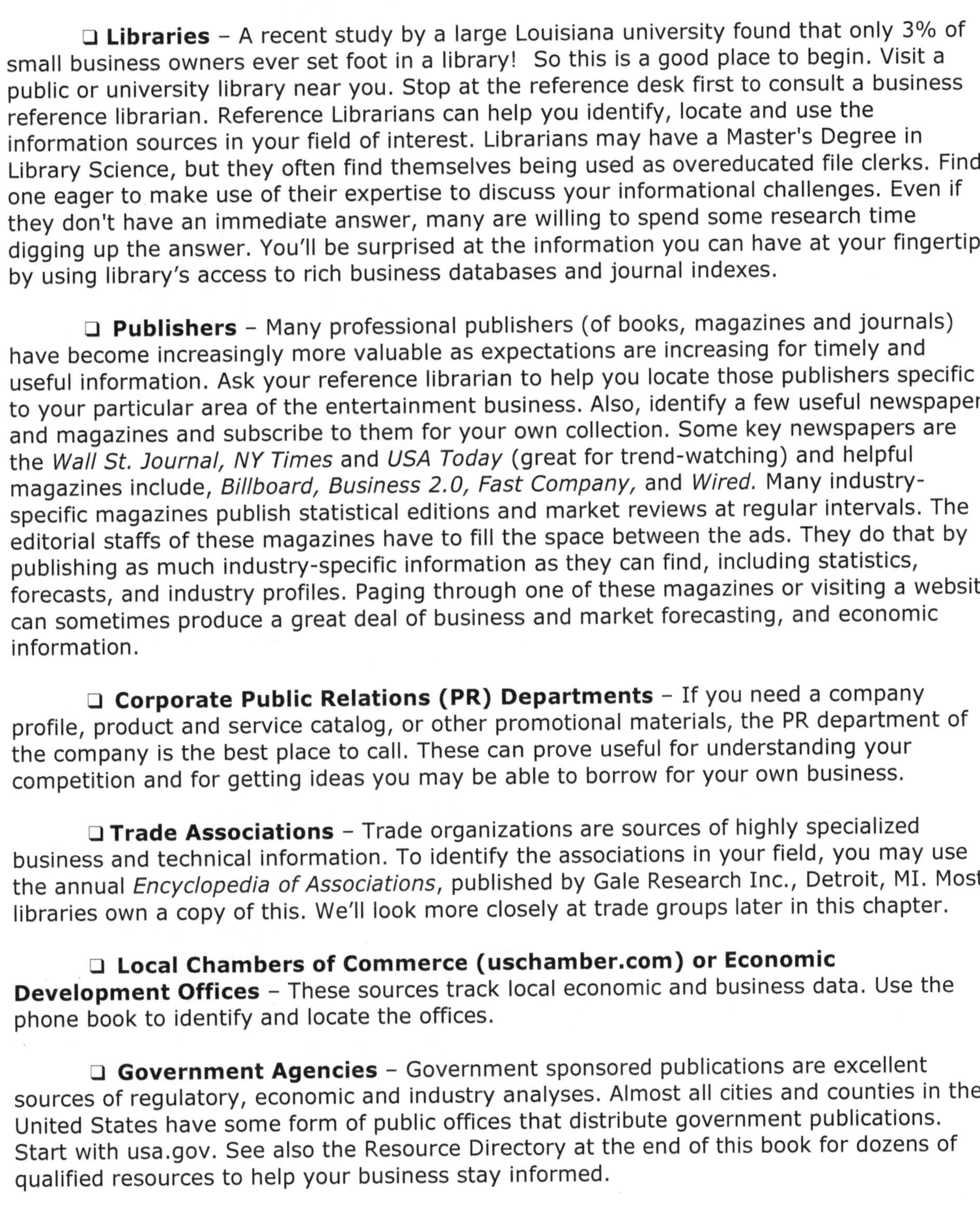

❑ **Libraries** – A recent study by a large Louisiana university found that only 3% of small business owners ever set foot in a library! So this is a good place to begin. Visit a public or university library near you. Stop at the reference desk first to consult a business reference librarian. Reference Librarians can help you identify, locate and use the information sources in your field of interest. Librarians may have a Master's Degree in Library Science, but they often find themselves being used as overeducated file clerks. Find one eager to make use of their expertise to discuss your informational challenges. Even if they don't have an immediate answer, many are willing to spend some research time digging up the answer. You'll be surprised at the information you can have at your fingertips by using library's access to rich business databases and journal indexes.

❑ **Publishers** – Many professional publishers (of books, magazines and journals) have become increasingly more valuable as expectations are increasing for timely and useful information. Ask your reference librarian to help you locate those publishers specific to your particular area of the entertainment business. Also, identify a few useful newspapers and magazines and subscribe to them for your own collection. Some key newspapers are the *Wall St. Journal, NY Times* and *USA Today* (great for trend-watching) and helpful magazines include, *Billboard, Business 2.0, Fast Company,* and *Wired.* Many industry-specific magazines publish statistical editions and market reviews at regular intervals. The editorial staffs of these magazines have to fill the space between the ads. They do that by publishing as much industry-specific information as they can find, including statistics, forecasts, and industry profiles. Paging through one of these magazines or visiting a website can sometimes produce a great deal of business and market forecasting, and economic information.

❑ **Corporate Public Relations (PR) Departments** – If you need a company profile, product and service catalog, or other promotional materials, the PR department of the company is the best place to call. These can prove useful for understanding your competition and for getting ideas you may be able to borrow for your own business.

❑ **Trade Associations** – Trade organizations are sources of highly specialized business and technical information. To identify the associations in your field, you may use the annual *Encyclopedia of Associations*, published by Gale Research Inc., Detroit, MI. Most libraries own a copy of this. We'll look more closely at trade groups later in this chapter.

❑ **Local Chambers of Commerce (uschamber.com) or Economic Development Offices** – These sources track local economic and business data. Use the phone book to identify and locate the offices.

❑ **Government Agencies** – Government sponsored publications are excellent sources of regulatory, economic and industry analyses. Almost all cities and counties in the United States have some form of public offices that distribute government publications. Start with usa.gov. See also the Resource Directory at the end of this book for dozens of qualified resources to help your business stay informed.

TYPES OF RESEARCH SOURCES

U.S. Government	• U.S. Census Bureau • U.S. Department of Commerce & U.S. Department of Labor • Internal Revenue Service	• Other government depts.. appropriate to your industry • Small Business Admin. • Securities and Exchange Commission (Edgar database)
State Government	• Sales Tax • Franchise Business Tax • City and County Governments	• Planning Departments • New Business Licenses
Quasi-Governmental Sources	• Regional Planning Associations	
Industry & General Business	• Trade Associations • Trade Publications	• Corporate Annual Reports • Thomas Register
Community Services	• Chambers of Commerce • Banks • Universities • Newspaper and Online •Libraries • Entrepreneur's Associations	• Merchants Associations • Real Estate Agents • Yellow Pages
Computer Databases	Business and Trade Information Individualized Research Services	
Market Research Sources	• Customers • Suppliers • Distributors • Independent Sales Representatives	• Managers of Related Businesses • Loan officers/Factors/ Venture Capitalists • Competitors
Paid Services	• Industry-Related Research firms • Survey/Polling Firms • Market Research Consultants	
Internal Data	• For existing business	

Internal Research Wisdom

You may be wondering why I haven't mentioned the Internet very much yet. It is because you can't always rely on the quality of information on the Net. Excellent resources reside along side the most dubious. The Internet is marked by the "publish then filter" dynamic, and you are the one now responsible to do the filtering. Evaluating the quality of information provided on a Web site involves more than determining its authenticity. An author may write with genuine passionate belief in that which he says, but the facts may not support his contention.

Evaluating Net-based information is no easy task, but there are a few guidelines to keep in mind that will help you winnow out the good from the bad. Before relying on Net-found information, you should:

❑ **Discover the author AND the publisher and review their credentials**. Who wrote this? Is the author a well-known and well-regarded name you recognize? Is biographical information about the author provided? Is there an email address or phone number available in order to request further information? Likewise, who is the publishing organization? In the print universe, this generally means that the author's manuscript has undergone screening in order to verify it meets the standards of the organization that serves as publisher. Is this organization recognized in the field in which you are studying?

❑ **Discover the date of the writing.** This gives the information historical context. For some types of information, currency is not an issue (e.g., Enrico Caruso's letters to his record company, Victor). For many other types, however, currency is extremely important, as is the regularity with which the data is updated. Look for a publication date of a "last updated" date.

❑ **Verify it.** Ensure an explanation of the research method(s) used to gather and interpret the data are included. See if the document relies on other sources that are listed in a bibliography or includes links to other verifiable sources. Find another reputable source that provides similar information and compare.

❑ **Tips for Smarter Searches**. The Web is a fantastic source of information if you know how to use its search engines effectively. These can be tricky and you may have been frustrated by a search engine more than once while doing a search.
Here are some guidelines for producing better search results:

- *Be specific:* Don't type "drums"; type at least three words in your search, such as "1965 Gretsch jazz drum set".
- *Use "and" or "not".* Adding "and" links two terms and focuses a search. Typing "not" narrows a search by excluding pages containing the second search term. Some engines assume you mean "or" if you don't use a conjunction between words. "Or" expands the search, delivering sites with any of the words you've typed.
- *Use quotes*: Most engines interpret quotes as "search only for sites with all words exactly as typed". So if you type, for example, music business resources you'll get results for every page on the Web with the word "music", "business", or "resources" on it. You'll drown
in your results. The correct way to type it would be "music business resources".
- *Don't use common words and punctuation:* Common terms like *a* and *the* are called stop words and are usually ignored. Punctuation is also typically ignored. But there are exceptions. Common words and punctuation marks *should* be used when searching for a specific phrase inside quotes. There are cases when common words like *the* are significant. For instance, Raven and The Raven return entirely different results.
- *Drop the suffixes:* It's usually best to enter the base word so that you don't exclude relevant pages. For example, *bird* and not *birds*, *walk* and not *walked*. One exception is if you are looking for sites that focus on the act of walking, enter the whole term *walking*.
- *Find variations of a keyword:* If you want to find variations of a keyword, you could use the symbol ~ just before the keyword. This might be helpful if you are not sure about the exact thing you are searching for. For example, if you type ~telephone into the search box, Google will look for not just telephones, but also mobile phones, smartphones and some other things relate to telephones.

Free Government Business Resources

Today, career- and business-planning information is hyper-abundant and easy to access, if you know where to look. The "small office, home office" (SOHO) trend has hatched an entire industry focused on entrepreneurs and what they need. Books, magazines, software, web sites, cable TV and radio shows designed for micro-businesses are popping up everywhere.

But besides *information* you'll also need *guidelines* for the ever-growing variety of business demands that you will face: What's the best office set up for my needs?, How do I hire help and where do I find it?, What's the most effective use of my time? How much should I spend on promoting my music service or product? Where can I find the answers to these questions without having to enroll in a MBA program?

Check out the Small Business Administration. The Small Business Administration, or SBA, is one of those quiet government programs in which pearls lie hidden. This is about the best return on your taxes you'll ever receive, so listen up.

The United States Small Business Administration (SBA) was created by Congress in 1953 to encourage the formation of new enterprises and to nurture their growth. It exists to serve small businesses by providing information and financial backing and speaking on their behalf in the corridors of Capitol Hill. Nearly 20 million small businesses have received direct or indirect help from one or another of those SBA programs since 1953, as the agency has become the government's most cost-effective instrument for economic development. In fact, the SBA's current business loan portfolio of roughly 262,000 loans worth more than $91 billion makes it the largest single financial backer of U.S. businesses in the nation. The SBA's mandate is very broad. The agency's definition of "small business" - service companies and retailers with annual revenues of $3.5 million or less, manufacturers with fewer than 500 employees, wholesalers employing fewer than 100 workers - embraces over 98 percent of the companies in the U.S.

The SBA's staff is over 4,000 nationwide, organized in 116 offices. So taking advantage of the SBA requires learning what it's equipped to offer, and then learning how to tap into its abundant resources.

Here are a few SBA programs you can tap into now.

- **SBDCs (Small Business Development Centers)**

When I was starting my consulting company (Music Business Solutions) back in 1991, I contacted an SBA program called the Small Business Development Center (SBDC) in Salem, Massachusetts. SBDCs operate out of about 650 colleges across the country providing management training and other start-up assistance to emerging businesses. SBDCs offer one-stop assistance to individuals and small businesses by providing a wide variety of information and guidance in central and easily accessible branch locations. The program is a cooperative effort of the private sector, the educational community and federal, state and local governments.

I was matched with a small business advisor who reviewed my business plan, provided me with my first computer training and offered suggestions and ideas galore for making Music Business Solutions a success.

Though untutored in the music business my advisor was *very* experienced in the ways of general business management and marketing. Together we forged a plan to launch and grow my business. In addition, he demystified the computer for me and introduced me to a whole new world of software resources I never knew existed.

Some SBDCs are general in scope and others specialize in particular populations like women and minorities. Some also focus on technology.
To find the SBDC office nearest you go to: http://www.sba.gov **>> "Local Resources".**

❑ S.C.O.R.E. (Service Corps of Retired Executives)

Unfortunately, if you don't live near a college with an SBDC, you generally won't be able to take advantage of their services. That's where S.C.O.R.E comes in. S.C.O.R.E. stands for the Service Corps of Retired Executives and complements the work of SBDCs. In fact, many S.C.O.R.E. representatives work out of SBDCs. More than 11,000 volunteers are available to consult without charge on topics ranging from writing a business plan to exporting your product. Both working and retired executives and business owners donate time and expertise as business counselors. "Their advice is geared to early-stage businesses," says Mark Quinn, acting district SBA director in San Francisco. "Lots of people seeking advice are individual proprietorships - very, very small."

Studies show that "managerial deficiencies cause 9 out of 10 business failures." Through in-depth counseling, S.C.O.R.E. volunteers help business owners and managers identify basic management problems, determine the causes and become better managers. S.C.O.R.E. also offers "pre-business" workshops nationwide at over 320 offices to current and prospective small business entrepreneurs, covering a vast range of pertinent topics. The great thing is now there is SCOREOnline and they've made it super easy to use: Just ask a question or enter keywords to find a mentor, make your choice, and then send a message thru the online form. You get a personal reply from your mentor, within 48 hours. Say you have a question about the pros and cons of setting your business up as a corporation, or you needed ideas for email newsletter options. You can describe your business, put the question to several consultants if you choose and then get back a group of substantial responses you can then apply to your specific company.

Almost any small independent business can get help from S.C.O.R.E. The approach is confidential and personal. Clients don't even need to have a business. Consultation and counseling *before* a business start-up is another important part of the service too. Some will even provide training in computer programs and bookkeeping, as well as some much-needed hand-holding through the process of writing a formal business plan. For those serious about growing their business, this will be the best return on your taxes you'll ever get.

To locate the S.C.O.R.E. office nearest you or to receive counseling via email, visit the organization's web site at **http://www.score.org**.

❑ The Small Business Training Network (SBTN)

A third SBA program is The Small Business Training Network (SBTN). The SBTN is a virtual campus providing quality (albeit brief) online training modules designed to meet the information needs of prospective and existing small business owners. It is an E-Government initiative, powering a comprehensive menu of business courses, designed to serve more customers, more efficiently. The Training Network operates like an electronic umbrella under which many SBA and agency resource training programs are captured, aggregated, sorted by content and made available in multiple formats.

Sample current online courses include "How to Prepare a Loan Package," "Surviving in a Slowing Economy," and "Technology 101: A Small Business Guide." Though the course modules are introductory and take only 30 minutes to complete, they are offered at no cost and can form a foundation from which you can learn the next phases of each subject.

Trade Associations as Information Centers

You may be wondering: How much do Americans spend each year on private music instruction? Or, what should my payroll, advertising, and rent be as a percentage of sales? Are my expenses too high or too low? What's on the horizon in my segment of the music business? All of these are real questions a start up business owner will be asking. Fortunately, finding answers to these questions is fairly easy, *if* one joins the appropriate business association.

Trade associations act as "grand central stations" of people and information specific to a particular kind of business or trade. There is one (or more) for just about every category of business. Some of the more well known music-related associations are:

- A2IM (Association of Independent Music)
- AES (Audio Engineering Society)
- AMC (American Music Conference)
- CMA (Chamber Music America)
- ESTA (The Entertainment Services & Technology Association)
- FMC (Future of Music Coalition)
- NAMM (National Association of Music Merchants)
- NAPAMA (National Association of Performing Arts Managers & Agents)
- NARAS (National Academy of Recording Arts & Sciences)
- NARM (National Association of Record Merchandisers)
- NAfME (National Association for Music Education)
- MPA (Music Publishers Association)
- RIAA (Recording Industry Association of America)

Trade associations are powerful pools of ideas and talent from which you can accelerate your learning curve and tap into market data your own budget may not allow you to obtain on your own. Most require a membership fee but it is money well spent. Associations regularly publish directories for their members, and the better ones publish statistical information tracking industry sales, profits, ratios, economic trends, and other valuable data. If you don't know which trade associations apply to your industry, find out by asking business owners in your segment. Besides having the most accurate and timely data in your industry, associations can additionally supply you with:

Newsletters & Journals which will identify new products, suppliers, money saving ideas and trends in your industry.

Trade shows and conventions. These are usually located in popular areas of the country and the entire trip becomes tax deductible. Also, you get to meet the industry tastemakers, network and ask questions.
See *The Directory of the United States Trade Shows, Expositions, and Conventions*, U.S. Travel Service, U.S. Department of Commerce, Washington, DC 20230; or check out The Ultimate Event Resource online (http://www.tsnn.com).

Periodic meetings. They will give you the opportunity to meet and discuss your common business problems. Most business owners are by nature very independent people, but joining an association is one of the best investments you can make.
There is a trade association for every business segment and you may not want to limit your association memberships to just music ones. Today many business categories overlap and blend into each other. Think about what other business categories may have an affinity with

yours. For example, if your company crosses over between music and fashion, you'll want to explore the key fashion trade groups too. If your company is a music performance space, you'll want to traffic a bit with a venue mangers and food & beverage associations as well.

Where to Find Association Data. Look for associations on the Internet:

• *The Encyclopedia of Associations* published by The Gale Group (http://www.galegroup.com) is probably the most established, respected source on associations. These cost several hundred dollars each and are normally available at reference libraries. This organization also offers the more updated Associations Unlimited online database of more than 400,000 organizations.

• Directory of Associations (http://www.directoryofassociations.com) has an associations database on the Web listing more than 10,000 associations.

• "Action Without Borders" (http://www.idealist.org) initiative from Idealist.org lists thousands of not-for-profit organizations.

Tracking Small Business Trends & Opportunities

You will also need a steady stream of ideas as you seek for better ways to build and market your business. To track emerging trends that can affect small businesses in general and your business in particular, you need to stay informed. To help this along, do the following:

❑ *Read a major metropolitan newspaper*, as well as one or two papers serving your local community. This way, you can stay informed of current events on both a local and a global scale. Publications like the *Fast Company* and *Wired* are valuable sources of trends that are developing on a national scale as well as detailed information on specific business opportunities. Just as important are local business journals that cover key developments in your own community so you can track new ideas and trends that appeal to that geographic market.

❑ *Again, join associations that serve your industry*. These are an excellent source of current news geared specifically to businesses like yours.

❑ *Contact manufacturers, wholesalers, and distributors* serving your industry. They can furnish information not only on the products they provide, but also on market research they may have done.

❑ *Subscribe to relevant trade periodicals* and newsletters. Again, many trade associations publish periodicals that report on your industry. These publications are usually filled with valuable management tips, industry trends, buying guides, etc.

❑ *Attend industry conventions and trade shows*. Again, these venues offer an exciting array of information regarding specific industries as well as new product and service ideas.

Taking the Pulse of Your Market

Most of what we've looked at so far is what's considered "secondary data", that is, information once removed from the "primary data" that only comes from talking directly with your potential market – in other words, your customers.

According to Dun & Bradstreet's Allbusines.com web site, among the many tools out there for primary market research, the *survey* stands out as a time-tested and popular option for many small businesses. Once you've collected a certain number of potential customer names (or piggybacked on another complementary business's list), you'll want to use one.

Telephone surveys are popular because they're inexpensive and easy to do. But you can also conduct surveys through the mail, in one-on-one interviews, via email, or on the Web. Internet surveys are a relatively new methodology for researchers. Today, they are a common and increasingly sophisticated part of many research plans. Your business' specific needs and budget will determine which type of survey to use.

Surveys can help you evaluate your customers' buying habits, compare your products with those of your competitor, or test a new ad campaign. In other words, surveys produce essential data that can guide many important business decisions. There are many survey services available, such as Zoomerang.com, SurveyMonkey.com and InstantSurvey.com. All offer various levels of creation, distribution and reporting. Of course, you can also craft your own survey and send it to your own qualified list of potential respondents.

Once you've determined your survey method and specific goals, you're ready to write the questionnaire. As you prepare the questions, remember a few basic rules:

- Keep the questions brief and to the point.
- Include no more than 12 questions per survey.
- Ask one question per sentence.
- Put your questions in logical order, usually from general to specific.
- Pretest your questions. Try out the questionnaire on friends, employees, and colleagues before you send out the real thing.
- Avoid questions that could trick or embarrass the respondent.
- Use neutral language. Try not to influence the response.
- Ask respondents their age and income level — have them choose from among a range of ages and income levels.
- Reveal your company's name and how you will use the information.
- Thank the respondents for their time and support.

Qualifying Your Data

Once you start compiling information, you might feel you have more facts than you know what to do with. Here are a few tips to keep in mind about the information you gather:

❑ ***Use the most recent data you can find.*** Printed information is often at least two years old and a lot can change in two years

❑ ***Translate data into units rather than dollars whenever possible***. Due to inflation, dollars may not give you consistent information from year to year.

❑ ***Give the most reliable source the most credence***. Generally, the larger the group sampled for information, or the more respected the organization that conducted the research, the more trustworthy the numbers you collect.

❑ ***Integrate data from one source to another in order to draw conclusions***. However, make sure the information is from the same time period and is consistent; small variations can lead to vastly inaccurate results.

❑ ***Use the most conservative figures***. Naturally, you'll be tempted to paint the brightest picture possible, but such information often leads to bad business decisions. Again, reference librarians are trained in scouring the best information so use their expertise whenever you have a question about the reliability of your data. Remember the words of the one-time ambassador Benjamin Disraeli which opened this chapter, "As a general rule, the most successful people in life are those who have the best information."

CHAPTER SUMMARY
KNOWING & USING YOUR RESOURCES

- **Info-Power is Yours**
  The most strategic factor in business today is knowledge. The Internet and, equally important your local library, bring tons of useful information within the grasp of every entrepreneurial citizen. However, while information is hyper-abundant, the key is getting to the right information for your particular needs. The music industry is a fairly complex industry and you really need as much industry knowledge as you can get. An understanding of your knowledge resources allows you to create a map that will get you to your destination in the most effective and efficient way possible. Having the best information always gives you the upper hand.

- **Free Tools to Help Your Research**
  As your revenue grows, you may need to hire more specialists for your information needs. Some places to go to get information costing very little, except for time: Libraries, publishers, corporate public relations departments, trade associations, local chambers of commerce and government agencies.

- **Internet Research Wisdom**
  The Internet is marked by the "publish then filter" dynamic, and you are the one now responsible to do the filtering. Evaluating the quality of information provided on a Web site involves more than determining its authenticity. Before relying on Net-found information, you should: discover the author and the publisher and review their credentials; discover the date of the writing; verify it; and do "smart searches."

- **Government Business Resources**
  Besides information you'll also need guidelines for the ever-growing variety of business demands that you will face. The SBA (Small Business Administration) exists to serve small businesses by providing information and financial backing and speaking on their behalf in the corridors of Capitol Hill. Some SBA programs you can tap into: SBDCs (Small Business Development Centers) provide management training and other start-up assistance to emerging businesses; S.C.O.R.E. (Service Corps of Retired Executives) is available to consult without charge on topics ranging from writing a business plan to exporting your product; and the SCTN (Small Business Training Network) is a virtual campus providing quality (albeit brief) online training modules designed to meet the information needs of prospective and existing small business owners.

- **Trade Associations as Information Centers**
  Trade associations act as "grand central stations" of people and information specific to a particular kind of business or trade. There is one (or more) for just about every category of business. Trade associations are powerful pools of ideas and talent from which you can accelerate your learning curve and tap into market data your own budget may not allow you to obtain on your own. Some of the more well known music-related associations are: A2IM (Association of Independent Music), AES (Audio Engineering Society), FMC (Future of Music Coalition), NAMM (National Association of Music Merchants), NARAS (National Academy of Recording Arts & Sciences), NARM (National Association of Record Merchandisers), RIAA (Recording Industry Association of America), etc.

- **Tracking Small Business Trends & Opportunities**
  To track emerging trends that can affect small businesses in general and your business in particular, you need to stay informed. To help this along, do the following: Read a major metropolitan newspaper in or near your business; visit online portals relevant to your industry; join associations that serve your industry; contact manufacturers, wholesalers, and distributors serving your industry; Subscribe to relevant trade periodicals and newsletters; and attend industry conventions and trade shows.

- **Taking the Pulse of Your Market**
  Surveys can help you evaluate your customers' buying habits, compare your products with those of your competitor, or test a new marketing campaign. There are many survey services available, such as Zoomerang.com, SurveyMonkey.com and InstantSurvey.com. All offer various levels of creation, distribution and reporting. Of course, you can also craft your own survey and send it to your own qualified list of potential respondents.

- **Qualifying Your Data**
  Once you start compiling information, you might feel you have more facts than you know what to do with. Here are a few tips to keep in mind about the information you gather: Use the most recent data you can find, translate data into units rather than dollars whenever possible, give the most reliable source the most credence, integrate data from one source to another in order to draw conclusions, and use the most conservative figures.

FURTHER RESOURCES

ONLINE RESOURCES

Association of Small Business Development Centers (ASBDC)
americassbdc.org
This organization offer business plan information and free one-on-one counseling, as well as resources on a wide variety of subjects.

Better Business Bureau
www.bbb.org
Offers information to help you check the reputation of potential clients (if they are also businesses). Membership in the organization is also recommended- it provides you with added credibility, services, such as informative quarterly newsletter and client conflict resolution services, are well worth the price. The BBB has chapters in most major metropolitan areas.

Bureau of Labor Statistics
www.bls.gov
Occupational and labor related data, as well as statistics on economics and related areas, can be found here. A great source of information if you want to know whether your particular business has any "staying power," what the government recommends/ considers normal in terms of education for a particular line of work, and so on.

Dun & Bradstreet
www.dnb.com
Offers member-based services that allow you to verify a client's ability to pay.

Hoover's Online
www.hoovers.com
Whether you go the "free" or "subscription" route on this website, you will definitely get quite a bit of information. Subscribers get more in-depth information, and this might be a wise investment for some businesses that need the information. Use it to research companies that might be good potential clients.

National Association for the Self Employed
nase.org
This membership-based organization offers political advocacy and member benefits such as health and financial programs.

SCORE (Senior Core of Retired Executives)
score.org
This volunteer organization is composed of retired executives who assist existing and startup small businesses. These services are free.

Small Business Administration
www.sba.gov
This governmental agency is charged with supporting smaller businesses, from starting a business to bidding on government contracts, to special loans, to providing resources businesses can use throughout their life cycle. Visit your local SBA (Small Business Administration) office, or find it on the Web. State, county, and local development offices might also offer some additional assistance.

State Department
www.state.gov
You might only think of this government department as being important when the United States is at war (or when the U.S government tells you what countries are unsafe), but it also offers extensive online information about business in foreign countries, if that is part of your plan.

5

RESEARCHING YOUR MARKET

I think there is a world market for maybe five computers.
– Thomas Watson, chairman of IBM, 1943

I am only a public entertainer who has understood his time.
– Pablo Picasso

Having the right information is half the battle today. Without it you can miss opportunities, find yourself taking the wrong paths and wasting precious time, money and energy in the process. Now that you know how to source good information, you're ready to apply this to your own potential customer-market. This chapter will help you focus your marketing lens; later, chapter 15 will guide you through the *organization* and *execution* of your marketing plan.

Introducing Market Research

Successful entrepreneurs do not launch companies without first gathering information about their market and their customer preferences. The idea is to look for similarities in this group, to understand what sort of people like your product or would use your service. Maybe most of your customers are teens, or producers, or families with small children. You may find that your people have similar values, or live similar lifestyles, or are of similar ages. Or that people interested in your business are also interested in the same other products, in the vein of Amazon's "people who bought *x* also bought *y*" recommendation system. Once you figure out what kind of people are interested in your business, you can figure out where those people spend their time and attention, and then you know where to reach them. What we are talking about here is *market* or *customer research.*

Hunches and intuition about your business will only take you so far. At a certain point you need to hear from your market with real data.

Any information you can obtain about your market will be helpful as you forge your business plan. "I first started by reading books and doing research online," writes Andreas Katsambas, owners of The End Records in Brooklyn. "Eventually I started making various contacts at media, other labels, and distributors. I would email or call them and talk to them. Any conversation helps especially when you ask the right questions". Panos Panay, founder of Sonicbids and Berklee's Institute for Creative Entrepreneurship, describes himself as a "voracious reader of all kinds of magazines and books" in order to keep his finger on the pulse of the entertainment market. "I have always been thirsty for information," says

Panay, "and have continuously sought to continuously upgrade my own knowledge-set - assuming that what got me 'here' won't get me 'there'."

Successful entrepreneurs develop new products and services that are based on real customer needs. This sounds pretty obvious, right? Maybe, but surprisingly few entrepreneurs develop products that meet a real need and most end up failing to generate any sales. Why? Unfortunately, many entrepreneurs become enamored of the idea of starting a company and do not pay enough attention to whether they can provide a product or service that is better than existing alternatives.

In our last chapter we became acquainted with some of the tools and resources you have at your disposal for entrepreneurial development. Now we are going to put those tools to work by focusing on the customers you will be connecting with about your own unique product or service.

Be sure to review the numerous tools from chapter 4 so you are fully apprised of them as you work on digging deeper into the general market niche you discovered for your business idea back in chapter 3. For example, if you're thinking of starting a venue-type business, you will probably want to speak with an advisor from the nearest SBDC. This advisor will have specific local knowledge that can prove extremely useful when planning your business. Chapter 3 resources and many more are included in the *Resource Directory* at the end of this book. Here are a few resource reminders and some additional tools to help your market research:

FAMOUS QUOTES FROM THE ANNALS OF MARKET RESEARCH

"A cookie store is a bad idea. Besides, the market research reports say America likes crispy cookies, not soft and chewy cookies like you make."
- Response to Debbi Fields' idea of starting Mrs. Fields' Cookies

"Computers in the future may weigh no more than 1.5 tons."
-Popular Mechanics, forecasting the relentless march of science, 1949

"Who the hell wants to hear actors talk?"
- H.M. Warner, Warner Brothers, 1927

"We don't like their sound, and guitar music is on the way out."
- Decca Recording Co., rejecting the Beatles, 1962

❑ ***Go surfing***

When you hit the Web, start with these recommendations and then let your instincts and your search engine take over:

• **Visit the websites of who you consider your competitors.** Check out how they present themselves, the brand attributes they highlight, and the new moves they're announcing to see what you're up against.

• **Go to the government websites.** Start with *www.census.gov* for information on the population and resident characteristics in practically any U.S. community. Then move on to the websites of the business development departments to the business resource center at your local chamber of commerce.

• **Search for organizations that serve the interests of your industry.** Enter your industry into a search engine and check out some of the top results in order to access facts and figures about the business arena in which you operate. For instance, when I enter "music products industry" in my favorite search engine, one of the first results is Namm.org, "the not-for-profit trade association that unifies, leads and strengthens the $17 billion global musical instruments and products industry." As another example, I enter "cellular phone industry statistics" into the search engine and one of the first results is for the Cellular Telecommunications & Internet Association, "the international association for the wireless telecommunication industry."

Similar industry groups probably serve your business arena.

❑ ***Hit the library reference shelves***
In addition to reference materials specific to your industry, check out these two marketing sourcebooks:

• **ESRI Community Sourcebooks:** These volumes contain population, demographic, and income data as well as other consumer information for every U.S. zip code, Direct Marketing Area (DMA), and Metropolitan Statistical Area (MSA). The information is valuable as you work to forecast demand for your products, note population trends, and analyze the composition of your target market area.

• **The Lifestyle Market Analyst:** Published by Standard Rate and Data Service (SRDS) and Equifax, this guide provides demographic and lifestyle data organized by geographic market area, lifestyle interests, and consumer profiles.
More similar resources can be found in this book's *Resource Directory*.

Getting to Know Your Market(s)

When CDs were more prevalent, you would often find small postcard mailers in new disc packages. They were usually 3"x4" and contained a series of questions in four point type on everything from where you purchased the CD to what music web sites you enjoy visiting. They also asked your gender, age, annual income, favorite magazines and how many CDs you tend to purchase each year. Why? Because record companies want to know you so they can sell more products to you in the future. They are doing customer research. Companies spend millions of dollars each year trying to figure out what makes their customers tick. Known in marketing lingo as *data mining*, industries have been capturing reams of data on every aspect of how we buy and sell in our consumer society. Data mining tools also predict future trends and behaviors, allowing businesses to make proactive, knowledge-driven decisions. Such techniques are the result of a long process of research and product development.

The type of business you're in will dictate the most appropriate approach. If your product is for a highly targeted market, and direct sales calls will be your method of selling, start by identifying the type of person you expect to sell to and engage in a mock sales call to understand what such people find interesting. If your product is aimed at a larger market, it may be more beneficial to recruit small numbers of people for focus groups until you have a feel for the market, and then validate it further using a survey.

The logic is simple: *know how your customers spend their time and you'll know better how and where to spend your marketing money*. There are numerous info-gathering methods you can use depending on the type of information you are seeking as the chart below illustrates.

INFORMATION-GATHERING APPROACHES		
Desired Finding	**Method**	**When to Call in the Pros**
Customer Profile	Information capture at first purchase, website registration, information requests on contest entry forms, information update requests, informal customer-intercept interviews	Seek assistance from website developers when creating online registration forms. You can handle the other methods yourself.
Customer awareness, interest, or satisfaction levels	Written or phone surveys	Seek professional assistance to develop survey questions that are clear and concise and don't lead or skew results and to analyze findings on complex issues.
Customer opinions of reactions to product or marketing ideas	In-person or phone interviews	Especially if the interview involves a sensitive issue, find a single, trained interviewer in your company or hire a professional so that all interviews are conducted in the same manner and by a person with whom the customer can be candid.
Customer input on product or marketing ideas (Crowdsourcing)	Focus groups	Involve a research professional to assemble the groups, to hold the sessions in rooms with two-way mirrors and recording capability, and to facilitate the discussion.
Customer behaviors	Observation, document review	No professional assistance is necessary. Watching your customers or studying their order history is relatively easy and requires no customer interaction.

Small business music entrepreneurs understand the value of this information and, while they may not employ all of the above techniques, they will use every tactic at their disposal and within their budget to understand exactly what their customers want and need.
For example, if you're marketing jazz products you'll want to be aware of the publications *Downbeat*, *Jazziz* and *Coda*, organizations like the Jazz Foundation of America and various cable TV and radio shows specializing in jazz performance, as well as the hundreds of generalist outlets for jazz music. Likewise, someone marketing reggae-related product will be acquainted with *Jamrock*, *Reggae Times* and *United Reggae*, record labels like Mango, Heartbeat and VP, and organizations like Reggae Ambassadors Worldwide. The same thing applies to folk, metal, EDM, blues, classical, country, Latin, world, experimental and all other music styles.

Let's just take one of these marketing vehicles – magazines. Did you know every magazine has a "media kit" available for potential advertisers? These media kits provide a rich array of facts and figures about the magazine's readership: average age, income level, amount of money they spend on music each month, other interests, etc. This is very valuable information you can borrow for your own market analysis. Why reinvent the wheel? Through learning about the who, what and where of your music's audience you also learn

about the best ways to reach that audience. This is a fundamental component of marketing. We've already gone over some of this topic in chapter 3 when discussing niches, but let's now go a little further into it.

We've all heard a business owner say, "My product is terrific! It appeals to everyone." Many of us have also seen small businesses that try to be all things to all people. This is a difficult, if not impossible, goal to achieve.

Market research is simply defining who your primary customer will be. Market research is a prelude to selling. It teaches you a great deal about what you will need to know to develop your offering for the market and whether your offering is even worth developing. A positive and aggressive attitude toward market research enables entrepreneurs to make that most critical of decisions: Should I spend the next several years of my life on this business?

Tagging the Net: A Dataminer's Dream Come True

"Everybody knows by now that the internet has shaken up the music business. Forecasts for the coming years are that Web 2.0 functionality will replace outmoded knowledge management systems. The reason is that application programming interfaces and social networking tools facilitate bottom-up contributions, whereas previous knowledge management systems were top-down tools that forced users to conform. In today's environment, users deploy "tagging" (attaching descriptive labels to Web content), which lets communities create their own "taxonomies" (hierarchical classifications of related items) – sometimes called "folksonomies" (folksonomy is the process of collaborative categorization through tagging, a process made popular by the social Web. Users rank favorite items by tagging them with freely chosen keywords, and as numerous users tag the same item, the categorization emerges)."

Source: *e-Preneur*

3 Steps to Understanding Your Customer

We already reviewed the three types of general markets in chapter 3. They are the Consumer, Business and Reseller markets. Hopefully, by now you are clear which of the three is your *primary* market. Once you understand this you can then begin to focus more clearly on your particular target market(s) within it.

Here are three steps to follow when researching your target market:

A. Step One: Identify Why A Customer Would Want To Buy Your Product/Service
B. Step Two: Segment Your Overall Market
C. Step Three: Profile Your Target Customer

STEP ONE - Identify Why A Customer Would Want To Buy Your Product/ Service.

People may rationalize their decisions based on facts, but they make those decisions based on emotions. Not the warm, fuzzy stuff of greeting cards, but emotions that allow people to see themselves experiencing the rewards of having taken action. Studies have demonstrated that lacking this emotional connection, people literally cannot decide! Therefore, the first step in identifying your target market is to understand what your products/services have to offer to a group of people or businesses. A good method to follow is to identify your product or service's *features* and those features' complimentary *benefits*.

For example, suppose I wanted to start a booking agency. Some features of this agency might be – three, dedicated agents; leading edge technology; and experience with a dozen different genres of music. These tell us *about the agency*. That's fine. The problem is, however, that an agency's market wants to know more about *what the service can do for it.* In other words, what's in it for the agency customers?

Putting the features and benefits in a table helps us see how one relates to the other:

FEATURES	BENEFITS
• **Dedicated agents** • **Leading edge technology** • **Multi-genre expertise**	• **Top shelf service** • **Smooth user experience** • **Choice**

The way you inventory and describe the benefits you offer customers will also provide you with the vocabulary you need for creating your marketing messages and materials. For example, say you offered a music transcription service that could be adapted to different languages. You describe this feature as "multi-lingual music transcription." That's fine. But the *benefit* of this feature can be described as "customizable to the particular language needs of each client." The word "customizable" (a powerful word in light of recent market trends) can then be used in all your marketing messages to help sell your service.
By knowing what your product/service has to offer and what will make customers buy, you can begin to identify common characteristics of your potential market.

STEP TWO: Segment Your Overall Market

It's a natural instinct to want to target as many people and groups as possible. However, by doing this your promotional strategy will never communicate *specifically* to any *one* group, and you will most likely turn many potential customers off. Your promotional budget will be much more cost effective if you promote to one type of customer and speak directly to them. This allows you to create a highly focused campaign that will directly meet the needs and desires of a specific group. This is called *market segmentation*.

For example, there are many music consumers who desire positive messages in songs as a benefit when purchasing a CD. Rather than targeting *everyone* in their promotional strategy, a record label may opt to target a specific group of consumers with similar characteristics, such as families with young children. This is an example of market segmentation.

As we saw, market segmentation is the process of breaking down a larger target market into smaller segments with specific characteristics. Each group requires different promotional strategies and marketing mixes (the variety of tools and tactics you chose to reach this segment) because each group has different wants and needs.
Segmentation will help you to customize a product/service or other parts of a marketing mix, such as advertising, to reach and meet the specific needs of a narrowly defined customer group.

Larger markets are most typically divided into smaller target market segments on the basis of the following:

1. ***Geographics:*** Potential customers or organizations are segmented in a local,

state, regional or national marketplace. If you are selling music instructional services, for example, you'll most likely need to be located in a fairly well populated area in order to ensure enough customers to support your company. Or, if you own a retail store, geographic location of the store is one of the most important considerations you can make. Decide if your business is going to do business on a local, regional, national or international level. Identify specific boundaries within which you will do business. Identify the geographic region your market is located in.

Of course, digital products (like recorded music) have been liberated from geographical constraints thanks to the Internet. The Net enables small entrepreneurs to have the whole world as a market. But even an international reach requires a marketer to have a very local message in order to be effective. Again, high tech requires ***high touch*** – always.

2. *Demographics*: Demographics are population or consumer statistics regarding socioeconomic factors such as age, income, sex, occupation, education, family size, and the like. Choose those characteristics of your demographic target market that relates to the interest, need and ability of the customer to purchase your product or service. For example, a target market for a general business band focused on the private party market, would include: Professional married couples approximately 30-50 years old with young children who have an income of over $100,000. Every decision from marketing to design is then based on the profile you develop of your target market.

A demographic for a business would include such factors as customer size, number of employees, type of products, and annual revenue. If you are a business to business (B2B) marketer, for example, you may want to consider segmenting according to your target market's size. A music production company, for example, may decide to target only Fortune 500 companies that produce more than a dozen video productions each month because they need high volume accounts to make a profit.

Identify the following demographic characteristics of your market:

For a Consumer Market

Age ______
Income ______
Gender ______
Profession ______
Education ______
Family Size ______
Homeowner ______
Marital Status ______

For a Business Market

Industry ______
Geographic location ______
Size of Company ______
Annual revenue ______
Number of Branches ______
Number of Employees ______
Age of Company ______
Company mission _______________

3. *Psychographics:* Many businesses offer products based on attitudes, beliefs, and the emotions of their target market. The desire for status, an enhanced appearance, and more money are examples of psychographic variables. The desire to be considered cutting-edge, discriminating and "cool" are other variables. They are the factors that influence your customers' purchasing decision. A seller of high-end audio would appeal to an individual's desire for status symbols. Business customers as well as consumers can be described in psychographic terms. Some companies view themselves as leading edge, high tech, others as socially responsible, stable and strong, and others as innovative and creative. These distinctions help in determining how to position your company and how you can use your company's position as a marketing tactic.

The following are some psychographic descriptions for both consumer and business markets. Identify which characterize your target market.

For a Consumer Market
Lifestyle:
Fun-Seeking ___
Family Stage ___
Trend-Setting ___
Hobbies ___
Status Seeking ___
Sports ___
Conservative ___
Forms of Entertainment___
Socially Responsible ___
Environmentally Conscious ___
Publication Subscriptions ___
Family Oriented ___
Technical interests ___
Other ___

For a Business Market
Business Style:
Industry Leader ___
Innovative ___
Conservative ___
Employee Relations ___
Trade Associations ___
Socially Responsible ___
Business Products/Services ___
Financially Stable ___
Services Used ___
Employee Friendly ___
Influencer ___
Publication Subscriptions ___
High Tech ___
Workforce Type ___
Management Style ___

4. *Behavioristic:* Products and services are purchased for a variety of reasons. Business owners must determine what the reasons are, including: brand, loyalty, cost, how frequently they use and consume products, and time of year. It's important to understand the buying habits and patterns of your customers. For example, a consumer does not rush and buy guitar lessons for their child from the first flier they see on a supermarket bulletin board. A fortune 500 company doesn't typically make quick purchasing decisions.
Try to answer the following questions regarding your customer-market's behavior:

- ❑ Reason/occasion for purchase?
- ❑ Number of times they'll purchase?

- ❑ Timetable of purchase, every week, month, quarter, etc.?
- ❑ Amount of product/service purchased?
- ❑ How long to make a decision to purchase?
- ❑ Where customer purchases and/or uses product/service?

Most businesses use a combination of each of the above to segment their markets. Some of this information may not even be available or relevant to your particular product of service. Demographic and geographic criteria will usually qualify your target markets because you need to establish if segment members have enough money to purchase your offering or if they're in a location that's accessible to the product or service. Most businesses then use the psychographic and behavioristic factors to construct a promotional campaign that will appeal to the target market.

Take a moment to decide which segmentation criteria will be most helpful to you in segmenting your target market: Geographic, Demographic, Psychographic and/or Behavioristic.

Next, you'll need to understand what your customers' interests are and identify what is most important to them. This is called "profiling your customer" and the knowledge you gain from this will give you the guidance needed to construct the most effective marketing and promotion plan for reaching your market.

STEP THREE: Decoding Your Target Customer

This is where you formally describe your target customer. Where to find the data: Use the information you've been gathering from the previous chapter as well as your own hunches. You will find loads of additional market research data in the resources at the end of this chapter.
Here are some suggestions for conducting your own market research:

❑ *Your current customers* can provide you with insight on *potential* customers and how to appeal to them. You may also discover an opportunity to produce additional products to serve this market or improve on an existing product. Ask yourself: What don't I know about my customers? You need to construct questions that will provide the answer. It can be as simple as asking a current customer: "Why did you purchase this product?" or, "How can this product be improved?"

❑ *If you have a retail outlet*, you have the means of distributing a customer comment card or questionnaire. A suggestion box is also a vehicle for obtaining information about your customers and their wants, needs and complaints.

❑ When mailing monthly invoices or statements, *include a questionnaire* and an envelope to return mail it. Those CD questionnaire postcards fall into this category. If you provide an incentive to those who return it, such as a free gift or discount, you increase the chances of getting it back.

❑ *Advertising Representatives*. Most major publications have demographic and behavioristic profiles of their readership. If you're a recording studio, a magazine focusing on regional musicians can provide you with valuable segmenting information. Simply call the advertising department and ask for a media kit. There's no sense in re-inventing the wheel.

❑ *Requesting an organization's annual report* will provide you with business demographic information. Public companies must make this available; private companies will at their own discretion. Hoovers.com can help with this segment.

❑ *Work with a local college.* If you need help in designing and executing a questionnaire, contact the marketing professor at an area college and offer your business up as a class project.

❑ *Trade associations,* as we saw in the previous chapter, provide valuable information for industries not only on demographic and company size, but competition and trends for growth areas as well. Trade associations usually sponsor trade shows too. For example, a maker of music stands would certainly want to attend the annual NAMM (National Association of Music Merchants) event in California. An American record label seeking to expand its market into Europe, will try to attend the winter MIDEM event in Cannes, France.

By the way, your local librarian can be a tremendous asset at this stage of your investigation. These people are specially trained in the art of tracking down hard-to-find information and will inevitably introduce you to valuable resources you've probably never heard of. Also, public libraries frequently subscribe to online research databases (e.g., Infotrac) that put an enormous amount of valuable information at your fingertips. Knowing where your customers "drink" (in a media sense) will help you decide on the best inlets and outlets for your marketing message. Use the following to record this info.

Where Do Your Customers and Fans Feed Their Interests?

What publications, web sites and events can help you monitor the lifestyles of your customers?

	Publications	Web Sites	Events
Fashion			
Food			
Music			
Sports			
Homes			
Hobbies			
Outdoors			
Politics			
Others			

Some important considerations when decoding your market:

1. If you pursue one segment of your target market and the demand for your product decreases, so will your financial strength. In essence, you are putting all your eggs in one basket along with its inherent risks.

2. When your firm becomes well established in a particular market segment, it may be difficult for you to move to another segment. This may occur due to your market reputation or popularity. For example, if a booking agency becomes known for securing college gigs, other entertainment buyers may perceive them as only having the expertise to serve that one market.

3. After you have mastered one particular segment, you can then begin to develop another. This strategy of directing your company's marketing efforts at one or more market segments by developing a marketing mix for each specific segment is known as the "Multi-Segment Strategy".

The marketing mixes for this strategy may vary by product, price, promotional material and distribution methods. It is not uncommon for a firm using the multi-segment strategy to increase its sales by focusing on more than one segment, since you would have marketing mixes aimed at each segment. Since this strategy would require additional processes, you will most likely incur higher production costs.

Additionally, different promotional plans and distribution efforts will result in higher marketing costs. Make sure the costs don't outweigh the benefits.
Now think about all the characteristics you have identified and start formulating the promotional campaign that will best address this specific target market. Start to formulate a picture or description of your ideal customer. Make sure everything you do from design to message, addresses your market.

Use the following chart to summarize your customer-market:

AT-A-GLANCE CUSTOMER DESCRIPTION
PROFILE: Our customers are predominantly [gender] living in [region] who [description of lifestyle facts such as: are married, own their homes, work as professionals, have young children living at home, and are members of business organizations and/or golf clubs].
WANTS AND VALUES: Our customers value [the attributes your customers value, for example Quality, Features, Convenience, Reliability, Expertise, Support, Service, Low Price, Prestige, or Exclusivity].
MOTIVATIONS: The top reasons our customers buy from our business are: [e.g., we're conveniently located, they get to work directly with the owner/s, they want the best and perceive us to be more exclusive than our competitors, we get things done quickly and on budget, and so on].

Learning From Competition

"Stand on the shoulders of those who've gone before you, and you'll see farther." -Anon

Here's a question for you. What happens when customers compare you to your key competitors? Unless you win 100% of those contests, that's a question worth answering.

Let's start with what happens when a prospect calls in. How personal is the attention they receive? If your competitor quickly connects them with a competent sales associate, but *your* system instead forces them to endure layers of automated phone instructions, only to tell them to leave a message, you've got a problem. Heck, you've got a problem even if your sales people sound too busy to care, or seem unsure of their answers.

Finding out the size of an existing market is barely research, you also really need to know exactly who the current providers are in that market, what their strengths and weaknesses are and what they are failing to provide. This sort of information is far more relevant and useful when developing a product or service, it can often identify your potential unique selling point and will certainly help you to assess the viability and potential of your idea.

Honestly evaluating your competition will help you better understand your own product or service and give potential investors or loan officers a reassuring sense of your company's strengths. It enables you to know how best to distinguish your company in the customer's eyes, and it points to opportunities in the market.

As you begin your competitive assessment, keep in mind that you need to evaluate only those competitors aiming for the same target market. If you own a small performance venue in Manhattan, you don't have to include Carnegie Hall in your competitive evaluation: you're not aiming for the same customer at the same time. On the other hand, if you are thinking of opening the first vintage drum shop in Alaska, you have to look far a field, at any such retail stores in Seattle or Vancouver, mail-order dealers from all over the country, and Internet dealers from all over the world, as that is where your potential customers shop now.

❑ ***Where to Look for Competitive Intelligence***. Start your competition research at the competitor's website. Consider this to be a book about the company. Read it "cover to cover" and print pages which interest you or which have information you want to double-check.

- Look at anything that says "News" or "What's New". This will give you the latest information on what is happening and possible clues about new opportunities.
- Read any mission or vision statements or description of services to see how this organization describes itself.
- Look for an annual report or strategic plan and read it carefully.

Check business directories and other employer information sources for outside profiles of the competitors. Tap your local library.

Depending on the size of the competitor, check the various web resources for information about the company's financial health (e.g. Yahoo! Finance, Bloomberg, CNN Financial, etc.). Check also with services like PRnewswire, BusinessWire, Canada NewsWire, etc. to see the latest press releases and news reports about the company.

There is also available some "semi-public" information about companies if you know where to look. This could include a brief profile with financials like Hoovers (www.hoovers.com), a copy of a annual report from the SEC's Edgar Database (www.sec.gov), or insider profiles like those from Vault.com (www.vault.com).

Finally, turn to the Search Engines, and, of course, speak to anyone you know who works there or who knows someone who knows someone who works there. That kind of "insider" information can often prove to be the most useful.

When preparing the competitive analysis portion of your business plan focus on identifying:

- Who your major competitors are
- On what basis you compete with them
- How you compare with them
- Potential future competitors
- How you plan on differentiating yourself from your competitors (see below)

Find out as much as you can about your key competitors. What do they talk about? What do they leave behind? Do they make it easy to move along to the next step in becoming a customer, even provide incentives to do so? Do they follow up? How?

Your goal, of course, isn't to mimic that competitor. For all you know, they might be dropping those very items or systems because they failed to produce decent results. Plus, every company is different. It's a mistake - and probably a very expensive one - for a small company to try to sell in the same way a huge worldwide competitor does. Sure, the Internet gives you the reach and efficiencies of a larger company, but you want to find the "gaps" in the larger firm's processes - the places where customer needs are not being fully met. *That's* your opportunity for innovation and differentiation.

You'll succeed when you understand more about what differentiates you from your competitors in your customers' eyes. Who in your company is in charge of knowing your competitors in the same way your prospects do? Without that knowledge, you'll never get closer to knowing why some choose that competitor over you. Or, to do something about it.

❑ ***A Differentiation Strategy*** is one of creating a product or service that is perceived as being unique throughout the industry. This has also been called your *USP* (unique selling proposition). The emphasis can be on brand image, proprietary technology, special features, superior service, a strong distributor network, or other aspects that might be specific to your industry segment.

In addition, some of the conditions that should exist to support a differentiation strategy include strong marketing abilities, effective product development, creative personnel, the ability to perform basic research, and a good reputation.

Here are some questions to help get you started –

1. What products and companies will compete with you?
   List your three major competitors (Names and contact info).
2. Will they compete with you across the board, or just for certain products, certain customers, or in certain locations?
3. Will you have important indirect competitors? (For example, used CD stores compete with record retailers, although they are different types of businesses.)
4. How will your products or services compare with the competition?

Sometimes you'll find that what makes a company unique may also be its Achilles Heel. "Our advantage is out biggest disadvantage," declares Andreas Katsambas of The End Records. "People say our music is not the most accessible, or we are quite diverse. But to me it feels the most challenging music is the one that offers the biggest reward as well. Also music needs to evolve and stay interesting." Leading with your strength, as in Katsambas's case, can also mean struggling to identify your market.

Building Your Database of Connections: The Lifeblood of Your Marketing

Successful marketing and promotion require intelligence, a little money, a fair amount of tact, a certain amount of push...*and contacts*.

What is your basic marketing goal? Answer: To let John and Jane Public know that you exist and that they should find out more about you. The way to achieve this is through *targeted* marketing and promotion. A targeted strategy insures maximization of resources; untargeted promotion, or "shot gunning," can waste gobs of time, money and effort. There are thousands of companies out there promoting their services and products, but only a handful do it effectively. It's the difference between hanging fifty posters that hundreds read and displaying one poster that thousands read. Targeting makes all the difference. So how does one go about it?

The first step is to compile your key contact lists and continue to add and delete from these lists throughout your company's history. They are the "Grand Central Stations" (a phrase you'll se again and again in this book) of all your marketing and promotion, and will allow you to feed the networking that is so crucial for business success today.

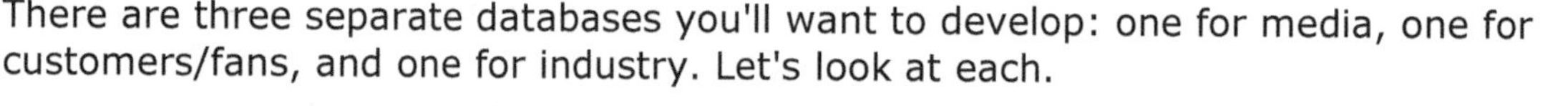
There are three separate databases you'll want to develop: one for media, one for customers/fans, and one for industry. Let's look at each.

❑ ***Media.*** Newspapers, magazines, radio programs, television and online media are all driven by common needs: To fill time and space with information of value to their readers, viewers and listeners. They're eager for this information and quite willing, at their own expense, to publish or air it. They need your news.

Begin your media database with the local scene and then branch out regionally, nationally and even internationally, depending on your marketing goals. A good public library is your key resource here. Tell the reference librarian what you're looking for and you'll be guided to the media directories you need. Several good ones are listed in the Resource Directory. You can find most local media information in the *Yellow Pages*. Pay attention also to writers, bloggers and radio D.J.'s who have helped break ground for other independent musicians and music companies. When the time is right, you can contact them with your promo

❑ ***Fans/Customers.*** This is your grassroots support network. The best ways to compile a fan database is at your gigs. Make it as easy as possible for people to join your fan list. Have pens and attractive cards on every table. Make them visible by announcing their existence throughout the night. Designate someone in the band or crew as the "Fan List Manager." Use your web site for the same purpose. Capture names at every juncture. As with all lists, the best way to store them is on a computer with a "contact management" or CRM (customer relationship management) program. This can be a mobile app (for example, *Insightly, Zoho*) or desktop-based. (for example. *Outlook, Act!)*. *FileMaker Pro* and other database programs can also serve you well here. Contact management programs will collect, file, and sort thru this information. They can also:

- link information from a message to a certain promo or company;
- time a phone call and generate a bill;
- send you a tickler beep or screen message to remind you of an appointment or phone call;
- make connections you might not otherwise think of and will save you time by organizing your activities; and *more...*

If you are selling from your web site there are some wonderful and robust shopping cart software products that can help manage your database along with many other marketing activities like order tracking, sales reporting, newsletter management, affiliate selling and more. Three I recommend are Mal's e-Commerce (http://www.mals-e.com), Squarespace.com and shopify.com. There are literally dozens of services like these out there.

❑ ***Industry.*** Your Industry database will be composed of people and organizations which can promote your music, hire you, use your songs, or book performances for you. This will include club owners, promoters, booking agents, managers of groups who might invite you to be a warm-up act for their group, blog gurus, music supervisors, music department heads at companies like Apple and Electronic Arts, artist and repertoire (A&R) executives at record companies, publishers, producers interested in buying new songs, and other from within as well as beyond the music space.

If you're a music production house or a record label, you'll want separate industry databases for such categories as music publishers, ad agencies, manufacturers, recording studios, music libraries, music supervisors, instrument rental services and other vendors. To obtain these look into the excellent series of industry directories published by The Music Business Registry (musicregistry.com). More local industry contacts can often be better obtained from published lists in local and regional music magazines.

Lists and directories always cost something but they're well worth it. If time is a factor or you don't want to do the research yourself, let others do it for you. No sense reinventing the wheel. These contact lists are an informational goldmine for the independent musician. Whenever you have a high profile gig, release a new product or plan an event, send a flyer, postcard or email announcing it to everyone on your mailing list. If you gig more than once a month you may want to do a monthly mailing. Don't forget to include any news about the band. Work to create a buzzzz. In this age of digits, it's sometimes beneficial to stand out with an analog snail-mail piece.

I recommended you work at least 30 minutes every day on your contact databases. Review them, study them, add to them and continue increasing their value.

Your databases can also provide you with valuable insight into your customers' relationship with your company. There are some important behavioral patterns to look for among your customer data. Each of the following can be set up as a "field" within your database:

- ❑ Date of last purchase
- ❑ Frequency of & momentum of purchases
- ❑ Monetary value of purchases
- ❑ Response to past promotions (offers, types of media, etc.)
- ❑ Product category & correlation between products purchased
- ❑ Billing & payment patterns
- ❑ Returns, cancellations
- ❑ Seasonality issues

Deciding On Your Marketing Mix

Everything we've done so far is "first-stage marketing", the essential foundation stones on which successful marketing is built. Most of this primary work is designed to help you develop a marketing "mind-set", one that will help you truly inform and render effective your more specific marketing aims.

Once you've reflected on unfolding trends, understood the benefits of your product, discovered and studied your target market, decided on your unique differentiation, and built a strong database of contacts - in other words, developed a clear sense of your niche-focus - your next step is to *communicate* it, that is, actively *market* it.

With your niche focus you can now decide which will be the most useful, the most effective, and the most profitable means to help you accomplish this. In marketing jargon, this is called deciding on your "marketing mix" - that combination of tools and tactics designed to get your message across to your target audience.

Most of us are not coming at this with deep pockets, nor are we playing with "monopoly money" from a parent corporation. The kind of marketing you will be doing has been given many names: *grass-roots marketing, guerrilla marketing, entrepreneurial marketing, expeditionary marketing, radical marketing, touch point marketing,* etc. No matter what you call it, all of these marketing approaches have the following features in common:

- ❑ low cost but effective communications
- ❑ doing more with less
- ❑ cooperative efforts
- ❑ leveraging resources

- ❑ tapping under-utilized resources
- ❑ using alternative channels
- ❑ using alternative media
- ❑ networking
- ❑ less use of money; more investment of time, energy, imagination
- ❑ acute focus in terms of products and services

Which Marketing Methods are Best for You?

All marketing activities come down to doing one or more of four things that we've done since kindergarten: WALK, TALK, SHOW, and TELL.

Some of us like to *talk.* For us, marketing activities from networking to making sales calls allow us to talk to our heart's content. Others of us enjoy being in the limelight, up on stage, so to speak. Activities like giving performances, speeches or seminars can be our forte. Still others of us prefer to remain in the background and communicate through the written word in brochures, advertising, direct mail and so forth. Some of us work best one-on-one through others like mentors and gatekeepers. Many of us want our work to speak for itself, and it can. We simply have to find ways to let those who might need or want it experience what we do firsthand through demonstrations, exhibits, or samples.
The best marketing activities will be those that enable you to be most fully yourself.

Effective marketing is a matter of identifying what you enjoy doing most, what comes most naturally to you, and what best fits into your schedule and your budget. There are plenty of options for us all.

Marketing Methods Exercise: *To find which kinds of business-generating activities are most comfortable and interesting to you, work through the following exercise. Check the statements that best describe you and select the activities that would be most appealing and easiest to fit into your schedule and your budget. Some of the following is drawn from Paul & Sarah Edwards' book, Getting Business to Come to You.*

❑ ***Making Personal Contact***

____ I like to meet people person-to-person.
____ I enjoy personally letting people know what I do and how I can help them.
____ I work well when I'm the center of attention, even in the spotlight.
____ I feel comfortable and would enjoy using (check any of the following):

- ____ Direct solicitation: selling in person or by phone or modem
- ____ Free consultations: working directly with prospective clients and customers
- ____ Networking: making business contacts at meetings and social gatherings
- ____ Sales speeches and seminars: selling to a group
- ____ Volunteering: contributing what I offer to trade, civic, or business concerns
- ____ Walking around the neighborhood: going door-to-door to meet my clients and customers

Example: Joe Cameron's secret for getting business is breakfast. Joe, an audio engineer and co-owner of a recording facility, woos prospects by inviting them to monthly networking breakfasts he hosts in elegant downtown restaurants. Each month he invites six people who don't know one another. He never gives a sales presentation but, instead, facilitates engaging discussions that highlight his expertise and experience.

❑ ***Getting Others to Talk About You***

____ I feel more comfortable letting other people promote and sell what I offer.
____ I enjoy working through and with peers and colleagues.
____ I like letting others know why they should promote my work.
____ I feel comfortable with and would enjoy using (check any that apply):

- ____ Gatekeepers and mentors
- ____ Gift certificates and coupons
- ____ Letters of reference, endorsements, and testimonials
- ____ Referrals
- ____ Sponsorships, donations, and events
- ____ Publicity:
  - ____ Newspaper
  - ____ Newsletter
  - ____ Magazine
  - ____ Radio and TV
  - ____ Business and trade publications
  - ____ Online publicity outlets/Social networking

Example – Glen and Jaya Kemp have a unique niche. Glen provides music backgrounds for Jaya's stories for African-American children. Publicity has been their best business generator. This special husband-wife team has been featured in *Essence, Black Enterprise,* and *Emerge* magazines, appeared on African-American talk shows, and been covered by the *Washington Post,* the *Detroit Free Press,* and the *Chicago Sun-Times.*

❑ ***Telling People All About It***

____ I'm good at explaining what I do in terms others can easily understand.
____ I'm good at motivating people with words.
____ *I feel comfortable and would enjoy creating (check any of the following):*

- ____ Advertising
- ____ Articles and columns
- ____ Blog posts
- ____ Brochures and flyers
- ____ Bulletin boards, tear pads, take-ones, and door hangers
- ____ Card decks and coupon packs
- ____ Catalogs
- ____ Direct mail
- ____ Fax-back, broadcast fax, and E-mail
- ____ Flyers
- ____ Inserts
- ____ Newsletters
- ____ Podcasts
- ____ Postcards
- ____ Product packaging and point-of-sale displays
- ____ Sales letters and proposals
- ____ Reply cards
- ____ Tweets
- ____ Web site
- ____ Yellow page and other directory listings
- ____ Your own book

Example – Jim Bernard's company is called, Step Up Productions. A leader and performer in several general business bands, Jim created an inexpensive, 10-page brochure called "Entertainment Planning for Your Wedding" and another called "Entertainment Planning for Your Private Party." These booklets have become his calling card. He sends them to event planners, caterers, banquet hall managers and others who traffic with people who are planning weddings and parties. In this indirect but helpful way, he introduces his own music groups to important influencers in this market.

❑ ***Showing Off What You Can Do***

___ I feel more comfortable letting my work speak for itself, and I don't mind finding ways to show it off.

___ I don't mind being the center of attention as long as the focus is on the work I'm doing or have done.

___ I feel comfortable and would enjoy using (check any of the following):

- ___ Podcasts/DVDs/CDs
- ___ Business cards as samples
- ___ Demonstrations
- ___ Displays
- ___ House parties, open houses, and occasion events
- ___ Media appearances
- ___ Video on Web sites
- ___ Photos and portfolios
- ___ Radio advertising
- ___ Having my own radio show
- ___ Samples and giveaways
- ___ Television – advertising
- ___ Having my own cable television show
- ___ Trade shows and special events
- ___ Video brochures on YouTube

Example: Erika Retallian deals wholesale in wooden music stands handmade in Indonesia. They are beautiful and functional, and they sell themselves when the right people see them. She makes sure they do so by taking a booth each year at the annual National Association for Music Education (NAfME) conference in Virginia and at the National Association of Music Merchants (NAMM) event in California. These shows put her products in front of important buyers and boost her credibility in her markets.

Hopefully, these examples have suggested a list of possible methods to help market your product or service, as well as some ideas for how to use them.

❑ ***The Time/Money Marketing Continuum***

Once you've settled on the most promising marketing tools for your product or service, you need to then decide how much time, money and energy you will put into each one. Until your sales are well under way, you should be willing to spend at least 60 percent of your time and money on marketing. If you don't have any business yet, you should spend your entire week (if possible) *marketing* until the business you generate starts filling your time.

The measure of a successful marketing campaign is the extent to which it reaches at the lowest possible cost the greatest number of people who can and will buy your product or service. Your goal should be to choose marketing methods that will provide you with the easiest and least costly access to the specific people you want to reach.
Every marketing effort takes a certain amount of time and money. For example, networking is a "high-time, low-money" marketing strategy, while traditional advertising is a "low-time, high-cost" marketing strategy. You need to decide where those precious few dollars will go as you promote your product or service.

Here is a comparison of how some of the various methods and tactics from the list relate on the **time/money marketing continuum**:

More Time					More Money
	Networking	Publicity	Direct Mail		
	Referrals	Internet	Sales Promotions	Advertising	
Less Money					Less Time

To find the right balance on the time/money continuum, ask yourself:

1. *How much business do I need?*

2. *What can I afford?*

3. *How much time do I have to invest?*

4. *How much effort will the activity I undertake require relative to the business it will generate?*

5. *What will I be motivated to do?*

As with many things in marketing, coming up with the right marketing mix isn't an exact science. It will take a combination of research, budget, instincts and experimentation to arrive at the best mix for your enterprise. We will re-visit this topic again in chapter 15.

The Ultimate Goal: Making Customers Not Just Sales

For your customers to have a good opinion of your business they need to have a positive experience when they interact with you and your team. Think about the last time you had a negative buying experience. Did the salesperson not have enough information to satisfy your query? Or maybe you were left on hold for too long when you called to place an order or to complain?

Most negative experiences are linked to poor customer service. Good customer service isn't that difficult if you follow these ten rules:

❑ *Commit to quality service*. It should be the focus of the whole team to provide service above and beyond the customer's expectations.

❑ *Know your products*. Conveying knowledge will help you win the customer's trust and confidence.

❑ *Know your customers.* This enables you to tailor your products and services to their needs.

❑ *Treat people with courtesy and respect.* Every contact with a customer leaves an impression - make it positive.

❑ *Never argue with the customer*. They may not always be right but concentrating on solving the problem, rather than laying blame, will encourage the customer to come back.

❑ *Don't leave customers hanging.* Today customers want quicker solutions - 95% of dissatisfied customers will return if their complaint is resolved on the spot.

❑ *Always provide what you promise*. Fail to do this and you loose credibility.

❑ *Assume that customers are telling the truth*. The majority of customers don't like to complain, in fact they will go out of their way to avoid it, so give them the benefit of the doubt.

❑ *Make it easy to buy*. Keep paperwork and forms to a minimum, make it easy to pay, help people find what they need and explain how products work.

❑ *Focus on making customers, not sales*. Keeping the customer's business over a long period of time is more important than making one big sale. Fact - *It costs 5-7 times more to secure a new customer than to sell to an existing one.*

When people have choices, they invariably go where they are made to feel special, important, and appreciated. The most effective strategy for leveraging your marketing efforts is to consistently communicate customer-centered information and advice that builds trust and confidence in you, your company, and your products or services.

A great example of this is the online indie music retailer, CDBaby. When I purchased my first CDs from this store my order came with a message on my receipt that said, "CDBaby loves Peter." Of course, I realize those who fulfilled my order did not know me from Adam, but nevertheless, this brief "extra value" message works in a subtle way to endear me to the service. CDBaby certainly doesn't *have to* include this message, but the fact it does tells me the company wants to go out of its way to make me feel special. The new economy requires us marketers to think holistically about our marketing tactics, working from the customer out, not from the medium in.

The following "Ten Demandments of Customer Service" should be kept before you always as you seek to turn the most demanding customers into the most delighted ones:

1. *Earn my trust* through respect, integrity, advocacy and quality.
2. *Inspire me* through immersive experiences, motivating messages and related philanthropy.
3. *Make it easy* with simplicity, speed and usefulness.
4. *Put me in charge* of making choices and give me control.
5. *Guide me* with expert advice, education and information.
6. *Give me 24/7 access*, from anywhere, at anytime.
7. *Get to know me* - listen, learn and study me, the real consumer, not just data.
8. *Exceed my expectations* with uncommon courtesies and surprising services.
9. *Reward me* with points programs, privileges of access or other worthwhile extras.
10. *Stay with me* with follow through and meaningful follow-up.

Adapted from, *The Ten Demandments: Rules to Live By in the Age of the Demanding Customer* by Kelley Mooney, with Laura Bergheim

Many business owners neglect the market research component, thinking they *just know* that there has to be a market for their wonderful service or product. Or, they feel their product or service is perfect just the way it is, and they don't want to risk tampering with it. Consider market research *an investment in your future*. If you take the time to examine your market and then make the necessary adjustment to your product or service now, you'll definitely save money in the long run.

SPOTLIGHT: GETTING TO *GO!*

Now, the moral of the story isn't *just go do things and be terrible at them and it'll work itself out probably,* because that's terrible advice. Research and planning are wonderful, essential things that you absolutely should be doing before you up and start a business. But at some point, you'll need to recognize that you've done enough, that you've reached the point of diminishing returns on your research, and that this thing is as organized as it's going to get. The idea is not to let the fear of failing, or not being exactly perfect, keep you from ever doing anything. Things will go wrong, no matter how much you plan, and you will find areas that need to be improved. You'll improve those things, you'll try again, and you'll find even more ways to make what you're doing better. And every time you put something out there and survive, it gets less scary to put work out there.

(Source: *Punk Rock Entrepreneur*)

CHAPTER SUMMARY

RESEARCHING YOUR MARKET

- **Introducing Market Research**

  Successful entrepreneurs make sure there is a real need for their product or service; assess customer preferences for the attributes of the new product or service; and identify the key dimensions of customer needs that their product or service is meeting. Here are a few resource reminders and some additional tools to help your market research: Surf the websites of those you consider your competitors, government websites, organizations that serve the interest of your industry; Hit the library reference shelves like *ESRI Community Sourcebooks* and *The Lifestyle Market Analyst.*

- **Getting to Know Your Market(s)**

  The logic is simple: know how your customers spend their time and you'll know better how and where to spend your marketing money. Through learning about the who, what and where of your music's audience you also learn about the best ways to reach that audience. Market research is simply defining who your primary customer will be. Market research is a prelude to selling. It teaches you a great deal about what you will need to know to develop your offering for the market and whether your offering is even worth developing.

- **3 Steps to Understanding Your Customer**

  Step One: Identify Why A Customer Would Want To Buy Your Product/Service. By knowing what your product/service has to offer and what will make customers buy, you can begin to identify common characteristics of your potential market.

  Step Two: Segment Your Overall Market. Segmentation will help you to customize a product/service or other parts of a marketing mix, such as advertising, to reach and meet the specific needs of a narrowly defined customer group. Larger markets are most typically divided into smaller target market segments on the basis of the following: Geographics, Demographics, Psychographics, and Behavioristic.

  Step Three: Profile Your Target Customer. The marketing mixes for this strategy may vary by product, price, promotional material and distribution methods. It is not uncommon for a firm using the multi-segment strategy to increase its sales by focusing on more than one segment, since you would have marketing mixes aimed at each segment.

- **Learning From Your Competition**

  Evaluating your competition will help you better understand your own product or service and give potential investors or loan officers a reassuring sense of your company's strengths. It enables you to know how best to distinguish your company in the customer's eyes, and it points to opportunities in the market.

- **Building Your Database of Connections: The Lifeblood of Your Marketing**
  There are three separate databases you'll want to develop: one for media, one for customers/fans, and one for industry. Media are all driven by common needs: To fill time and space with information of value to their readers, viewers and listeners. Begin your media database with the local scene and then branch out regionally, nationally and even internationally, depending on your marketing goals.
  Fans/Customers. This is your grassroots support network. The best ways to compile a fan database is at your gigs. Make it as easy as possible for people to join your fan list. Your Industry database will be composed of people and organizations that can promote your music, hire you, use your songs, or book performances for you.

- **Deciding on Your Marketing Mix**
  Your "marketing mix" is the combination of tools and tactics designed to get your message across to your target audience. The best marketing activities will be those that enable you to be most fully yourself. Effective marketing is a matter of identifying what you enjoy doing most, what comes most naturally to you, and what best fits into your schedule and your budget.

- **The Ultimate Goal: Making Customers Not Just Sales**
  When people have choices, they invariably go where they are made to feel special, important, and appreciated. The most effective strategy for leveraging your marketing efforts is to consistently communicate customer-centered information and advice that builds trust and confidence in you, your company, and your products or services.

FURTHER RESOURCES

ONLINE RESOURCES

Google's Marketing Almanac
thinkwithgoogle.com/marketers-almanac/
Great portal into the whole field of market research.

Federal Government Data
A great deal of demographic data is either free or inexpensive because it is collected and published by the federal government. Your tax dollars fund it. The following publications are from the Commerce Department and Census Bureau.

Every ten years, the United States Census Bureau, in its attempts to count the number of people in the U.S., gathers a vast array of data about its citizens. The 2000 Census is available in print format in many libraries. The Census is also available for the first time in CD-ROM format. In addition, the Census Bureau monitors the population through its regular surveys, including monthly Current Population Survey (CPS). The March issue of CPS contains household and income data. Go to www.census.gov and then click on 'Data Tools'.

Data For American States:
The simplest way to collect state and local data is to make a telephone call to the appropriate source. The phone numbers for other state data centers can be obtained from the Bureau of the Census at 800-923-8282. City or county planning departments often compile demographic data. Additional sources for local information are chambers of commerce, local business associations, regional economic development groups, Realtors and school boards. Local experts may also be able to help you with detailed data. Sources listed under "Federal Government Data" and "On-line Demographic Information" also contain state data.

Online Demographic Information
Online databases and their companion CD-ROM products have made it possible to sift through the mountains of information created by the Census Bureau and other sources quickly and easily. For a complete listing of demographic and other databases, consult the *Quandra Directory of On-line Databases* (available at most large libraries).

The following databases are available online:

United States Data
American FactFinder (FREE)
factfinder.census.gov
Provides users with the capacity to browse, search, and map data from many Census Bureau sources.

County and City Data Book (FREE)
www.census.gov

Contains statistical tables for 220 data items at the US, census region & division, state, and county levels. Also contains statistical tables for 194 data items for cities, and population and income data for smaller places. Updated every six months.

State & Metropolitan Area Data Book (FREE)
http://www.census.gov/library/publications/2010/compendia/databooks.html
Contains a collection of statistics on social and economic conditions in the United States at the state and metropolitan area levels.

Statistical Abstract of the United States (FREE)
http://www.census.gov/library/publications/2010/compendia/databooks.html
A collection of stats on social and economic conditions in the U.S.

Official City Sites (FREE)
http://officialcitysites.org
Just what it says – local, hometown directories of Chambers of Commerce, businesses, happenings and news from all over the country.

International Data
International Database (FREE)
https://www.census.gov/population/international/data/idb/informationGateway.php
A data bank containing statistical tables of demographic, and socio-economic data for 227 countries and areas of the world.

Statistics Directorate (FREE)
http://www.oecd.org/std/
The OECD [Organization for Economic Co-operation and Development] collects stats needed for the analysis of economic and social developments by its in-house analysts, committees, working parties, and member country governments from statistical agencies and other institutions of its member countries.

United Nations Statistics Division (FREE)
http://unstats.un.org/unsd
The Statistics Division compiles statistics from many international sources and produces global updates.

- Music Market Research Companies

Audiokite
audiokite.com

Big Champagne
bigchampagne.com

Forrester Research
Forrester.com

Music Watch
musicwatchinc.com

NPD Group (owned by Ipsos)
npd.com

ResearchMusic
researchmusic.com

BOOKS

Crossing the Chasm, 3rd Edition: Marketing and Selling Disruptive Products to Mainstream Customers by Geoffrey Moore (2014, HarperBusiness).

Hispanic Marketing & Public Relations: Understanding And Targeting America's Largest Minority by Elena Del Valle (2005, Poyeen Publications).

Market Research in a Week by Judy Bartkowiak (2012, Teach Yourself).

The Daily You: How the New Advertising Industry is Identifying Your Identity and Your Worth by Joseph Turow (2013, Yale University Press).

The New Mainstream : How the Multicultural Consumer Is Transforming American Business by Guy Garcia (2005, Rayo).

6

PLAN TO SUCCEED: MAPPING OUT YOUR BUSINESS PLAN

Planning is bringing the future into the present so that you can do something about it now.
– Alan Lakein

Chance favors the prepared mind. –Louis Pasteur, Chemist

With an understanding of the times, your market research in hand, and a firm grasp of your available resources, you are now ready to map out a plan for your business.

The Challenge of Planning Your Vision & Mission

There are two words that can strike fear in the hearts of new business owners. These two words are *strategic planning*. Strategic planning is something we'd prefer to avoid. We resist business planning for any number of reasons. Here are some common ones:

"My business is simple, plans seem too complex." A plan is simply a "map," and a map helps you see *your* path more clearly to your destination.

"Business plans are only for the big guys. My business is only me, so I really don't need a plan". Size make no difference and it's a lot cheaper working things out on paper than trying them in real life and failing.

"I'm too busy trying to get everything else going in my business to write a business plan". Don't let the tail wag the dog. A plan will act as a compass in the storm; and there *will* be storms.

"What if I change my mind after I've written my plan? I'm afraid I won't be able to stay as flexible". Plans are not written in stone; they will change and adapt as you change and adapt. No plan is final.

"I don't know how to write a business plan." There's no single "right way" to write a business plan. This chapter will walk you through the process. It's not rocket science. Fear not!

First, the benefits...

The Power of Writing a Business Plan

The purpose of the business plan is to form a picture - to yourself, potential investors and company employees - of what the company is about and why this particular company is going to be a stand out enterprise within its market.

If you are preparing your plan for investor formation, then it is important to realize that investors are generally looking into companies that are bringing something new and creative to the music market, something that has not yet happened in the music industry, and this must show in the business plan. More on investor formation in chapter 8.

There are a number of specific benefits to the process of writing a music business plan. A well-thought out business plan will:

- ❑ **Clear the way for creative thinking**
- ❑ **Pinpoint strengths and weaknesses**
- ❑ **Identify obstacles and problems**
- ❑ **Expose hidden opportunities**
- ❑ **Set proper priorities**
- ❑ **Coordinate your marketing program**
- ❑ **Take the guesswork out of budgeting**
- ❑ **Allow for meaningful review and revision**

A plan let's you mentally rehearse and process different scenarios your business may face. And this mental practice puts the mind in a greater state of readiness when such scenarios become reality.

Is a plan absolutely essential for business success? No. Some plans were no more than a few rudimentary thoughts written on the back of a napkin or envelope. "I wrote a basic outline of ideas but everything was so new to me I didn't even know how to write a proper one," says Andreas Katsambas of The End Records. "I believe a general outline always help. If you don't need to seek a loan or investment then keep it simple so you can modify and update easily. It will work as roadmap."

The critics of formal planning contend that it runs counter to what's at the heart of the entrepreneurial spirit: the ability to learn and adapt through experience. Too, many business concepts are "transitional in nature," meaning there are competitive advantages to starting the business quickly and by the time you write a full business plan the "opportunity will be gone." Entrepreneurs like Chris Hicks, CEO of Emissary Media Group, caution against "analysis paralysis." Sometimes "you just have to go *do*."

Sean Hagon of Music Media Solutions agrees. "Business plans are necessary if the company, product or service involves complex functions of legal structure, marketing and/or targeted promotion, venture capital, investment, and the involvement of multiple constituents in order to get the company, product or service launched. As a film & TV composer, my concept was quite simple, required very little upfront investment and involved just me as the sole proprietor. So I felt a detailed business plan wasn't necessary."

Jay Andreozzi of Amalgam Digital initially launched his business without a written plan but then quickly saw how difficult it was keeping track of all his ideas. "I decided I wanted to expand and needed more clarity and definition of exactly what it was that I was doing so I began to draft my first business plan as a plan for expansion and also a handbook for future staff members to get a complete understanding of the company. The fringe benefit was that it ultimately led to more thinking and more ideas giving birth to the concept for my latest business. Now, I am an advocate for putting it all on paper."

The type of business plan this book recommends is a 15-20 page provisional document that maps out the essential components of the business: purpose, market, structure, management and costs. Plans, while not always perfect, *can* help nascent entrepreneurs nail down important aspects of their concept, and sometimes prevent costly mistakes.

A Good Planning Framework

Here are some fundamentals to help get you in the right mental framework for writing your plan:

- ❑ **Scope out the Environment.** Consider the *external* factors that impact your business, such as market demand for your products or services, your competition, your customers' needs, the status of your suppliers, market trends, new technology and governmental legislation and regulations that may impact your industry.
- ❑ **Organizational Analysis.** This includes both the *internal* examination of your value and the *external* assessment of your available resources.
- ❑ **Mission Statement.** Every business, no matter how large or how small, needs one of these. A mission statement provides direction for your company – it tells you (or your employees) where you (and they) should be headed and why. It's the driving mantra of your creative enterprise.
- ❑ **Goals & Objectives.** Based on your analysis and mission statement you next decide on objectives, both general and specific, for your business. Get others who are close to you involved in this process and, together, commit to them.
- ❑ **Strategic Resource Planning.** Once your objectives are set make sure you have sufficient resources in place to meet them. These resources will include everything from financing and facilities to people and support services.
- ❑ **Implementation Strategy.** Many businesses prepare a plan, but then don't consider steps to implement it. The key is to phase in your plan in a smart, sequential way.
- ❑ **Communicate it in Writing.** Write out your plan in a simple, straightforward format. It doesn't have to be fancy or elaborate. It just needs to be clear, concise and understood by yourself and anyone involved with your business.

With this framework in mind, you can now hunker down with the various phases of creating your plan.

Phase 1: Summarizing Your Business Concept

This summary of your business concept will eventually become the "Executive Summary" of your business plan. You'll want to define the business you're starting, the type of products/services it will offer, and its role in the context of the overall music industry, particularly how your business concept is unique in that context. If you can't put the whole thing into 200 words or less, you're not ready to go on to Phase 2. Be clear and concise.

Here is an example:
"The purpose of Revolver Records is to find the best, upcoming dance artists in the world, form strategic partnerships with them, fund their recording and development, and then use both traditional and new media outlets to promote their "brand" to the world. Complimentary to promoting the artist is promoting the Revolver Records brand as an exciting source of new dance sounds".

Here's another from Jeannie Deva Voice Studios:
"To provide singers around the world with a simple, direct method of voice training that is physiologically factual and non-style specific; to develop the full functionality, health and expressivity of a singer's voice while maintaining and enhancing the unique identity of each vocal artist. To empower singers of all genres and styles with confidence in their instrument and their own vocal identity in live and studio performance; to raise the bar on vocal

excellence within the world music community, thereby contributing to a planetary artistic renaissance elevating the culture".

Phase 2: Choosing a Name for Your Company

If you're like most business owners, your business means a lot to you – in some ways, you consider it your child. You've planned for it since its conception, nurtured it from birth, given it tender loving care, and have great hope for its future.
It makes sense, then, to consider naming your business with the same intelligence and care that you would exercise in naming a child. Your business name will be your number one asset so take care in choosing one!

Here are five guidelines to help you name your company for the long term:

❑ **Make the name meaningful** – since your company name is often the first thing someone knows about your business, consider it an important *marketing* tool (e.g., think of "Delicious Vinyl," "Noteworthy Children," etc.).

❑ **Make sure the name is easy to pronounce and remember** (for example, "Mountain Records" rolls off the tongue easily; "Stanhope House Records" does not).

❑ **Make sure it's available**. You want to ensure your company name is not being used by anyone else. See chapter 9 for guidelines on clearing your business trademark.

❑ **Choose a name that you can live and grow with.** Be forward-thinking in your choice of a business name, so that it can expand as you do. Some newer music companies choose to avoid the use of words like "records" and even "music" in their names and, instead, go with terms like "productions" or "media" instead to reflect changing technology and to allow the expansion of their company into other areas of entertainment and media.

))) ILLUMINATING TRIVIA (((

Did you know...

...that Clive Calder and Ralph Simon named their company Zomba, after the then-capital of Malawi, where legend holds that local tribe members were blessed with superior hearing?

❑ **Make it unique.** Your name must also be unique, since two businesses in the same geographic area cannot legally operate under the same name. In Elizabethtown, Kentucky, Victor Moseley used the name Victor's Secret when he opened his adult gift and lingerie shop. Victor's Secret did not remain secret when the legal department of Victoria's Secret sent a letter to Moseley claiming trademark infringement. In haste, the name was changed to Victor's Little Secret, but the change was not enough for Victoria's Secret who then filed a lawsuit. For more information on doing a name search (also called, a *trademark* search), see chapter 9, "Securing the Required Paperwork".

❑ **Link it to a Domain Name**. Once your name is selected, see if you can obtain the domain name for it too. I started Music Business Solutions in 1992 and when I set up my web site in 1996, I had to decide on an internet address for it. Mbs.com was taken; musicbusinesssolutions.com was too long; I settled on mbsolutions.com – a happy compromise. Check for existing domain names on an Internet registration site, such as godaddy.com or register.com. See chapter 7 ("**Creating & Registering Your Domain Names"**) for more information on this topic.

The right business name will help distinguish you from a sea of bland competitors, provide your customers with a reason to hire you, and aid in the branding of your company.

Phase 3: Identifying Start-up Expenses

You'll need a basic estimate of what your start-up costs will be going forward for at least the first year of business. You will use this estimate later in your business plan when you come to the "Financial Information" section ("Startup Costs") starting on the next page and continuing later in the chapter.

Chris Hicks of Rights Emissary Media Group has this advice: "Plan 10-20% above every number on your spreadsheet and go quality but cheap (gear, furniture). Don't shoot yourself in the foot, invest in gear you *need* to do your job (e.g., kick ass scanner/copier), not what you want (e.g., leather couches)."

A budget is, of course, only as good as the estimates that go into creating it. You can maximize the accuracy and usefulness of your first-year budget by building a comprehensive list of start-up costs for your business. Here is a list of some typical start-up expenses:

1.	**Legal costs** (incorporation, trademark clearance, etc.)	**$** ____________
2.	**Fees and licenses**	**$** ____________
3.	**Design (logos, letterhead, etc.)**	**$** ____________
4.	**Sales literature**	**$** ____________
5.	**Fixing up/equipping the office, etc.**	**$** ____________
6.	**Hardware/software expenses**	**$** ____________
7.	**Rent before start-up**	**$** ____________
8.	**Insurance before start-up**	**$** ____________
9.	**Office supplies**	**$** ____________
10.	**P.O. box rental fee**	**$** ____________
11.	**Web site development/maintenance**	**$** ____________
12.	**Industry expenses** (subscriptions, travel, etc.)	**$** ____________

As for format, I recommend you create a spreadsheet. This should be a digital spreadsheet using a program such as Excel or Google Docs. Depending on your situation, you may have only a few items for some categories and an entire page for others.

It's also advisable to sort your start up expenses into one of four categories. This will help immensely when tax time arrives each year. The categories are: *Startup deductible expenses, Ongoing deductible expenses, Startup not deductible* and *Ongoing not deductible*.

• *Startup deductible expenses*. These occur only once, when starting your business, and are deductible as a business expense. An example would be a phone you purchase to use in your business. (You aren't likely to need to replace the phone for some time, so this would be categorized as a startup expense).

• *Ongoing deductible expenses*. These are ongoing, and they are also deductible as a business expenses. An example of an ongoing deductible expenses is copy/printer paper. Whenever possible, list in the spreadsheet the cost of this expense for one month.

• *Startup expenses that are not deductible*. These are expenses you will incur as a result of beginning your business, but they are not deductible as a business expense. For example, let's say that you switch your daughter's bedroom with the spare room so that you can use her current room for your home office. You will repaint her new room to the color she desires. This will still cost you – but you cannot deduct that as a business expense.

• *Ongoing expenses that are not deductible*. These are expenses you will incur as you operate your business, but are not a reasonable business expense. For example, let's say you decide to send laundry out rather than go to the laundromat. This gives you additional time to invest in your business because you are spending a few minutes to gather it and a few minutes to put it away rather than two hours or more at the laundromat. But this isn't a business expense *per se*, so you will not be able to deduct it as such. Whenever possible, list this as a monthly expense. This allows you to view a monthly picture of your expenses easily. Come tax time, you'll be able to run a report and get an annual total in a snap for your tax forms.

Also, don't forget exploratory and investigative costs like researching possible business ideas, traveling to a potential location or paying for a market survey. Keep in mind that any expense that would qualify as a business deduction once you are in business qualifies as a *startup cost* if you incur it *before* you launch your new venture.

Your estimates need not be perfect, but they should be as realistic as possible. This exercise may take several hours or several days; the important thing is that you stick with it until you have identified *all* start-up expenses.

You can find a simple and useful "Start-up Costs Calculator" online at:
http://www.bplans.com/common/startcost/index.cfm
Adapt it to your own needs.

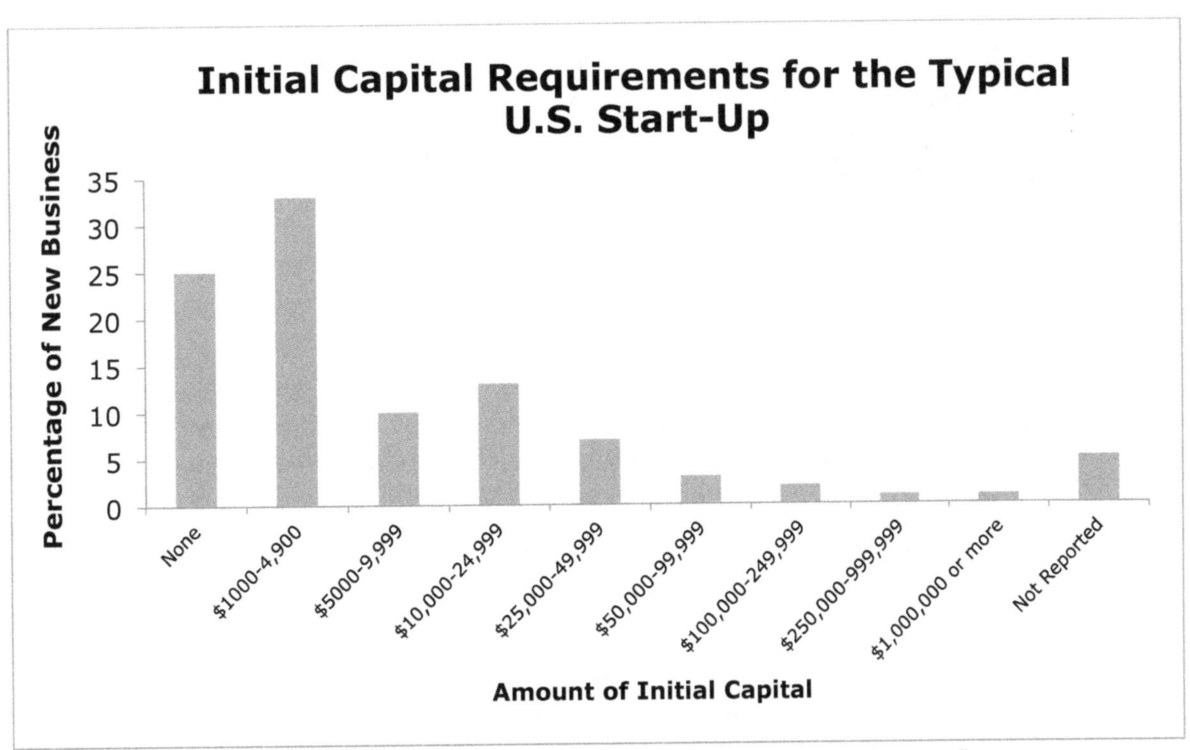

Source: Adapted from "Characteristics of Business Owners," U.S. Department of Commerce, Bureau of the Census, 2016

Getting Help with Budgeting and Accounting. I highly recommend that you get professional assistance with budgeting and financial management if:

- You have little or no experience in these areas
- You are really uncomfortable with numbers
- You *hate* anything to do with bookkeeping and budgeting

Don't worry – you're not alone. That's why there are professional accountants. Find one who can help you set up your books and first-year budget (chapter 11). Check to confirm that every expense you have in a "deductible" category is truly a deductible expense. (Don't rely on the preceding examples – your circumstances might be different!). Your business and personal peace of mind will benefit from it. Don't be afraid to shop around for the best person. Ask other business owners who they use and talk to your banker or attorney for recommendations. Sometimes your local college's accounting department can be a good source for referrals as can your local SBDC or even SCORE online. Call the Society of Certified Public Accountants in your state. Many, though not all, have referral services. Ask your accountant to identify any first-year expenses you may have overlooked. The goal is to have the most comprehensive inventory of expenses possible. When it comes to money and your business you want as few surprise expenses as realistically possible.

It is also recommended you download "Publication 334: Tax Guide for Small Businesses" and "Publication 4035: Is it Too Good to Be True? Home Based Business Tax Avoidance Schemes" to help you determine whether an expense is truly considered a business expense. These publications, and much other helpful information, can be found at the IRS web site, www.irs.gov. More about smart tax practices in chapters 9 and 14.

Phase 4: Deciding on the Legal Form of Your Business

As a business owner you must choose from one of several legal forms for your business. Each one has its own procedures, tax and liability implications so it's a good idea to check with an attorney and accountant in selecting the best legal form for your specific company. Essentially, there are three main forms: sole proprietorship, partnership, or corporation, which can itself take several forms.

See page 123 for an "at a glance" chart on the different business legal structures. Let's look at the most common ones and how to set them up.

❒ Sole Proprietorships

A sole proprietorship is a business that is owned by one person and that isn't registered with the state as a corporation or a limited liability company (more on these forms later). Of the over 28 million small businesses in the U.S., almost 74% of them are sole proprietorships. Being a sole proprietorship means *you* are the company. You have total control over its operations. Entrepreneurs who chose this route are truly their own bosses, and as we noted in chapter 2, that is one reason why many people choose to become entrepreneurs in the first place.

These benefits come at a considerable cost, however. The most important of these involves the fact that owners of sole proprietorships are subject to *unlimited personal liability.* Under a sole proprietorship, company assets and personal assets are, from a government (and tax) perspective, treated as one. If the company goes "belly up", the owner can lose his entire investment *and* his own personal assets come into play if the business is deeply in debt.

Despite its drawbacks, however, the sole proprietorship is still the most popular form of business and one has the option of converting from this form to another (say a corporation)

once the company's assets grow to a point where that makes sense.
Form to file: DBA (doing business as)
Where to file: County Clerk's Office/Town-City Hall
Fees: $0-$50, depending on the state

Note: Some states require you to announce the formation of your new business in the local press. They will let you know at the time you file your form.

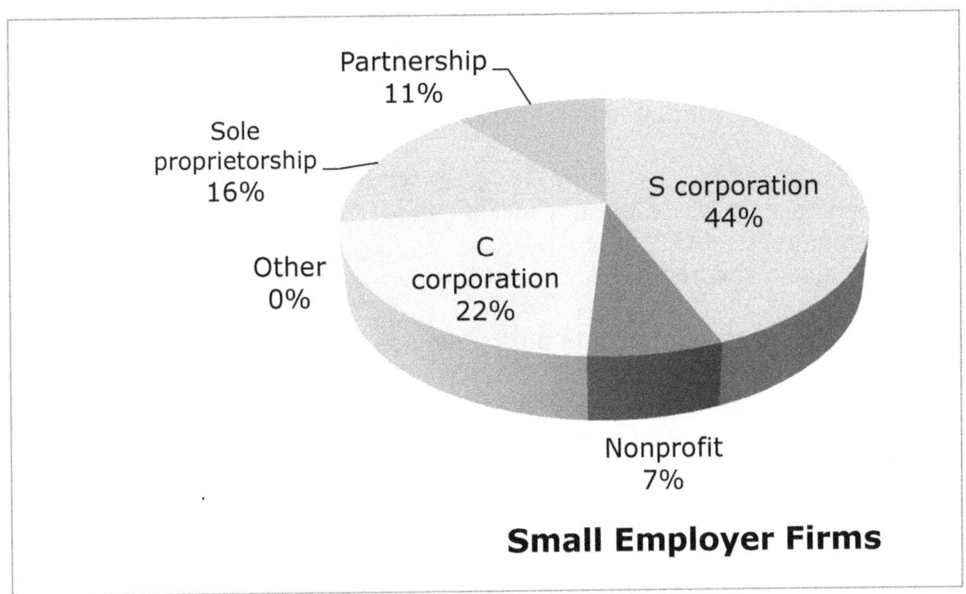

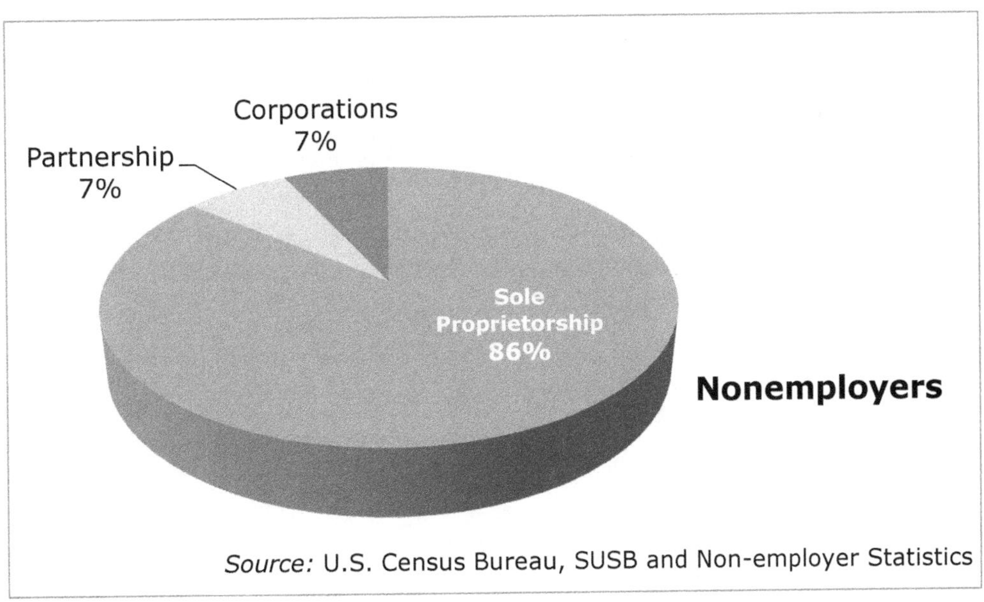

Source: U.S. Census Bureau, SUSB and Non-employer Statistics

❒ Partnerships

A *partnership* is a formal partnering of you with at least one other person. Forming a partnership generally requires an attorney. The main reason to form a partnership is to increase the money, labor, expertise and skills available to the business.

There are two kinds of partnership: General and Limited –

• ***General Partnership:*** Partners share control, profits, as well as liabilities for debt, etc.

• ***Limited Partnership:*** Some partners invest money or property in return for a cut of the profit, but their control is limited to the amount of their investment (sometimes referred to as "silent partners").

If you are a home-based business, you might not be allowed to form a partnership unless it is with your spouse or domestic partner (depending on the regulations of home businesses in your area). Forming a partnership with someone not living with you is a bit trickier. But this is the twenty-first century – the era of the virtual company. If this is someone you know you can trust, and zoning regulations (see chapter 9) allow it, there's no reason why two people in different cities – or even different states or countries – can't use this business form.

- *Form to file:* Certificate of Conducting Business as Partners or similar form.
- *Where to file:* County Clerk's Office/Town-City Hall
- *Fees:* $0-$150
- Sign a Partnership Agreement (see sample below).

For more guidelines on forming partnerships, see chapter 11, "Building Your Team".

What if a partnership doesn't work out?... It has been said that a partnership is like a marriage – easy to get into, not so easy to get out of. Ariel Hyatt of Cyber PR Music in New York City shares some painful memories when it comes to partnerships. "I fell down a lot with partnerships. It turns out I'm not a fantastic judge of character and tend to trust what people say at face value. I learned some very key lessons about doing serious due diligence, and I skipped that part with a couple of people that I worked with early on and it ended up definitely coming back to haunt me".

In the event that things do not work out between you and your partner(s), you will need some kind of written agreement for dissolving the partnership.
This is known as a *Notice of Dissolution*. Here is a sample:

NOTICE OF DISSOLUTION OF PARTNERSHIP

Notice is hereby given in accordance with the provisions of (Section and Code of State) that:
The partnership heretofore existing between (partner A) and (partner B) , under the fictitious name of(fictitious name of partnership) at (address) , City of , County of , State of ______________________________ is now dissolved by mutual consent.
That (partner A) , of the City of , County of , State of , has withdrawn from ______________________ and is no longer associated in the conducting of said business, and (partner B) , of the City of , County of , State of will conduct said business hereafter, has assumed all of the outstanding obligations of said business incurred both heretofore and hereafter, and is entitled to all of the assets of said business.
Said partnership is dissolved as of ______________(date).
/S/ _______________________ /S/ ____________________

❑ Corporations

A corporation is a legal entity separate from the shareholders and employees. It is formed after an individual or group applies to the state for a charter. A corporation needs to file its own taxes and have its own bank account. Income and losses are taxed to the corporation. Any income generated by the corporation for the stockholders is also taxed in most cases.

Corporations offer some distance between you (an officer in the corporation) and the entity itself, which might be helpful when dealing with liability. However, these rules have changed in response to scandal, and vary from state to state, so you will need to talk to an attorney for a current understanding of benefits and limitations. Some forms of corporation can even be one person, so check the laws in your state to determine if this is the best organization for you. As with partnerships, your city or county might restrict or forbid this type of business from operating from a private residence.

Example: If the company makes $100, and your share is $50, the government would tax the $100 at the *corporate* rate, and then tax your $50 at the *individual* rate. This "double taxation" is one of the more onerous drawbacks to most corporate arrangements.

There are essentially two different kinds of corporations you can set up (Limited Liability Companies and non-profits are types of corporation too, but will be treated separately). Before deciding to incorporate the business owner should consider these questions:

- ❒ How much *risk* are you willing to absorb?
- ❒ How will the *laws* of the incorporating state influence your decision on method of incorporation?
- ❒ What are your *prospects* for attracting capital?
- ❒ Are you willing to share *control* of the businesses with outsiders?
- ❒ Is there a *tax advantage* or incentive for you to incorporate?

***Regular, or C Corporation*:** A regular (also known as "standard") corporation gives owners liability protection, and taxes are paid by the business itself, at a corporate rate. Being able to deduct health care expenses for employees and his or her family – including insurance premiums, deductibles, and co-payments – is an increasingly popular motive to start a C corporation. *As with all tax matters, this may change, so it's important to have your legal and financial advisors review all such matters.*

Subchapter S Corporation*:** Think of this option as a blend between a corporation and a sole proprietorship. You receive all the benefits of a corporation's liability protection, but taxes are assessed to you at a personal level (corporate rate is significantly higher) There is also an entity known as a ***Professional Corporation, sort of a mix of partnership and corporation aspects. This corporation type is usually available only to certain types of businesses, however, and often limited to high-risk occupations such as doctors, lawyers, and accountants.

The Incorporation Process: It *is* possible for a small business owner to incorporate *without* legal counsel, or at least to do the lion's share of the work before hiring an attorney. To minimize legal fees, consider obtaining and filling out all forms for incorporation yourself. Forms and guidelines are available from your state secretary of state's office. Have them reviewed by an attorney before you file.

You can obtain free or low-cost legal forms and tools at do-it-yourself sites like:
Nolo Press (nolo.com**), Find Law (findlaw.com) and Legalzoom (legalzoom.com)**

Incorporation forms require the following:

1. **Company name:** Name must have the words *Corporation, Inc., Limited, or Ltd.* contained within to indicate that the liability of the shareholders is limited.

2. **You need to reserve that name with the Secretary of State Corporate Division office**. Once your name has been accepted by the state, your corporation

3. can officially do business under that name. Of course, the same guidelines regarding trademarks apply here as well (see chapter 9).

4. **Mailing address:** In some states a P.O. Box or home address is not an acceptable address. Be sure to check.

5. **Lawful Reason or a specific purpose for the business:** In other words, what the company will do to make a profit. Educational or not-for-profit organizations may have to submit additional documentation to support their organizational purpose.

6. **Number of shares to be issued and their different classifications with the rights, preferences, privileges and restrictions of each series included.**

7. **Number of Directors, names and all addresses:** If you are the only director, you will most likely be named president and secretary as well. Individuals can serve dual roles as officers and board members.

8. **Name & address of the incorporator.**

9. **Date when corporation's existence will begin.**

10. **Notarization of documents (required in some states).**

11. **Name & address of registered agent:** This is the individual who is incorporating the business and who received all the formal information about incorporating the business from the Secretary of State (you or an attorney representing you).

Why do people so often incorporate in Delaware and Nevada? – The states of Delaware and Nevada have positioned themselves as among the friendliest for would-be corporations in the United States. Anyone may form a corporation in Delaware without ever having to visit the state. Delaware has kept its fees low and is one of the friendliest states to corporate businesses. Indeed, over 50% of all companies listed on the New York Stock Exchange are Delaware Corporations.

Here are some facts about incorporating in this state:

- Names and addresses of initial directors need not be listed in public records.
- The cost to form a Delaware corporation is among the lowest in the nation. The annual $50 Franchise Tax compares favorably with that of most other states.
- Delaware maintains a separate court system for business, called the "Court of Chancery." If legal matters arise involving a trial in Delaware, there is an established record of business decisions.
- No minimum capital is required to organize the corporation and there is no need to have a bank account in Delaware. Just one person can hold all the offices of the corporation: President, Vice President, Secretary and Treasurer. There is no state corporate income tax on Delaware corporations that do not operate within the state.
- Shares of stock owned by persons outside of Delaware are not subject to Delaware personal income tax.
- There is no Delaware inheritance tax levied on stock held by non-residents.
- A Delaware corporation can be formed quickly and easily by phone in as little as 15 minutes.

Nevada too is becoming increasingly friendly to corporations with its privacy and liability protection status as well. Numerous companies are relocating their business entities to Nevada in order to receive the numerous tax benefits. Listed below are some of the reasons why Nevada is attracting more and more businesses each day:

- No state corporate tax on profits.
- No state annual franchise tax.
- No personal income tax.
- Stockholders are not on public record which permits complete anonymity.
- Just one person can hold all the offices of the corporation – President, Vice President, Secretary and Treasurer.
- Stockholders, directors and officers need not be residents of Nevada.
- A Nevada corporation can be formed quickly and easily by phone too in as little as 15 minutes.

Notwithstanding the ease of incorporating in these states, it's still a good idea to get professional legal advice on your decision whether or not to incorporate.

❑ The LLC (Limited Liability Company)

The LLC has emerged as one of the most popular forms of incorporation. Why?

Because it allows the business owners to adopt a *corporate* business structure while permitting them to operate like a traditional *partnership*.

Such a structure distributes income and income tax to the partners (reported on their individual tax returns) but also protects them from personal liability for the business's debts, as with the corporate business form. The downside to an LLC is that you don't get the free transferability of ownership, perpetual existence, and the ability to be totally owned by a single individual that you'd get with a Corporation. That is the trade off you make to get the Partnership tax status and greater management flexibility.

LLCs also have distinct advantages over the S Corporation: 1) LLCs can issue several different classes of stock (S corps can issue only one), and, 2) LLCs can have an unlimited number of stockholders (S corps can have only 35 U.S. stockholders).

However, if the company's business plan includes raising capital by someday admitting new owners or going public, then a Corporation is probably the more desirable form for the business. Limited Liability Companies generally restrict the transfer of ownership interests in the business to make sure the business is classified as a Partnership under federal tax law.

LLCs have become the preferred business form for music-related companies where two or more partners are involved.

❑ *The Benefit Corporation*

In the United States, a benefit corporation is a relatively new type of for-profit corporate entity, authorized by 30 U.S. states and the District of Columbia that includes positive impact on society, workers, the community and the environment in addition to profit as its legally defined goals. Additionally, the demand for corporate accountability is at an all-time high, with many consumers already aligning their purchases with their values. The benefit corporation status is a great way to differentiate your company from the competition and capitalize on these customers. Downside is expanded reporting requirements vis-a-vis shareholders.

COMPARING LEGAL STRUCTURES FOR YOUR BUSINESS (+= positive, – = negative)

Sole Proprietorship

+ Controlled by owner
+ All profits to owner
+ Little regulation
+ Earning taxes at personal level retirement/death

- Personal liability for business debts
- Limited Resources
- Potential increased risk of IRS audit
- Likelihood of no continuity at

General Partnership

+ Joint ownership and responsibility
+ Access to more money and skills
+ Earnings taxes at personal level

- Conflict of authority
- Partners liable for actions of others
- Profits divided
- Possible end of business at retirement or death of one partner

Limited Partnership

+ General partner(s) runs business
+ Limited (silent) partners have no liability beyond invested money
+ Earnings taxed at personal level

- Limited partners have no say in the business
- General partners have a personal liability for business debts
- More regulations than general partnerships

Limited Liability Company

+ Limited personal liability
+ Unlimited number of shareholders
+ Profits and losses taxed at personal level

- Relatively new entity with untested legal issues
- Costly to form and maintain
- Closely regulated by the state and IRS

S Corporation

+ Limited personal liability
+ Legal entity with transferable ownership
+ Earnings taxed at personal level

- Closely regulated by the state and IRS
- Costly to form and maintain
- Restricted to 75 or fewer stockholders
- Not recognized by all states

C Corporation

+ Limited personal liability
+ Legal entity with transferable ownership
+ Employee benefits deductible

- Closely regulated by the state and IRS
- Costly to form and maintain
- Potential double taxation on personal and corporate income

B (Benefit) Corporation

+ Certified by third party
+ Institutionalized social mission
+ Possible money savings

- Untested in the court system
- Third party auditing
- Lots of paperwork

❑ The Non-Profit Option

If you decide to operate your business as a corporation, chances are you'll form either a C corporation, an S corporation, or perhaps an LLC. But you should be aware of another kind of corporate structure as well: the Nonprofit Corporation.

Each state permits people to form nonprofit corporations, also known as "not-for-profit" corporations. The main reason people form these is to get tax-exempt status under the Internal Revenue Code (Section 501(c)(3)). If a corporation is tax-exempt, not only is it free from paying taxes on its income, but people and organizations who contribute to the nonprofit corporation can take a tax deduction for their contributions. Because many nonprofit organizations rely heavily on grants from public agencies and private foundations to fund their operations, attaining 501(c)(3) status is critical to success.

Tax-exempt status isn't the only benefit available to a nonprofit corporation. An organization that plans to do some heavy mailing may be attracted by the cheaper postal rates charged nonprofits. And the nonprofit label seems to create an altruistic aura around the organization and the people running it. The message is, "We're not in this for the money – we really do love kids (or music or animals)."

The legal standard for tax-exempt status is that the corporation has been formed for religious, charitable, literary, scientific or educational purposes.

Of course, being "non-profit" doesn't mean the company can't make a "profit". Most non-profits rely at least partially on donations from individuals and corporations, as well as grants from government and foundations to offset their operating costs. However, most nonprofit organizations also earn money directly, through mechanisms such as membership dues, fees-for-service, or thrift shops. Nonprofits can even make more money than they need for operating expenses. However, they are limited in how these profits can be made and spent. "The only difference is that if we generate more revenue than we spend we must reinvest that money into the organization," says Matt McArthur, Executive Director of The Record Company, a non-profit recording studio and training program in Boston. "It cannot be distributed as a dividend to the owners because there *are no owners*." Non-profits can have no owner shareholders who benefit from surplus revenues.

What kinds of groups should consider becoming nonprofit corporations? Here's a partial list:

- child care centers
- shelters for the homeless
- community health care clinics
- museums
- hospitals
- churches, synagogues, mosques and other places of worship
- schools
- performing arts groups
- conservation groups

How about a non-profit record label? Why not? New Amsterdam Records was started in 2006 as a way to get "indie classical" music out to the world and as an antidote to the stranglehold traditional labels have had on the music that get distributed. Threadhead Records grew out of an online chat room on nojazzfest.com, eventually morphed into a fundraiser for the post-Katrina New Orleans Musicians Clinic, and is currently a full-blown label producing and releasing a variety of New Orleans recording artists. Other non-profit record labels include Sunstruck (Tucson, AZ) and Croquet (Raleigh, NC).

Most nonprofit corporations are run by a board of directors or trustees who are actively involved in the work of the corporation. "Board recruitment and management continues to be one of the most challenging parts of the work," says Matt McArthur of The Record Company. "In the beginning we needed a board with a lot of practical skills, a 'working' board to help actually operate the organization. Five years later we're transitioning to what is called a 'governing' board, or a board with a more strategic role and less involvement in the operations of the organization."

Because both profit and nonprofit corporations can take a tax deduction for the reasonable salaries of their employees, there may not be too much difference in the operation of the two types of corporations.

Keep in mind that if you put assets into a nonprofit corporation, you give up any ownership or proprietary interest in those assets. They must be irrevocably dedicated to the specified nonprofit purposes. If you want to get out of the business, you can't just sell it and pocket the cash. The nonprofit corporation goes on; if it ends, any remaining assets must go to another nonprofit.

Should you consider the non-profit a viable form for your business? Here is McArthur's advice: "If your idea is primarily about community benefit and you're willing to contribute to an organization that will always belong to the community (and not you!), then non-profit might be the way to go."

This book is addressed primarily to people starting and running business *for profit*, so you'll find little here on the specifics of nonprofit corporations. For plenty of further info on this topic visit: nonprofits.org and idealist.org. The pro-bono legal organization, Volunteer Lawyers for the Arts (vlany.org), can also help should you decide to go this route.

❑ **Franchising**

The concept of *franchising,* another form of business, was introduced in chapter 2 when we explored today's music-related opportunities. Franchising is a system of distribution in which semi-independent business owners (*franchisees*) pay fees and royalties to a parent company (*the franchisor*) in return for the right to use its trademark, sell its products or services, and, in many cases, use the business model and system it has created. For more information on franchising as a business option, go to www.franchising.com and re-visit chapter 2 in this text.

Ok, let's assess where we are now in the business planning process. So far, you've named your company, thought through the market for your product, worked out a startup budget, and what legal form your particular company will take. Now you're ready for:

Phase 5: Solidifying Your Business Concept

This phase helps you develop your "elevator pitch" – your opportunity to succinctly communicate the core elements of your business idea. If you can't answer all of the following questions, then you're not ready to write your business plan.
Work on these foundations first and you'll have the solidity needed to build solid walls for your company.

- Can you describe the product or service you intend to sell in 25 words or less?
- Can you convincingly explain why there is a *need* for your product or service?
- Who will buy your product or service and why?
- What are your (and your partners') management qualifications?
- What will make your company unique in the marketplace?
- What approach will you take to maintain your unique advantage in the future when competitors try to imitate it?

How did you do? If you felt doubt in your mind about any of these questions, then it may be you need to re-visit a previous phase (or chapter) first.
The clearer you are about your business idea, the stronger the foundations you'll establish, and the stronger your plan will be.

Phase 6: Write Your Plan!

Below is an outline of a basic business plan. There are many, many other plan outlines in the world of business entrepreneurship. This one, however, is not too detailed and not too sparse. It may not be the kind of outline you would use to attract investors, but it is one you can use along with your bank loan application. I believe it affords start-up entrepreneurs the essential areas needing attention if an effective business plan is to be constructed. Explanation and commentary on each component follows. First the outline:

I. Summary statement

II. Foundations of your business
- A. History and background of you and your business idea
- B. Management description and experience
- C. Business legal structure

III. The market for your product or service
- A. Market description
  1. Primary market description & data
  2. Secondary market description & data
  3. Referral markets
  4. Competition profiles
- B. Marketing (Branding) strategy
  1. Positioning statement
  2. Marketing mix
  3. Pricing philosophy
  4. Method of sales/distribution
  5. Customer service policies

IV. Operations
- A. Facilities and equipment
- B. Organizational dynamics
- C. Plans for growth and expansion
- D. Threats & Risks

V. Project timeline

VI. Financial information
- A. Start up costs
- B. Three-year financial projections

I. Summary Statement. Here you want to answer the following questions as succinctly as possible: Who are you?, What will you do? (your business goals), Why will the business be successful?, How will it be financed?, and, When do you think it will turn a profit? (Remember, a 'profit' is not how much money you *make*, but how much you *keep*). Be as clear and realistic as possible.

It is also in the summary statement that you list the products or services being offered as well as the names and positions of all personnel involved. The summary should close with a strong statement about what is unique about your company.

It essentially summarizes the whole plan. For this reason I advise clients to write the complete Summary Statement *last* and write a more bare-bones one for now.

II. Foundations of your business

This section begins to flesh out the summarization above.

A. Begin first with the history and background of your project. This provides the overall context in which to view your current enterprise. List all data that pertains to the various facets of your present business. Don't pad it with your whole life story, just the pertinent highlights that have brought you to the present moment.

B. A management description should follow next. How is your business project organized? What does the leadership (it's style and command chain) look like? How are decisions made and facilitated? What kind of staffing will be necessary to operate the business? What ongoing business meeting schedule will be followed to ensure smooth operation? It's sometimes helpful to create a visual team flow-chart (see p. 129) to illustrate company functions.

C. Describe the business structure you will use (i.e. sole proprietorship, partnership, corporation, etc.) and why you chose that particular form. Remember, your answer to this question has many legal and tax implications, varies greatly from state to state, and from time to time. Again, seek the advice of your small business advisor at your local SBDC office, your attorney or your accountant if you have any nagging questions.

INSPIRATION: EPITAPH RECORDS

Epitaph, for one, has made itself into a household name, but it started out as just a logo and a PO box. They pressed a record with a $1,000 loan from Brett Gurewitz's dad and sold 10,000 copies in a year, mostly through mail order. This wasn't a guy with a Harvard MBA and country club connections, this was just a guy that wanted to get his music out there, who got involved in something and found out that he had the skills to contribute to a community of people like him. You learn a lot as you go. If Epitaph had started out as big as it is today, it probably would have been completely overwhelming.

III. The Market for your Product and/or Service

Now we are getting into the essence of what your company is uniquely about. Marketing ultimately results in *selling* and it is an absolute truth that unless a start-up business can sell its offerings it will not survive. Getting orders – selling or licensing your products and services to paying customers – is of fundamental importance to a new business. This part of your plan is your opportunity to demonstrate how it will happen. The marketing section of your plan breaks down as follows:

A. Description of the market for your product/service. In Chapter 5 you explored the details of your target market. You will draw on this information for this part of your plan. That research helps you correctly *position* your product in your *primary* and *secondary* markets and find your own unique niche (your USP) within them. You will also include here what *Referral* markets might be relevant and useful for your product or service. More on that in a moment.

Like all of your planning, market research should be viewed as an ongoing process.

1. Primary Market Description/Data. Your primary market can be very broad, but you'll obviously need to narrow it down in order to describe it effectively. Who or what does the business provide these services or products to? Are there specific industries or geographic locations services are provided to, or are they offered internationally? Is the entity business-to-business, business-to-consumer, or both? Are you planning to sell mainly through retail? Your web site? Others' web sites?

Here you will want to ask: What part of this larger market do I fit into? In other words, who are my *specific* customers? You might say "all musicians" or "every recording artist", but that's obviously too broad to be useful. "All musicians" may be your primary market, but you'll want to focus on the most relevant segment of the musician market for the most effective marketing strategy, like "musicians over 40 years old" or "formally trained musicians in the Dallas-Fort Worth region".

Provide a detailed description of your ideal customer. This doesn't mean that you cannot have customers who don't fit this description, but you should have a good sense now of who your *primary* target customer is.

If you can see a number of markets for what you're planning to sell, then list them all and give each a general description. For each one, try and get a sense of what makes that market 'tick' – what it values, where it feeds media-wise, what motivates it, and how it matches to what you are offering.

2. Secondary Market Descriptions/Data. You will probably have more than one target customer (or market segment), and it is important to provide details of each. For instance, as a music publicist you might provide services to individual clients as well as to large record labels. Or, say you're a commercial music producer. Your primary market may be ad agencies and your secondary markets may be corporate video producers, college AV departments, and radio stations. Include as many secondary markets as make sense.

3. Referral markets. These are complementary businesses that can *refer* customers to your business (and that you can refer your customers to when appropriate). For example, a college music teacher you know refers parents of young kids to your local private music instruction service. Or a Drum Circle workshop leader you know refers attendees to your percussion instrument store. Referral markets are endless but are only as valuable as the relationships they're built on. Online marketing strategies like "link exchanges" and "affiliate marketing" arrangements are the digital complements to traditional referral marketing.

4. Competition profiles. In addition to your customers you'll also want to describe your competition. Be as specific as possible. Gather the research of your three or four most pertinent competitors from chapter 5 (pp. 98-100), assess the relative strengths and weaknesses of each, and compare your product or service with similar ones in terms of price, promotion, distribution and customer satisfaction.

Remember, information is readily available if you know where to look. The Web will be your key resource. But you should also visit retail stores if possible and speak with buyers in your particular category of music product or service, study relevant trade magazines, or see who listens to your company's genre of music, check statistics from RIAA and SoundScan, go to public libraries and tap into the skills of a reference librarian; even call the company you want to become or be similar to.

B. Marketing (Branding) Strategy. Now that you've gathered information on your primary, secondary and referral markets, and your competitors, you're now ready to develop your marketing strategy or implementation plan. This too can be broken down into several component parts. Feel free to tap the guidelines provided in chapter 15 where I discuss managing your marketing program, as well.

1. Positioning statement – "Positioning" is related to finding your market "niche", filling the gap you've discerned through studying your market and your competition. It establishes the desired perception of the way you want your target market to perceive, think, and feel about your services compared with the alternatives.

Here are a couple positioning statements drawn from sample business plans at Bplans.com.

The first is from a music instrument shop in Albuquerque, NM:
For our target clientele, including those who feel abandoned by the local retailers, MusicWest will provide a complete one stop shopping experience that will address all the needs of the aspiring musician. By offering repairs and unique marketing programs such as our "You play, we pay" and our "100% of purchase price trade up policy" we can exceed the local client base's expectations of what a music store can be. Unlike the vast majority of our competitors, MusicWest will more selectively stock products with value in mind and not just the lowest price, and we will always strive to provide the highest level of attention to our customers in order to gain their trust and purchasing power.

And, another from a non-profit music-related co-op:
Gamehenge Tapers Co-op is a not-for-profit organization that was created to serve the Portland tapers community. The tapers community is a hobby based community that trades live recordings for personal use, never for commercial gain. The Co-op will provide this community with the equipment needed to further the taping of shows which in effect supports the trading community as well (people who trade these live shows for personal consumption only). The Co-op sells the recording equipment at wholesale prices + a low overhead percentage. By offering the members heavily discounted rates, it encourages them to become more active tapers. Because the organization is a not-for-profit co-op, members are willing to volunteer their time to help the organization allowing it to become successful. The organization exists to support the trading community.

No matter what products or services you provide, you can carve out a niche for them based on your experience, skills, resources and interests and deepen that niche as you work to serve it. Ask yourself questions like: Who needs what I'm offering the most? Where can I provide that product or service that will give me a chance to expand what I do to utilize my other interests? What do I have to offer that is special or unique? The answers to these questions will help you "position" yourself to most effectively promote what you're selling. Ultimately, the place you want to position yourself is in *your customers' minds*. It's a matter of how your market "sees" you in its mind's eye that ultimately matters.

2. Marketing Mix - As we saw in chapter 5, the particular combination of marketing methods you choose for your marketing campaign is referred to as your "marketing mix." Methods can include news releases, sponsorships, social media, personal contact, publicity fliers, contests and giveaways, classified ads, trade shows, radio spots, charitable donations and literally hundreds more.

When making your selection, keep in mind this fundamental rule of successful marketing: The measure of a successful marketing campaign is the extent to which it reaches at the lowest possible cost the greatest number of people who can and will buy your product or service.

Generally speaking, the more of your time a marketing activity requires, the less money it costs you, and vice-versa. For example, networking costs almost nothing in money but lots in time. On the other hand, advertising in a city newspaper costs a bundle while requiring relatively little in time. Let's review **the time/money marketing continuum** chart from chapter 5:

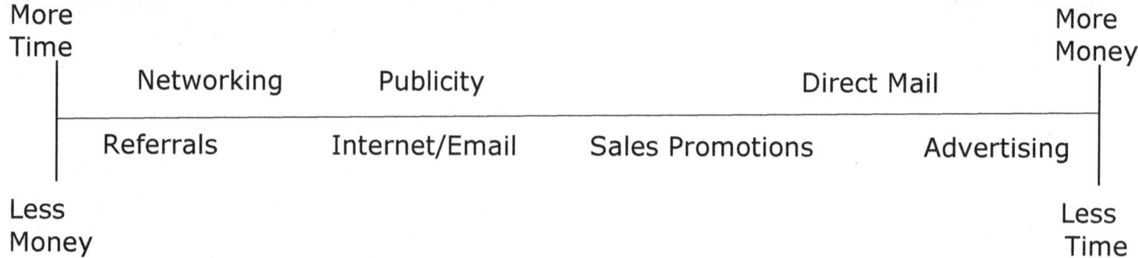

You will ultimately be choosing your methods and tactics from the long list of possibilities in chapter 15 ("Organizing Your Brand Introduction Tactics").

3. Pricing Philosophy - How much you charge for your product or service will depend on many factors. Here is where the research about your competitors comes in especially handy.

Undercutting your competition is one common way to gain market share. But there is another approach. Research has shown that buyers, when making a purchase decision, select what they consider to be the best *value* - all things considered. And this suggests that value is equal to the benefits they perceive divided by the price. *Price, therefore, is only one part of the purchase decision process.* Accurate Records of Cambridge, Massachusetts, for example, has routinely sold its CD releases for $4-5. *above* average retail price. It has been able to do so because of the high-quality, unique music its founder, Russ Gershon, signs and produces.

If you want to increase your customers' perceived value of your product, you can do so by either increasing the benefits or decreasing the price. It is almost always preferable to work on the benefits, both tangible and intangible, both rational and emotional, both large and small, that will make it possible to sell at a higher price.

4. Method(s) of Sales/Distribution - This, of course, is related to your marketing mix and details the methods you will employ in implementing the various parts of your mix. Methods can include direct marketing, retail consignment, working through brokers, sales agents or wholesalers. Also known as "sales channels", these methods need not only distribute goods (for example, a record label might use of a regional distributor as a sales channel). They can also distribute "awareness" of your company and its offerings. For example, say you invented a unique guitar strap and you placed it in a national mail order catalog targeted to musicians. That catalog would be distributing awareness of your company towards making sales.

It's helpful to analyze the distribution channels of your competitors before deciding whether to use the same type of channel or an alternative that may provide you with a strategic advantage.

5. Customer Service Policy – As we saw in chapter 2, one of the clearest market developments of the past 30 years is the increasing power of the consumer to drive production and the marketplace. It's a buyer's market and customers are demanding more and more from businesses. This has forced companies to give increasing attention to developing their customer service standards.

Meeting the needs and expectations of customers requires that you know your customers as individuals. That means consistently collecting their input, removing barriers to communicate with them, and taking steps to foster a long-term relationship with them rather than just a limited, transactional one. In other words, making *customers,* not just *sales*.

See if you can translate elements of this customer dynamic into your own customer service policy. Write down your customer philosophy and then list all applications you can imagine related to your business. Clear, straightforward customer-friendly policies should accompany your vision. For example, think of ways you can build rapport with customers, how you can show appreciation to them, ways you can make a lasting impression. Consider how can you go the extra mile with your clients. Find ways of distinguishing yourself from your competitors in this area and you will ensure a faithful clientele for years to come.

When considering customer service it is always useful to ask yourself why *you* continue to frequent certain businesses. More than price, more than product quality, you will often return again and again to these businesses because you feel taken care of. The people of those businesses go the all important "extra mile" to make you feel special. They anticipate your needs and provide for them in the various ways they deal with you.

IV. Operations

Operations has to do with the overall physical and logistical operations of your company. How are you actually going to run your business? The Operations section of your plan is where you begin to explain the day-to-day functions of your company. As such, this section becomes the preamble to your company's "Operations Manual". This eventual manual should describe the specific details of the processes by which you produce, distribute, maintain and manage your products and services.

Examining your basic operation is particularly important for internal planning. A capable manager does not take any activity in the business process for granted. Each step is worthy of evaluation and improvement. In fact, a little bit of extra planning in the operational area can mean marked improvements in profit margin.

The Operations section of your plan typically has four parts to it: Facilities & Equipment, Organizational dynamics, Expansion Plans, and Risk Assessments.

A. Facilities and Equipment will encompass such things as your location, office space, studio facility, computer technology, instruments, gear, sound and light equipment, and vehicles you use to haul it all around. Chapter 10 ("Equipping Your Work Space/Office") provides much greater detail on these maters and you may want to scan it for ideas to help with the Operations section of your business plan.
In this section of the plan, you'll answer these three questions:

- Where is the business located? How much space is rented/owned/allocated?
- What relevant equipment do you own, and what remains to be purchased?
- What arrangements have been or need to be made with other businesses in order to provide the products and/or services offered by your business?

When evaluating your **facilities**, examine those aspects most important for your particular business. Do you need a prestigious address in a downtown office building? Do you need to be close to key suppliers for your manufacturing processes? Do you need access to transportation resources? When record label distributor Jay Andreozzi looked for a spot to set up shop, he made sure he found one near the Boston's Logan Airport in order to expedite shipments to his international customers.

What aspects of your facilities are most likely to affect your company's success? Are you near your target market? Are you in a convenient location? Does your lease have particularly favorable terms? Will you be able to grow in these facilities without moving? Or, if you're a home-based business, how will that affect the company's bottom line and image? What is your neighborhood like? Are there special amenities nearby? Is there something you wish were close by, but isn't? How does that affect your business? Finally, describe *where* your office will be located within your home.

In this section of the plan, list what **equipment** your business will need and whether you currently own or must purchase that equipment. Also in this section, describe the necessary supplies you'll use in your business. Imagine the complete cycle of meeting your ideal customer, convincing her to hire you, performing work for her, and being paid. What supplies do you need at each step? What about software? Beyond word processing and spreadsheets, you will probably need software to store and manage client information, invoices and orders. What about music production software like ProTools, Logic or Ableton Live, and hardware like outboard gear and computers?

A brief note on equipment **insurance** should also be included here, if relevant. Investors and lenders also appreciate seeing the founders of a company have a cash investment in the business, in addition to "sweat equity," so a mention of what you yourself will be bringing to the business in terms of hardware, software and other assets would be appropriate to mention.

We will cover office setup and equipment in chapter 10. For now, just identify and generally describe the location of your business and the essential equipment you will need to launch it. Draw from the Startup Budget you created earlier in this chapter for the equipment inventory.

B. Organizational Dynamics. How is the company set up to ensure smooth, efficient (that is, 'non-money/time/energy-wasting') operations? Every manufacturing business has a production process – the way it goes about fabricating a raw or component material and creating an item with greater usefulness or desirability. But even if yours is a service or retail business, you have a method of "producing" something of value for your customers, whether it's music lessons, media visibility, better-sounding recording studios or successful music performances.

Take time to evaluate and assess your production plan to see if you can enhance efficiencies, improve the quality of the finished product/service, and, in the long run, increase your profit margin. Look at the various stages involved in creating your product or service: Can these stages be shortened? If so, you will be able to produce more and sell more in less time.

Examine also how you plan to organize and orchestrate your work force. What role does each worker have in this process? Do you use a team approach – with one group of workers responsible for a job from start to finish? Or, do you use a production-line approach, with a worker doing the same portion of each job and then passing it along to someone else?

Increasingly, companies are using *variable labor* in addition to permanent employees, as an integral part of their workforce. Variable labor – employees hired to perform a specific task for a specified period of time – is particularly useful for seasonal work or unusually large or special orders. Temp workers are a form of variable labor, as are interns and sub-contractors. More on these in chapter 11.

Sometimes it helps to draw an organizational chart that graphically represents work flow and structure, like the staff chart on the following page for a mid-size indie record label

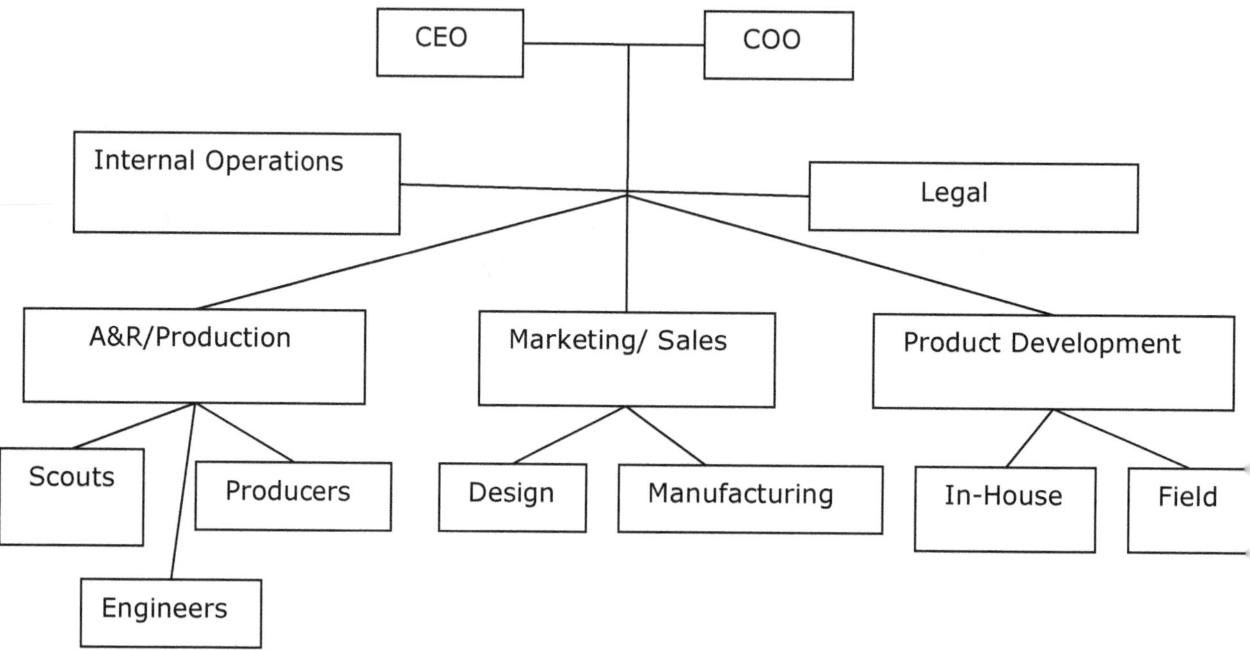

C. Plans for Growth or Expansion. Here is where you project some of your general goals into the future. *Where do you want to go? What do you want your business to look like in three, five or seven years?* What will you need when you progress from local to regional success? Regional to national? National to international?

In founder-led and small companies, the personal goals of the entrepreneur and the goals of the business should reasonably relate to one another. Otherwise, the inherent tensions will undermine the success of the business.

Perhaps you'll want to develop other divisions within your primary company. Maybe a publishing wing, or a video division, or perhaps branch out into an entirely new market. Maybe you aspire to be a niche leader, carving out a narrow place in the market that your company can dominate; or perhaps your goal is to be an innovator in your business category.

Whatever the goal, in the course of your planning process you will find it useful to establish *markers* – milestones – to keep you on track. By developing specific objectives, you have signposts to measure progress along the way. Think it through as clearly and completely as possible, and leave some flexibility built in for creative surprises.

A variety of possible expansion strategies are explored in greater detail in Chapter 16, "Enriching & Enlarging the Score".

D. Threats & Risks - Not only does risk assessment show you're being open and honest with your financing source, but it forces you to consider and assess alternative strategies in the event your original assumptions do not materialize.

List possible *external* events that might occur to hamper your success: a recession, new competition, shifts in customer demand, unfavorable industry trends, problems with suppliers, or changes in legislation. Also, identify potential *internal* challenges such as income projections not realized, long-term, illness or serious injury. Then generate a contingency plan to counteract the most significant risks. Think them through.

V. Project Time Line

Here you want to lay out the schedule for your business goals, both short-range (e.g., producing a CD, licensing a track, setting up an internship program, launching a new business division, procuring distribution, etc.) and long-range (e.g., signing a joint-venture deal, licensing your catalog to an Asian record company, expanding into a new city, etc.). This is also a good place to schedule the unfolding of your marketing plan. Think through the essential steps needed for the attainment of each goal and then estimate how much time each will take.

Your project timeline can also list your future milestones. A milestone list allows you to see what you specifically plan to accomplish, and it sets out clearly delineated objectives. For example: Initial Financing Secured, Product Design Completed, Trademark Secured, First Products Shipped, etc. Break it down month-by-month with 3-5 significant activities.

VI. Financial Information

People in business usually fall into one of two categories: those who are fascinated by numbers, or those who are frightened by them. If you're in the first category, you're probably delighted to have finally gotten to this section. If you are one of those in the second category, however, you're probably intimidated by the very prospect of having to touch financial matters.

Take heart: Numbers are neither magical, mysterious, nor menacing. They merely reflect other decisions you have made previously in your business planning. Every business decision leads to a number, and taken together, these numbers form the basis of your financial forms.

After defining your product or service, market, and operations, you need to address the real backbone of the business plan – the financial information. No matter how wonderful your plan is it isn't going anywhere without capital investment, whether it's yours or someone else's. Most business plans will have four separate financial forms or spreadsheets: *Startup Expenses, Income Statement (*shows whether your company is making a profit), *Cash-Flow Projection* (shows whether the company has the cash to pay its bills), and *Balance Sheet* (shows how much the company is worth overall). In this chapter, you'll create only the first two and your Income Statement will cover three years. The additional forms are very helpful in an already functioning business, but in this book we are concerned with an entrepreneurial start up, and so the financial information is simpler and also more concrete.

However, next to your competitive differentiation, this is the part of the plan potential investors and lenders will concentrate on the most. So if you will be using your plan to secure a loan or to attract investors, you'll need to approach the financials in more depth. This is where a SCORE or SBDC advisor can prove indispensable.

The task of *raising money* is taken up in greater detail in Chapter 8.

Financial *management* issues and strategies are addressed in depth in Chapter 14.

Some guidelines for preparing your financial forms (or, how *not* to act like the Wall St. 'giants'):

- Be conservative: avoid the rosy picture
- Be honest: expect to be asked to justify your numbers
- Don't be creative: use standard formats and financial terms
- Be consistent

A. Start up costs. You have already worked out your startup expenses earlier in this chapter, so draw on that information. Of course, for both sections you want to create spreadsheets to hold and display the financial data.

B. Three-Year Income Projection. Financial projections provide your team with an idea of where you plan to take the business. Perhaps more importantly, they tell a lot about your intrinsic good sense and understanding of the difficulties your company faces.
It "normally" takes a well-run business with a marketable product or service about 3 years to turn a profit. So, to start with, think through all the possible expenses you'll have over a 36-month period. These are "the costs of doing business".

They will include:

- All *start-up* costs (e.g., licenses, trademark, office equipment, etc.)
- All *operating* costs (e.g., rent, utilities, insurance, marketing, etc.)
- All *production* costs (e.g., studio time, engineers, manufacturing, etc.)

No need to break each year down into monthly projections, just three annual columns with side itemizations of projected revenues and costs. The first column will also contain your startup costs for the first year.

Whatever you decide you need financially, make sure it's based on a hardheaded assessment of the true costs of achieving your goals. A basic rule of thumb in estimating costs is to always add 15% onto whatever figure you come up with. This covers all those "hidden" and unexpected costs that inevitably arise.

Often, financial projections are optimistic to an outlandish extent. They are usually prefaced with words like, "Our conservative forecast is..." Do not use the word "conservative" when describing your forecast. Be careful also not to use the "hockey stick" approach to forecasting, that is, little growth in sales and earnings for the first couple of years followed by a sudden rapid upward surge in sales and totally unrealistic profit margins. Excessively optimistic projections ruin your credibility as a responsible businessperson.

In making financial projections it is a good idea to include "best guess," "high side," and "low side" numbers. An important fact to remember when preparing your income projections is that you will often not receive full payment at the time of an actual sale or transaction. While most customers will pay within 30 days, some may take as much as 120 days, and some will never pay at all. Projecting cash flow solely on the sales made, rather than cash actually received, will leave you seriously short on money.

The spreadsheet on the following page, illustrates the financial cash flow and three-year projections of the fictional, regionally successful jam band, Ping

Three Year Cash Flow

	Year 1 (2016)	Year 2 (2017)	Year 3 (2018)
Revenues			
Record Sales	40,000	90,900	204,525
Merchandising	47,000	100,000	225,000
Personal Appearances	42,000	85,000	191,250
Sponsorship	0	15,000	35,000
Licensing (Music Publishing)	2,700	5,400	12,150
Recording Studio	12,000	18,000	40,500
Total Revenues	**143,700**	**314,300**	**708,425**
Cost Of Sales			
Record Sales (Manufacturing)	8,800	19,998	44,995
Merchandising (Purchasing Inventory)	10,340	22,000	49,500
Personal Appearances	9,240	18,700	42,075
Sponsorship	0	0	0
Licensing (Music Publishing)	594	1,188	2,673
Recording Studio	2,640	3,960	8,910
Total Cost of Goods Sold	**31,614**	**65,846**	**148,153**
Gross Profit			
Operating Expenses			
Record Production	5,500	8,000	9,000
Post Production	700	1,200	1,500
Digital Distribution Costs	60	20	20
Overhead	27,130	28,487	29,911
Total Operating Expenses	**33,390**	**37,707**	**40,431**
Selling General & Administrative Expenses (Touring & Promotional Costs)	**41,950**	**51,268**	**62,556**
Net Income	**36,746**	**159,479**	**457,556**

Staying Flexible

Don't worry if you feel a bit overwhelmed by the avalanche of detail your business plan requires. Who wouldn't? Give yourself time. It's helpful to set yourself a goal for completing the first draft of your plan - say three months from now.
Begin with one section at a time and meet periodically with your small business advisor to review your plan's development. He or she will be able to discern blind spots as well as affirm the plan's overall direction. When performing songwriter Gilli Moon began working on her business plan it went from one version to another over a long period of time. "In fact," she says, "I'd sit with my mentor once a month and revise it, for about four years. Now I do it once a year".

Remember too that your business plan is just a provisional guide that will evolve over time. It is never really "finished". Patrick Faucher of Bose Corp., states unequivocally, "One thing is for sure, whatever plan you write, it is imperfect and will always change over time". This provides no reason, however, to not write your plan, says Faucher. "It's a valuable tool to help you focus effort and measure against what you set out to do. I can't imagine starting a business without one because it causes you to define what success is for the project".

If you're thinking of foregoing the effort altogether and just "winging" it, remember that no planning inevitably leads to wasted time, money and energy - all three in short supply for startup businesses! Remember too that your plan is *primarily for you.* It's an opportunity to direct your passions and energy. This is also how Panos Panay, founder of Sonicbids, sees it: "I don't think that you should write a plan necessarily for raising money; you should write it as a road map for you." A map is a good metaphor and your plan should be designed to get you to your destination (business goal) in the most effective and efficient way possible.

The rest of this book details the best entrepreneurial tools and tactics to help you do this. Getting out of the planning stage and into the getting-it-done stage is what makes you an entrepreneur instead of a person with a cool idea who is sort of thinking about maybe pursuing it one day.

SAMPLE GENERAL PARTNERSHIP AGREEMENT at the end of this chapter to give you a sense of the issues requiring your attention in this type of business arrangement.

AGREEMENT by and between the Undersigned ("Partners").

1. Name. The name of the partnership is:

2. Partners. The names of the initial partners are:

3. Place of Business. The principal place of business of the partnership is:

4. Nature of Business. The partnership shall generally engage in the following business:

5. Duration. The partnership shall commence business on ________________ and shall continue until terminated by this agreement, or by operation of law.

6. Contribution of Capital. The partners shall contribute capital in proportionate shares as follows:

7. Allocation of Depreciation or Gain or Loss on Contributed Property. The partners understand that, for income tax purposes, the partnership's adjusted basis of some of the contributed property differs from fair market value at which the property was accepted by the partnership. However the partners intend that the general allocation rule of the Internal Revenue Code shall apply, and that the depreciation or gain or loss arising with respect to this property shall be allocated proportionately between the partners, as allocated in Paragraph 6 above, in determining the taxable income or loss of the partnership and the distributive share of each partner, in the same manner as if such property had been purchased by the partnership at a cost equal to the adjusted tax basis.

8. Capital Accounts. An individual capital account shall be maintained for each partner. The capital of each partner shall consist of that partner's original contribution of capital, as described in Paragraph 6, and increased by additional capital contributions and decreased by distributions in reduction of partnership capital and reduced by his/her share of partnership losses, if these losses are charged to the capital accounts.

9. Drawing Accounts. An individual drawing account shall be maintained for each partner. All withdrawals by a partner shall be charged to his/her drawing account. Withdrawals shall be limited to amounts unanimously agreed to by the partners.

10. Salaries. No partner shall receive any salary for services rendered to the partnership except as specifically and first approved by each of the partners.

11. Loan by Partners. If a majority of partners consent, any partner may lend money to the partnership at an interest and terms rate agreed in writing, at the time said loan is made.

12. Profits and Losses. Net profits of the partnership shall be divided proportionately between the partners, and the net losses shall be borne proportionately as follows:
Partner ________________________________ Proportion________

13. Management. The partners shall have equal rights and control in the management of the partnership.

14. Books of Accounts. The partnership shall maintain adequate accounting records. All books, records, and accounts of the partnership shall be open at all times to inspection by all partners, or their designated representatives.

15. Accounting Basis. The books of account shall be kept on a cash basis.

16. Fiscal Year. The books of account shall be kept on a fiscal year basis, commencing January 1 and ending December 31, and shall be closed and balanced at the end of each year.

17. Annual Audit. The books of account shall be audited as of the close of each fiscal year by an accountant chosen by the partners.

18. Banking. All funds of the partnership shall be deposited in the name of the partnership into such checking or savings accounts as designated by the partners.

19. Death or Incapacity. The death or incapacity of a partner shall cause an immediate dissolution of the partnership.

20. Election of Remaining Partner to Continue Business. In the event of the retirement, death, incapacity, or insanity of a partner, the remaining partners shall have the right to continue the business of the partnership, either by themselves or in conjunction with any other person or persons they may select, but they shall pay to the retiring partner, or to the legal representatives of the deceased or incapacitated partner, the value of his or her interest in the partnership.

21. Valuation of Partner's Interest. The value of the interest of a retiring, incapacitated, deceased, or insane partner shall be the sum of (a) the partner's capital account, (b) any unpaid loans due the partner, and (c) the partner's proportionate share of the accrued net profits remaining undistributed in his drawing account. No value for goodwill shall be included in determining the value of a partner's interest, unless specifically agreed in advance by the partners.

22. Payment of Purchase Price. The value of the partner's interest shall be paid without interest to the retiring partner, or to the legal representative of the deceased, incapacitated or insane partner, in monthly installments, commencing on the first day of the second month after the effective date of the purchase.

23. Termination. In the event that the remaining partner does not elect to purchase the interest of the retiring, deceased, incapacitated, or insane partner, or in the event the partners mutually agree to dissolve, the partnership shall terminate, and the partners shall proceed with reasonable promptness to liquidate the business of the partnership. The assets of the partnership shall first be used to pay or provide for all debts of the partnership. Thereafter, all money remaining undistributed in the drawing accounts shall be paid to the partners. Then the remaining assets shall be divided proportionately as follows:

Partner ______________________________________ - Percentage ________________________

24. This agreement shall be binding upon and inure to the benefit of the parties, their successors, assigns and personal representatives.

Signed under seal this day of ____________________.

_________________________________ Partner _____________________________ Partner

CHAPTER SUMMARY

PLAN TO SUCCEED: MAPPING OUT YOUR OPPORTUNITY PLAN

- **The Challenge of Planning Your Vision & Mission**
  Strategic planning is something we'd prefer to avoid. We resist business planning for any number of reasons: "My business is simple, and plans seem too complex", "I don't know how to write a business plan." There's no single "right way" to write a business plan. This chapter will walk you through the process.

- **The Power of Writing a Business Plan**
  The purpose of the business plan is to form a picture – to yourself, potential investors and company employees – of what the company is about and why this particular company is going to be a stand out enterprise within its market. A plan let's you mentally rehearse and process different scenarios your business may face.

- **A Good Planning Framework**
  Some fundamentals to help get you in the right mental framework for writing your plan: Scope out the Environment, Do an Organizational Analysis, Create a Mission Statement, Set Goals & Objectives, Gather Strategic Resources, Map out an Implementation Strategy, and Communicate it all in Writing.

- **Phase 1: Summarizing Your Business Concept**
  The summary of your business concept will eventually become the "Executive Summary" of your business plan. You'll want to define the business you're starting, the type of products/services it will offer, how your business concept is unique, and how it will generate revenue.

- **Phase 2: Choosing a Name for Your Company**
  Five guidelines to help you name your company for the long term: make the name meaningful, make sure the name is easy to pronounce and remember, make sure it's available, choose a name that you can live and grow with, make it unique, and link it to a domain name.

- **Phase 3: Identifying Start-Up Expenses**
  You'll need a basic estimate of what your start-up costs will be going forward for at least the first year of business. You will use this estimate later in your business plan when you come to the "Financial Information" section ("Startup Costs"). It's also advisable to sort your start up expenses into one of four categories. This will help immensely when tax time arrives each year. The categories are: Startup deductible expenses, Ongoing deductible expenses, Startup not deductible and Ongoing not deductible.

- **Phase 4: Deciding on the Legal Form of Your Business**
  There are three main legal structures: sole proprietorship, partnership, or corporation, the latter of which can itself take several forms. A sole proprietorship is a business that is owned by one person and that isn't registered with the state as a corporation or a limited liability company. A partnership is a formal partnering of you with at least one other person. Forming a partnership generally requires an attorney. A corporation is a legal entity separate from the shareholders and employees. It is formed after an individual or group applies to the state for a charter.

- **Phase 5: Solidifying Your Business Concept**
  This phase helps you develop your "elevator pitch" – your opportunity to succinctly communicate the core elements of your business idea. The clearer you are about your business idea, the stronger the foundations you'll establish, and the stronger your plan will be.

- **Phase 6: Writing Your Plan!: A Step-By-Step Guide**
  An example of basic business plan outline:
  I. Summary statement

II. Foundations of your business
  A. History and background of you and your business idea
  B. Management description and experience
  C. Business legal structure
III. The market for your product or service
  A. Market description
    1. Primary market description & data
    2. Secondary market description & data
    3. Referral markets
    4. Competition profiles
  B. Marketing (Branding) strategy
    1. Positioning statement
    2. Marketing mix
    3. Pricing philosophy
    4. Method of sales/distribution
    5. Customer service policies
IV. Operations
  A. Facilities and equipment
  B. Organizational dynamics
  C. Plans for growth and expansion
  D. Threats & Risks
V. Project timeline
VI. Financial information
  A. Start up costs
  B. Three-year financial projections

- **Staying Flexible**

Begin with one section at a time and meet periodically with a small business advisor to review your plan's development. Your business plan is just a provisional guide that will evolve over time. It is never really "finished". If you're thinking of foregoing the effort altogether and just "winging" it, remember that no planning inevitably leads to wasted time, money and energy - all three in short supply for startup businesses!

FURTHER RESOURCES

ONLINE RESOURCES

- Business Planning Resources

Business Plan Center
businessplans.org
Sample business plans and planning
Guidelines for business owners
(800) 423-1228

More Business
morebusiness.com
Sample business forms, agreements and marketing plans, as well as informative articles and links

Web Site 101
website101.com/
Free online tutorials, surveys and articles related to business planning.

- Software

Business PlanPro (Palo Alto Software)
bplans.com

Business Plan Software (freeware)
planware.org

SCORE Template Gallery
www.score.org/template_gallery.html

- Business Legal Structures

I recommend the books put out by Nolo Press (nolo.com). They have volumes on forming corporations, LLCs, partnerships and nonprofits, as well as numerous free online resources to help you get started with any of these business structures.

- Non Profits

Artspace

artspace.org
Organization helping people start arts-related non-profits.

Idealist.org
This site offers has a lot of tools and information, simply presented. Check out The Nonprofit FAQ—" based on questions and answers about nonprofit organizations exchanged on the Internet since 1994" -it's very extensive.

Free Management Liberty
www.managementhelp.org
This "Complete, highly integrated library for nonprofits and for-profits" is another general site with special focus on new nonprofits. It has a list of 675 books and articles indexed by 675 topics and continuously updated. There's also a Free Complete Toolkit for Boards—www.managementhelp.org/boards/boards.htm—that contains a wealth of information for board members and those who would evaluate board members and Human Resource Management Information for Nonprofit Organizations—www.managementhelp.org/hr_mgmnt/np_spcf.htm—that does the same for staff.

National Council of Nonprofits
councilofnonprofits.org/
This Web site offers guides to assessment tools, strategy, financial reporting, budget and cash flow, starting a nonprofit, accounting rules and regulations, human resources, organizational policies, audits, and book-keeping systems and accounting software. If you need help with finances this is a good place to start.

Financial Management in Nonprofits
managementhelp.org/nonprofitfinances/
Free Management Library-All About

Council of Nonprofits: Financial Management
councilofnonprofits.org/tools-resources/financial-management
This Web page shows another aspect of the Council of Nonprofits: it maintains a materials covering all facets of nonprofit financial management.

Energize, Inc.
energizeinc.com
This is a fine Web site aimed at managing volunteers, a vital topic for all nonprofits but especially small or new organizations. See its library and referral networks.

- Sample Marketing Plans Online

mplans.com/spm/

articles.bplans.com/outline-for-a-marketing-plan/

- Financial Planning

Financial Statement Templates
http://forms.entrepreneur.com
For each statement you want to use, click on the link, save the spreadsheet onto your hard drive, and then work on it.

BOOKS

A Marketing Plan for Life : 12 Essential Business Principles to Create Meaning, Happiness, and True Success by Michael Fried (2005, Perigee Trade Paperback).

Business Model Generation: A Handbook for Visionaries, Game Changers, and Challengers by Alexander Osterwalder (2010, John Wiley & Sons).

The Marketing Plan Workbook (The Sunday Times Business Enterprise Guide Series*)* by John Westwood (2004, Kogan).

Powerhouse Marketing Plans: 14 Outstanding Real-Life Plans and What You Can Learn from Them to Supercharge Your Own Campaigns by Winslow Johnson (2004, AMACOM).

Successful Business Plan: Secrets & Strategies by Rhonda Adams (2014, Planning Shop).

7

PUTTING THE WEB & ECOMMERCE TO WORK FOR YOUR BUSINESS

The Internet is the world's largest library. It's just that all the books are on the floor.
–John Allen Paulos

I have an almost religious zeal - not for technology per se, but for the Internet which is for me, the nervous system of mother Earth, which I see as a living creature, linking up.
–Dan Millman

With the Internet, the information explosion of the past few decades has finally found a technological partner. Entertainment conglomerates and arts-grant bureaucrats still hold the strings to attractively fat purses. But their power is being tempered by the reach of the Internet and the resourcefulness of creative minds paired with cheap, versatile tools. The Internet is a technology and though technology seems to be about machines, it's really about *people*. Technology allows you to maintain control of your relationships, saves time for you and your customers, and increases your ability to please your customers.

Publishing in all its forms has been revolutionized by the Net. It's often been said that "freedom of the press belongs to those who own one." The Net enables *everyone* to own the press. Rather than competing with other media outlets for the public's attention, the media is suddenly competing with the *public itself.* Individuals can decide *on their own* what's important and what's not, set up their own information "filters" (rather than rely on the editorial judgment of faceless media conglomerates), and get closer to sources of information than ever before.

But that was merely Web *1.0* – the Internet's first generation.

Today we are all an integral part of the Web *2.0* business economy because every time you click on Google, Wikipedia, eBay, or Amazon, you are sparking "network effects." Web *2.0* turbocharges networks because online users are no longer limited by how many things they can find, see, or download off the Web, but rather by how many things they can *do, interact with, combine, remix, upload, change,* and *customize* for themselves. More on this in a minute.

This seismic shift isn't just limited to how works are created. Already, digital technology has caused sweeping changes in how people gain access to creative works. Independent musicians have long turned to the Internet in their struggle for recognition outside traditional industry channels such as radio and MTV. Now, in the wake of the dot-com bust, many are discovering that savvy online marketing may never catapult them to stardom – but it *can* give their careers an important lift. I recently read a story of how Death Cab for Cutie's Ben Gibbard discovered an artist named Devin Davis on a site called *Music for Robots* (http://www.music-for-robots.com). He liked Davis's music and began an email correspondence, which eventually led to Gibbard inviting Davis to open a show for his band. An unlikely discovery. You never know who is watching or who is listening on the Net.

Smart music entrepreneurs are diving head long into opportunity-rich world of Internet commerce. "We use all social networking tools – MySpace, Facebook, Twitter, and Imeem to improve our internet marketing,' says Jay Andreozzi of new media outfit Amalgam Digital. "We also used our blog as well as establishing relationships with hip-hop related blogs to promote our projects. We use Google Analytics to look at traffic, website referrals, where our traffic is coming from, and keywords used to arrive at our site."

Web 2.0, 3.0, 4.0...: Tapping Into The Social Media Revolution

What is Web 2.0, anyway? Essentially, it encompasses the set of tools that allow people to build social and business connections, share information and collaborate on projects online. That includes blogs, wikis, social-networking sites and other online communities, and virtual worlds. The phrase was coined by Tim O'Reilly who organized the first Web 2.0 conference in 2005. Web 2.0 meant a number of things, but mainly highlighted an online progression from *reading to participating*, from *thinking to acting*, from *individual to community*, from *contemplating to interacting*.

While "Web 2.0" is a nice catch-all phrase for the natural progression of the Internet, it's important to point out the limitations. Even the smartest players on the web, such as Google, are struggling to monetize Web 2.0 applications, despite nearly unlimited funds provided by their Web 1.0 business – text search and text ads. There is still a lot of room here for pioneers to figure this stuff out.

Web 1.0 (1995-2004)	Web 2.0 (2004-present)
Personal websites	Blogging
Doubleclick	Google AdSense
Ofoto	Flickr
Britannica Online	Wikipedia
Directories ("taxonomy")	Tagging ("folksonomy")

Source: O'Reilly Media

In other words, don't think of social media or Web 2.0 as a revenue-generating channel, but as another *customer touch point*. This underlines an important truth about the Internet in general that bears repeating. The Net should be viewed as a *complement* to your business, but it will not provide your business with a crutch if your real-world venture isn't taking care of the basics – good organization and management, strong communications, and award-winning customer service. But as a *companion* to your main business – as a marketing tool and outreach to customers – it is unsurpassed.

Another limit – be ready for the incoming! Beware of the "hundreds of posts on one subject effect." Maintaining a "conversation" with customers and potential customers can be time consuming. Would you be able to set aside 3-4 hours or so every week? Or, how about an hour per day? The Net is your Open Mic *to the world* and customers will find you from far and wide. You should be ready.

Web 2.0 Business Models – A quick survey

Type of Service	Values to users and content generators	Business model
Virtual world, virtual goods	Emotional values (be who you want to be, be present, be cool/romantic, meet other people, etc.)	Virtual goods fee, advertising
Online (office, video/picture adding, project management, communication, etc) tools	Replacement of desktop tools, collaboration, productivity	Subscription for premium service, funding from complementing services
Market/broker platforms	Mediation, effective tools, lower costs/risks	Service fee, advertising
Social media sites	Easy ways to publish, find and subscribe to sources, revenue sharing for content generators	Advertising
Social networking sites	Emotional values (share things with friends, make new friends, keep contact with friends, etc.)	Advertising, service brokerage fee
Blog, podcast engines, wiki	Emotional values (let people know what I know/like/do, be known to the world, popularity, etc.), sharing the knowledge	Subscription for premium service, advertising, funding them complementing services
Mapping tools	Find location, driving direction, local stores, etc.	Local advertising, funding from complementing services
Mashups	Find related information, access to large audience	Funding from related services, service fee, commission, advertising
Widgets, Web portals, feed engines	Easy-to-use tools to publish and track consumption, to select information to consume; access to large audience	Funding from related services (media, related services, etc.)
News engines	Easy way to select and get trusted news	Advertising, funding from media companies and other companies benefit from PR
Social bookmarking, dipping	Easy way to select and let others know what you find interesting	Advertising

Managing Your Social Media

The popularity of social networking sites is a phenomenon worth noting. According to *Social Media Today*, at the end of 2015 there were nearly 1.4 billion Facebook users, 285 million Twitter users and 300 million Instagram users. With numbers like that, you simply can't afford to ignore social networking as a promotional tool if you want to attract business.

The following chart illustrates how your web site will serve as the hub around which all your social media revolves, and what the primary purpose is of each.

Basic Social Media Strategy Outline
Showing The Primary Movement Of Customers And The Purpose Of Each Tool

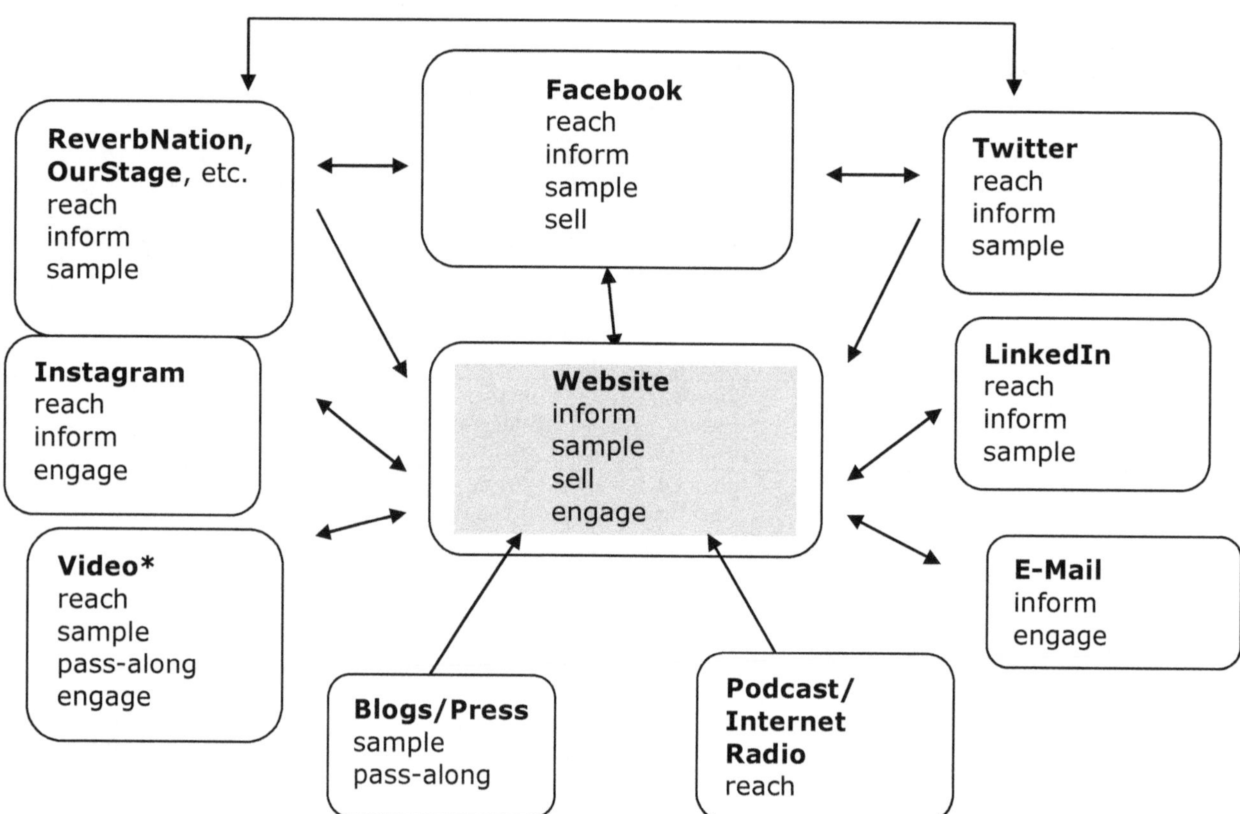

Social networking sites – like Facebook, Twitter, Xanga, LinkedIn and others – make it easy for people to create a profile about themselves and use it to create a virtual network of their offline friends and to make new friends online.

The "social web," by definition, has two meanings: (1) it is an online *place* that people visit to meet, discuss, hash out, vent, and share their thoughts, comments and opinions. The second definition is, (2) a present *network* that is an open global distributed data sharing network similar to the Web, except instead of linking documents, the Social Web will link people, organizations, and concepts.

Social networking sites are becoming increasingly more popular. If you want to stay atop of the latest trends, then you would benefit from setting up a business profile on Facebook, whether you are a solo artist or a mega entrepreneur. Change happens quickly in this space, so you need to take an experimental stance towards social media. "I use social media experiments and technology in a rotating series of tests to grow the reach of my artist," says artist manager Ralph Jaccodine. A wise approach.

The six goals of a social media strategy for a band or artist are to reach more people, to keep their fans informed, to allow people to sample their music, to sell their music and merchandise, to have content that people pass along to friends and to engage their fans to encourage continued interest. Each goal can be reached with the following popular tools. Of course, there are dozens of others that are not included here as well.

❑ ***Reach:*** Twitter, video, blogs/press, Facebook, Instagram, Reverbnation, Ourstage, LinkedIn, podcast/internet radio.

❑ ***Inform:*** Facebook, Twitter, Reverbnation, Ourstage, LinkedIn, website, e-mail.

❑ ***Sample:*** Facebook, Reverbnation, Ourstage, website, video, blogs/press, podcast/internet radio.

❑ ***Sell:*** Facebook, website (w/Paypal button or integrated online store).

❑ ***Pass-along:*** video, blogs/press, social bookmarking (tagging).

❑ ***Engage:*** video, Twitter, LinkedIn (groups), website/artist blog, e-mail.

ONLINE STORE OPTIONS

1. **Paypal -** Basically, if you have an account with PayPal you can download HTML code from PayPal that allows you to put a payment button on your website pages. You can edit prices, and if you have multiple products/services, just add extra buttons. When customers click on the button, they will be sent to PayPal's site to checkout and pay. Free to set up + 2.9% and $.30 fixed fee per transaction ($30/month for *PayPal Pro*).

2. **Word Press** - If you are tech-savvy and want to build a highly-customized online store for your business, WordPress gives you the most options. You can edit almost any aspect of your business website and online store. Also, using WordPress's plug-ins, you can add almost any functionality to your site via third-party sources.

3. **Shopify -** Create wholesale, phone, or custom orders right in Shopify. Send invoices directly to your customers and accept payments without any fuss. Accept credit cards anywhere. There are many others. Just Google "online stores".

Social networking is not the only way to make it as an artist. In my opinion social media is simply a fan management extension. Social networking's purpose is about building a bridge between you and your fans who, in turn, will use word of mouth to promote you. Therefore, it's better to look for your fans and build up your online social presence. The main objective is to get your fans to your website and take them on a journey into your story. That way they can discover you, share, interact and, eventually, support and buy.

Tracking Your Social Media Presence

One can easily begin to feel out of control when it comes to social media. In fact, due to the explosion of social media *reputation management* has now become a crucial component in one's career management. We all know that one of the first things hiring managers check when someone applies for a job is their social media presence. If you ever posted a less-than-admirable photo of yourself, or if you released an unfiltered stream of consciousness rant on some topic, or even a "prank" video, it might later come back to bite you. We are all leaving digital footprints.

The best way to fight this is, of course, to never post anything unsavory. But if there is personal stuff online you don't like, you can suppress unwanted content by flooding the Web with good, positive content. This content might include a solid, professional LinkedIn profile, a blog, a personal website, and more. The important thing is to keep this content clean and professional, without anything that might raise a potential employer's eyebrow. That's a career tip you can take to the bank.

Tracking all the conversations, band mentions, fan questions, comments and feedback can become almost impossible for one person (even one band!). Thankfully some services have emerged to help with the online bustle. Here are a few savvy artists are using to monitor their mentions in social media:

❑ ***Google Alerts:*** Set up multiple Google Alerts for your company, band, name, products, leaders, industry terms, etc. The alerts will get delivered directly to your email inbox at the frequency you indicate (e.g. daily or as they happen) and is a great way to help you track mentions of your brand and relevant keywords on the web on news sites, in blogs, etc.

❑ ***Twitter:*** Monitor mentions of your brand on Twitter with tools like Twitter Search or HootSuite. CoTweet is also a great tool to help manage multiple tweets.

❑ **Artist Data** - Artist Data (which was acquired by Sonic Bids) actually allows you to update everything from your profile info and status to things like music and events on all of your existing social networks like Facebook, Last.fm, Reverbnation and a whole list of others.

❑ **Ping.fm** - Similarly to Artist Data, Ping.fm allows you to update information on many different social networks (http://ping.fm/networks/). The difference here is that Ping.fm is for general use, and not specifically for artists, so while it has a much larger reach to more social networks and blogging platforms, it has less capability to meet the specific needs of an artist.

❑ ***Google Reader and RSS Feeds:*** Set up RSS feeds in Google Reader of searches of your brand or industry keywords in other popular social media sites such as Flickr, Digg, Delicious, etc. Scan the results in your reader daily for mentions.

❑ ***Facebook Insights:*** Helps you stay on top of and participate in discussions occurring on your company's Facebook Fan Page. Use your Fan Page's "Facebook Insights Dashboard" (found in the left sidebar when you're on your page as an administrator) to show you stats such as fan growth and page views to gauge your page's interaction and engagement.

Notes to the Social Media Optimist

Social Media isn't the only way to market your band or brand, though you have to wonder in light of all the press it gets. This is the number one mistake because it can absolutely cripple a band from ever finding success. Some artists are sitting out the Twitter revolution completely (i.e., Mumford & Sons) and others are finding it a distraction no longer worth the time ("[Twitter] started to make my mind smaller and smaller and smaller. And I couldn't write a song," lamented John Mayer).

Far too many artists forget that social media is a device to be used within a strong, well-rounded marketing campaign. If you, as an artist, expect to just sit in front of your computer, friend thousands of people and wait by the phone for the call from a talent scout, you will be severely disappointed when that call never comes.

Too, social networking is causing artists to draw lines between what is public and what is private very clear. They have to be careful not to overuse any one social media platform and censor the type of information they share: Promoting a contest or showcasing new merchandise for the tour? Awesome. The lead singer's girlfriend when they're on a date? Not so much.

I'll focus on Facebook because of its ease of use, but the following guidelines are applicable to other social networking sites as well. It takes about a half hour to set up your basic Facebook account and website, and here are some tips for getting the most out of it:

- First, **switch your personal profile to a Facebook Page.** A Facebook Page is a better option for promoting your music. For one, using a Facebook Page allows you to keep your personal details private. Facebook Pages also have key features that will help you market your music. Note: You need to have a profile before you can create a Page.

• **Use location targeting to promote** shows, tours, album release parties and other events. Use it to determine where you'll have more success in terms of touring, physical CD distribution, street-team investment, and media coverage. Playing in Denver in two weeks? Develop a Facebook ad for the upcoming performance and target it to Facebook users who fall into your demographics and who live in Denver.

• **By collecting additional contact information** from your fans through a sign-up form, you can augment your Facebook campaigns with mass emails and mobile promotions. But, be sure to show your followers a side of yourself that enhances their connection to your music, and not solely based on promoting it.

• **Target ads based on interests**. If you've been told you sound like Radiohead meets Bob Marley, target your ads to fans of Radiohead and Bob Marley, and be sure to communicate your similarities to those brands. Also, if a noteworthy music critic is the one who said this, be sure to include his/her quote.

• Many top musicians, including Coldplay and Shakira, **create separate Facebook events for each of their concerts** to drum up awareness and gain exposure for their Pages. This may seem like overkill for an indie artist, but there may be a high-profile show that merits it. With just a little foresight and coordination, you can easily invite everyone your band knows on Facebook. Just be careful to delegate one band member to post the event so fans don't receive multiple invites.

• **Live chats allow you to webcast video** of yourself responding to questions which fans pose through a text-based chat room interface. These provide vivid, intimate virtual face-to-face interaction with fans that is cheap in terms of dollars and an artist's time.

Getting Buzz on Social Networks

No matter which of the social networks you use, there are broad principles you can apply to each to attract attention and maximize your effectiveness.

• Complete your profile completely wherever appropriate. List all your products, services, qualifications, specialties, partners, and so on. Many people will find you by conducting a keyword search on the social network or at Google.com, so make sure you've seeded your profile with all the relevant details.

• Include testimonials from happy customers or well-known people in your field. Anyone can have a profile on a social network, but the ones that are taken seriously have credible people vouching for their trustworthiness.

• Have the largest number of friends possible within your target market. The more complete your list, the better the odds that new people in your target market will discover you promptly.

• By **hosting a forum** where users can interact with each other and voice their opinions, Pages like that of Jack Johnson and Amanda Palmer draw fans back by providing a sense of community in addition to more formal content.

• **"Serialize" your content** by spreading videos, MP3 giveaways, tour diaries, photos, essays, and status updates across your Twitter, Facebook, and other social profiles, as well as your blog. When you do, make sure folks know they can find other kinds of content in those other locations.

Facebook is a continuously improving social media platform and keeping up with all the changes is an arduous task. Your best bet is a weekly visit to facebook.com/help, which informs users of these developments and suggests ways for how to best make use of them.

Here are other leading social networking sites. You can navigate to each of these sited by adding a .com to the end of the names:

- ❑ **LinkedIn,** known as a business-to-business social network, helps professionals find and contact one another to find new jobs or leads by referral only. LinkedIn is to cyberspace what networking groups once were to local business communities.

- ❑ **YouTube** is the 800 lb. gorilla in social media, serving out over 3 billion videos each day. A great way to tap its potential for your business is to tap its own *Creator Playbook* to help you learn the best tips for building your audience and taking your channel to the next level.

- ❑ **Pinterest.** Serving as a giant virtual idea and inspiration board, Pinterest has made a huge impact on social media in the last few years.

- ❑ **Vine** offers users the chance to share and view brief video clips. While that theoretically offers a virtually endless range of uses, most of Vine's content is entertainment-focused, with a heavy preference towards "viral" and "meme" clips that are easy to share.

- ❑ **Instagram,** like Pinterest, is a visual social media platform that is based entirely on photo and video posts. The network, which Facebook owns, has over 300 million active users, many of whom post about food, art, travel, fashion and similar subjects.

- ❑ **Tumblr** is different from many others in that it essentially hosts microblogs for its users. Individuals and companies, in turn, can fill their blogs with multimedia (like images and short video clips).

- ❑ **Renren**. Literally translating into "everyone's website," Renren is China's largest social platform. Hugely popular with the younger crowd, it works in a way similar to Facebook, allowing users to share quick thoughts, update their moods, connect with others, and add posts or ideas to a blog-like stream.

- ❑ **Google+.** Social media's big up-and-comer has really arrived over the past few years. By combining the best of Facebook and Twitter into one site – and backing it by the power of the world's largest search engine, Google has given users a social site that has a little something for everyone.

Of course, as with any technology, there are some downsides to social networking too. We all have to be very careful about what words and images we post. While social networks can indeed spark creative collaborations, our "digital shadow" will follow us for the rest of our lives, and company hiring managers routinely use the Net as a vetting tool for job candidates. We also know that predators and hackers of every kind are trolling the Web for victims. Sharing personal information can also put us at risk for identity theft (called "phishing") – one of the most widespread crimes today thanks to, yup, the Internet. Finally, we need to beware of the excesses of social networking. It can be a time sink if we're not careful.

But as a tool for outreach and feedback social networking is unsurpassed.

Of course, if you want to go beyond the freebie options, then you'll want to design your own web site. This gives you full control over the look and functions of your online presence.

Purpose: Deciding What Your Online Business Presence Will Be

A fundamental question to answer before you create your own Web site is: what do you want it to do? In other words, what is its purpose? Having a *web plan* is as important as your original business plan. First, decide what kind of experience you want your online customers to have. Think not only about today but also two and five years down the road. Your internet plan starts with web site goals. Who are your target customers? What do they need? Are they getting information only, or can they buy products at your site? These key questions, asked and answered early, will determine how much time and money you'll need in order to develop and maintain your online presence.

Second, decide what products or services you will offer. How will you position and display them? Will you offer both online and offline purchasing? How will you handle shipping and returns? Additionally, don't overlook the customer's need to reach a live person.

Basically, you have three strategic options when deciding on the purpose of your web site:

- Sell products and services
- Generate leads
- Establish credentials (i.e., your personal brand)

Option 1, an e-commerce site, requires the biggest development and marketing budgets. It produces direct revenue and measurable profit, as well as sales leads.
Option 2, a lead-generation site, can be developed and marketed for less (generally speaking), but still requires a hefty investment. It produces qualified, trackable sales leads.
Option 3, a credentials site, is the simplest and least expensive option. It makes a good impression on people who know who you are, but won't help you find new leads or customers.

Creating & Registering Your Domain Names

One of the first things you should do when you start your business is to pay for the rights to your name on the Internet. This is called your "domain name". It is the "Web address" that your visitors will become familiar with and use to access your site. We looked briefly at this last chapter under "Choosing a Name for Your Company," but let's now delve a little deeper.

Why is domain name registration imperative? Because more than 40 million new domain names have been registered since 2010 alone! Everyone wants a catchy name, so registering yours ensures that no one else can use it as long as you maintain your registration. For a small investment, you can hold your place on the internet until you launch. As some companies and individuals have found out the hard way, there are plenty of so-called cyber-squatters who will buy up preferred and popular names, like plumber.com or weddingplanner.com, and then sell them to others at highly inflated prices.

The 10 Most Expensive Domain Names

1. Insurance.com, $35.6 million
2. Vacationrentals.com, $35 mill.
3. Privatejet.com, $30.8 million
4. Internet.com, $18 million
5. 360.com, $17 million
6. Insure.com, $16 million
7. Sex.com, $14 million
8. Hotels.com, $11 million
9. Porn.com, $9.5 million
10. Fb.com, $8.5 million

From the available names, choose one that is the easiest to spell and remember. Once you've chosen a name, prompts on the domain registration site will guide you through a simple registration procedure. You will generally be offered one-, two- or three-year registration packages. It's also good to link your Web pages to that URL as soon as possible. In addition, a name that closely mirrors that of your business is far easier to remember than a Geocities name full of subdirectories and backslashes. For example, if your business is called Music by Justin, buying the rights to the URL www.musicbyjustin.com makes sense. When it comes to getting your own Web address, however, be prepared for disappointment – odds are, you won't get your first choice. Be flexible and creative, and keep in mind that the name should be intuitive and easy to remember – and to spell. You can check out the availability of your name choices easily at either register.com or godaddy.com.

Given how cheap domain names are (around $10 a year), you might also want to buy a few variations that are close to your primary address that could be easily confused with it. Or, perhaps, purchase the same name with different top-level domains like .org, .net or .info. If the .com name of your choice is taken, you might try the alternatives.

Getting Serious: Building Out Your Web Presence

When it's time to move beyond the limitations of free web pages like those offered at Wix, Squarespace or Weebly.com, your options multiply considerably. A web site is a multimedia representation of your company. Because it's *multi*media you have an opportunity to create and experiment with elements that include color, line, texture, graphics, animation and sound. It's tempting to want to go all out and incorporate as many "bells & whistles" into your site as possible. But just because you can doesn't mean you should. Simple is usually best. Aim for clarity and functionality, keeping the end user always in mind.

Web site construction costs can range from free to well over $10,000, depending on the information included, the complexity of the design and who does the actual coding of your site. Off-the-shelf software packages like Apple's iLife (comes with every Mac computer, or $99), Adobe Dreamweaver ($29.99/mo.), and Microsoft's ExpressionWeb ($149) make web site design a snap for the do-it-yourselfer. You'll find a rich list of resources to help you design your site in the "Resources" section of this book.

However, if you need higher functionality and specialized database systems built into your web site, you would be wise to tap the talents of a web designer.

There are plenty of web designers for hire and costs vary *a lot*. If you're a startup business on a shoestring budget, and nobody on your team feels ready to tackle HTML (hypertext markup language), you're going to have to find an economical solution. One idea is to tap into the talent of your customers or fans. See if there is someone on your mailing list who would like to help you create your site in exchange for the service or products you provide. Or, look into art schools with New Media Design or Computer Graphics programs. Students in these programs are often looking for opportunities to grow their portfolios. For a quicker solution tap Craig's List (http://www.craigslist.com), an international collection of local community classifieds and forums.

As you begin the planning of your company's web site, here are some tried and true tips to help guide you:

1) ***Get organized.*** Start visualizing your Web page before you ever turn on the computer. Think about what you want to put on your home page, what you want the reader to get out of it, how the information will relate, and how you want everything to look. Some Web experts recommend creating a storyboard or flowchart – small sketches of

each page in outline form – before you start writing. I like to use the "journey" metaphor when designing. Take your visitor on a journey into your company story.

2) ***Take a look at other web sites.*** No sense reinventing the wheel. Check out which sites you like the best, put them in your Favorites file, and then study them. What features make the site easy for you to use? What content appeals to you? What designs do you like best? Select the best elements of your favorite sites and incorporate those features into your own site.

3) ***Add value.*** Don't waste people's time with a page that provides only a list of links to other Web sites, unless, of course, that is your purpose. You should think about providing content that is of value to your site visitors. For example, if you're an avid blues lover and want to create a Web page on the subject, tell visitors where the best blues clubs are in your area and provide directions. *Pull* people in with useful information.

4) ***Keep it simple.*** The home page is to the rest of your Web site as a book's cover is to its contents or as the front door is to a place of business. The design should be bold and understandable at a glance. Don't clutter it up with unnecessary details or over-complicated layouts. Online, people skim pages, grabbing information from headlines, clicking on easy-to-understand buttons, and stopping only when they see information that seems to meet their needs. To catch the attention of these fast-moving page skimmers, avoid long blocks of text in favor of quotes, testimonials, headlines, graphics, and a design that's clear, clean, and capable of conveying your brand image at a glance.

5) ***Get visual.*** Use imaginative layouts and good-looking typography to give your Web pages a unique and identifiable look. Graphical content should be of some practical value. Avoid empty window dressing.

6) ***Observe limitations.*** Many people have "technologically challenged" hardware and not everyone is on broadband. The World Wide Web becomes the World Wide *Wait* when huge graphics or audio files are downloaded for viewing. Keep graphics to no more than 50k and your site will be a delight to visit.

7) ***Make it easy to navigate.*** One of the home page's primary roles is as a navigational tool, pointing people to information stored on your Web site or elsewhere. Make this function as effortless as possible. Also, don't bury information too deep in the page hierarchy. Stepping through five or more links can get pretty tedious. Finally, don't leave your visitors looking for bread crumbs to find their way to you. Provide a clear navigation signs and an e-mail gateway so people can contact you if they wish.

8) ***Include the essentials.*** Here are a few things most every home page should have: a header that identifies your Web site clearly and unmistakably, an e-mail address or form for communicating and reporting problems, copyright information as it applies to online content, and contact information, such as email address and phone number.

9) ***Make it fun***. What causes people to come back for return visits? According to IntelliQuest, 56% return to entertaining sites, 54% like attention grabbing sites, 53% extremely useful content, 45% information tailored to their needs, 39% imaginative sites, and 36% highly interactive sites.

10) ***Be sure to title your home page*** with a headline that will attract the most viewers to your web site. Many search engines use the title as one of their main ways of selecting sites to show to requesters. The first paragraph of text after your title is also often used by search engines to rank listings, so be sure your first paragraph contains key words about the contents of your site. As a matter of practice, you should add proper titles to the

rest of your pages as well. Follow the same basic principles for all your pages.

12) ***Keep it fresh.*** Visitors could get jaded if your Web site never changes. Encourage return visits by giving them something new to look forward to. Include your Web site in your established publicity program, so that new information (such as press releases), appears concurrently on your Web pages.

GUIDELINES FOR HIRING A WEB SITE DESIGNER
Prepare a list of questions, and interview three to five designers. Some questions to begin with are:

- What are the steps in the design process?
- How long will it take?
- What will I need to provide?
- Will you be doing the work yourself?
- Will you host the site? How much will that cost?
- What kind of tech support do you offer?

Be sure to get an estimate, including both price and deliverable dates, in writing. Ask if you can contact their other clients. When you call or email references, ask if the designer was easy to work with and good about returning calls.

Once you have selected a web designer, develop a written contract that includes:

- A *detailed description of the work to be done*, including number of web pages and features and functionality.
- *Timing* – Including check-in points and a final completion date.
- *Costs* – Specify dates for payments. The final payment shouldn't be due until your web site is completed.
- *Additional Terms* – Such as who owns the site design and handling of updates/maintenance to the site.

Content is Still King. Content describes electronically delivered information, including text, photos, or graphics. As you plan the content for your website, keep the following tips in mind:

- **Build your site page-by-page.** Don't think of your site as a single unit with many pages. Think in modular terms, with an introductory home page and links to pages that each covers a single topic.
- **Think of your home page as the welcome mat to your entire site.** Just as you wouldn't try to tell your whole story on the cover of your brochure, don't try to tell your whole story on your home page. Use your home page to establish your company image, convey your brand values, and invite users to click for specific information.
- **Use keywords to your advantage.** Keywords are words or phrases that people enter into search engines when they're seeking information or a particular website. As you develop each page on your site, think of the keywords that describe the content of your page. Then use those words in the page headline and several times in the page copy so that, when consumers seek information through keyword searches, your page has a chance of appearing in the search results.

Keyword searches may send users to internal pages of your site rather than to your home page, so be sure that every page identifies your brand and provides an easy link back to your home page.

These are some things you can do in the design phase of your web site to help maximize its visibility to Web surfers and searchers. We'll cover more ideas and tips on this subject in a later section of this chapter titled, "Creating Your internet Marketing Plan."

Host With the Most

So you now have an awesome web site that runs beautifully on your computer. Now, how does it all get on the Net? You have two basic options. The first is to host it yourself on a computer that can be dedicated as a web server (or a computer that's permanently connected to the Internet) and has a broadband connection. This will prove costly to set up and maintain. The second option is to use a web hosting company, which stores and manages web sites for businesses, among other services. Many businesses swear by some of the bigger names in web hosting, such as Network Solutions (networksolutions.com), Bluehost (bluehost.com – my company, Music Business Solutions, uses this service), 1&1 Internet (1and1.com), Go Daddy (godaddy.com), Hostaway (hostaway.com), iPower (ipower.com) and Yahoo! (yahoo.com).

Some companies, however, prefer local, small hosting providers, since they offer a direct contact – especially important if your site has an outage. Most of these companies also offer domain name services, mentioned above, so you can sign up when you choose your name. Whether buying from a large or small provider, a basic hosting service – along with basics like domain name registration and email accounts – starts at about $10 per month.
Free Hosting. There's also the "free" hosting option. A number of companies offer small businesses their own domain name, a website with up to 150 MB of space, and numerous email accounts. The tradeoff with most, however, is that you agree to allow ads (banners, pop ups, text link, etc.) to appear on your web pages, the content of which you have no control over. This is not recommended for a new business. To review the variety of free hosting options go to: free-webhosts.com.

Creating Your Internet Marketing Plan

Having a web site, hosting company and ecommerce package are the fundamental ingredients for an effective web business. Now you must put a plan in place that will make your business site visible to your target audience. But first a caveat.
The Internet may be the biggest breakthrough in the history of marketing, but it is not marketing itself. Effective marketing depends on certain qualities that transcend technology: understanding your customer, clear and consistent communication, and the highest levels of customer service. Technology will amplify your reach and add efficiencies to your business, but it is these more basic practices that will ultimately make your company visible and give it staying power in the marketplace.

With that said, it is undeniable that the Internet has afforded businesses of every size an opportunity to galvanize global customers through creative communications. Internet marketing has become so complex, whole courses are being taught and books written on all of the following topics:

- Affiliate Marketing
- Article Marketing
- Attribute Bundling
- Banner Advertising
- Blogging
- Google Ad Sense/Adwords
- Co-Registration
- Conversion/Testing
- Web site Design
- Link Strategies
- Mobile advertising
- Relevant Inbound Links
- Local Marketing
- Shopping Carts/Transactions
- Online PR
- Online Video Marketing
- Opt-In Email Lists
- Pay Per click

- Site Usability
- E-Commerce Design
- E-Mail Marketing
- Geo-Targeting
- Google Analytics
- Landing Page Strategy
- Paid Search/Paid Placement
- Podcasting
- Search Engine Optimization
- Shopping Cart Abandonment
- Social Media/Networking
- Text Ads

While we cannot deal with all these internet marketing tactics in this book, I do want to focus on several that have proven to be most effective when done right.

❑ ***Email – Your Best Friend in Marketing.*** While providing online payment options is crucial to making money using the Internet, the single most important element of your marketing will always be communicating with your customers. And email provides quick, nearly free communication with large numbers of people. The benefits are clear:

- *Low cost*: You may pay monthly charges to get access, but the money you save on fax and mailings by using the Net instead will more than make up for these fees.
- *Extremely fast delivery*: Most email arrives at its destination (around the corner or around the world) in seconds.
- *Permanent records*: A copy of all your email messages will be stored on the server host of your email program, for as long as that server is in existence.
- *Flexibility*: It's not unusual to send a two- or three-word email message. Email provides the considered thoughtfulness of mailed correspondence with the quickness and informality of a phone call.
- *Ease of communication*: Replying to an electronic letter is simple and fast.
- *Ease of replication*: Because email is digital, you can replicate a message as many times as you'd like. For example, a band with 100 fans can alert them to a surprise performance and encourage the 100 to forward the message to three friends each, bringing the total distribution to almost 1000 people in minutes.

❑ ***Networking Etiquette Online***:

1. Never confuse advertising with networking. While there are ways to advertise online both for fee and for free, when networking online, you must exercise restraint in promoting yourself. People are looking for ideas, advice, friends, and help. Most people resent a sales pitch or even a self-serving promotion.

2. Think collegial and interactive. Just as face-to-face networking is a two-way process among colleagues and peers, so is online networking. Visit groups and forums and join Internet mailing lists that relate to your field, reviewing ongoing conversations and think about how you could join in the dialog and make a contribution based on your expertise and your curiosity. Asking good questions is a contribution, too.

3. Visit promising sites often. Just as attending in-person networking meetings regularly is important, being visible online regularly is also important. You don't build relationships by dropping a message here and there and rushing on to other sites. You will develop online business through establishing ongoing relationships.

4. Provide personal responses. The more personal you can make your communication the better, so respond to concerns and queries of particular individuals whenever possible.

5. Provide valued information. When leaving messages for an entire forum or newsgroup, focus on tips, trends, new information, or recent discoveries you've made in your work that would be of high interest and practical use to others. You might want to post a tip sheet, your newsletter, or segments from your informative booklet if you have one. Just be sure the information you post is informative, and no more than subtly 'promotional'.

❑ ***SEO: Helping Search Engines Find Your Site –*** Search engine optimization (SEO) is the ongoing process of improving the page ranking of your web site in a search engine result. On average business-to-consumer companies allocate 45% and business-to-business companies allocate 36% of their online budgets to SEO. According to Internet marketing research firm *Media Post*, SEO is estimated to be the fastest growing expenditure in companies' net marketing efforts, projected to reach a staggering $45 billion in 2019.

Your SEO strategy begins with your site's design. Search engines, such as Google, are the 411 operators of the Internet. Many of your potential customers will use a search engine to find products and services (such as those your business offers) by searching on a specific word or phrase. Search engines operate by looking at "keywords" from a web site. Your web designer should be able to maximize your site by ensuring that all the most important keywords and phrases appear in your site content. That way, searches will return your site's web address, and prospective customers can readily find you when they are searching for your particular business.

Google powers the majority of online searches, and the goal of most website owners is to achieve good Google presence. After all, as far as your online presence goes, *you are what Google says you are!*

An outstanding resource for achieving this victory is *Building your Business With Google For Dummies* by Brad Hill (Wiley), which includes these tips:

- Build pages around core keywords that define each page's topical focus.
- Incorporate core keywords into the page's content.
- Place core keywords in each page's <META> tags, which are the hidden HTML code commands that search engines scan.
- Fill in the <TITLE> tag, using core keywords.
- Use <alt> tags, with keywords, on page graphics.
- Use text, not graphical buttons, for navigation links.
- Register and use domains that describe the site's business.
- Avoid *splash pages*, which are entry pages that visitors must click through to get to your home page.
- Devote one page to a comprehensive site map.
- Keep pages focused, and write new pages for divergent subjects.
- Build a network of incoming links from other sites to your site.
- Don't use spamming, keyword stuffing, or cloaking. All three techniques aim to trick search engine spiders into heightening a site's ranking in search engine results.

They're considered unethical approaches, and when discovered, they prompt search engines to take action ranging from lowering the site's rank to banning it from the index.

❑ ***Google Adwords and similar services.*** Placing text ads through services like Google Adwords, Yahoo Advertising, Bing Ads (Microsoft) and Ask.com are additional ways you can optimize your online presence. In these you, as the advertiser pay on a "per-click" basis; in other words, you pay a few pennies for each time a web visitor clicks on their sponsored link.

If, for example, you specialize in "internet radio promotion," you will want to come up with all keywords and phrases a searcher might use when seeking this service. You'll probably create a list containing all or most of the following: "internet radio promotion," "net radio promotion," "internet music promotion," "internet music marketing," "internet radio airplay," "airplay radio promotion," "streaming music promotion," etc. Google's keyword tool and Wordtracker are two free tools to help research what people are searching for. Google's AdWords, by far the most popular program, are text ads that are clearly labeled as "sponsored links" so consumers do not confuse the ads with the natural listings Google generates. AdWords works on an auction-based system that assigns particular words to whichever company bids the most for them. Google makes its billions by taking the money advertisers have bid every time a user clicks on an ad. There is no minimum spending requirement for Google AdWords - the amount you pay is completely up to you. For example, you can set a daily budget of ten dollars and choose to pay ten cents each time your ad is clicked.

In order to prevent bidders securing words that are completely unrelated to their businesses, Google monitors how popular each ad is. If an ad receives few clicks, meaning that consumers do not find the ad particularly relevant to the search they have performed, Google determines it is not relevant and downgrades it in its sponsored link ranking system.

This also ensures that in the long run the most relevant, and therefore most lucrative, ads appear the most frequently.

Making that "Sig" (Signature) File Work for You

This was a musician's signature file in an email message sent to me:

What would you get if you combined Yanni, Hans Zimmer, and Kitaro, threw in a dash of Pink Floyd, set to simmer, and served it for dinner? Click here: http://www.kellykendall.com to find out!

❑ ***Affinities & Affiliates.*** One of the many benefits of online commerce is the ability to link your site to others. The Net easily allows you to find and link up with businesses your company may have an affinity with. This is called *Affinity Marketing*. For example, a client of mine who specializes in producing recordings of traditional Irish music discovered all kinds of affinity partners, ranging from gift shops to Irish travel companies. With each one she created a media swap where she displays banner ads or links to their sites in exchange for the same at theirs. Within a month of initiating these exchanges her business doubled.

These online "affinities" are all about related businesses teaming up and combining skills, products, services and resources to create new streams of income and profit. One great way to profit through joint ventures is to seek out products or services that would benefit your visitors, and then approach the companies that provide those products or services. Ask them if you can recommend their product or service on your site for a portion of the profits. Most companies will gladly agree to this arrangement – after all, there's no risk for them since they only pay you when you refer a paying customer.

Affiliate programs are similar to "affinity marketing" but are also a bit different.

An ***affiliate program*** (also referred to as a *reseller* or *associate program*) is a way to get other people to promote and sell your product or service. For every customer your affiliates send to your site, you pay them a commission. Your affiliates send visitors to your site using banner ads, text links, letters of referral, and other methods of promotion. Then you track these visitors using special software. For every visitor who decides to buy, you pay your affiliate a commission, usually once a month. There are two ways to do this:

- ***Recommend affiliate products.*** Recommending affiliate products creates a "no-risk" partnership that allows you to promote another company's products or services on your site to earn a percentage of their sales. As one of the company's "affiliates" or promotion partners, you earn a commission each time someone you've referred to their site makes a purchase. To advertise their wares, you might post a banner on your site that links to the affiliate program's site, or you might publish an article about the company and their products in your newsletter.

• ***Start an affiliate program.*** With your own affiliate program, you can recruit an army of people (your affiliates) who will recommend your product on their web site for a percentage of any sales they refer. You have the power to exponentially increase your income as more and more affiliates sign up and you continue to teach your existing affiliates how to increase their commission checks (and your income).

❑ ***Videocasting.*** According to many estimates, broadband penetration has reached 80 percent of the U.S. market, making streaming videos a must marketing tool. In fact, eMarketer reported that 123 million Americans watch a video at least once a month, and three quarters tell a friend or business colleague about it.

Of all the online video options, YouTube.com is without a doubt number 1. Founded in 2005 and acquired by Google for $1.65 billion in 2006, YouTube is an ever-growing online community that allows you to post video clips on the world wide web, and watch a huge array of clips in hundreds of categories. Every day people watch hundreds of millions of hours on YouTube and generate billions of views. The variety of videos is truly staggering. There are clips from popular TV shows, obscure music videos, sports highlight, and every choice of instructional video.

What makes YouTube a hit is its ability to transcode anything and produce an easy-to-watch and easy-to-embed streaming flash movie. You simply upload a video you made on a digital camera or camcorder, and YouTube's computers turn it into a flash video. Producers, the public, wannabe actors, corporations out for publicity, and clip collectors all use YouTube. Musicians and music-related companies – from 'Obama Girl,' who crooned about her crush on Barak Obama, to the tread-milling band OK Go, to lesser-known songwriters like Julia Nunes – are finding opportunities to connect on a visual (and emotional) level with potential fans and customers through online video.

Here are some tips for making the most of your online video presence:

Production – It all comes down to good planning, so hunker down and absorb the following advice:

- *Make it short:* 15-30 seconds is ideal; break down long stories into bite-sized clips.
- *Design for remixing:* create a video that is simple enough to be remixed over and over again by others. Example: "Dramatic Hamster".
- *Don't make an outright ad:* if a video feels like an ad, viewers won't share it unless it's really amazing. Example: "Sony Bravia".
- *Make it shocking:* give a viewer no choice but to investigate further. Example: "UFO Haiti".
- *Use 'fake' headlines:* make the viewer say, "Holy Toledo, did that actually happen?!" Example: "Stolen Nascar".

Promotion – How do you get the first 50,000 views you need to get your videos onto the Most Viewed list? It'll take some work, but here are some tips:

- *Post to relevant blogs* (see next section below).
- *Post to relevant forums:* Even start new threads and embed your videos.
- *Facebook:* Share, share, share.

- *Email lists:* Send the video to a qualified email list. Depending on the size of the list (and the recipients' willingness to receive links to YouTube videos), this can be a very effective strategy.
- *Friends:* Make sure everyone you know watches the video and try to get them to email it out to their friends.

Also, if you have multiple videos, post all of them at once. If someone sees your first video and is so intrigued that they want to watch more, why would you make them wait until you post the next one? Give them everything up front.

BREATHING DOWN YOUR BROWSER

The data-collection machine in the United States is a behemoth. Data broker Acxiom told the FTC it has some 3,000 data segments for nearly every consumer in America. Datalogix, which works with Facebook, has personal information about almost every U.S. household, according to the FTC. Counting four types of interactions with company websites in addition to the hits from advertisements served from advertising networks, there is the potential for collecting upward of 2,500 pieces of data on average per user per month!

There are plenty of other resources for promoting your act or business via YouTube, Google Video, Vimeo and other online video outlets. Check the Further Resources section. YouTube is a style now, an aesthetic of its own. It didn't take very long, but it has lodged itself into our consumer psyche as a recognizable visual, aural and narrative convention. In that sense, it's a huge and notable success deserving of a special footnote in media history.

❑ ***Blogs.*** The essential ingredient of a blog is its short entries or posts. They're arranged in reverse chronological order, with the newest at top. Posts can be a few sentences long, or many paragraphs long, and often link to outside information like other blogs, newspaper stories, or multimedia clips hosted elsewhere on the Web.

Nearly any tidbit of information relevant to your audience can be spun into a blog post of some type:

- **Informational** - new development or news-oriented blurb.
- **Question/Answer** - easy to write, and fun to read.
- **Instructional** - can be a longer post; perhaps a tutorial that explains how to do something related to your niche.
- **Link posts –** link to an interesting blog post and add your own spin.
- **Rant** - let off some steam, and let it rip. Interesting blogs don't play it safe, they take sides.
- **Book review** - review a book related to your field.
- **Product reviews** - the word "review" is a popular search terms. Give your frank opinion, and encourage your readers to chime in with their own views.
- **Lists** - write about the "Top 5 Ways" to do a task, or the "Top 10 Reasons" for such-and-such. Readers love lists. If someone else publishes a list, you can summarize it or critique it on your own blog.
- **Interviews** - chat with someone in your field. Provide a text summary on your blog. You can also add a transcript even an audio file.
- **Case studies** - report on how so-and-so does such-and-such. You don't have to call it a "case study," just tell the story.
- **Profiles** - profiles focus on a particular person, a personality. The person

profiled can be someone well known in your field, or perhaps a newcomer nobody's heard of.

Most blogs are conversational and informal, but that doesn't provide a license to be sloppy. You want your blog to reflect favorably on your business, and that requires attention to detail. It's worth proofreading and spell-checking your posts before publishing. Keeping your paragraphs short will minimize your rewriting chores.

One helpful feature for you and your readers is blog categories. Assign each post to one or more categories, such as "technology," "marketing," "features," "reviews," or however you can best divide your material. Category headings can be listed on your blog's margin, and are especially valuable for new readers.

❑ **MP3 Blogs**. Music blogs – weblogs that present audio files from their host's collections, one at a time – are another opportunity for music promotion. Nobody's sure who came up with the first MP3 blog, and the evolution of the form was gradual enough that it's hard to pinpoint the date of its origin, although it was probably around 2002.

According to Technocrati, there are approximately 11,000 music blogs, specializing in everything from hard-core punk to pre-World War II gospel. The music blogosphere has developed into a subculture with its own unofficial leaders and unwritten rules, and it's becoming a significant force in the recording industry, which mostly seems to be smiling on the phenomenon. Aggregators such as The Hype Machine (hypem.com) and Music Blogtrotter (http://musicaggregator.blogspot.com) track MP3 blog posts and display the most recently updated posts on their respective front pages.

There's a relatively standard format for MP3 blogs that's unofficially evolved: one or two songs a day, each one accompanied by a paragraph or two about the song or the artist. Some bloggers also include photographs or links to places where their readers can buy the CD on which each song appears.

Most focus on little-known musicians or rare and out-of-print recordings; few will post something that's already a huge radio hit or by a very famous artist, and it's frowned upon to post more than a single song from a given album.

Of course, one of the first questions a lot of people ask about MP3 blogs is if they're legal. The answer is that it's a gray area, and MP3 bloggers tend to work from the principle that it's easier to get forgiveness than permission. None has been sued, and nobody's yet talking about suing them. In fact, Universal Music Group's European division is paying Matthew Perpetua, the curator of Fluxblog (fluxblog.org), to be a talent scout (he sends them an annotated CD-R of his favorite new music once a month)!

All a prospective blogger needs is a site, a way to host the files, and a means to get the word out. The site part is easy enough: free services such as Blogger.com or wordpress.com provide the basic setup for a lot of music bloggers.

It was just a matter of time for popular music blogs to begin spawning the next record labels. Indeed, music blogs are organizing concerts, being quoted in television, and releasing independent albums – just like a record label. Wired.com's Eliot Van Buskirk agrees, and points out that these blogs, 1) have the audience, 2) fans already think of them as tastemakers, 3) they have lots of experience in judging new music (hmm...that one's questionable), and 4) they can submit songs to digital distribution networks such as The Orchard, IRIS, Tunecore and so on, just like anyone else can.

To the extent that all next generation entrepreneurs need a point of entry, blogs do provide that for free. Time will tell if they can indeed deliver the A&R filtering and marketing dynamics traditional labels provided.

Having an e-commerce plan is as important as your original business plan. The internet allows you to communicate with anyone anywhere with email. Advertising your product or service, showing potential customers your wares and allowing them to purchase immediately, doing test marketing and surveying, joining discussion groups with like-minded individuals, sending a monthly newsletter, and linking with affiliated businesses are all part of what you can do on the web. The power of Web 2.0 is allowing entrepreneurs to take their enterprises to a whole new level of business engagement and the more you can bring these dynamics into your business, the stronger it will be.
The Internet is indeed your open mic to the world.

CHAPTER SUMMARY

PUTTING THE WEB & ECOMMERCE TO WORK FOR YOUR BUSINESS

- **From Web 1.0 to 2.0: Tapping Into the Social Media Revolution**
  Web 2.0 encompasses the set of tools that allow people to build social and business connections, share information and collaborate on projects online. That includes blogs, wikis, social-networking sites and other online communities, and virtual worlds.

- **Managing Your Social Media (added section needs summary, after following paragraph)**
  Social networking sites are becoming increasingly more popular. If you want to stay atop of the latest trends, then you would benefit from setting up a business profile on Facebook, whether you are a solo artist or a mega entrepreneur. Other leading social networking sites: LinkedIn, YouTube, Pinterest, VIne, Instagram, Tumblr, Renren and Google+.

- **Purpose: Deciding What Your Online Business Presence Will Be**
  Having a web plan is as important as your original business plan. First, decide what kind of experience you want your online customers to have. Second, decide what products or services you will offer. Some detailed list of the possible web site purposes: selling, product design, marketing, support to customers, manufacturing, expertise, human resources, and general administration.

- **Creating & Registering Your Domain Names**
  One of the first things you should do when you start your business is to pay for the rights to your name on the Internet. This is called your "domain name". It is the "Web address" that your visitors will become familiar with and use to access your site. From the available names, choose one that is the easiest to spell and remember. Once you've chosen a name, prompts on the domain registration site will guide you through a simple registration procedure.

- **Getting Serious: Building Out Your Web Presence**
  A web site is a multimedia representation of your company. Because it's multimedia you have an opportunity to create and experiment with elements that include color, line, texture, graphics, animation and sound. However, if you need higher functionality and specialized database systems built into your web site, you would be wise to tap the talents of a web designer.

- **Host With the Most**
  You have two basic options. The first is to host it yourself on a computer that can be dedicated as a web server (or a computer that's permanently connected to the Internet) and has a broadband connection. The second option is to use a web hosting company, which stores

and manages web sites for businesses, among other services. There's also the "free" hosting option. A number of companies offer small businesses their own domain name, a website with up to 150 MB of space, and numerous email accounts.

- **Creating Your Internet Marketing Plan**
  Effective marketing depends on certain qualities that transcend technology: understanding your customer, clear and consistent communication, and the highest levels of customer service. Some examples of marketing tactics: Email, Networking Online, SEO: Helping Search Engines Find Your Site, Google Adwords and similar services, Affinities & Affiliates, Videocasting, Blogs, and MP3 Blogs.

FURTHER RESOURCES

ONLINE RESOURCES

• Internet Stats and Surveys

Clickz
www.clickz.com

Cyber Atlas
www.cyber-atlas.com/

Living Internet
http://livinginternet.com

• Web Site Development Tools

Bandzoogle
bandzoogle.com

Prestashop
prestashop.com

SiteInspire
siteinspire.com/
Web Design Inspiration

Wix.com
wix.com

• Domains & Hosting

Go Daddy
http://godaddy.com

Hostbaby
http://hostbaby.com

Network Solutions
http://www.networksolutions.com

Register.com http://register.com
Domain Name Registration & hosting

WhoIsHostingThis
whoishostingthis.com/
Discover who is hosting any websites

• Sound Utilities for the Web

Adobe Audition
http://www.adobe.com/products/audition.html

Audacity
audacity.com

The Freesite
thefreesite.com

Freeware
freeware-guide.com

Goldwave
www.goldwave.com

Harmony Central
harmonycentral.com

• Video Editing Tools

Flash Player
adobe.com/software/flash/about

Shortcut
shotcut.org/

WeVideo
https://www.wevideo.com/

• Online Business Development

Entrepreneur.com
entrepreneur.com

Idea Site for Business
ideasiteforbusiness.com

Smart Cart
smartcart.com

• Online Store Options

Amazon Advantage Program
amazon.com/advantage

Paypal
paypal.com/us/webapps/mpp/merchant

Shopify
shopify.com

Wordpress Simple Shopping Cart
wordpress.com

Yahoo Stores
smallbusiness.yahoo.com/ecommerce

8

RAISING CAPITAL FOR YOUR VENTURE

The amount of money one needs is terrifying.
- Ludwig von Beethoven

Enough is abundance to the wise.
- Euripides

You may have heard the old saw:

Q - How do you make a million dollars in the music business?
A - Start with two million.

Without a doubt, the music business is fraught with risk. People have made - and lost - millions of dollars throughout its history. You would think that by now we'd have it figured out; you would think we'd know the secret of creating a hit record, securing an artist's future, or succeeding with a fantastic new music service. But we don't.

This makes the investor community a bit shy when it comes to valuing new music properties (like upstart labels or internet music companies). A number of music ventures were part of the dot com boom and bust (1998-2001), and then the revenue drain from file-sharing didn't help instill much confidence when investors assessed the music business. You can think of the music industry as having a pyramid shape, reflecting the existence of many small companies, few medium-sized firms and a very few major companies. A UK study, *Banking on a Hit*, suggests that this may be due to the music industry's "management anxiety about growing any bigger, and a desire for early exit routes."

Such companies are usually not suitable for venture capital (VC), which tends to focus on ambitious companies with high growth prospects and top-notch management. Venture capital investors have lately become elusive. VC is most likely to be given to an established company with an already proven track record. If you are a startup, your product or service must be better than the wheel, sliced bread and the PC - with an extremely convincing plan that will make the investor a lot of money. And even that might not be good enough.

> If you have built castles in the air, your work need not be lost; that is where they should be. Now put foundations under them.
>
> - Henry David Thoreau

Some capital is needed to properly launch your company, though maybe not as much as you may think. Derek Sivers, founder of CDBaby, believes resourcefulness rather than capital is the key ingredient: "Entrepreneurs don't say, 'I need $20 million to get my idea started,' unless they're building an airline. A real entrepreneur can find a way to get a prototype launched for almost nothing, make it profitable almost right away, and build on that".

Jay Andreozzi of Amalgam Digital started his company with less than $500. That initial seed money has tuned itself into a $1.5 million company in less than five years. But even that $500 may not be crucial: "If you are having a difficult time financing your start up, use the lack of financial resources to get creative and think outside the box. You really don't need any capital to start. With $0 you can start offering human service solutions. Sell your services to generate small amounts of working capital."

On the other hand, underestimating what you'll need can cause paralysis. "After you spend a good amount of time planning and researching and budgeting, take the amount of time and money you think it will take to make the business sustainable and triple it, right off the bat, " says Patrick Faucher, of Bose Corp. Faucher continues: "Be prepared to not get paid for two years. Be very careful when taking on outside investors, be sure that they are completely on board with your plan and that they will be patient through the tough times because it is guaranteed there will be tough times".

Surveys show that many self-employed business people start their businesses with $5,000 or less – sometimes much less. For many small service businesses, this amount is enough to establish the business, create some marketing materials, and invest in inventory or materials (if it's a product-based business). In contrast, if you're planning a business that requires expensive equipment or a startup fee (as in franchises), $5,000 might seem on the low side.

What the $5,000 startup figure does not include are your daily living expenses. According to financial advisors, if you're launching a business that will be your only income source, you should have a financial cushion equal to six to nine months of income. This serves as your security blanket and allows you freedom from financial worries. With this in the bank, you can focus exclusively on launching your business and building a new income stream.

Do-It-Yourself Financing

The best place to begin is by looking in the mirror. Self-financing is the number-one form of financing used by most business startups. In addition, when you approach other financing sources such as banks, angel investors or the government, they will want to know exactly how much of your *own* money you are putting into the venture. After all, if you don't have enough faith in your business to risk your own money, why should anyone else risk theirs?

Begin by doing a thorough inventory of your assets. You are likely to uncover resources you didn't even know you had. Assets include savings accounts, equity in real estate, retirement accounts, vehicles, recreation equipment and collections. You may decide to sell some assets for cash or to use them as "collateral" for a loan (*Collateral* is an item of value that is pledged in exchange for a loan. This minimizes the lender's risk by ensuring there is an item of value to recoup his investment from in the event you stop paying on the loan. The less credit you have, the more likely it is a lender would demand collateral in exchange for payment).

❑ ***If you have investments***, you may be able to use them as a resource. Low-interest margin loans against stocks and securities can be arranged through your brokerage accounts. The downside here is that if the market should fall and your securities are your loan collateral, you'll get a "margin call" from your broker, requesting you to supply more collateral. If you can't do that within a certain time, you'll be asked to sell some of your securities to shore up the collateral.

❑ ***If you own a home or property***, consider getting a home equity loan on the part of the mortgage that you have already paid off. The bank will either provide a lump-sum loan payment or extend a line of credit based on the equity in your home. Depending on the value of your home, a home-equity loan could become a substantial line of credit. Nimbit co-founder Patrick Faucher says he re-mortgaged his house several times to keep the company afloat in its early years, though he doesn't recommend going quite that far. However, if you have $50,000 in equity, you could possible set up a line of credit of up to $40,000. Home equity loans carry relatively low interest rates, and all interest paid on a loan of up to $100,000 is tax-deductible.

❑ ***Consider borrowing against cash-value life insurance***. You can use the cash value built up in a cash-value life insurance policy as a ready source of cash. The interest rates are reasonable because the insurance companies always get their money back. You don't even have to make payments if you don't want to. Neither the amount you borrow nor the interest that accrues has to be repaid. The only loss is that if you die and the debt hasn't been repaid, the money is deducted from the amount your beneficiary will receive.

❑ ***Income from a primary or secondary job*** is another source of capital. Many entrepreneurs "moonlight," or conduct their business during the off-time hours from their regular job. This is the approach Claire Chase took to finance the start of the International Contemporary Ensemble: "I worked 60-80 hour weeks and dumped all of the extra money I earned into the company. For the first three months I lived alternately in the kitchen at work, on friends' couches and in the practice rooms at Northwestern University, so that I could save money on rent and get a head start on financing ICE".

Moonlighting is a great way to ease into a new business. It also gives entrepreneurs a chance to develop their skills without the pressure of generating a lot of income right away. Starting your business "part time" may be another option. If you're confident that your new business can generate at least half your income, consider cutting back your full-time job to part-time, and dedicate the remaining time to focusing on your new business. These days, more employers are willing to consider this option, since it can save them money. "Piggybacking" is a third approach. This is when new businesses are launched with the support of an employed spouse or partner. With one full-time salary to cover basic needs, the would-be entrepreneur can focus on the new business. If you choose this approach, don't overlook the potential psychological stresses this can put upon a relationship. Some spouses mutually establish a set length of time or a cutoff date for funding the business effort. This arrangement often serves as a strong motivator and a realistic boundary for the commitment.

❑ ***Credit.*** Finally, take a look at your ***personal line of credit***. Some businesses have been successfully started on credit cards, although this is one of the most expensive ways to finance yourself. The obvious drawback to "debt financing" is the high interest rates; if you use the cards for cash advances rather than to buy equipment, the rates are even higher.

About 60% of businesses that use credit cards pay off the balances in full each month (this is *required* by American Express). This practice helps them avoid debt, which can mount up quickly because of the way credit card debt is structured. It works like this: The card minimum payment is typically set so low that it doesn't cover the cost of the monthly interest charged. If a business owner pays only the minimum amount, unpaid interest is added to the principal owed. Interest is then charged on interest (known as compounding interest), thus increasing the debt without the card user even making any purchases. In this way, business owners can find themselves quickly burdened with enormous debt if they don't make sufficient monthly payments.

Typically, credit cards extend debt of $1,500 to $15,000 at interest rates of 12% to 22%, plus fees for cash advances or renewing cards. The interest is calculated assuming that the principal will be paid back in three or four years, even though that may not happen. Some entrepreneurs take advantage of low-interest credit card offers they receive in the mail, transferring balances from one card to another as soon as interest rates rise (typically after six months). If you use this strategy, keep a close eye on when the rate will increase. If you are good at juggling payments, your startup needs are low, and you are confident you'll be able to pay the money back fairly quickly, this could be the route to take.

Tapping Other Sources of Capital

When businesses grow faster than the capital they generate, they often turn to external sources for financing. These sources may include family and friends, bank loans, state-sponsored micro-loan programs, venture-backed capital, and angel investors. Before looking for outside financing, the savvy business owner will tighten up cash flow and narrow cash gaps. So the first thing to do is assess ways you can make your company look more financially attractive. The guidelines on diagnosing your company's financial health and streamlining operations in chapter 14 should be carefully considered here.

Too, if your company is stalled at a certain size and you want to grow, you will certainly need an in-flow of money to take things to the next level. To secure this capital you will need to thoroughly review your business plan and get a firm grasp of the financials. So get it out and visit it again, reviewing the numbers, and updating any sections that may need it. While your initial thought may be to ask for cash exclusively, there may be other resources that would help you even more. Perhaps what you really need is some personal assistance, or office space, or perhaps a new computer. These can sometimes be provided more easily than cash. So broaden your definition of "financing".

Financing most commonly comes in the form of debt, such as loans, or equity, such as a piece of the business sold as stock or as a partnership.
Before asking for that money, however, you'll need to answer the following questions:

- What is the money **needed** for specifically? (Your answer yields the loan *amount* needed.)
- Is it a **short-term** or **long-term** need? (Your answer determines the *length* of the loan.)
- What will the **owner** give up for the **capital**? For example, will the owner or the business itself take on the debt, or will the owner give up equity or management of the company? (Your answer determines what sort of *requirements* the owner must adhere to in order to get the money.)
- What **rate of return** can be expected from the success of the business? (Your answer indicates how much *interest* on a loan or how much of a return on investment money a business owner can afford to pay.)

Based on your answers to these four questions, you can focus on the sources of funding most likely to match your need: small loans, big loans, non-loan sources and equity. For small loans — from $1,000 to $50,000 — you will pay higher interest rates, from 12% to 22%, because the loans are usually short-term and it costs the lender as much labor to prepare as a longer-term, $1-million loan.

Always make sure your *debt-to-capital ratio* is sensible - something like 25 percent debt and 75 percent investment or working capital or 10 percent and 90 percent investment working capital. If your debt-to-capital ratio is 50/50, or worse 40/60, you're in big trouble. A company can't grow on quicksand. Too much debt in the early years of a business is just that. Not only can it pull your business under, it can also drag your personal life down with it. Never put your future at risk - only your present.

Remember too that it is your business leadership, not so much the business idea, that people invest in or loan money to. Panos Panay saw this when starting his company. "My feeling is that people invest in people, not ideas," says Panay. "When I was trying to get some money from friends and family to start Sonicbids, many people came forward and said, 'I only have $2,000, but I want to give it to you because I believe in you'. Ideas don't inspire confidence – people do."

❑ ***Friends and family:*** A bank may be the first place you expect to turn to for loans, but more than half of all small businesses are launched with money from the owner's personal savings or from friends and family. The reality is, you always have to start with sources close by, because they know you best. If these friendly sources do not have much money in savings, they may have other assets that can be converted into cash. They may own a home on which they could obtain a second mortgage. Or they may have stocks, bonds, or other assets that could be pledged.

If those individuals won't lend you the money you seek, it could be a signal to reevaluate your plans. Your business may be riskier than your friends and family can accept, or it may not meet their income expectations. There's no free ride just because they're family members. Even relatives and friends expect to be repaid or to receive a profitable piece of the business. To avoid disputes later, all agreements should be verbalized, discussed and put in writing.

Family and friends typically lend amounts ranging from $5,000 to $50,000, and sometimes more, depending on their financial status. They often will accept a return at only slightly above bank savings account rates of 3-4% and may wait longer for repayment. But in a family economic crisis, they might suddenly demand all the money back to meet their own needs.

Another source of "friendly money" is crowdfunding, first mentioned in chapter 3 under the trend, "Rise of the Customer-Creator". Crowd*funding* is a type of fundraising and occurs for any variety of purposes, from disaster relief to citizen journalism, and from political campaigns to artists seeking support from fans. It makes it possible to reach out to a group of potentially interested supporters at very low cost. Its popularity is being driven by people getting big responses from their networks as they leverage their niche communities to spread the word about their projects.

Crowdfunding can replace the need for specialized grant applications or other more formal and traditional fundraising techniques with that of a more casual, yet powerful, approach based on crowd participation. This "diffused patronage" approach is used widely among music industry artists to bypass music publishing companies and go direct to their fans who are now seen as much as investors as listeners. For example, songwriter Jill Souble raised nearly $90,000 for her 2009 album, *California Years*, by holding a virtual telethon on the site Jillsnextrecored.com. A whole rack of music services have emerged based on the crowdfunding idea including ArtistShare.org, KickStarter.com, and Fundable.com.

Of course, the process of asking people for money can be daunting. "Learning how to raise money was also a huge hurdle for me," remembers Claire Chase. "I'd never done it before, and I was terrified of asking anyone for money. I didn't come from money, I'd never asked anyone for money, and I was allergic to the whole idea. But I quickly realized that this skill was essential to accomplishing anything I wanted to do creatively, and I realized that it was a skill that could be learned, not just born, and that I could overcome my fears and face this challenge with creativity and gratitude." Chase eventually went on to raise $10,000 for a weeklong festival of free new music concerts in Chicago and, from there, "things really started to pick up speed".

❑ ***Government Help***: The SBA (Small Business Administration) guarantees loans from other institutions; it does not make loans directly. If you are seeking financing, the SBA can provide you with a list of lending institutions active in giving loans to small businesses. These banks and institutions must approve your application, so you must meet bank criteria to qualify. Typically, new businesses do not qualify for SBA-guaranteed loans Government funding is also often available to help small companies train employees and develop work skills. While some funds come as grants, much of it gets allocated to states or local work-force boards which decide what industries and areas to support. The trick is to identify programs aimed at your region or industry.

Start at the federal level. Representatives at the U.S. Department of Labor's Business Relations Group will work with you to identify programs you could use. Tell them what industry you're in and what you're hoping to accomplish with worker training. They know about programs in the works and can put you on lists to be notified about future opportunities.

In addition, look into:

- State training programs – They use a variety of names, so when searching online for those available in your state, use a variety of keyword and keyword phrases.
- Community colleges and public universities – They often run government-funded training programs and can help you with writing the program grant.

❑ ***Micro-loan programs:*** Micro-loans have become popular in the United States. In most programs in this country there is often a requirement that owners complete business or technical training. Lenders are typically community development agencies that target specific geographical areas or groups, such as minorities or victims of disasters and economic downturns. Creation of new jobs is often a requirement. The SBA (Small Business Administration) also recently started its own micro loan program for business startups, so be sure to look into this too. A good aggregator of government-sponsored business loan programs is business.gov.

Loan amounts can range from $10,000 to $100,000, with interest rates from 12% to 15% for one to three years. Besides connections to these people, you'll also need your business plan and financial statements.

Special bank programs: Because banks have come to realize that small loans can be profitable, and because they have responsibilities under the federal Community Reinvestment Act, many banks are targeting certain groups or businesses for loans ranging from $5,000 to $50,000. With loans this small, banks make a profit by eliminating some of the human labor involved in evaluating the loan.

They substitute computers in a process known as "credit scoring." In credit scoring, points are accumulated for income, years of experience in business, loan payback history, number of employees and other characteristics that banks prefer to keep to themselves. Once enough points are accumulated, the loan is approved.

As with many computer programs, computer scoring must fit certain categories. Banks often lack flexibility to lend outside those parameters. Typically, banks provide lines of credit or loans at prime interest rates (the most favorable short-term loan rate charged to corporations), plus 2% to 4%, with a loan fee of 1% or 2% of the total loan amount. Besides the basic application, a financial statement is required.

Even though your loan request may be small, you must still present your business comprehensively and professionally via your business plan and in person.

Loans range from $5,000 to $25,000, with some as high as $50,000, over one to five years at 10% to 16% interest. Besides business training, lenders also require a cash-flow chart, financial statements and, sometimes, collateral. The assumption is that the business owner will seek the next loan from a traditional lender. It should be noted, however, that the current recession has made these programs much more conservative in their lending.

❑ ***Grants:*** There's a persistent lie traveling through the entrepreneurial community that there are millions of dollars in grants available to start a business. The truth, however, is that few groups give individuals money to finance a startup. The majority of the available grant money is really targeted at nonprofit organizations and government agencies. These groups use the money to fund a variety of special projects such as community revitalization, job training, cultural enrichment (that's where the arts fit in) or research, similar to the "micro loan" programs mentioned above. The money is allocated by a variety of foundations. The following list will give you a general idea of what could be available to you:

- Organizational grants for arts programs
- Special projects
- Art career fellowships
- Short-term fellowships
- Travel and study
- Mentoring grants
- Emerging artist grants
- Distinguished artist grants
- Arts collaboration grants
- Productions grants to finish a work or collection in any discipline, pre- and postproduction for film and media projects
- Peer learning grants for artist who also work in nonprofits.

One funding area that is strong right now in light of the sluggish economy is small business "stimulus" grants. These range from "business story" competitions like the one sponsored by software giant Intuit, to the small business grant program from the National Association of the Self Employed (NASE). Search the Web for these opportunities and check out the Resource section of this book for further information.

❑ ***Angel Investors:*** High-net-worth individuals are like friends, family and a very liberal bank rolled into one. But a small-business owner is usually referred to these people; angels are not on public lists. In most cases, they are professionals such as attorneys, accountants and doctors, with money to invest. Successful entrepreneurs, especially retired ones, are especially likely to become angels.

Although the figures vary widely, angels are believed to provide billions of dollars in capital to entrepreneurs every year. Based on demographics, studies characterize angels as follows: wealthy, usually self-made as opposed to being rich through inheritance, usually in their fifties and sixties, and almost never below forty. They prefer to invest in companies

they are familiar with or have a personal affinity for. They usually seek out small and growing companies in their own industry.

How do you find an Angel for your business?

• The first place to look is among your own *business associates*. You have a greater chance of securing financing from people who know you. Then ask your business associates to ask their acquaintances. However, the farther the relationship is from you personally, the lesser the chances of securing the investment unless they have a unique understanding of your business.

• *Network, network and network.* Join a professional organization or trade group for your industry. Begin attending meetings on a regular basis. This is the best way to get acquainted with successful business owners in your field or related fields.

• Stay local. You don't need to go beyond your geographic area to find investors willing to take their chances with your venture. Be sure to join and participate in your local Chamber of Commerce.

• Discreetly inquire about people who appear to be the most *successful members of your industry.* Pitch the idea to your lawyer or accountant - they may be interested or know someone who could be interested. They may have clients who frequently invest in a new and growing businesses.

• *Research the Internet*. Being an "angel" investor has become more popular over the years, and there are now organizations or groups of angel investors. As a last resort, some online resources provide listings of angel investors per geographical location, while others provide focused advice on getting investors for your particular small business category. Check out the following sites:

- ❒ Angel Capital Association: http://www.angelcapitalassociation.org/directory
- ❒ Angel Investor Directory: http://www.secondventure.com/angel-investor-directory.asp
- ❒ Boogar: http://www.boogar.com/resources/venturecapital/angels.htm
- ❒ Zelnick Media: http://www.zelnickmedia.com

The rule, however, is always to raise money at the *right time.* Convincing angels (or anyone else) to part with their cash to support your venture takes a lot of time and diligence. Be sure to dedicate enough time and budget in your search for financing.

Once you find a prospect, send a letter requesting a short meeting to discuss the proposal. An even more effective approach is to be personally introduced to the angel investor by a common friend. People are more inclined to be receptive to offers from other people if the request comes from people whom they trust.

In the event that the prospective angel shows interest in your business idea, make sure that you have prepared a well-researched and detailed business plan. Your plan should emphasize why you need additional financing and exactly what you plan to do with the money. Write an executive summary for the plan that spells out in one page why someone should invest money in your business. Explain too, how you can repay the money and when. Better yet, have presentation materials ready based on your business plan in order to have a more effective discussion with your prospective investor. You want to appear relaxed, confident and as knowledgeable as possible.

If the investor is interested, bring in your lawyer and accountant to the negotiations. Informal investors usually invest from $10,000 to $100,000 in each venture. While angels may be able to invest considerable money in your venture without requiring the kind of documentation that other investors do, be sure to put your arrangement in writing to reduce any misunderstandings. Angels may prefer to make straight loans at rates comparable to banks or at a slightly higher rate. They generally expect to lend their money from three to seven years, with some requiring guaranteed exit provisions such as a mandatory buy-out. Others may want to be repaid in stock if your company eventually goes public. Be sure to tailor the financial arrangements to fit your angel's needs.

Angels can also provide you, not just with money, but guidance, advice and a mentor relationship. Also called "advisory investors," they are generally not interested in controlling the business, but may require you to meet certain business goals or follow certain business practices. If possible, encourage your angel to become a member of your advisory board (more on this in chapter 11, "Pulling Together Your Team").

Many angels like to keep a close eye on their money, plus they can offer you valuable advice. If your angel is well connected in the local business community, he or she may help you find additional investors, introduce you to a banker or an attorney, or bring in new customers. An angel may also help you gain membership in a club or professional society that will benefit your business. Remember that every relationship is different. The key to success is doing everything you can to increase your angel's comfort level so the person's investment and relationship with you and your business will be longstanding and profitable.

Venture-Backed Capital & Investor Formation

Typically, financing is necessary because the entrepreneur's vision is greater than his or her wallet. Thus, most entrepreneurs need others to buy into their vision in order for that vision to become a reality.

Why is raising money for a new venture so difficult? The answer lies in what entrepreneurs are asking investors to do. Entrepreneurs identify uncertain new venture opportunities based on research that other people either do not have or do not recognize. As a result, investors must make decisions about funding new businesses of very uncertain value with less information than the entrepreneur has. This can often be complicated by the fact that entrepreneurs are reluctant to share all the information they've discovered with the investor for fear of the business idea being "borrowed" and used elsewhere (This is where a signed & dated *Confidentiality Agreement* comes in handy).

As you search for money, you probably will hear the term "venture capitalist" (VC) quite often, but those who use the term may be referring to different entities. True venture capital firms are among the most sophisticated investors available, typically providing an entrepreneur with more than money. Their knowledge, experience, and connections may prove to be as important to your company as the dollars they bring. They differ from angel investors in that, rather than investing their own money, venture capital funds are corporate entities that pool money from a range of institutional and individual investors.

Whether you're looking for a small, short-term loan or actively pitching venture capitalists, strong preparation and planning can improve your chances of finding funding. You need to put your small business in the best possible financial light to make a good impression on prospective sources. Take time up front to get yourself ready for this process.
Venture capitalists and other financiers tend to back companies with the following features: they are in attractive industries that are large and growing, produce products or services for which customers have a high need, have high operating margins, and appeal to markets that are not (yet) crowded.

While music properties are seen as "high risk", there are several venture companies who focus on the music sector including, DN Capital, Benchmark Capital, Ventech, and Power Amp Music. See the Resource section for more relevant investor groups.

If you're seeking to launch a company with funding needs in excess of $200,000, then you will have to look to the investor community for support. The following section applies to formal capital investment for your company, whether angel financing or venture capital. When preparing for investor formation, it is a good idea to consult with a SCORE business counselor or other small business consultant to ensure your documentation and presentation are optimally prepared.

WHY ENTREPRENEURS SEEK VENTURE CAPITAL

TYPE OF ADVANTAGE	REASONING
Capital	Venture capital is a major source of high-risk capital for new ventures.
Credibility	The prestige of venture capital backing makes it easier for entrepreneurs to persuade customers, employees, and suppliers of the value of their new businesses.
Connections to investment bankers	The high volume of venture capital backed initial public offerings means that venture capitalists have close ties to investment bankers, facilitating going public.
Connections to suppliers and customers	Venture capitalists often link the companies that they finance together as suppliers and customers of each other.
Assistance in recruiting the management team	Venture capitalists have strong ties to executive search firms and can help entrepreneurs attract CEOs and other senior management talent.
Operating assistance	Many venture capitalists were former entrepreneurs and have significant experience building new companies.

Improving Your Chances of Being Funded

Here are 9 things you can do *before* you seek financing to help your chances of getting that needed investment. They are:

- ❑ Get your business plan in shape
- ❑ Put your paperwork in order
- ❑ Be prepared to show how you'll use the money
- ❑ Examine your ratios
- ❑ Check your credit
- ❑ Incorporate your business
- ❑ Practice
- ❑ Make your applications impeccable
- ❑ Be patient

Let's look at each in turn.

1. *Get your business plan in shape.* Review the latest version of your business plan to make sure it tells the story of your company accurately and effectively. Is it easy for a potential investor to get a handle on your company by skimming the plan? How effectively have you demonstrated that you understand how to market your music product or service and can turn a buck doing so? How strong is your executive summary? Do your financials show when and how you will obtain long-term profitability? How honest have you been in your assessments of the market and your competition? Do you have third-party corroboration to back up the key assumptions you're making in your plan?

2. *Put your paperwork in order.* A standard loan or investment application requires specific documents and numbers. You should take some time before going through the loan process to get this information in order. It's always a good idea to schedule a

meeting with your accountant or other financial advisor to do this.
Among the documents you'll need are:

- ❒ Accountant-prepared business financial statements (profit & loss, balance sheet) for the past three fiscal years (if available);
- ❒ Business federal tax returns for the past three years (if available);
- ❒ Most recent federal tax returns for each principal owner;
- ❒ Personal financial statements for each principal owner;
- ❒ Organizational papers, such as articles of incorporation, DBA papers, business licenses, etc.;
- ❒ Lists of business and personal assets that could be used as collateral;
- ❒ Names and contact information for at least three credit references.

3. *Be prepared to show how you'll use the money.* In addition to the previously listed documents, you may want to include a *pro forma* that includes projected financial statements for the next 5 years. You can use your 3-year projection from your business plan and expand it two additional years. In your pro forma, give a clear description of how you'll use the proceeds and how you intend to pay the money back. Be specific. Show how you'll use the money to open up new markets, introduce new products & services, or other business developments that will positively impact your bottom line.

Vague terms like "need working capital" won't work because these words don't give lenders and investors the confidence that their money will be well spent. Try to tailor these presentations to the needs of the funding source. If you're looking for debt financing, you'll want to emphasize your ability to repay the loan. On the other hand, equity investors will want to see the potential for a strong rate of return on that portion of the company they will be receiving in exchange for their investment.

4. *Examine your ratios.* You might be tempted to provide overly optimistic projections (the "hockey stick" sales curve) in your pro forma financial statements, but that would be a big mistake. Bankers want to see business projections that are in line with industry averages, which they get from the operating ratios published in the *Annual Statement Studies* from Risk Management Associates. See the Risk Management web site for further information, particularly its "Knowledge & Training Center": www.rmahq.org Those that differ markedly raise an automatic red flag, and immediately put your loan application in jeopardy.

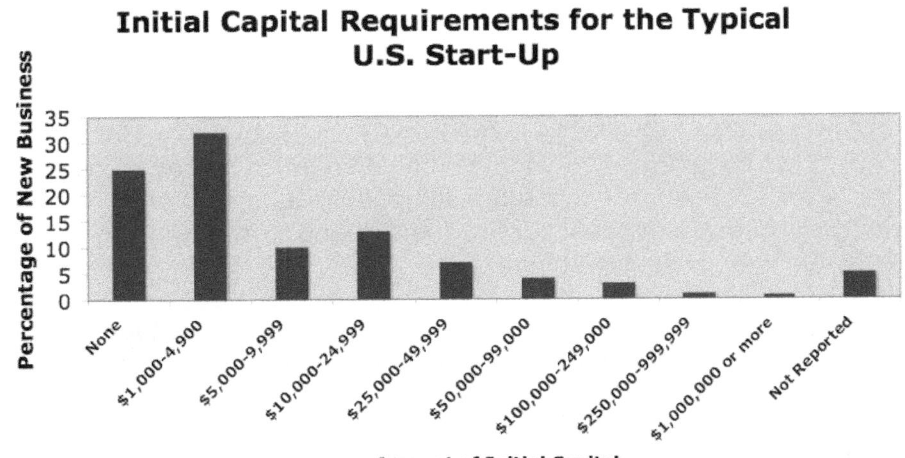

Source: Adapted from "Characteristics of Business Owners," U.S. Department of Commerce, Bureau of the Census,
Washington, DC: SSGPO, CB087-1, Table 15C, p. 10.

5. Check your credit. As mentioned, most banks now use "credit scoring" to determine whether you qualify for a loan or not. Investors will do the same. Commonly used for consumer loans, credit scoring uses factors such as credit history to determine whether or not you're a good risk. Be sure to contact the major credit bureaus – TRW/Experian, CBI Equifax, and Trans Union – to get a copy of your credit reports to ensure their accuracy and correct any possible mistakes before you start looking for capital.

6. *Incorporate.* You don't *have to* be incorporated to get financing, but it can help (see chapter 6 for more on incorporating). Even though other structures are equally appropriate for many businesses, there is a certain cachet to corporate status for lenders and investors. They will likely feel more confident about your business. Incorporation will also make it easier for outside investors to acquire equity in your business in return for their money (via stock options, etc.).

7. *Practice.* Many small business owners find it useful to conduct a mock interview before speaking with financing sources. This lets them prepare strong, effective answers for any possible questions that might come their way.
Remember, you only have one shot at a potential investor, so you need to get it right the first time. Don't make these practice sessions casual. Get help from your accountant, a peer who has recently sought financing, or a banker acquaintance. Your SCORE advisor may be a good stand-in here. Make sure they ask questions as tough as those you'll get from the funding source.

8. *Make your applications impeccable.* Your financials are probably the most important criteria for helping you get financing, but neatness counts too. Don't forget about the little things that will help you impress money sources and reinforce your image of professionalism. Make forms neat and easy to read because sloppy reports will do nothing but work against you. Dress in appropriate, conservative business attire for meetings. Do everything possible to demonstrate trustworthiness and show that you are highly capable.

9. *Stay patient.* Finding financing, no matter what stage your business is at, is a time-consuming and exhausting process. Many small business owners vastly underestimate the time it will take them to find the money they need, and it's not uncommon for businesses to run out of cash during the process. Be sure you factor in time for all the tasks

you'll need execute – from refining your business plan to weeding through lists of banks, lending institutions, or outside investors.

"Staging" the Investment

New ventures typically raise money from investors in a series of *stages,* rather than all at once. That is, investors provide a small amount of money to create an *option* – a right, but not an obligation – to make additional investments later. Why? For two main reasons: to minimize their exposure to the risk and to see how the entrepreneur manages the money for the business in the interim.

The chart on the following page illustrates the several stages or "tiers" of capital investment. Each stage has different sources of financing, different uses of capital, and different expected rates of return.

"The Elevator Pitch". When considering a prospective investment, venture capitalists and other investors often want to hear what they call the "elevator pitch." An elevator pitch is a brief summary of your business or a short story that you can tell in the course of a elevator ride (and not an elevator in a skyscraper! – think 6 floors tops). It's an exercise in condensing value and content in a message. Here are some famous elevator pitches:

"Ning lets you create your own social network for anything. For free. In 2 minutes."
– Marc Andreessen, founder of Netscape and Ning

"To empower musicians to build effective websites for their music." – Chris Vinson, Bandzoogle

"Lion's Bridge Recording is a conduit, facilitator, enabler, and champion of creativity."
– Rick Pontalion, owner

Your elevator pitch doesn't have to be made in an actual elevator to be useful. You'll find you'll use it often: in emails to prospective financing sources, to introduce yourself and your company at networking events, to describe your business to potential customers. It's a succinct, distillation of your company's core mission.

"STAGES" OF FINANCING

STAGE	CONDITION OF THE VENTURE	SOURCES OF CAPITAL	USES OF CAPITAL	COST OF CAPITAL
Pre-seed stage	The entrepreneur has an idea, but has not yet formed a company or written a business plan	Entrepreneur Friends and family Business angels Corporation	Write a business plan. Form a company.	70-100% rate of return
Seed stage	The entrepreneur has formed a legal entity, has a partial venture team, and has written a business plan.	Entrepreneur Friends and family Business angels Venture capitalists Corporations	Develop a prototype of the product. Fill out the venture team. Conduct market research.	60-80% rate of return
First stage	The entrepreneur has organized the company, and the product development and initial market research are complete.	Entrepreneur Friends and family Business angels Venture capitalists Corporations	Make initial sales. Establish production. Buy fixed assets.	40-60% rate of return
Second stage	The entrepreneur has produced and sold initial versions of the product and the organization is "up and running."	Business angels Venture capitalists Asset-based financiers Corporations	Scale up production. Hire additional people for sales and for production	20-40% rate of return

If you are raising money for your company, you can increase the chances of raising the capital you need through preparation, research, and cultivating contacts. Research your recipients and tailor the presentation of your plan to the recipient's interests and concerns, whether that person is a relative, friend, banker or investor.

This is where a good business plan comes in. Your plan needs to communicate the message of your business - why the need is there, how you are going to solve it, why you are going to make money, and so on - in a clear and compelling way.

Choose your potential funding sources wisely; remember that your funding source will become an ongoing participant in your business. And be realistic. You must always give something in return for the money you receive.

CHAPTER SUMMARY

RAISING CAPITAL & GATHERING RESOURCES

- **Do-It-Yourself Financing**
  Self-financing is the number-one form of financing used by most business startups. In addition, when you approach other financing sources such as banks, angel investors or the government, they will want to know exactly how much of your own money you are putting into the venture. Begin by doing a thorough inventory of your assets. You are likely to uncover resources you didn't even know you had. Assets include savings accounts, equity in real estate, retirement accounts, vehicles, recreation equipment and collections. You may decide to sell some assets for cash or to use them as "collateral" for a loan.

- **Tapping Other Sources of Capital**
  When businesses grow faster than the capital they generate, they often turn to external sources for financing. These sources may include family and friends, bank loans, state-sponsored micro-loan programs, venture-backed capital, and angel investors. Before looking for outside financing, the savvy business owner will tighten up cash flow and narrow cash gaps. So the first thing to do is assess ways you can make your company look more financially attractive.

- **Venture-Backed Capital & Investor Formation**
  Whether you're looking for a small, short-term loan or actively pitching venture capitalists, strong preparation and planning can improve your chances of finding funding. You need to put your small business in the best possible financial light to make a good impression on prospective sources. Venture capitalists and other financiers tend to back companies with the following features: they are in attractive industries that are large and growing, produce products or services for which customers have a high need, have high operating margins, and appeal to markets that are not (yet) crowded.

- **Improving Your Chances of Being Funded**
  9 things you can do before you seek financing to help your chances of getting that needed investment: Get your business plan in shape, Put your paperwork in order, Be prepared to show how you'll use the money, Examine your ratios, Check your credit, Incorporate your business, Practice, Make your applications impeccable, and Be patient.

- **Staging the Investment**
  New ventures typically raise money from investors in a series of "stages," rather than all at once. Investors provide a small amount of money to create an option - a right, but not an obligation - to make additional investments later. Why? Two main reasons: to minimize their exposure to the risk, and to see how the entrepreneur manages the money for the business in the interim.

FURTHER RESOURCES

ONLINE RESOURCES

Enterprise Zones
www.usa.gov
Areas where incentives can be provided if you set up a business or hire employees, these can be found by contacting your state or local government offices.

Independent Community Bankers of America
www.icba.org

Internal Revenue Service (IRS)
www.irs.gov
Whether you were raised to pay your taxes up front or avoid them at any cost, the IRS website is a must (and an ideal starting place in your research). Get current and previous year tax forms, publications that specifically address business issues, and more. Be sure to check out the special page for small/ home-based businesses and self-employed individuals.

Small Business Investor Alliance
sbia.org/

Small Business Administration (SBA)
sba.gov
For possible funding sources beyond your local bank, check with your local Small Business Administration office (or go online).

• Grants

Arts Grants Opportunities:
earts.org

Creative Capital:
creative-capital.org

National Endowment for the Arts:
arts.gov

National Endowment for the Humanities
neh.gov

New York Foundation for the Arts:
nyfa.org

• Crowdfunding

Artistshare.org
CASHmusic.org
Crowdfunding.com
Fundable.com
GoFundMe
Kickstarter.com

BOOKS

Angel Financing for Entrepreneurs: Early-Stage Funding for Long-Term Success by Susan Preston (2007, Jossey-Bass).

Finding an Angel Investor in a Day: Get It Done Right, Get It Done Fast! By Joseph R. Bell (2007, The Planning Shop).

Investors in Your Backyard: How to Raise Business Capital from the People You Know by Asheesh Avani (2006, Nolo Press).

Persuasive Business Proposals: Writing to Win More Customers, Clients, and Contracts by Tom Sant (2012, AMACOM).

Where to Go When the Bank Says No: Alternatives For Financing Your Business by Steven Replin (2011, Barbers Chair Press).

• Grants Directories & Books on Grant Writing/Sponsorships

The Annual Register of Grant Support (annual, Information Today). Check your local library.

The Grants Register (annual, Palgrave Macmillan). Check your local library.

Grant Writing for Dummies by Bev Browning (2014, Hungry Minds, Inc.).

How to Get Sponsorships and Endorsements: Get Funding for Bands, Non-Profits, and more! by Simon S Tam (2012, Simon Tam).

Made Possible By: Succeeding With Sponsorship by Patricia Martin (2003, Jossey-Bass).

The Only Grant-Writing Book You'll Ever Need: Top Grant Writers and Grant Givers Share Their Secrets by Ellen Karsh and Arlen Sue Fox (2009, Basic Books).

The Sponsorship Seeker's Toolkit by Anne-Marie Grey et. al.(2014, McGraw-Hill Book Company).

LICENSES, PERMITS, & TAXES, OH MY!

The Lord's Prayer contains 56 words. Lincoln's Gettysburg Address has 268 words. The Declaration of Independence is 1,322 words long. Federal regulations governing the sale of cabbages are 26,911 words long.

– Bernard Kamoroff, *Small Time Operator*

All businesses must deal with various levels of legal paperwork. Some require more paperwork than others. For example, a solo eBay retailer can probably get by with just a simple DBA (doing business as) license. A record label with two employees, on the other hand, must deal with all the basic licenses, permits, insurance and tax regulations required of all businesses with employees, *plus* a rack of additional specialized documents like artist contracts, copyright forms, licensing agreements, distributor one-sheets and more. And let's not forget about trademark registration, annual corporate reports, marketing plans, and the occasional joint-venture proposal!

It takes a good deal of persistence and resolve to stay on top of all this paperwork. It's easy to ignore the need for licenses and permits, especially when you're embroiled in all the excitement of starting a new business. But failing to do so – and do it right from the beginning – is one of the most common (and costly) mistakes entrepreneurs make. Yes, it's a red tape jungle. But think of it as an obstacle course set up to test the intensity of your desire and your willingness to go the extra mile to make your company happen.
In this chapter we'll look at what paperwork you will need to launch and grow your business and where to get it. In chapter 13 we'll tackle ways to organize and manage all your paperwork and information successfully. It's a good idea to work through your company's paperwork requirements with your small business advisor or SCORE counselor (see chapter 4 for more info about SCORE and other sources of free small biz advice).
We'll start with the basic licenses you will need to set up your company.

Securing the Required Paperwork

Basic Business Licenses

❑ **Fictitious Name (DBA)**. When a business goes by any name other than the owner's real name, the business is being operated under a 'fictitious name' or D.B.A. (Doing Business As). "Mack's Music", "Sound Mirror Mastering" and "Geffen Records" are all examples of fictitious names.

In some cases this license may be required by your bank for you to open business checking/savings accounts.

How to Obtain: Call the licensing bureau of the city you plan to operate and find out their licensing requirements and application procedure. Some states require you to place an ad in the local newspaper for a certain amount of time, announcing the opening of your business. Expect to pay anywhere between $50-100.

❑ **General Business License**. Contact your city's business license department to find out about getting a general business license, which grants you the right (after paying a fee, of course) to operate in that city. When you file your license application, the city planning or zoning department will check to make sure your area is zoned for the purpose you want to use it for and that there is enough parking spaces to meet the codes. We'll look more closely at zoning issues in a moment.

❑ **Seller's Permit or Resale Certificate.** A Seller's Permit may exempt you as a business from paying sales tax to your vendors (i.e., suppliers, printer, CD duplicator, photographer, etc.) since you are considered a wholesaler. To get this exemption (only on business purchases) you need to be authorized to do so from your state. You'll need to apply for a State Sales Tax Vendor ID/Certificate of Authority with your state department of taxation and you'll be given a sales tax vendor ID number which identifies you as a manufacturer/wholesaler.

The point to remember is that your business is exempt from paying sales tax on *resale* items – elements that are part of the raw materials in your product for sale. But the tax is not eliminated, just *deferred*. You will need to submit the sales tax you do collect to your state department of revenue each year.

This certificate authorizes you also to collect sales tax on retail sales, that is, sales directly to the public. As a small business, you will probably only have to file this once per year. Keep good records!

If you operate a service-based business (like a music licensing company, music instruction service, or booking agency), your activities may or may not be subject to sales tax, depending on your state regulations, and so this permit will not be necessary.

❑ **Other possible licenses & permits**. Always check with your local town or city hall for other licensing requirements. Depending on your business, other requirements may include:

- *Liquor, Wine & Beer License* – Allows you to sell alcohol products.
- *Health Department Permit* – If you plan to sell food, either directly to customers or as a wholesaler to other retailers, you will need a county health department permit.
- *Fire Department Permit*- If your business uses flammable materials or if your business will house large numbers of the public, you may need this.
- *Air & Water Pollution Control Permit*- If you burn or discharge anything into the sewers or use gas-producing products (e.g., paint-sprayers), this will be required.
- *Agent License* – This is required in some states for representing artists as an agent and/or personal manager.
- *Noise Permit* – If you use amplified sound you'll usually run into "residential noise limits" requiring a certain time restriction and decibel limit.
- *Sign Permit* – Some cities and suburbs have sign ordinances that restrict the size, location and sometimes the lighting and type of sign you can use outside your business.

A note on federal licenses. In most cases you won't have to worry about federal licenses. However, a few types of businesses do require federal licensing, including meat processors, radio and TV stations, and investment advisory services.

Getting Around the Red Tape

I suggest you contact your local government before you open your doors. If you do not get the proper permits or the local building codes, the city or county can shut you down or bring you uninvited aggravation. Speak also with a SCORE advisor who lives in the area in which you're setting up shop. He or she will know the best ways to navigate the legal requirements for your business in that locale.

Many cities, particularly smaller ones in economically challenged areas, are eager to help new businesses locate in their jurisdiction, especially businesses that may have minor zoning or building code problems.

Some cities even have a "grant fund" - free money - to help fund local start-ups. Ask at city hall if they have any kind of economic development program or assistance available. These programs are related to the "micro-loan" options mentioned in the last chapter on raising capital.

As long as your situation is routine, there will not likely be any issues that hold up permits or licenses for your operation. However, if your circumstances are subject to some agency or governmental ruling that could delay or alter your plans, you should be prepared to deal with the situation in order to overcome any obstacles and allow enough time for all these matters to be settled.

Working Within the Zoning Laws

Zoning has to do with the way the governments control the physical development of land and the kinds of uses to which each individual property may be put. Zoning laws typically specify the areas in which residential, industrial, recreational, agricultural or commercial activities may take place.

When it comes to zoning, be in the Know. Before you sign a lease, check with the local zoning department to make sure the building is zoned for your use. Find out about any special requirements, such as off-street parking or sign limitations. Don't rely on the landlord for this information. Just because a similar business previously occupied the same building without zoning problems, it is no guarantee you'll have no problems. The old business may have been there before current zoning laws were in effect (called "grandfathering") or maybe they had a special arrangement or variance that may or may not be transferred to you.

While many communities have modernized their zoning ordinances, some states still have zoning laws against home-based businesses. Many date back to the early 1900s and were designed to protect against "sweat shop" conditions for work-at-home textile employees. In recent years, larger recording studios in metropolitan areas have taken to reporting home project studios in residential areas to local zoning boards. If you operate a music production business out of your residence, and there are zoning restrictions in your state against home-based businesses you could get fined (and even shut down).

It's important to find out what *is* and *is not* allowed in your community regarding home-based businesses. A call to your municipal clerk's office will get you started. After that, a big part of staying out of trouble with zoning problems is *common sense* and *common courtesy*. Here are some guidelines:

1. *Be a good neighbor.* Keep your business out of sight and it will be out of mind.

2. *Be sensitive to the traffic you create.*
3. *Keep parking accessible for neighbors.* If you have employees or operate a business that requires customers to visit your home, make sure that you plan for adequate parking.
4. *Consider obtaining a P.O. Box for your business mail.* Or you may consider using one of the numerous mail service centers that have sprung up around the country – they offer mailbox rentals, shipping, photocopying, faxing, and other support services for small businesses.
5. Other considerations:
   - ❒ Building Codes: Does your business meet all health, safety and environmental regulations? If you are operating a recording studio, what about sound insulation, etc.?
   - ❒ Conversion: Permission is required to convert buildings of historical or architectural importance, so check with local authorities before undertaking any construction projects.

Checklist of Business Regulations, Permits & Licenses

Getting licenses and permits is about as much fun as visiting the dentist. Although you can wade through various bureaucracies to find out what burdens you face, you would do well to seek competent advice from a lawyer and accountant to insure that everything pertaining to your specific operation is nailed down.

Depending upon the size and nature of your business, some of the following licenses, permits, and compliances may be required. Put a check next to the ones you think may pertain to your business and be sure to figure their cost into your startup budget:

- ❒ Articles of incorporation filed with the state (only corporations)
- ❒ Annual corporate reports filed with the state (only corporations)
- ❒ Registration as a foreign corporation if your company is based in a state other than the one in which it's incorporated (only corporations)
- ❒ Securities and Exchange Commission (SEC) regulations and registration (mainly corporations; if you're seeking equity investors or selling limited partnerships; there are also varying laws among states dealing with sales of stock and partnerships)
- ❒ State sales permit (if you sell retail, you'll have to collect sales tax on behalf of the state; this might also apply to your city)
- ❒ State resale tax exemption certificate (so you won't have to pay sales tax if you purchase from vendors as a wholesaler; deferred until tax time)
- ❒ Property tax assessment filing (all businesses with real estate; usually with your county)
- ❒ Local business license (all businesses; usually with your city)
- ❒ Fictitious name registration (all businesses; usually with your state)
- ❒ Employer identification number (optional; IRS form SS-4)
- ❒ Trademark registration (usually with your state, but also federal)
- ❒ Workers' compensation (only businesses with employees; usually with your state)
- ❒ Employee withholding allowance certificate (only businesses with employees; IRS form W-4)
- ❒ Employee withholding exemption certificate (only businesses with employees; IRS form W-4E)
- ❒ Withholdings of income and social security taxes from employees must be deposited with the IRS either semi-monthly, monthly, or quarterly (only businesses with employees; obtain form 501 from the IRS)
- ❒ Quarterly filings of IRS form 941 detailing employee withholdings (only businesses with employees;)
- ❒ IRS form W2 supplied to each employee by January 31 stating amount of wages paid

and taxes withheld during the preceding calendar year (only businesses with employees;)

- City and state withholding forms (similar to W2) supplied to employees if applicable
- State and federal unemployment taxes and disability insurance be required as withholdings; also IRS form 1099 detailing payments to independent contractors (must be filed with the IRS by February 28 for work done during the preceding calendar year)
- Various state and federal laws concerning hours and conditions of work, minimum wage, health and safety standards, discriminatory hiring practices, etc., if applicable.

Sony Ericsson Patents Theme Music Technology to Match Your Mood

Here's some pretty future tech for you. Sony Ericsson has filed a patent for phone technology that will recognize your facial expressions and automatically select music for you according to your mood.

Your handset will use the front facing camera to capture your image and, although there may be some initial calibration involved, the system will then pick the next track from your collection that best suits your mood.

If it works, there could be some alarming revelations about your neutral expression. I'd like to think my general demeanor would sound like the poppier end of The Who's catalogue but I guess I'll have to wait and see what Sony Ericsson thinks.

Intellectual Property Assets

Ideas may be your greatest asset. When you begin to transfer them into names, inventions, product designs, logos, music, writings or other forms, they become intellectual property. Just as you would protect your *physical* property against theft and damage, so you should protect your *intellectual* property from the same. In this age of digital copying and rampant piracy, it's important to understand what intellectual property is and how to best protect it.

There are three types of intellectual property protection: patent, trademark and copyright. They serve different purposes and shouldn't be confused with one another. A *patent* is granted to the inventor of a new or useful idea. It's a grant of property rights that excludes others from making, using or selling the same invention, and it expires after a number of years, depending on the type of invention patented. A *trademark* protects the distinguishing identity of goods and services. A word, name , symbol , phrase or slogan, or a combination of these items, can be trademarked. A *copyright* protects original works of authorship such as literary, musical, dramatic, pictorial, graphic or architectural works, motion pictures and sound recordings. It protects the form of expression, preventing others from lifting from your idea and reworking it for their use and requires them to obtain your permission to reproduce any part of it.

We'll look at each one in turn.

- **Patents.** A patent allows the inventor the exclusive rights to make, use, and sell an invention throughout his country during the term of the patent. Any other party that makes, sells, or uses the patent invention during the term of the patent – without consent of the patent holder – is ***infringing*** on the patent.

There are three forms of patents: design, utility, and plant.

• **Design patents** are granted for any new, original, and ornamental design for an article of manufacturing. Design patents cover the aesthetic appearance of an invention such as the appearance of a fax machine or a lamp. Design patents have a term of 17 years in the United States. Some people believe that design patents are the weakest form of patent because a competitor can avoid infringing on your patent by changing the design only slightly.

• **Utility patents** cover the functional features of an invention and are granted for any new and useful process, machine, manufacture, or composition of matter, or for any new and useful improvement. For example, the switching mechanism in an effects pedal or the electronics in a microphone could fit this category. A utility patent lasts 14 years.

• The third type of patent, a **plant patent**, protects a new form of greenery or plant.

• Recently, the courts have allowed inventors to patent ***"business methods,"*** such as Amazon.com's "One Click" system, which permits repeat purchasers to make purchases without reentering information about themselves. The patent was granted in 1999, reexamined in 2006, and modified in 2007. However, Amazon's "one click" method was denied patent protection in Europe.

We often think of patents in relation to inventions. But patents are granted for a wide range of creations including the "look" of a product. CD-only label Rykodisc distinguished itself early on by patenting its own green-tinted CD jewel box. This not only resulted in greater visibility in retail racks, but it also provided a small but sure additional revenue stream for the company through licensing the use of these jewel cases to others.

Patent Facts

- The authority of a patent is limited to the country in which you have applied for that patent.
- Most U.S. patents have a life span of no more than 20 years. Patents cannot be renewed.
- To be awarded a patent, an invention must be considered novel and "non obvious".
- A basic patent application fee can be several hundred dollars, depending upon the size of your business. It's a complex process and you'd do well to hire a patent attorney.

Applying for a Patent. In order to obtain a patent, you must file an application with the U.S. Patent and Trademark Office (USPTO) where examiners determine the originality of your invention and request through a series of steps. To patent something may take anywhere from one and three years, and can easily cost between $10,000 and $20,000 depending on the size of your business and the number of claims in the patent application. You must apply for a patent within one year of the time a product is first offered for sale or disclosed publicly.

The protection you'll get from your patent is effective only when a patent is granted, not during the "patent-pending" period. Also, a patent only protects you in the United States. A U.S. patent will not stop someone in another country from manufacturing and selling your product outside the United States. If you want to protect yourself in other countries, you need a patent in each one.

For patent information, and applications visit **The U.S. Patent and Trademark Office** web site at: **http://www.uspto.gov.** Google Patent Search can be a goldmine for historical trivia on patents. There you'll find everything from a music string with different vibration behaviors to a toy that illuminates itself with music, and more.

❑ **Trademarks.** Unlike patents and copyrights, trademarks affect *all* businesses. When you use the name of your business publicly, you are using it as a trademark. When you sell products using a brand name, you are using that brand name as a trademark. If you are providing a service, the brand name for that service is a *servicemark* or, essentially, a trademark for services. A trademark or service mark may consist of letters, words, graphics, or any combination of these elements. A trademark *distinguishes* the goods and services of one company from those of another.

For the sake of convenience I will use the words "trademark" and "servicemark" interchangeably.

Both the federal government, through the United Stated Patent and Trademark Office (USPTO), and states have the power to grant trademarks and servicemarks. Federal law requires marks to be used in interstate commerce (i.e., doing verifiable business between two or more states), while state registrations can be used to protect a regional mark from competitive use. The ® symbol means the USPTO has reviewed and registered the mark. A "TM" or "SM" symbol, on the other hand, indicates that the word, phrase or design is being used and claimed as a trademark or servicemark, but is not yet federally registered. Many states, including Colorado, do not have any review process associated with the registration of marks.

Next to you, *your company name* is your #1 asset so it's crucial to select it carefully and protect it relentlessly. You automatically have some protection for your trademark if you were the first person to use that trademark in commerce, even if you did not formerly register your trademark with the USPTO. For example, when PBS television launched the series "Nova," the show's producers failed to register the trademark with the USPTO. Several years later a gentleman started a science fiction magazine called NOVA and proceeded to register the name with Washington. He was granted the mark and then sued PBS for trademark infringement.

He lost. Even though he had the formal trademark, PBS had been *using* it for several years on a national and international basis. *Use* superseded *formal registration* and the magazine owner had to relinquish the mark.

Notwithstanding, it is usually easier to prove an infringement case and collect damages, if the mark has been formally registered.

A Note on Protecting Artist/Band/Names

To make sure artist and band names are free to use before signing any contracts, you should search some of the online artist and band directories, like the Ultimate *Band List* (www.ubl.com) and the *All-Music Guide* (http://www.allmusic.com).

An entrepreneur may lose the exclusive right to a trademark if it loses its unique character and becomes a generic name. *Aspirin*, *escalator*, *thermos*, *brassiere*, *super glue*, *yo-yo*, and *cellophane* all were once enforceable trademarks that have become common words in the English language. These generic terms can no longer be licensed as trademarks.

Trademarks are granted for 20 years and may be renewed indefinitely if a firm continues to protect its brand name. If a company allows the name to lapse into common usage, it may lose protection. Common usage takes effect if a company seeks no action against those who fail to acknowledge its trademark. Recently, for example, the popular brand-name sailboard Windsurfer lost its trademark. Like trampoline, yo-yo, and thermos, *windsurfer* has become the common term for the product and can now be used by any sailboard company.
By the way, some marks are ineligible for federal registration. The USPTO won't register any marks that contain:

- Names of living persons without their consent
- The U.S. flag
- Other federal and local governmental insignias
- The name or likeness of a deceased U.S. President without his widow's consent
- Words or symbols that disparage living or deceased persons, institutions, beliefs or national symbols, or

- Marks that are judged immoral, deceptive or scandalous.

Do-it-Yourself Trademark Search. You came up with a business name back in chapter 6 when setting out to draft your business plan. Now you need to know if the trademark you've chosen is available. You can do your own trademark search for free on the Internet by visiting the U.S. Patent and Trademark Office's Website at http://www.uspto.gov. Or you can visit one of the Patent and Trademark Depository Libraries, available in every state. These libraries offer a combination of hardcover directories of federally registered marks and an online database of both registered marks and marks for which a registration application is pending. Most of these libraries also have step-by-step instructions for searching registered and pending marks.

In addition to searching for registered or pending marks, you can employ less formal methods of searching. For example, you may also use product guides and other materials available in these libraries to search for possibly conflicting marks that haven't been registered. This can be important because an existing mark, even if it's unregistered, would preclude you from:

- Registering the same or confusingly similar mark in your own name, and
- Using the mark in any part of the country or commercial transaction where customers might be confused.

To find the Patent and Trademark Depository Library nearest you, see PTO's list at http://www.uspto.gov/go/ptdl/.

Use the Web: The Web is a ready-made source of business names. Any of the top search engines (e.g., google.com) will let you type in the name and search for it on all the indexed web pages of that engine. Because no search engine is 100% complete, a thorough search will necessarily include several additional search engines.

Another helpful place to search for unregistered trademarks is The Thomas Register of Goods and Services, at thomasregister.com. You have to sign up as a member (free) before it will let you search.

A good place to find **domain names** being used by Web-based businesses is the dotcom directory at http://www.dotcomdirectory.com/nsi/basic.hm. Simply describe the type of product or service you're looking for. The site then returns a list of websites that provide it. It's a worthwhile resource.

In addition, it is wise to scan some of the top offline music industry directories, like the *various directories published by the Music Business Registry (musicregistry.com)* and the many annual *Billboard* directories. Look for the same or similar names under a variety of categories.

Formal Trademark Registration. *Again, rights to a business name come through use, not a formal registration with the USPTO in D.C. But registering with the USPTO can have several benefits. It:*

- Provides notice to everyone that you have exclusive rights to use the mark;
- Entitles holder of mark to sue in federal court for infringement;
- Establishes incontestable rights regarding use of the mark for commerce;
- Entitles you to use the trademark registration symbol® as opposed to simply ™;
- Provides a basis for filing trademark application in foreign countries.

The trademark registration process is fully explained at the USPTO web site (www.uspto.gov). You can either register electronically or print out a form and mail in your registration. The current cost (c. 2016) for trademark or servicemark registration in the U.S. is $375. ($325 if you file electronically).

To register a trademark with the USPTO, the mark's owner must first put it into use "in commerce that Congress may regulate." This means the mark must be used on a product or service that crosses state, national or territorial lines or that affects commerce crossing such lines – for example, a record label selling CDs in other states, or a touring band providing performances in other states.

Once the USPTO receives a trademark registration application, the office must answer the following questions satisfactorily:

- *Is the trademark the same as or similar to an existing mark used on similar or related goods or services?*
- *Is the trademark on the list of prohibited or reserved names?*
- *Is the trademark generic – that is, does the mark describe the product itself rather than its source?*
- *Is the trademark too descriptive (not distinctive enough) to qualify for protection?*

If the answer to each question is "no", the trademark is eligible for registration and the USPTO will continue to process the application. You can expect to receive a "Filing Receipt" within eight weeks. After that you will receive a notice that your band or business name will be published in a government publication known as *The Trademark Gazette*. If there is no opposition to your mark, your registration will be issued. The whole process may take anywhere between 12 and 18 months.

Your intent to establish a mark can be shown by affixing the letters TM or SM next to your company name or logo. Once the registration is complete, you may begin using the ® symbol.

❑ **Copyright.** Items protected by copyright law include books, magazines, software, advertising copy, newspapers, music compositions, movies, audio recordings, and artwork. Items not protected by copyrights include concepts or ideas, titles, names, and brands.

In its most basic sense "copyright" means "the right to make copies". In fact, a copyright is actually a bundle of rights, each of which can be copyrighted independently and sold, assigned, leased, and/or licensed separately.

In the U.S., copyright protection *automatically* extends to any material once fixed in a form. This is the case whether you file for a copyright notice or not. So through *creation* a work is copyrighted, not through any formal registration process. Copyrights extend to creators for their entire lives and to their estates for 70 years thereafter.

Formal registration of copyrights, however, is recommended as it provides some extra insurance and a 'path' to the work's creator if someone wants to make contact. It also makes infringement cases move more quickly through the courts.

• ***Where to Register Your Copyrights***. The U.S. Copyright Office website is the place to register (copyright.gov). Remember, the Copyright Office receives and registers copyright claims – *it doesn't evaluate them or make decisions about whether a song has already been copyrighted by someone else.* If ten songs with the same title come in, they'll all get registered. It's up to you to take responsibility for not infringing on copyrights and monitoring your own copyrights.

As your business grows, your copyright registrations may become increasingly frequent –

along with the number of checks you cut for the filing fees (currently $50-65 per registration; $35 per online). If you make at least 12 filings a year, however, the Copyright Office will accept a $250 advance payment. The payment gets deposited into an account, the fees for future registrations are deducted, and statements are sent to you for your records. This saves time and streamlines the payment process.

The Copyright Office was mandated several years to streamline and simplify its processes, and so it is currently phasing out the multi-form system it has used for years (i.e., Forms TX, VA, SR, PA and SE), for a new, single one called the eCO (electronic copyright office) Form. Learn more at copyright.gov/help/faq/

• ***Who Owns the Copyright?*** As an independent contractor or freelancer, you usually own the rights to what you create unless you sign a contract giving rights to your client. If ownership is not stipulated in a contract (often done so with the phrase, "work for hire"), the creator owns the copyright to the work.

Before you sign any contract, be sure you know who will own the work you create during your employment. Oftentimes, the entity paying you will try to lay claim to all work, not just what you were hired to create, during the term of the contract, *so be on the lookout for this type of clause in all contracts!*

If you hire someone to create a work for your business and you want to own it – public relations material or ad copy, for example – you will want to have the agency or individual sign an agreement assigning rights to you.

You may have heard the term *fair use*. This rule says that portions of works may be reproduced for educational, news, commentary, parody or research without infringement under some circumstances. Fair use is decided on a case-by-case basis using the following criteria:

- Purpose of use. For example, whether it is commercial or for non-profit, educational purposes.
- The nature of the copyrighted work.
- The effect of the use upon the potential value of or market for the work.
- How much of the entire body of the work is used.
-

• **When You're Planning on Using Other Peoples' Music...**
If you're using someone else's copyrighted recorded composition(s), you need to obtain a mechanical license in writing. A mechanical license cannot be denied (it is a statutory right, set by Congress), but it can be a cumbersome process. There are three ways to get one: First, find out who owns the copyright on the composition by contacting BMI (212-220-3000 or www.bmi.com), ASCAP (212-621-6000 or www.ascap.com) or SESAC (800-826-9996 or www.sesac.com). Search their online databases. Armed with this info, you can contact the publisher and negotiate your own rates.

If you don't want to negotiate your own rates, **contact the Harry Fox Agency** (212-834-0100 or harryfox.com) which is authorized to issue mechanical licenses at the statutory rate of 9.10 cents per song up to five minutes. Songs over five minutes are calculated at 1.75 cents per minute, per song. To figure out your royalty fee, multiply the cost per song by the number of units manufactured. [E.g., one seven minute song on 1,000 CDs would cost 1,000 x (7 x $0.175) = $175.].

There are additional separate rates for Permanent Digital Downloads and Master Ringtones. Statutory rates change every two years. You can find them listed at: http://www.harryfox.com/license_music/what_mechanical_royalty_rates.html

If you're a community group, religious organization, school/ university or individual, and not an existing Harry Fox customer, and would like to obtain a license to make and distribute within the U.S. 2500 or less recordings, you can now get an HFA mechanical license at **SongFile.com**. This would apply to most artists or artist-owned labels in the U.S.

If you can't afford the standard fee, contact a group like the Volunteer Lawyers for the Arts (go to vlany.org to find the chapter nearest you). They can often help negotiate reduced royalties for schools and non-profit groups.

Are samples licensed? Yes! The sample has to fit a 30 second time frame and there's no certain amount of samples that you can use without getting clearance or permission from the owner of the license.

• ***Copyright Infringement***. **I**nfringement of copyright happens when works - paintings, books, computer software, films and music - are reproduced without permission from the copyright owners. Infringement can also occur when works such as plays and films are performed, screened or made public in other ways without permission from the copyright owner. A person who sells infringing versions of a work, even if somebody else made them, is also in breach of copyright, as is a person who authorizes someone else to make an infringement. If a work is very distinctive and original, reproducing part of it may be a breach of copyright.

There are many different ways copyright owners may find their copyright has been infringed upon. For example infringing activities include:

- *Bootlegging* - where illegal recordings are made of live performances;
- *Piracy* - the illegal copying of music products that have been released without permission from the copyright owner. Common ways this is done are by uploading tracks to file-sharing service like Limewire or Bitorrent, copying CDs onto cassettes or copying them onto other CDs using a CD-burner. Pirate products are not necessarily packaged in the same way as the original, whereas;
- *Counterfeiting* - involves duplication of both the music product and of its packaging. For this reason unwitting buyers are less able to recognize counterfeit copies than is the case with some pirate copies.
- *Sampling* – the practice of digitally copying or transferring snippets or portions of a preexisting (copyrighted) master to make a new composition. An artist will take a piece of a preexisting recording and use that piece (i.e., "sample") to create a new recording. Sampling exists mostly in rap, hip-hop, street, or dance records.

A person doing any of the above can be sued, as can most parties involved in the manufacture, distribution, sale, and performance of such works. If you are a record company and your artist is using the copyrighted song, you as the record label are in jeopardy. Copyright infringement is a federal offense so beware!

Contracts & Agreements

You take a lot of risks as a business owner. One way to help protect you from extra liabilities is through the use of written contracts. A written contract or agreement is a lot easier to prove in court than a verbal one, but verbal contracts are just as legal and binding – unless it is for the sale of goods over a certain amount.

It is smart, however, to have written agreements for recording artists, songwriters, musicians, record producers, vendors or any other contracted party you plan on trafficking with.

A contract is any agreement between two or more parties that is enforceable in court. As such, it must meet six conditions. If all these conditions are met, one party can seek legal recourse from another if the other party breaches (i.e., violates) the terms of the agreement.

1. ***Agreement***. Agreement is the serious, definite and communicated offer and acceptance of the same terms.
2. ***Consent***. A contract is not enforceable if any of the parties has been affected by an honest mistake, fraud, or pressure.
3. ***Capacity***. To give real consent, both parties must demonstrate legal "capacity" (competence). A person under legal age (usually 18-21, depending on the state) cannot enter into a binding agreement.
4. ***Consideration***. An agreement is binding only if it exchanges considerations – that is, items of value. Note that items of value do not necessarily entail money. For example, a tax accountant might agree to prepare a music teacher's tax return in exchange for a certain amount of music lessons for her son. Both services are items of value. Contracts need not be rational, nor must they provide the best possible bargain for both sides. They need only include legally sufficient consideration. The terms are met if both parties receive what the contract details.
5. ***Legality.*** A contract must be for a lawful purpose and must comply with federal, state, and local laws and regulations.
6. ***Proper form.*** A contract may be written, oral, or implied from conduct. It must be written, however, if it involves the sale property or goods worth more than $500. It must also be written if the agreement requires more than a year to fulfill. All changes to written contracts must also be in writing.

Keep in mind, also, that while there are "standard industry practices" in the contract arena you are free to design the contracts that best meet your values and approach as a label, production company or other type of music business owner. See page 258 for some helpful contract negotiation tips as well as a note on "form" contracts.

The important thing is to cover all aspects and eventualities that may arise in a certain situation or set of circumstances.

No contract is written in stone. The terms can be modified by the parties according to their particular situation and according to what it is the parties want to achieve. As long as the terms are equitable and the contract can stand in a court of law, you are free to negotiate the terms of your contract. Every initial contract, therefore, should be viewed as *a draft*, and nothing more.

Other Paperwork

Barcodes and How to Get One

If you plan on selling recordings and you would like those sales to show up in SoundScan reports and other tracking systems, you will need to obtain a Universal Product Code (UPC), which is kind of like a bar-coded social security number for your products.

Most music chains no longer carry non-UPC products (because they can't scan them at the cash register), and major label A&R departments conduct much of their market research on unsigned bands and indie labels by checking Sound Scan sales on the retail level.

"It's a great idea to put a UPC on your CD," says Kevin Williamson, VP of A&R at Atlantic Records. "A UPC helps tell the truth concerning how many [CDs] are actually being sold. It can also really help a band to attract interest from us. That's a way we found Hootie & The Blowfish. Our research saw that their self-released CD had already sold thirty to forty thousand units on the local level." Hard data helps get more attention. "The more data you can give to a potential label, manager, agent, talent buyer, venue, etc., the better," says Lou Plaia, founder of ReverbNation. "If you can show all these people that you are selling a lot of your music in markets where you play, it proves you have fans willing to buy something from you."

Soundscan now also accepts live show CD sales reports, the place, after all, where most indie artist sales happen. However, only labels, distribution companies and retailers can report these sales directly to SoundScan. Individual bands and artists can use an intermediary service like Indiehitmaker.com (for a fee, of course) to get their data submitted.

A UPC consists of twelve digits: The first six numbers uniquely identify your organization, the next four (which *you* choose) specify the release, the following number corresponds to the format (CD or single track), and the last number is used to check that the scanner read the product correctly.

If you'd like to receive an application for a UPC or need more information, contact GS1 (formerly, The Uniform Code Council) online at **http://www.gs1us.org** (GS1 is a non-profit organization dedicated to standards development and maintenance for automated product identification and electronic data.) The fee is determined by the number of products you need to identify and your company's gross sales revenue.

A less expensive (and easier to follow) barcode service is provided by Buyabarcode.com. It has a one-time registration and set-up fee and the code lasts a lifetime. CDBaby.com and most other online music storefronts and services will also set you up with a barcode for very little cost.

Music Metadata: Getting the Right Coded Information into Your Music Tracks

If you plan on releasing music on the Internet, through satellite radio, or via music services like Muzak, you'll need to understand the following. A lot of information on a music CD isn't music. Some of it is codes that help trace the uses and sales of your music online. Without them there is a good chance you'll miss out on royalties owed you.
The four important codes you'll need are:

- ***UPC (Universal Product Code)*** – See information in previous section above. Nielson Soundscan collects UPC sales data from over 15,000 outlets in the U.S. and Canada to compile its weekly list of music sales, which are published online (http://titlereg.soundscan.com/soundscantitlereg/).

- ***ISRC (International Standard Recording Code)*** – The ISRC is the international identification system for sound recordings and music DVDs. Each ISRC is a unique and permanent identifier for a specific recording, to help identify recordings for royalty payments. It is assigned *per track*, not per CD. It's smart to identify your recordings this way. They are embedded in the metadata of your CD during the mastering phase. For further information on ISRCs go to: http://usisrc.org.

❑ ***CD Text*** - CD Text is information about the release that can be encoded as a separate file on an audio CD. It stores such information as the album title and song titles. When playing back an audio CD containing CD Text information on a CD Text-enabled player (usually an LCD screen), the listener will be able to read this information on the display panel. It's displayed only on CD or DVD players, not on the desktop of most computers. Since its part of the *Red Book* standard CD Text info can be entered onto a CD master quite easily using the "table of contents" in the appropriate CD sub-channel.

Insurance Tip

Keep detailed records of the value of your office or store's contents off-premises. Include photos of equipment plus copies of sales receipts, operating manuals and anything else that proves what you purchased and how much was paid.

That way, in case of a fire, flood or other disaster, you can prove what was lost. It's also important to be able to prove your monthly income so you are properly reimbursed if you have to close down temporarily.

❑ ***CDDB (Compact Disc Data Base)*** - A database for software applications to look up CD information over the Internet. It was designed around the task of identifying entire CDs, not merely single tracks. The identification process involves creating a "discid", a sort of "fingerprint" of a CD created by performing calculations on the track duration information stored in the table-of-contents of the CD. There are alternatives to Gracenotes's proprietary CDDB. These include FreeDB, MusicBrainz and All Media Guide's AMG LASSO. To submit to Gracenote's database go to: http://gracenote.com and read the FAQs under "Company Info".

Covering Your Assets: Getting Business Insurance

When it comes to insurance, half of us are probably insurance poor (from paying on several necessary insurance policies), and the other half so *under*insured we're worried to death about what will happen if 'the worst' happens. Some of us have both problems. Insurance is one of the most important considerations for your enterprise, however, because lack of the right coverage can put you out of business overnight. Some music-related businesses, like record labels and production companies have special insurance needs beyond the standard ones for most businesses.
For example, a record company's biggest *exposure* (insurance lingo for liability) is in the contracts it signs with its distributors, product manufacturers, retailers, and most importantly, with its artists. To ensure the proper protection of these contractual liabilities, a label should purchase insurance that protects its exposures such as errors and omissions. Since some music company personnel are considered "invaluable" for their "ears," the company may also want to explore "key man" life insurance coverage or long-term disability plans as well.

The following info will alert you to dangerous situations you might have overlooked and will help you ask the right questions the next time you meet with an insurance agent.

❑ **Buy a business owner's policy if necessary**. If you are a home-based business and have employees - and in some cases, if you use a name other than your own - you will have to buy a business owner's policy in order to obtain liability coverage. This is also true if your business assets are so great that they cannot be covered by extending your homeowner's policy. This is similar to the kind of policy businesses outside of the home would purchase; it provides important coverage for items such as product liability, general liability, business interruption, and property damage.

❑ **Extend your car insurance**. If you use your regular car in the course of your business and you infrequently have customers in your car, most insurance companies will let you pay a little more for business use under your personal auto policy. Auto policies do not cover the contents of a car, so if you travel with valuables, make sure your product policy covers loss outside your home. If other people will be driving your car for the business, put their names on your policy. If your employees use their own cars in the course of working for you, you may need to get a *Non-owned-auto insurance policy* that provides coverage in case something happens when they are working for you. If you have a van that is used primarily for business, you will most likely have to buy a separate business auto policy.

❑ **Determine if you need professional liability insurance**. Professional liability insurance is the service equivalent of product liability and includes coverage for malpractice and errors and omissions. Some states and professions require it by law. Even if you are not mandated, it is wise to have it if the service you provide could inadvertently harm another person. The professions for which it is recommended or required include, but are not limited to, computer technicians, systems analysts, accountants, hairdressers, lawyers, and consultants.

❑ **Determine if you need product liability insurance**. Most business owner's policies include this coverage. If for some reason you do not have this coverage through a business policy, and your product runs the risk of inflicting harm on other people, you may need to buy product liability coverage separately, which can be expensive. A "product" is anything that is tangibly used, touched, or consumed. It is recommended for businesses including, but not limited to, toy makers, candy manufacturers, caterers, cake decorators, computer hardware, food sellers, and garment manufacturers.

❑ **Obtain workers' compensation insurance**. Most states will require you to have workers' compensation insurance for all employees you have on payroll. This is the insurance that covers employees in case of a work-related accident. Some states (New York, for example) also require that you purchase *disability insurance* which covers employees in case of any accident, no matter where it happens.

❑ **Consider disability insurance**. Disability (or loss-of-income) insurance covers you in case you cannot work because of illness or injury. You can insure up to 60 per cent of your gross income. If you want to cover yourself for disability, you can also set yourself up as a corporation, and cover yourself with workers' compensation. Expensive, but it does bring peace of mind.

❑ **Buy extra equipment coverage**. If your computer equipment isn't adequately covered by your other insurance, you can buy a *rider* or separate policy to cover it. Not all insurance companies offer this kind of coverage, but one of the vendors specializing in it is Safeware – (800) 800-1492. Computer data is expensive to cover, but in some cases, insurance companies will write a policy that will partially pay for time spent on data restoration.

❑ **At least consider life insurance**. If you have only yourself to worry about, even insurance agencies admit that you may be better off putting your money back into your business than investing it in life insurance. If you have a family or other people depending on you, however, life insurance is recommended. There are "term" plans that are reasonably priced for most people. You can conveniently get comparative quotes on most insurance policies at sites like **insure.com**.

Calculating the Cost of Health Insurance

Pick up any newspaper, visit any new site on the Internet, and the current health insurance situation screams from the headlines. Health insurance can be expensive, tough to get, and insufficient when it comes to covering chronic illnesses or prescription drugs.
Consider these options:

- Check whether your spouse or partner's employer can cover you.
- Join a group offering health insurance. Check with your local chamber of commerce or professional industry group. These plans often allow participation without minimal restrictions on prior conditions, and are less likely to require a physical exam or reject you for a prior health condition.
- Choose to form a partnership or corporation, which might qualify you for group rates. Talk to a benefits specialist about the minimum requirements for obtaining group insurance and the difference in pricing between an individual and group policy.
- Continue your employer's coverage via COBRA (Consolidated Omnibus Budget Reconciliation Act), national legislation enacted that allows an employee to continue health insurance through his or her employer, even after leaving. There are a number of restrictions and requirements—for example, you must be working for an employer with at least 20 employees or more and be currently enrolled in the health plan. If eligible, you (and possibly dependents you also covered via your employer's health plan) would be able to continue this coverage for 18-36 months, depending on your circumstances.

Taxes as a Plus-Minus Formula: How to Figure Your Taxable Income

- You receive various types of income -or "pluses". Examples: wages, fees, commissions, pensions, savings account interest, stock sale gains, unemployment compensation, Social Security benefits, lottery winnings.

- Various kinds of deduction- or "minuses"- reduce your income. Examples: IRA contributions, business expenses, union dues, charitable contributions, mortgage interest, gambling expenses.

- You subtract the minuses from the pluses. What you are left with is "taxable income".

- You pay tax on your income. That's why it's called income tax. Therefore, the more minuses, the less tax you pay.

However, this does not mean that you will pay the same amount currently deducted from your paycheck—you will be paying your employer's contributions to your health premiums as well, making the total cost higher, and often prohibitive. (For more information, visit https://www.dol.gov/ebsa/cobra.html.)

There are clearly no easy answers when it comes to health insurance. Most entrepreneurs opt for a high-deductible "catastrophic" policy that convers large health issue (e.g., operations) and pay out-of-pocket for more routine care (e.g. a checkup). Stay informed at healthcare.org and Ehealthinsurance.com.

Tax Basics for the Entrepreneur

When it comes to taxes, there's no getting around the fact that you have to pay them regularly. Federal, state and local taxes combined can take a big chunk out of your company's money, leaving you with leas cash to operate your business. That's why it's important to keep up with your business's tax situation and work with a qualified accountant to understand all that's required of you by federal, state and local governments. The task is by no means simple. New business owners face a host of tax requirements and ever-changing rules.

U.S. TAX FACTS FROM THE IRS (2014)

According to the IRS –

• The top 1% pay 33.1% of taxes (annual gross income over $364,657)

• The top 5% pay 54.36% of taxes

• The top 10% pay 65.84% of taxes

• The top 25% pay 84.88% of taxes (annual gross income over $134,300)

• The top 50% pay 96.54% of taxes

The top 1% pay more than one third of all income taxes. Almost half of Americans pay no income taxes. We don't need more *taxes*, we need more tax*payers*!

Personal finance tools like Mint.com and Quicken (Intuit, the same company that makes *TurboTax*) can help self-employed individuals categorize and keep track of their business and personal income and expenses separately.

Your business will be required to identify itself on tax forms and licenses by either of two numbers:

- ❒ A Social Security Number (SS#), or,
- ❒ A Federal Employer Identification Number (called "FEIN" but, more often, simply "EIN", it is a nine-digit number issued by the IRS).

Use your **Social Security number** as your sole proprietorship's identifying number, unless:

- You must withhold taxes from a subcontractor you've hired.
- You hire one or more employees.
- You set up a self-employed retirement plan.
- You deal in products that require you to file a federal excise or alcohol, tobacco, and firearms return.

Federal Employer Identification Number (EIN)
If one or more of the above applies to your business, you will be required to obtain a nine-digit EIN. You can receive your EIN immediately by phone or by going online. To apply online, go to www.irs.gov, click on "Businesses," then "Employer ID Number."
Partnerships, corporations, and LLCs must have a federal EIN whether they hire employees or not.
If you obtain an EIN, use it for all your business correspondence with the federal government. Don't use your Social Security number for this purpose unless specifically asked for both numbers. You should have only one EIN even if you have two sole proprietorships. Never use someone else's EIN. If you buy a business you cannot use a previous owner's EIN.

Required Taxes - For U.S. business owners your taxes will include the following:

- ❒ *Local taxes* (possibly) - check with city or town hall.
- ❒ *State & Sales taxes* - these include Income Tax, Employee Income Tax, Unemployment Tax (if you have employees).
- ❒ *Federal Taxes* - included are Corporate Income Tax, Employee Income Tax & Unemployment Tax (if you have employees).
- ❒ *Social Security Taxes* - When the profit on your tax report reaches $400 or more (2016), you must file a Self-Employment Form along with your regular income tax form and pay into your personal social security account at a rate and wage base that is continually being increased.

Understanding Self Employment Taxes. Yes, the choice of self-employment comes with its own special tax category and obligations. While income tax is paid on any kind of taxable income, self-employment tax is paid only by people who work for themselves. It is the Social Security and Medicare tax for self-employed and is paid on a self-employed *net* earnings (after expenses are deducted).

Self-employment comes with tax advantages as well. You are in control, so in many instances...

- You have more influence over business expense deductions
- More business expenses are actually deductible.
- You get more flexibility in how much tax you'll pay and when you'll pay it.
- You can influence when you receive income.
- You can distribute income to family members by hiring them as employees.
- You have a wide range of pensions choices.

But in order to make the most of these advantages, you first need to understand how self-employment taxes work from the inside.

Here are some key points to keep in mind and to help clear the fog around this subject of the self-employment tax. Take a deep breath; ready?:

❑ ***Self-employment (SE) tax kicks in if net profit from self-employed income is $400 or more.*** You must file a tax return if your net profit is $400 or more no matter how much or how little your other income; no matter how young or old you are; no matter if you're collecting Social Security or in grammar school; no matter if you're married or single.

❑ ***SE tax is paid on 92.35 percent of all net profit*** (don't worry about why this is; just accept it as an IRS fact).

❑ ***The SE tax rate is 15.3 percent and is made up of two components:*** 12.4 percent Social Security tax plus 2.9 percent Medicare tax. Social Security benefits are available to self-employed persons just as they are to wage earners. Your payments of SE tax contribute to your coverage under the Social Security system, which provides you with retirement, disability and survivor benefits. Medicare coverage provides hospital insurance benefits.

Many self-employed people (usually the younger ones) confuse Social Security payments and unemployment compensation. Employees receive coverage for both benefits. If a W-2 (that is, employed) person has worked for a certain amount of time and leaves work under certain conditions, she can receive payments while not working. This is called unemployment compensation. It is also taxable income. Self-employed never receive unemployment compensation.

❑ ***Payments toward the Social Security tax portion of SE tax stop when earned income reaches a specified amount.*** In 2015, for employer, employee, or a self-employed, the cutoff was $118,500. That means if any combination of Social Security wages, tip income, and/or net earnings from self-employment reached $118,500, no more Social Security tax had to be paid. The cut-off point rises a little every year.

If as a salaried employee you earned $118,500 in 2015 and you had a sole proprietorship as well, you would not have to pay any of the Social Security tax portion of SE tax no matter how high your net earnings from self-employment.

If your total net earnings from self-employment or your salary or a combination of both were $118,500, you would pay the same amount of Social Security tax as your neighbor who earned five million dollars.

❑ ***All earned income is subject to the 2.9 percent Medicare tax.*** There is no limit. You and your high-earning neighbor will pay very different amounts of Medicare tax.

❑ ***An employee pays one half of his Social Security and Medicare tax and his employer pays the other half.*** As a self-employed you pay both the employer's half and the employee's half of Social Security and Medicare taxes.

You pay both halves and you get to deduct one half. The deduction is taken as an adjustment to income on the front of your tax return, in the same section as self-employed health insurance premiums and your pension contribution. The deduction reduces only income tax. It is not a deduction against net earnings from self-employment.

❑ ***The amount of Social Security you receive in your golden years is based upon your earnings over a lifetime.*** The Social Security Administration gets its figures on earnings from your tax return. If you've shown little or no income over the years, you will receive little or no Social Security when you get old. That's what happens to all the under-the-table musicians and nannies: no Social Security when the arthritis sets in and they can't work anymore.

❑ ***Special Tip - Estimated Tax Payments***: Some tax assessments require payments or deposits in advance based upon your projected sales or earnings. You're naturally confident the venture you're launching will meet its projections, and you'll be inclined to tell all and sundry how well you expect to do. But don't volunteer your optimism to a tax assessing authority. Rather, you should adopt an attitude of, "Gee, we just hope we can keep our doors open long enough to pull in some business." You want to pay the least amount possible where advance payments are required. Why tie up working capital to pay taxes on income you've not yet earned?

❑ ***How to Report Earnings.*** We'll re-visit the subject of taxes in chapter 13. There we will address business deductions and general long-range tax planning strategies to help maximize your money.

For now, you should know that you must complete the following federal tax forms by April 15 after any year in which you have net earnings of $400 or more:

- Form 1040 (U.S. Individual Income Tax Return);
- Schedule C (Profit or Loss from Business) or Schedule F (Profit or Loss from Farming) as appropriate; and
- Schedule SE (Self-Employment Tax).

You can get these forms from IRS.gov and most banks and post offices. Send the tax return and schedules along with your self-employment tax to the IRS. Even if you do not owe any income tax, you must complete Form 1040 and Schedule SE to pay self-employment Social Security tax. This is true even if you already get Social Security benefits.

Protecting Your Independent Contractor Status

Your status as an independent contractor is important because if you are someone's employee and not an independent contractor, the employing organization can be held responsible for your taxes, employee benefits, and related items. Nevertheless, you will run into potential clients who want you to be an independent contractor, but will want to also treat you as an employee. They do not want to pay your taxes, benefits, or anything other than a project fee, yet they will try to insist that you come to their office and perform work for them onsite during specific hours.

Does this mean that you should never go to a client's location? Of course, not. What it means, however, is that you need to understand when it is problematic. Attending a meeting at a clients location, regarding a project or potential project, in and of itself, is not a problem. A client asking you to attend a staff meeting, or asking you to arrive at 8 a.m. and leave at 5 p.m., every day, signals a potential problem.

Working as a W-2 employee also has numerous disadvantages for you as a home business owner. After all, how much marketing can you reasonably do if you are sitting at another company's cubicle from 8 a.m. to 5 p.m., Monday through Friday? You need to have more than one client, and it's tough to do that if you are sitting in another client's workplace, using its phone and email.

To make the situation even worse, such an arrangement tends to be a slippery slope. After all, if you are at a desk during regular hours and show up every day, most of your colleagues will assume that you are an employee and treat you accordingly. This means that they will include you in office parties, ask you to order office supplies for the company, attend staff meetings, and do all the other things you thought you had left behind. So instead of being a business owner, you are now an employee again—but this time without the benefits.

So how do you avoid the W-2 trap? Follow these guidelines:

1. Review the IRS guidelines mentioned previously, and be familiar with them. If you still have questions, read the additional recommended material or consult your accountant or attorney.
2. Whenever a client or prospect edges you toward specific no-nos, such as requesting that you spend more than a few days of set work hours at their place or employment, educate them about the IRS constraints. Make it clear, too, that you cannot provide the same services as an employee. You have other clients to think about, and your office is based at your home, not at their address.
3. Be sure that your contract has clear language indicating that you are an independent contractor and won't be expected to remain on site for set hours or perform other tasks that would make you an employee.
4. In addition, your contract should be very clear as to the scope of your duties, and, most likely, these duties are tied to a very specific project (and set amount of time). If the prospective client tries to add language that sounds vague, such as a job description, explain why that isn't acceptable.

Amazingly, many prospective clients will not know about this distinction. By educating them in a positive tone, you help them avoid unnecessary problems and keep the door open for actual work in the future.

As the comedian Denis Healey once said, "The difference between tax avoidance and tax evasion is the thickness of a prison wall." Though an annoying part of life, there are strategies you can use to minimize the pain of taxes in your business. We'll explore these in chapter 14 when we discuss the entrepreneurial management of money.

But now, let's get your own workspace organized.

CHAPTER SUMMARY
LICENSES, PERMITS & TAXES, O MY!

- **Securing the Required Paperwork**
  Some Basic Business Licenses you may need: Fictitious Name (DBA), General Business License, Seller's Permit or Resale Certificate, Other possible licenses & permits (Fire Department Permit, Agent License, Sign Permit , etc.).

- **Getting Around the Red Tape**
  If you do not get the proper permits or the local building codes, the city or county can shut you down or bring you uninvited aggravation. Speak also with a SCORE advisor who lives in the area in which you're setting up shop. He or she will know the best ways to navigate the legal requirements for your business in that locale.

- **Working Within the Zoning Laws**
  Zoning laws typically specify the areas in which residential, industrial, recreational, agricultural or commercial activities may take place. Before you sign a lease, check with the local zoning department to make sure the building is zoned for your use. Find out about any special requirements, such as off-street parking or sign limitations. It's important to find out what is and is not allowed in your community regarding home-based businesses.

- **Checklist of Business Regulations, Permits & Licenses**
  Depending upon the size and nature of your business, some of the following licenses, permits, and compliances may be required. For example: Local business license (all businesses; usually with your city); Fictitious name registration (all businesses; usually with your state); Employer identification number (optional; IRS form SS-4); Trademark registration (usually with your state, but also federal); Workers' compensation (only businesses with employees; usually with your state), etc.

- **Intellectual Property Assets**
  Ideas may be your greatest asset. When you begin to transfer them into names, inventions, product designs, logos, music, writings or other forms, they become intellectual property. In this age of digital copying and rampant piracy, it's important to understand what intellectual property is and how to best protect it.

- **Patents**
  A patent allows the inventor the exclusive right to make, use, and sell an invention throughout his country during the term of the patent. Any other party that makes, sells, or uses the patent invention during the term of the patent – without consent of the patent holder – is infringing on the patent. There are three forms of patents: design, utility, and plant. Design patents are granted for any new, original, and ornamental design for an article of manufacturing. Utility patents cover the functional features of an invention and are granted for any new and useful process, machine, manufacture, or composition of matter, or for any new and useful improvement. A plant patent, protects a new form of greenery or plant.

- **Trademarks**
  When you sell products using a brand name, you are using that brand name as a trademark. If you are providing a service, the brand name for that service is a servicemark. Trademarks are granted for 20 years and may be renewed indefinitely if a firm continues to protect its brand name. If a company allows the name to lapse into common usage, it may lose protection.

- **Copyrights**
  Items protected by copyright law include books, magazines, software, advertising copy, newspapers, music compositions, movies, audio recordings, and artwork. Items not protected by copyrights include concepts or ideas, titles, names, and brands. Formal registration of copyrights, however, is recommended as it provides some extra insurance and a 'path' to the work's creator if someone wants to make contact. It also makes infringement cases move more quickly through the courts.

- **Contracts & Agreements**
  One way to help protect you from extra liabilities is through the use of written contracts. A written contract or agreement is a lot easier to prove in court than a verbal one, but verbal contracts are just as legal and binding – unless it is for the sale of goods over a certain amount. A contract is any agreement between two or more parties that is enforceable in court. It must meet six conditions: agreement, consent, capacity, consideration, legality and proper form.

- **Bar Codes**
  If you plan on selling recordings and you would like those sales to show up in SoundScan reports and other tracking systems, you will need to obtain a Universal Product Code (UPC), which is kind of like a bar-coded social security number for your products.

- **Music Metadata**
  If you plan on releasing music on the Internet, through satellite radio, or via music services like Mood Music (formerly, Muzak), you'll need to understand the these codes that help trace the uses and sales of your music online. Without them there is a good chance you'll miss out on royalties owed you. The four important codes you'll need are: UPC (Universal Product Code), ISRC (International Standard Recording Code), CD Text , and CDDB (Compact Disc Database).

- **Covering Your Assets: Getting Business Insurance.**
  Insurance is one of the most important considerations for your enterprise, because lack of the right coverage can put you out of business overnight.
  Some issues you'll want to address include: Buying a business owner's policy if necessary; Extending your car insurance; Determining if you need professional liability insurance; Determining if you need product liability insurance; Obtaining workers' compensation insurance (for employers); Considering disability insurance; Buying extra equipment coverage; and seriously considering business interruption insurance.

- **Calculating the Cost of Health Insurance**
  Health insurance can be expensive, tough to get, and insufficient when it comes to covering chronic illnesses or prescription drugs. Consider these options: Check whether your spouse or partner's employer can cover you; Join a group offering health insurance; Choose to form a partnership or corporation, which might qualify you for group rates; Continue your employer's coverage via COBRA (Consolidated Omnibus Budget Reconciliation Act).

- **Tax Basics and the Entrepreneur**
  It's important to keep up with your business's tax situation and work with a qualified accountant to understand all that's required of you by federal, state and local governments. Some required taxes: local taxes, state & sales taxes, federal taxes and social security taxes.

- **Protecting Your Independent Contractor Status**
  Your status as an independent contractor is important because if you are someone's employee and not an independent contractor, the employing organization can be held responsible for your taxes, employee benefits, and related items. Some guidelines to avoid the W-2 trap: Review the IRS guidelines mentioned previously, and be familiar with them; Educate clients about the IRS constraints; Be sure that your contract has clear language indicating that you are an independent contractor; and your contract should be very clear as to the scope of your duties.

FURTHER RESOURCES

Independent Insurance Agents and Brokers of America
iiaa.org
This listing of insurance agents provides you with referrals to agents who are not affiliated with a particular company. Because they can offer products from one or more organization, these agents are likely to search for a product that best suits your needs and budget.

Music Industry Forms: The 75 Most Important Documents for the Modern Musician (Music: Business) by Jonathan Feist (2014, Berklee Press).

National Association for Women's Business Owners
nawbo.org
Resources and networking opportunities for women-owned businesses.

Online Insurance information
www.insureme.com and www.equote.com
These are just two of a number of consolidated, one-stop shopping sites that offer health insurance. Check any site's privacy policy, so you're comfortable providing information for a quote. You'll also want to check out the company providing the insurance, so you know they're legitimate before sending any premiums.

Patent and Trademark Office
uspto.gov
A visit to this website will not only provide information about the trademark process, but also help you make a decision whether you need the help of a lawyer. (For websites, you'll also want to check for existing domain names on an Internet registration site, such as Register.com.)

Social Security Disability Coverage
ssa.gov/disability/
See this site for information about Social Disability coverage, including a screening tool that allows you to put in possible scenarios based on your personal circumstances.

BizFilings
bizfilings.com
Information on incorporating and related services for business owners, including forms, advice and tools needed.

Small Business Notes
smallbusinessnotes.com
Useful site that features a wide variety for business articles and resources, including legal issues and record-keeping.

10

ORGANIZING YOUR OFFICE & WORK SPACE

For every minute spent organizing, an hour is earned. – Benjamin Franklin

---

Finding the Right Space

Where should you locate your business? One expert will tell you location is absolutely vital to your company's success; another will argue that it really doesn't matter where you are – and they're both right! How important location is for your new company depends on the type of business and the facilities and other resources you need, and where your customers are. Superstar videogame composer Norihiko Hibino saw that in his line of work it was imperative to present a certain image to potential clients by locating in a big city, in this case, Tokyo. "Better to have an office in the center of the city. It shows your seriousness in the business, especially for the people who are outside the entertainment business...The only way they can trust you is not by the quality of work (because they may not appreciate the value), but the solidness of your company as evidenced by your central location."

Sometimes multiple locations are called for, as in the case of the International Contemporary Ensemble. Its director, Claire Chase, recalls: "I wanted to set up a multi-city company – the original idea was to have a chapter in Chicago, a chapter in New York that would form 3-4 years later, and eventually a chapter on the West Coast, to be formed when the company expanded into its 10th or 11th season – to provide truly national exposure for our music and our mission."

If you're in retailing, venue ownership or manufacturing, then geographic location is extremely important. If your business is information- or service-related, the actual location takes back seat to whether the facility itself can meet your needs. It's only recently that we truly have been unchained from fixed phone numbers, office resources and the need for face-to-face with colleagues. Internet connectivity, powerful mobile versions of office tools and new phone services are loosening the ties that bind and making physical location more about convenience than necessity.

Leased Office Options

In cities across the country, commercial vacancy rates are 10 percent or higher, and growing currently (2016). With square feet emptying out in cities all over the country, vacant cubicles have become legion and commercial lease holders very nervous. These conditions put renters and lessors in a very good bargaining position. If your business needs commercial space then you should feel very bold in negotiating lowers costs and shorter lease terms with owners and landlords.

Executive suites, or business centers, provide another type of leased option. These individual private offices and suites offer meeting rooms complete with visual equipment, corporately appointed reception area, phones answered in your company name, copiers, video conferencing and fax equipment, coffee service, online access, and even kitchen facilities.

Administrative and secretarial support services are also available on an as-needed basis. Leased suites offer businesses of all types and sizes the opportunity to open an office and operate at maximum efficiency while controlling overhead expenses.
Features usually include:

❑ **Flexible lease terms**, sometimes as short as 30 days, are available, reducing the uncertainty and expense of the traditional three-to-five year lease. If you're looking to expand into new markets, executive suites are a cost effective way to "test the waters" in new territories without long term commitment or capital outlay.

❑ **Support services**, which are available as needed and typically billed in 10 minute increments, eliminate the salaries and benefits associated with hiring and managing permanent and often under utilized administrative personnel. With office equipment such as telephone systems, copiers and fax machines provided, clients are free from binding equipment leases and/or the cost of purchasing and maintaining such equipment. Executive suites offer immediate occupancy, with furniture selection customized to best suit your needs, or you may bring in your own office furniture.

Resource: Online Office Suite Directory – http://www.offices.org/

Another Option: "Incubating" Your Business

Just as a poultry hatchery incubates new chicks, a business incubator (sometimes known as a business *accelerator*) incubates your business for a set time until the business is ready to 'walk on its own.' A business incubator's main goal is to produce successful firms that will leave the program financially viable and freestanding.

Today there are over 1200 incubators in North America alone and, for the right kind of business, they can be a huge help. Incubators provide essential office equipment, office space and the advice and guidance of seasoned business consultants to help entrepreneurs test their business ventures. They also afford opportunities to network and create mentoring relationships with other entrepreneurs. Most incubators (about 94 percent) are nonprofit organizations focused on economic development. The remaining 6 percent are for-profit entities, usually set up to obtain returns on shareholders' investments.

Who sponsors business incubators? Incubator sponsors – organizations or individuals who support an incubation program financially – may serve as an incubator's parent or host organization or may simply make financial contributions to the incubator. According to The National Business Innovation Association (www.nbia.org):

- Most North American business incubators (about 93 percent) are nonprofit organizations focused on economic development. About 7 percent of North American incubators are for-profit entities, usually set up to obtain returns on shareholders investments.
- 54 percent are "mixed-use," assisting a range of early-stage companies.
- 37 percent focus on technology businesses.

- About 6 percent focus on service businesses, serve niche markets or assist other types of businesses.
- 3 percent serve manufacturing firms.
- About 47 percent of business incubators operate in urban areas, 28 percent operate in rural areas and about 25 percent operate in suburban areas.

The National Business Innovation Association estimates there are about 7,000 business incubators worldwide.

Is your business idea a good match for an incubator? A good way to gauge this is to visit the web sites of incubators like, for example, LaunchBox Digital and YCombinator, two of the more noteworthy incubators. LaunchBox Digital (launchboxdigital.com) focuses on startups in sectors including social networking, mobile-phone applications, online gaming and TV set-top convergence. It provides some seed capital, mentorship in various areas and access to strategic partners. YCombinator (ycombinator.com) helps startups find big-money investors or acquisition firms. It will also help entrepreneurs fine-tune their goals and products. Y Combinator can provide some seed money ($20,000 or less), too.

Of course, it can be argued that even eBay can be viewed as a business incubator in the area of ecommerce. eBay has enjoyed a reputation as a 21st century path to the American Dream. It is a unique online platform that connects buyers and sellers, an idea that *Business Week* once called "nothing less than a virtual, self-regulating global economy." Started in 1995, eBay today has over 159 million active users in 190 countries. Numerous businesses have gotten their start on eBay and is an option you should definitely explore. Other services like Café Press, Zazzle and Printfection afford online entrepreneurs the chance to test market their products, adjust as necessary and gradually build a loyal customer base. If your business is information-based, then these can be good and inexpensive places in which to develop your company, or even as a supplement to a customized web site or storefront you already have.

Home-Based Businesses

I assume most people reading this book will start their business from their home or apartment. This make the most financial sense and poses a low-risk scenario for the nascent entrepreneur. Hundreds of well-known companies started from home, including Microsoft and Dell Computers, both of which were launched from dorm rooms.

There are lots of benefits to having your business at home. Living where you work is cost-efficient and certainly convenient. "It enables me the convenience and flexibility necessary to balance work and family," says Rhode Island music publicist, Ginny Shea. "I've never had to send my kids to day care. If the kids get sick, I can adjust my day to take care of them and then put in the extra hours on the weekends or evenings".

Working from home also means you don't have to fight traffic because you don't have to worry about being late, and there is no dress code - you can have "casual Friday" every day. Home-based offices provide significant tax benefits, don't require commuting, and generally involve lower start-up costs, fixed costs and rent expenses.

However, home offices can also have their drawbacks. Working at home can create tension between you and family members (or, housemates) who may feel ignored (or intruded upon). Entrepreneurs who merge workplace and home may eventually find themselves sleeping late every morning or, conversely, working late into the evening because the work is *always* there. The secret to success lies in setting up a distinct place for business activities that separates your personal and professional lives, then establishing a regular work schedule to help family, friends and clients know when they can and cannot interrupt you.

If you live in a small space, check the nooks and crannies and you just might see a space for a file cabinet or a small desk. If you want to work out of your room, imagine how you can organize it to separate your personal items from your office supplies. Working out of your garage means that you can have some privacy and maybe space for inventory. Sometimes a particular portion of your home environment will do double duty. Your kitchen can be your office during the day and a place to serve meals at night. It's incredible how many uses a kitchen table can have, from doing paperwork to shipping merchandise.

The chart below will help you evaluate the best place in your home to set up shop:

Questions to Ask & Answer When Choosing Your Workspace
When trying to find a good place to put your home office, you should ask yourself several important questions:

- ❑ Will distractions be kept to a minimum?
- ❑ Is the space comfortable year round?
- ❑ Is the ambient temperature and humidity computer-friendly?
- ❑ Is there sufficient lighting?
- ❑ Is the electrical wiring sufficient to support your needs?
- ❑ How difficult would it be to run a phone line into the space?
- ❑ Is there room to display samples of your work?
- ❑ Is there room for everything you need (desk, file cabinet, computer, printer, and so on)?
- ❑ Is there enough storage space?
- ❑ Can you meet clients comfortably in this space if need be?
- ❑ Is there a way to keep clients from seeing the rest of your home?

Some good possible sites are:

- ❑ the spare room (dedicated room)
- ❑ the basement (watch out for moisture)
- ❑ the attic (may need air conditioner)
- ❑ the converted garage (might need separate business entrance)

Not recommended are:

- ❑ the guest bedroom
- ❑ your bedroom
- ❑ the kitchen

Developing a new attitude about your home surroundings will help you transform your domestic space into a professional environment that can become the breeding ground of your success. You should be motivated enough to want to organize your space, because pleasant working surroundings help you maintain a positive and productive attitude. The ideal situation is to have a permanent room for your work area, both from a productivity and taxation point of view. A distinct workspace helps condition your mind that this is a place where you do work. Moreover, having a separate area that is used exclusively and regularly for your business is an important criterion to qualify for tax deductions for your home office, a subject we will re-visit later.

Setting Up Your Four Work Centers

Did you know corporate executives waste an average of forty-five minutes everyday looking for things they can't find? If the primary reason for business failure is management incompetence, and if *organization* is the primary ingredient for good management, then it is crucial for you to set your office up in a way that will keep you organized and efficient. A helpful way to do this is setting up separate "work centers" focused on specific daily tasks. No matter where you finally decide to set up shop, you will need to equip and organize your work space to maximize your production and minimize distractions.

The "L-Shaped" Office

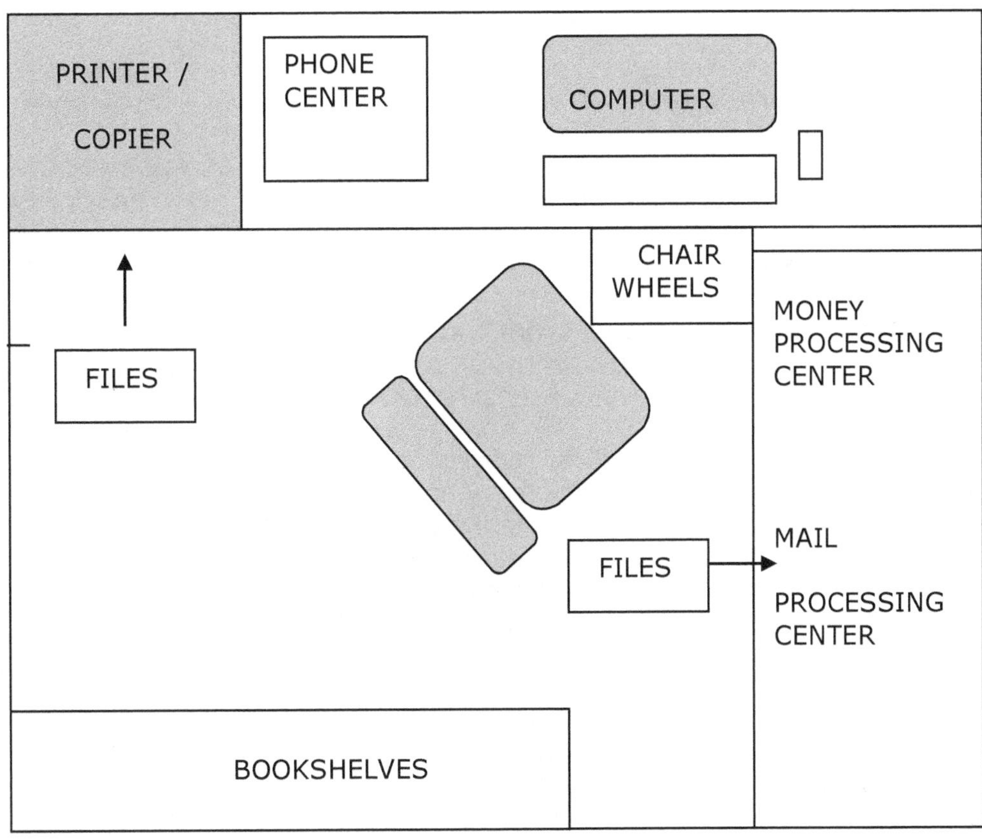

There are, minimally, four work centers most small businesses need:

- ❑ **Telephone work center** – Have a place near your work phone where you keep your card file of names and addresses, answering or voice-mail machine, and all phone messages.
- ❑ **Mail work center** – Have a place where you process all your mail. Have bins or boxes in which to place incoming and outgoing mail. Keep stationery, envelopes, stamps, cards, publicity materials, and anything else you need to send out regularly. You might also want to keep a postage scale, overnight and priority shipping envelopes, and a paper cutter at hand.
- ❑ **Money-processing work center**. If you want to make sure you have enough money, you have to mind your money. That means having a time and space for processing your financial transactions such as making deposits, invoicing, bill paying, and keeping bank records.
- ❑ **Filing work center**. If you have a place for each file and a file for each type of written material you need to keep, you'll have no need for piles. The key is organizing your information early on in your business and staying on top of it. To keep your desk and other surfaces clear and still have quick access to what you need, create three filing areas: *Immediate* file (files you refer to daily or are working on currently); *Current* files (files that you use on a weekly or monthly basis; these can be kept in a filing *cabinet*); *Archives* (info

materials that you are keeping for reference or for purposes of documentation can be kept in a remote location). Chapter 13 delves more deeply into practical strategies for managing information.

Of course, all of these work "centers" revolve around "Grand Central" - your computer - the single most important piece of equipment for your business. Here's a look at a well-organized home office space:

Optimizing Your Office Space. There are several "best practices" you can apply to the physical organization of your work space:

❑ **Keep the most frequently used objects**, tools and supplies closest at hand. The "L"-shape work space is recommended for this purpose and is illustrated above.

❑ **Avoid built-in desks or other fixtures**. Use adjustable shelving. Buy a pair of two-drawer file cabinets rather than a four-drawer unit. Think *modular*, not fixed.

❑ **Pay attention to lighting**. Poor lighting can lead to eyestrain, headaches, irritability and overall lower efficiency. Two types of lighting are necessary: *ambient light* (a blend of natural light and artificial light, usually provided by a ceiling fixture or halogen pole lamp), and *task lighting* (provided by lamps at each work area). More on this in a minute.

❑ **It's easier to look down than up**. If you are using a computer, always position it so that the center of your monitor is about 17" in front and about six inches lower than your eye level, or square with your chin, when you are sitting in your normal work chair.

❑ **When using a telephone**, try to find a way to keep your hands free. This enables better production and minimizes neck strain. Good telephone headsets are available for about $40 (Plantronics).

❑ **Be health conscious**. Avoid the coffee-to-get-up, alcohol to come down syndrome. This can set your body and mind on a roller coaster. Good health requires that you stand up and move around often. After reviewing your work area, can you honestly say that this is the most functional, comfortable, safest, and logical way to set up the area? Or, do certain tasks or pieces of furniture and equipment stand out as awkward, difficult, even painful to use? Use your common sense to eliminate the barriers to performance that you find. "Ergonomics" (lit., *work economics*), is the science of designing the job, equipment, and workplace to fit the worker. The science of Ergonomics addresses the many ways office workstations can be optimized for ideal comfort and productivity. Ergonomic chairs, desks and computers are important, as are fresh air, visual diversion, and control of noise levels. We'll look at some of these ideas in more detail below ("Greening Your Office").

VIRTUALLY REAL

"Virtuality" is a term of art that is becoming an important part of our everyday lives. Per the American Heritage Dictionary, it refers to those simulated equivalents of real-world objects and concepts we now use without a second thought. Thus, we have cyberspace, cyber communities and cyber criminals; e-mail, e-commerce and e-tail where e-cash is spent; virtual memory, virtual drives, virtual offices and a strong vibrant virtual economy. The concept of virtuality originated with computer and network design, but our use of all things virtual tracts very closely with our quick uptake of all things internet.

A spin-off of virtuality is the concept of presence—particularly relevant if you belong to any of the virtual communities created by instant messaging, VoIP, blogging, podcasting or online gaming. Presence doesn't refer to your physical presence but, rather, when you're online and available for communications.

New conventions like these keep providing more mobility and more convenient ways of doing things and opening new markets in the real world.

Equipping Your Office

Since whole books have been written about how to best equip an office, I will concentrate on only the most important elements a new company should consider. Every business is different though there are some general principles that should guide your equipment choices.

In general, you need to balance form, function and budget when outfitting your base of operations. Once you've decided where you will establish your office — either in your home or a commercial space — the next important decisions involve furnishing and equipping it. If you're starting out on your own and you have a very tight budget, you may not need to buy any equipment at all. Many towns now have business centers from which you can fax, e-mail, access the Internet, photocopy and so on. Though cheaper than actually buying equipment in the short-term, this option is inconvenient and can be very expensive in the medium-to long-term. Eventually you will want to purchase and own your own equipment. Here are some questions to consider:

❑ Do you have a budget in mind? (Even if you don't know what your budget will allow per item, have a total figure—it saves time for everyone involved.). It's a good idea to make a list of the supplies you'll need. A list of "Must Haves" and "Can Do With Outs" will help you in making certain decisions about how you should budget.

Statistics have proven that a well-prepared office layout can lead to higher productivity and employee satisfaction for you and your staff. Therefore, you'll need to bring along answers to the following questions as well:

❑ How many people will be working in the office?
❑ Do you have a floor plan? (There are some great software tools - like, Ikea's *Office Planner* or *Live Interior 3D* - to help you visualize your office layout. These will give you a very good idea of how the area will look prior to making your decisions.)
❑ Do you have a preference for workstations or regular desks?
❑ What type of filing system will you need (for everyday use and for storage)?

Office Supplies. An experienced office products salesperson can quickly assist you in putting together a list of the items needed for your new office. Some essential items to consider are the following:

- An extra phone line
- Filing supplies
- Appropriate software
- Copier supplies
- Paper supplies
- Storage containers/supplies
- Shipping supplies
- Warehouse supplies
- Presentation supplies
- Miscellaneous desk items (calculator, stapler, tape, pens, clips, etc.)

There are many ways you can place your office supply orders today, including faxed requisition forms, telephone contact and the Internet. Ordering office products should be a smooth experience with very little hassle. Companies like W.B. Mason (wbmason.com), Staples (staples.com) and Office Depot (officedepot.com) pride themselves in their quick turnaround and customer service.

Office Technology. *CRM, EDMs, VoIP, WiMAX, RFID, VPN* - all these techno acronyms can make one dizzy and it's often difficult for the entrepreneur to keep up with the spate of tools and technologies coming to market. These days, choice rules. New Web-based office and telephony tools and wireless data services are rocking the once-simple tech universe of the small business. Plus, one unfailing characteristic of consumer and small-business technologies is that each new version delivers more for less. Depending on how much mobility you need, you may find yourself buying more individual pieces of equipment than in years past, but the price tag on each one is guaranteed to be lower than last year and the year before that. In fact, prices fall so rapidly that office technologies depreciate at an unusually high rate. It's not that they're shoddy – quite the contrary. But their resale values are continuously being undercut by cheaper, better successors.

You can be so sure that any class of computer or telecommunications equipment will leapfrog its predecessors in functionality that you should treat your purchase as a simple business expense rather than the investment in capital equipment over years. Yes, the products will work just fine and continue to deliver productivity for years. But their costs are recovered within weeks or months with no depreciation calculations required. Therefore, you should think about office tools slightly differently than you do other durables. Here are a few truisms that need to be taken into account when buying hardware:

- Even the most expensive office item, the personal computer, is dirt cheap by historical measures.
- Whatever you buy and whenever you buy it, it will appear expensive and underpowered compared to succeeding versions.
- Office equipment pays for itself in a very short time by enhancing your productivity; it then helps you make money by letting you do whatever you do faster and better.

However, with all the changes, one thing is certain: *Technology is the key to small business success.* A micro-business lives and dies by email, phone/voicemail, the internet, faxes, and postal and delivery services. In fact, it can be said that technology (particularly desktop technology) is the "great leveler", enabling even the tiniest company to have the look, reach and efficiencies of its much larger counterparts.

We will look at each tool in a minute. For now, I just want to suggest some guiding principles on this subject. Trying to decide what you need in the fast-changing business technology market can be trying. "I was feeling overwhelmed with all the mediums of communication," remembers Ginny Shea, owner of Mixed Media. "It has grown from phone calls and snail mail, then to faxes, now email, texts/instant messaging not to mention keeping up on the social networks". It took a while for Shea to figure out what was best for her particular business. "I finally developed an efficient time management system. It's impossible to stay on top of everything but thanks to tools like iCal/blocked time/schedule alerts and the iPhone – you can be productive waiting in lines or getting your nails done!" Whenever you're considering purchasing a new piece of office technology, always ask yourself these questions:

- ❒ Will it reduce my expenses?
- ❒ Will it increase my income?
- ❒ Will it save me time?
- ❒ How much will maintenance and supplies cost?
- ❒ How long will it take me or how much will it cost to install?
- ❒ Am I willing to make the effort to learn how to properly use and maintain the equipment and software I need?

By first asking and answering these questions you'll lessen the "technostress" that's common with new technology purchases.

Before you decide what you need to purchase, let's look at what you *truly* need (and what you already have). Bear in mind, however, that this chapter can only speak in generalities.

We'll be focusing here on the most commonly needed technology. Your own business might need more, or less, depending on the specific business you operate, your client base, and other factors. Minimally, you'll want to have the following:

• **Computer(s)** – Only 35 years ago, there were 50,000 computers in the world; now that many are being installed daily. PC or Mac? Who cares? Both are now integrated and can run each other's programs. The big issues, however, continue to be cost (PCs are cheaper) and reliability (Macs have less problems). Besides a desktop computer, you might also need a laptop or iPad. Consider your need for mobile computing when making this decision, though most new hand-held devices have become uber-gadgets providing enough computer power for most on-the run uses.

• **Software** – There's an old saying in the computing world: "Start with the software, then get the hardware." Your first job must be to list all the specific things you'd like a computer to do for you – and this includes far more than the basic business tasks described in this chapter. Because there is such an overwhelming variety of programs, you must either do a lot of self-study to find out what you should buy, or work with a knowledgeable computer consultant who is familiar with currently available software. You may not even have to "buy" software any longer. There's a revolution afoot making desktop software a thing of the past, replaced by free, simple, Web-based applications (apps) that do everything from spreadsheets to email – and more. Making it possible is Ajax (Asynchronous JavaScript and XML), a programming technique that gives Web sites the same kind of interactivity and speed that desktop programs have traditionally had. All these Web-based applications take place in that nebulous realm called the "cloud." Whether you purchase your software or use these free apps, first choose your software then buy a computer that's optimized for those programs.

• **Peripherals**

❑ **Printer(s)** – Whether this is color or black and white will largely depend on your specific business and the expectations of your clients. Laser printers, both color and B&W, dropped in price significantly overt the past decade. Because of their superior print quality, and this price reduction, they became the standard. Unless your business requires voluminous internal reports or has other special needs, avoid dot matrix, inkjet or other types of printers.

❑ **Fax machine or fax software** – If the majority of faxes you send and receive are documents created in a word processing or spreadsheet program, you can use fax software rather than a fax machine. Fax software lets you fax these types of documents directly to and from your personal computer, bypassing the need for a fax machine. If you're uncomfortable with fax software, however, and need faxes primarily for reference or communication only (rather than to manipulate their content), you might want to stick with a regular fax machine.

OUT AND ABOUT

There's work going on out there often in unusual places, thanks to mobile tools and internet connections. When asked when they had worked this month by The Dieringer Research Group, a sample of America's 135 million workers reported:

- 45.1 million from home
- 24.3 million at client or customer businesses
- 10.6 million in an automobile
- 16.3 while on vacations
- 15.1 million at a park or outdoor location
- 7.8 million on a train or airplane

The 45 million-plus Americans working from home report having thee to four regular workplaces!

❑ **Copier** – If you are right across the street from a copy shop, you might be able to put this off initially. You can get a small personal copier for $150 or less, but don't count on more than six pages per minute (ppm). Some copiers are also scanners (devices that take documents and images and transfers them to digital files on your computer), which will add to the price but also deliver some additional functionality that can prove quite useful.

❑ **Mobile technology** – Personal digital assistants (PDAs) are lightweight, hand-held computers designed for use as a personal organizer with communications capabilities. A typical PDA has no keyboard, relying instead on special hardware and pen-based computer software to enable the recognition of handwritten input, which is entered on the surface of a liquid crystal display screen. In addition to including such applications as a word processor, spreadsheet, calendar, and address book, PDAs are used as notepads, appointment schedulers, and wireless communicators for sending and receiving data, faxes, and electronic-mail messages. Gradually, cell phone technology is being added to these tools (e.g., iPhone Touch) and you can count on other "apps" (applications) being integrated in the near future.

❑ **Long-Term storage** – Always, always, *always* back up your data, and the best way to do this is to use a portable zip drive you can take with you. The cost for portable digital storage has come way down in price and because of this, it is smart to back up your data in three places (just in case). As broadband internet access becomes more widespread, *remote backup* services (such as iDrive, Rhinoback and Carbonite) are rising in popularity. Backing up via the internet to a remote location can protect against some worst-case scenarios such as fires, floods, or earthquakes which would destroy any backups in the immediate vicinity along with everything else. However, you will need to trust the third party to maintain the integrity and confidentiality of your sensitive data.

Office Ecology

Greening Your Office. Did you know that you can increase your productivity and that of your employees significantly by cleaning up indoor air quality, keeping temperatures even and ideal, and providing high-performance lighting?

❑ **Air quality.** The US Environmental Protection Agency (EPA) cites indoor air pollution as one of the top five public health threats in America. Pollutants can range from carbon monoxide to formaldehyde, particulate matter to volatile organic compounds (VOCs). Soy-based printer inks lower levels of VOCs. Houseplants are an often-overlooked helper in ridding the air of pollutants and toxins, counteracting outgassing and contributing to balanced internal humidity. Best plant choices for this are the Areca Palm, Reed Palm, Boston Fern, English Ivy and Rubber Plant.

❑ **Temperature.** The U.S. industrial sector uses more than one-third of all the energy consumed throughout the country, most of which comes from natural gas and petroleum. This consumption comes in the forms of heating, ventilation and air conditioning. Studies done by the National Institute of Standards and Technology have shown that improvements in windows and insulation are very cost effective, providing potential reductions in heat loss greater than 50 percent, reducing energy use by the same amount, and increasing comfort levels significantly. Use automatic setback thermostats to adjust the temperature for weekends and evenings.

❑ **Lighting.** Besides being another energy and money drain, the wrong amount or kind of lighting can result in eyestrain, glare, headaches and irritability – in short, employee inefficiency. Use "full-spectrum" light bulbs for more natural light; replace old fluorescent lighting fixtures using T-12 lamps with T-8 fluorescent lamps for better color, less flickering and 20 percent less energy use.

Other ways to create a better office ecology: Turn office equipment off at night; activate sleeper mode for printers, copiers and fax machines; buy and use recycled paper, folders and envelopes; monitor paper usage; and consider tapping into the power of aromatherapy. Studies show that the essential oils bergamot, peppermint and jasmine boost alertness, while lavender, lemon and rosewood reduce stress and tension.

Telephone Wisdom

Communication is the lifeblood of every business, and your telephone line is one of your most basic, yet multi-functional, tools. You should look at your needs for phone service in much the same way that you evaluate your needs for equipment: Think about how much time you spend on the phone, and how you will be using your fax (if applicable).

Most phone companies have staffs devoted to helping home office customers determine what combination of phone lines and services they need to set up or expand a home office. They can also help you figure out how to lower your phone bills. It's a smart thing to evaluate every six months or so.

Should you forego a landline entirely and just use your cell service? Many have but, if image is important to your business, then the unreliability of signal clarity will not put your company in the best light. If resources (or lack thereof) necessitate you using your cell phone exclusively, then plan for this and get the best phone possible with the most reliable service available.

Getting Tech Help When There's No Tech Department

If you are a small business owner and you run into a technical problem, the first place you should turn is the software or hardware vendor who sold you the equipment. Have their phone numbers written down in an easy-to-find location during a technology crisis. Also, follow these tips:

❑ *When all else fails, read the directions.* Most software and hardware come with "Help" files. Learn to use these. Most of your solutions will be found there.

❑ *Check out online user discussion lists* (see http://groups.google.com). These often have indexed archives to help you find answers to your problem. If your problem doesn't need immediate response, post your problem on the technical bulletin boards of an online service.

❑ *Research the location and hours of the nearest computer facility* at which you could work for a day or an afternoon in case you have a technical problem when you are working under deadline. Many of these places are open twenty-four hours a day. As with your other emergency numbers, post this information somewhere other than in a file on your computer, so you can easily put your fingers on it when you are having a problem. Chains like Kinkos provide these computer suites.

❑ *Try to anticipate when a problem might occur.* Part of coping with home office computer problems is figuring out how to anticipate them. One step is to use some of the gadgetry on the market that will alert you to problems before they reach the critical stage. Programs called utilities (e.g., Norton Anti-Virus Utilities) periodically test and analyze your system for things like errors on the hard drive. You can also get virus detection software that checks your system for viruses whenever you switch it on.

❑ *Hire a consultant* who will fill the role of a corporate technical department by coming to your home office. The best way to find a good consultant is through a referral from a friend or colleague, or by contacting a local computer users group which will have listings of local experts in various technologies. Keep in mind that a referral from a users group is not an endorsement, so hire carefully.

Look for someone who asks a lot of questions about your system and your problem. Authorized service providers are another option. These are usually computer stores or service organizations that specialize in certain kinds of hardware and software. Look for them in the *Yellow Pages* under "computers" and be sure they are authorized by a computer vendor. Services, like Best Buy's "Geek Squad," are another option.

❑ *Take precautions.* Keep your keyboard covered when you're not using it, to avoid debris buildup; don't eat or drink at your desk; clean your drives regularly (using compressed air); and regularly back up your hard drive and frequently used CDs so you don't lose all your data if you have a problem. Scrubex sheets can keep your laser printer, copier, or fax machine from breaking down. They are solvent-coated sheets that pick up the residue that can cause printer problems. To prevent mishaps from blackouts, brownouts, or electricity quirks (one of the most common causes of damage to computers in the home office), you can also buy an uninterruptable power supply. This device will maintain power in your office for twenty or thirty minutes during a power outage, so you have time to save what you are working on. Be sure to get one with a built-in surge protector.

This section on organizing and equipping your work space begins the transition from a focus on "Business Arrangement" (*setting up* your business) to "Business Conducting" (*managing your business*). Part one puts all the requisite pieces in one place; part two ensures all the pieces are working together in harmony.

CHAPTER SUMMARY

EQUIPPING YOUR OFFICE & WORKSPACE

- **Finding the Right Space**
  How important location is for your new company depends on the type of business and the facilities and other resources you need, and where your customers are. If you're in retailing, venue ownership or manufacturing, then geographic location is extremely important. If your business is information- or service-related, the actual location takes back seat to whether the facility itself can meet your needs. Internet connectivity, powerful mobile versions of office tools and new phone services are loosening the ties that bind and making physical location more about convenience than necessity.

- **Leased Office Options**
  If your business needs commercial space then you should feel very bold in negotiating lowers costs and shorter lease terms with owners and landlords. Administrative and secretarial support services are also available on an as-needed basis. Leased suites offer businesses of all types and sizes the opportunity to open an office and operate at maximum efficiency while controlling overhead expenses. Features usually include: Flexible lease terms and administrative support services.

- **Another Option: Incubating Your Business**
  A business incubator incubates your business for a set time until the business is ready to 'walk on its own.' A business incubator's main goal is to produce successful firms that will leave the program financially viable and freestanding. Is your business idea a good match for

an incubator? A good way to gauge this is to visit the web sites of incubators like, for example, LaunchBox Digital and YCombinator, two of the more noteworthy incubators. Also, remember that home-based offices provide significant tax benefits, don't require commuting, and generally involve lower start-up costs, fixed costs and rent expenses.

- **Home-Based Businesses**
  There are lots of benefits to having your business at home. Living where you work is cost-efficient and certainly convenient. The secret to success lies in setting up a distinct place for business activities that separates your personal and professional lives, then establishing a regular work schedule to help family, friends and clients know when they can and cannot interrupt you.

- **Setting Up Your Four Work Centers**
  No matter where you finally decide to set up shop, you will need to equip and organize your workspace to maximize your production and minimize distractions. There are four work centers most small businesses need: Telephone work center, Mail center, Money-processing center, and Filing center. There are several "best practices" you can apply to the physical organization of your work space: Keep the most frequently used objects within reach, Avoid built-in desks or other fixtures, Pay attention to lighting,

- **Equipping Your Office**
  In general, you need to balance form, function and budget when outfitting your base of operations. Once you've decided where you will establish your office — either in your home or a commercial space — the next important decisions involve furnishing and equipping it. Minimally, you'll want to have the following: Computer(s), Software, Peripherals (Printers, Fax Machine, Copier, Mobile Technology, Long-term storage).

- **Office Ecology**
  You can increase your productivity and that of your employees significantly by cleaning up indoor air quality, keeping temperatures even and ideal, and providing high-performance lighting. Other ways to create a better office ecology: Turn office equipment off at night; activate sleeper mode for printers, copiers and fax machines; buy and use recycled paper, folders and envelopes; monitor paper usage; and consider tapping into the power of aromatherapy.

- **Telephone Wisdom**
  You should look at your needs for phone service in much the same way that you evaluate your needs for equipment.

- **Getting Technical Help When There's No Tech Department**
  If you are a small business owner and you run into a technical problem, the first place you should turn is the software or hardware vendor who sold you the equipment. Some tips: When all else fails, read the directions; Check out online user discussion lists; Research the location and hours of the nearest computer facility; Try to anticipate when a problem might occur; Hire a consultant; and Take precautions.

FURTHER RESOURCES

ONLINE RESOURCES

American Home Business Association
www.homebusinessworks.com

Mother's Home Business Network
www.homeworkingmom.com

Equipment Leasing and Finance Association
elfaonline.org

National Business Incubation Association International Business Innovation Association
https://www.inbia.org/
Provides incubator location assistance.

SECTION TWO

BUSINESS 'CONDUCTING'

The act of directing a musical performance by way of visible gestures;

the direction of an orchestra or choir;

direct the course of; manage or control;

directing of a group of musicians.

11

BUSINESS CONDUCTING: BUILDING YOUR TEAM

The conductor is the only musician who doesn't make a sound. His power lies in his ability to make other people powerful. He is a silent releaser of the players' energies.
- Benjamin Zander, Boston Symphony Orchestra

It is typical for new entrepreneurs to fill multiple roles in the first phase of their company's development. The DIY (do it yourself) principle is strong in the music space. But this principle can easily be misunderstood. Derek Sivers, founder of CDBaby is fond of describing DIY as "*decide* it yourself" but don't try and *do* everything yourself. Likewise, artist Steve Kercher eventually found himself committed to a principle that just didn't work: "I made the mistake of thinking that I could do *everything* myself. WRONG! You cannot solve every problem in your business, no matter how good you are. Business is about creating something new through solving problems. You can't do that alone. You will get nowhere."

This doesn't mean music entrepreneurs won't have to fill a lot of different roles on their way to profitability. When The End Records began, founder Andreas Katsambas found himself wearing a variety of hats. "I had to get better at everything: accounting, marketing, A&R, promotions, graphics, etc. It was so tough at times but I couldn't afford a staff with experience". Eventually Andreas saw the value of this experience: "It really helped me develop extensive skills and see the big picture, which is now invaluable."

Independence is great, but once you have a clear idea of what you want and how to get it, you will likely need to pull together a team to help you become more successful. That can be a challenge because you'll need people who are passionate about the company's mission *and* capable of contributing to the group without a lot of wasted energy. ***Organizing people in the most effective way and getting them to work as a unit is the heart of leadership***. If two or more people work exceptionally well together, you'll want to use the combination to move the team forward. If two people on the team don't get along, you'll need to find a way to help them contribute to the group without destroying morale.

Skilled individuals and people who can quickly learn critical skills can be hard to find and recruit. Not to mention the lack of funds to pay top talent. Some entrepreneurs, like videogame composer Norihiko Hibino, see a way around this. He explains, "I had a lot of friends early on helping my business without any exchange of money. It was just because I helped a lot of my friends in many situations as well. So, even before you start up, show your 'love' to people. Paying for that expertise alone will not give you the best results anyway." What "goes around comes around," and sowing those seeds of generosity will often bear fruit.

When is it the right time to hire more help? If there just aren't enough hours in the day for you to get all your work done and you simply have more orders than you can fulfill, that's one signal it might be time to hire. Another: when you start to lose customers or receive a lot of complaints about anything from missed orders to poor quality. "If things start to fall through the cracks, it's a pretty good indication it's time to bring someone in," says Ron Finklestein, who heads AKRIS, a small business consulting firm in Akron, Ohio. But, above all else, hire only when the cash flow is positive enough to support hiring.

Defining Your Talent Requirements

A talent profile is a "wish list" of the type of person you want for your team. It's not a job description by itself, but can be used to develop one later. A talent profile is a tool that can help you decide whether to hire or outsource, figure out the best ways to recruit candidates, and help you screen candidates.
What do entrepreneurs look for in their potential team mates? Here is what Claire Chase requires for the International Contemporary Ensemble: "Passion. Commitment. Generosity. An unstoppable work ethic. A willingness to disagree, and to engage in dialogue about why we disagree. An eagerness to have one's mind changed by a better idea, or to change someone else's mind in a similar way. Everyone who works for ICE – the staff, the musicians, the interns, the volunteers – all have these qualities." This seems like a tall order, but Chase doesn't see it that way. "It's really pretty simple. We surround ourselves with people who speak this language and it's infectious – like a virus – but a good virus, one that makes you dream big and fly high and give more than you think you had to give."
Here are several points to consider as you develop your own talent profile:

❑ ***Don't delegate this work to someone else.*** You know best where your company is headed and what kinds of people will help you get there.

❑ ***Always start by asking yourself*** whether this position is really needed. Is there some way to combine tasks or positions in a more effective way?

❑ ***Consider what type of person will fit*** into your current work environment. Do you need someone who can work well in a team or operate on their own? Do you need someone who can work in a small room?

❑ ***Think about your personal and team skill gaps***. Can you find someone who will shore up your own weaker skills or fill in any gaps?

Small Business Advantages For Recruiting Top Talent

• Small business is slower to layoff in times of uncertainty. Big companies are the first to cut in the wake of economic crisis.

• Big corporations have a culture that is often distanced from the actual vision of top management. In small companies, everybody works together where the vision, integrity, and passion of the owner creates a positive, warm culture for employees.

• Being a small cog in the large corporate machine makes employees feel as if their results have no impact on the organization. In small business, the results of an employee's work can be felt immediately. This quick feedback mechanism creates stronger employer-employee relationships and mentoring.

• Staff in large companies, rarely feel the use of their full potential and talents. In the small firm, everyone knows and needs the full talents and contribution of each employee to succeed.

– Darrell Zahorsky, *About.com*

Finding Talent

Every small business owner wants to hire the best possible talent. But finding the appropriate candidate can be expensive and time consuming. "We have grown so much that I am in need of hiring more staff to keep up with the demands," writes Sara Wheeler about her company, Little Groove. "There are so many more exciting ways we can expand our company, but finding the right people to do the work can be challenging."

One of the biggest challenges is deciding *where* to look. Whether you've decided to hire a full-time employee or pursue another option, there are many sources of talent available to you.

❑ ***Use your own Network.*** First and foremost, put the word out to your colleagues and contacts that you're looking for help. Your own web of relationships will be the most valuable source for finding people. "The people that are closest to you are the ones to start with," advises Steve Kercher of Cartwheel Galaxy. "They know you well and will be honest with you. They will tell you whether you are going down the wrong path, or if the project and career move you are about to make, makes sense for you. You have to build great relationships and keep them nurtured." If you're a member of social networks like Facebook, LinkedIn and GuruNation, you already know how valuable these networks can be. Use your own internship program as a development lab for new recruits too. In fact, in the music business, internships account for over 50% of all hires.

❑ ***Use online employment postings:*** If you post your position online, you may want to avoid the monster-size job sites, like Monster.com, and craigslist.org, and focus instead on more music-specific sites like entertainmentcareers.com, and lamn.com. Another smart move is to contact music business department chairpersons at colleges and universities, and ask them to refer their top talent to your job opening. You can find a directory of these programs at http://meiea.org/member.schools.html

❑ ***Consider hiring "Virtual Assistants":*** The Virtual Assistant industry across the world is becoming a thriving, extremely valuable and very affordable resource for companies feeling the pinch in these uncertain times. Many Virtual Assistant's (commonly known as VA's) started out as corporate professionals, having spent a number of years working in the 'real' world and were looking for a flexible work-from-home solution. Not only can a company save significant costs when working with a Virtual Assistant, they will also find that VA's are efficient, knowledgeable, experienced, very dedicated and highly motivated people. Because VA's run their own businesses, they want to do a great job for their clients. Neither the location of a company or a VA is a barrier, because everything can be done online. You can source VAs at some of the more popular sites like upwork.com and guru.com.

HIRING "CREATIVE TYPES"

"There are plenty of good reasons why traditional executives ignore or dismiss professionals who came up through the creative side. And plenty of ammunition, based largely on the reinforcement of stereotypes that can keep us away from just about every management job, at every level. We're flaky; we lack the proper college degrees; we're outspoken, improperly trained, unreliable, too liberal, and unlikely to focus on any truly important topic for more than a few minutes-you know, we all have ADD, and we all suffer from short attention spans. What's more, we don't understand the numbers. And if we elevate the creative leader, who is going to take her place?"

– Harold Blumenthal, *The Creative Professional*

Outsource or Hire?

Even if you are sure you need to staff a position, you still need to decide whether you should hire a full-time employee or outsource the work to an independent contractor on a temporary basis. Entrepreneurs I spoke with outsource any of the following to contractors: marketing, legal, managing online social media, graphic and web design, bookkeeping, managing accounts, taxes, editing materials, and various promotional services. Follow these steps to evaluate the benefits and costs of both options.

❑ ***Review your growth goals and operating budget***. You need to have both your goals and your budget in mind as you make the "outsource vs. hire" decision.

❑ ***Determine the tangible and intangible benefits you could realize if you hire***. Forecast the extra income a new employee could generate in his/her first year with your business. If you're hiring a sales associate, for example, forecast the amount of new business he or she could bring in. If the individual's work is not so directly connected to the bottom line, make your best estimate of his/her impact on your business profitability. Consider other less tangible ways a new worker could help you achieve profitable growth. For example, could a new hire free you up to do the following:

- Spend time with valued customers to ensure their continued business?
- Attract and win new business?
- Develop new products or services?
- Work on operational or financial projects to make your business more profitable or accelerate its progress toward your growth goals?

All of these are fantastic reasons to consider hiring help. But then you must...

❑ ***Determine the costs of hiring***.

- Calculate the minimum salary and benefits, or contractor fees, you would have to pay the first year;
- Add the extra costs involved in recruiting and hiring a full-time employee (see p. 223f);
- Add the costs of orientation, training, mentoring, and supervision.

For tax purposes, the IRS differentiates between contractors and employees by the amount of power the employer has over the worker in terms of assigning duties, schedules and supervision. If the employer dictates not only what the worker is doing, but also when, where and how, this is an *employee.* If the worker is assigned other projects besides the specific task that they were originally hired for, then this is also falls under the category - *employee*.

❑ ***Compare benefits with costs and decide whether to hire***. If the benefits (tangible and intangible) exceed the costs of hiring, you can justify hiring a full-time employee. But if the costs exceed the benefits, you should explore the following options instead:

- Part-time employees
- Independent contractors and VAs (virtual assistants)
- Temporary help
- Leased staff
- Student interns or volunteers

When you do outsource some work, be careful of the temptation to go with the lowest bidder. "Cheap is tempting," says voice instructor Jeannie Deva, "but is usually more expensive. It is usually the sign of someone who is not as competent and who will give one a sub-par product that does not properly represent the company and image; has to be done over again costing more time and money, and often is being done by someone who turns out to be a nightmare to deal with personally." So hiring manager beware!

ADVANTAGES AND DISADVANTAGES OF HIRING WORKERS FROM VARIOUS SOURCES

	Advantages	Disadvantages
Paid employees	• Stable workforce • Loyalty to the organization • Can develop long-term relationships	• Cost of salary/wages • Cost of benefits, taxes
Contracted employees	• Can hire for special skills • Can hire for limited periods • No need to pay benefits or taxes	• Per-hour cost may be higher • Less loyalty to the organization • Constant need to train new workers
Outsourcing	• Can hire for special skills • Don't have to manage employees • Can build community relationships	• Per-hour cost may be higher • Little of no loyalty to organization • Company policies may differ
Volunteers/Interns	• No cost to organization • Can seek special skills • Can build community relationships	• Constant need to retrain • Organizational instability • Potential lack of skills/experience

How to Draft a Job Description

Creating a job description is a key step in the recruitment process. It is important to know what your requirements are, and potential candidates need the necessary information to determine whether they are suitably skilled to apply. It can also help you determine whether a full or part-time member of staff is required. You may wish to consider the following points in drawing up a description:

❑ **Determine salary** - make sure you are aware of the market/industry rate for the job you are recruiting for.

❑ **Title** - make sure it accurately describes the job that you are recruiting for.

❑ **Location and hours** - will the candidate be expected to travel, or can you foresee

a need for this? And what are the core working hours?

❑ **Who is the boss?** Who will the candidate be reporting to? In turn, will anyone be reporting to them? What are the overall supervisory responsibilities, if any?

❑ **Role overview** - a paragraph to summarize the job, perhaps including why it exists and how it might develop.

❑ **Functional responsibilities** - draw up a list of at least five duties here, in order of importance. Also indicate frequency of tasks, deciding what is routine and what is not.

❑ **Deliverables** - what will you expect of the candidate? Make sure these goals are well-defined, taking both short-term and long-term views.

❑ **Education, experience, skills** - define what is essential and desirable for the post.

❑ **Personality/style** - what sort of person would best fit this role? A couple of keywords will give yourself and a potential candidate a rough idea about the right sort of person.

The guiding principles of creating a job description are not only to get the right staff for your business, but to keep staff focused once they are hired. You will also be able to see if they have met your expectations. A good job description can be used throughout the employee's tenure in that position, helping both employer and employee to determine development and growth.

One full-time position you will most likely develop is that of Administrative Assistant (AA) – the engine that keeps your business humming. The following chart details the common areas an assistant can help with, divided into two columns. The first depicts basic functions requiring the ability to follow specific instructions any beginner, or even someone who is experienced but less confident, should be able to perform. The second column describes higher-level functions requiring greater judgment that a more experienced, seasoned, or competent assistant can master. Use these lists to speed your efforts to get the most out of your AA. In general, it is best to start with the basics, and then increase responsibilities to the more advanced functions.

ASSISTANT	**BEGINNER**—Requires Ability to follow directions	**EXPERT**—Requires Judgment and experience
PHONES	Take complete messages and forward to appropriate dept.	Filter calls and troubleshoot problems
MAIL & EMAIL	Presort into categories Toss/delete junk Assemble packages Type stock letters Address packages Send faxes	Read, summarize mail Stock answers—certain inquiries Forward to relevant others Draft letters, edit boss's drafts Custom assemble materials Draft faxes
FILING	Maintain existing system Put things in right places	Design/streamline system Weed folders out post-project

SCHEDULES	Type in appointments Type to-dos Confirm appointments day before Arrange transportation Get directions Make reservations Type itinerary	Prioritize and schedule appointments Remind boss of upcoming dates Pull relevant files and brief boss Keep boss on time Meeting planning Block out time to do projects Assist on to-dos
MANAGE CONTACTS	Enter new contacts Vigilantly update changes	Weed database/re-categorize Merge for mass mailing
CLIENT/STAFF CARE	Send birthday cards Order flowers/gifts	Clip and send articles of interest Write thank-you notes
REPORTS/MEMOS	Type as dictate	Generate reports—requires writing, editing, financial software skills
SUPPLIES/EQUIP.	Keep supplies in stock Call and supervise repairs	Troubleshoot computers Research vendors/reduce costs
MARKETING	Send out packets Assemble huge mailing	Oversee brochure production Design mailing materials
MEETINGS	Book space Confirm attendees Order refreshments Order A/V Assemble materials	Pull relevant files Take notes Attend in place of boss

Developing An Internship Program

It's been said that the music business is built on the backs of interns and that may be true! In a business as relationship-driven as music, it only makes sense that internships are so important. They allow industry careerists an opportunity to get their foot in the door and begin building their careers from within.

Internships can prove to be very rewarding for both the company and the intern. There are several routes to finding top-notch interns. Many colleges have career centers or specialized offices that coordinate internships for the entire campus. Some people go directly to department heads and ask for recommendations, while others tap their industry associations (for example, MEIEA.org or NAMM.com).

If there is a Music Business, Arts Administration or Communications program in a nearby college or university, you'll have a large pool of potential interns. A little known way to find top candidates is by visiting classrooms. Speak to classes in exchange for the chance to solicit for students. Start early! Make calls in February and March for the fall semester. Once you've found the ideal intern, follow these nine rules of student hiring.

❑ ***Be prepared to teach.*** Even if your intern is a self-starter, don't forget she is there to learn. Expect to spend about 10 percent of the allotted time instructing her.

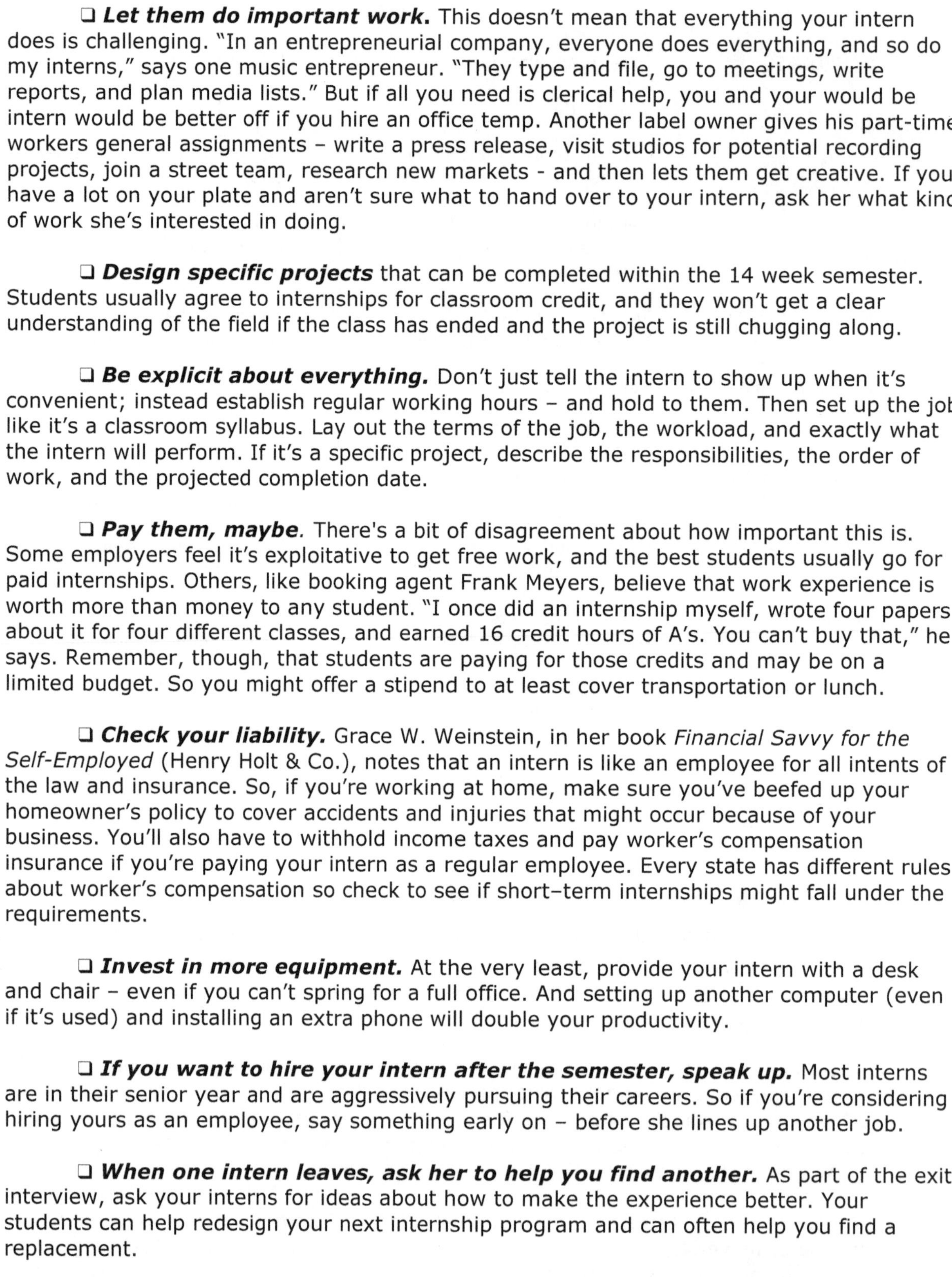

❑ ***Let them do important work.*** This doesn't mean that everything your intern does is challenging. "In an entrepreneurial company, everyone does everything, and so do my interns," says one music entrepreneur. "They type and file, go to meetings, write reports, and plan media lists." But if all you need is clerical help, you and your would be intern would be better off if you hire an office temp. Another label owner gives his part-time workers general assignments - write a press release, visit studios for potential recording projects, join a street team, research new markets - and then lets them get creative. If you have a lot on your plate and aren't sure what to hand over to your intern, ask her what kind of work she's interested in doing.

❑ ***Design specific projects*** that can be completed within the 14 week semester. Students usually agree to internships for classroom credit, and they won't get a clear understanding of the field if the class has ended and the project is still chugging along.

❑ ***Be explicit about everything.*** Don't just tell the intern to show up when it's convenient; instead establish regular working hours – and hold to them. Then set up the job like it's a classroom syllabus. Lay out the terms of the job, the workload, and exactly what the intern will perform. If it's a specific project, describe the responsibilities, the order of work, and the projected completion date.

❑ ***Pay them, maybe***. There's a bit of disagreement about how important this is. Some employers feel it's exploitative to get free work, and the best students usually go for paid internships. Others, like booking agent Frank Meyers, believe that work experience is worth more than money to any student. "I once did an internship myself, wrote four papers about it for four different classes, and earned 16 credit hours of A's. You can't buy that," he says. Remember, though, that students are paying for those credits and may be on a limited budget. So you might offer a stipend to at least cover transportation or lunch.

❑ ***Check your liability.*** Grace W. Weinstein, in her book *Financial Savvy for the Self-Employed* (Henry Holt & Co.), notes that an intern is like an employee for all intents of the law and insurance. So, if you're working at home, make sure you've beefed up your homeowner's policy to cover accidents and injuries that might occur because of your business. You'll also have to withhold income taxes and pay worker's compensation insurance if you're paying your intern as a regular employee. Every state has different rules about worker's compensation so check to see if short–term internships might fall under the requirements.

❑ ***Invest in more equipment.*** At the very least, provide your intern with a desk and chair – even if you can't spring for a full office. And setting up another computer (even if it's used) and installing an extra phone will double your productivity.

❑ ***If you want to hire your intern after the semester, speak up.*** Most interns are in their senior year and are aggressively pursuing their careers. So if you're considering hiring yours as an employee, say something early on – before she lines up another job.

❑ ***When one intern leaves, ask her to help you find another.*** As part of the exit interview, ask your interns for ideas about how to make the experience better. Your students can help redesign your next internship program and can often help you find a replacement.

If You Decide to Take on Partners...

If you're considering going into business with a friend, or several friends, you're joining in a basic human dream – running your own show, being your own boss and hopefully gaining some control over your economic destiny. There can be many benefits of shared ownership of a business. The chemistry and spirit of two, three or more minds and souls working together can often produce exciting results. There's more energy and enthusiasm, and – at least as important – more cash, skills and resources. And it's a lot easier to arrange time off if you have partners than if you're trying to run a business all by yourself.

Those who choose to run their own company will almost inevitably go through periods of stress, and their survival will depend on their mastering quickly and competently all sorts of unfamiliar skills and tasks. In a partnership business, there are also the stresses and risks that can come with shared ownership. Money can be incendiary stuff, and when you share money, you're inevitably involved in an intimate relationship with your fellow partners. Here are some guidelines for developing and nurturing strong partnerships:

- ❒ Find someone whose strengths complement your weaknesses.
- ❒ Set up a trial period to see if you can work well together.
- ❒ Make no promises or financial commitments until you are sure the chemistry is right.
- ❒ Consider rotating positions and titles.
- ❒ Communicate regularly to avoid power grabs and misunderstandings.
- ❒ Define who will contribute the cash, property, or expertise.
- ❒ Specify the percentage of ownership each person will have.
- ❒ Prepare a business plan and financial forecast for the life of the partnership.
- ❒ Figure out who will provide additional cash if it is needed.
- ❒ Be sure the tax profit-and-loss allocations are consistent and fair for all the partners involved.
- ❒ Provide a way to remove or buy out partners who fail to meet their obligations.
- ❒ Define how, when, and in what order the profits will be distributed to partners.
- ❒ Communicate openly and honestly with your partners.

As explained in chapter 6, a partnership can take a variety of legal forms: General Partnership, Limited Partnership, Limited Liability Corporation (an interesting hybrid of a partnership and corporation), and a Limited Liability Partnership. It is beyond the scope of this book to address these. I would refer you to an excellent primer on business alliances called, *Teaming Up: The Small Business Guide to Collaborating with Others to Boost Your Earnings and Expand Your Horizons* by Paul and Sarah Edwards (Jeremy Tarcher/Putnam).

Selecting an Attorney

Sooner or later you will need legal counsel as a small business owner and it's important to know how to select the best counsel for your particular needs. So many issues can arise when developing a business. "We used a trademark lawyer to apply and receive each of our registered trademarks," writes entrepreneur Jeannie Deva. "When it came time to create important contracts for licensing my certified voice teachers, we definitely took on a lawyer. As well, when we sold our Boston voice studio in order to restructure the business and our corporation and move to Los Angeles, we used a lawyer to plan for and draw up the contractual agreements". The list can go on and on.

When it is time to see an attorney here are a few tips to help you with the screening process:

❑ ***Get a Specialist***. Music-related businesses should be cautioned against the natural inclination to use a friend, relative ("My Cousin Vinny"), or family lawyer to fill their entertainment law needs. This is fine if they're qualified. However, the trend today is toward greater legal specialization than ever before because of the increased complexity of our commercial society and the music industry itself.

Unless a lawyer regularly deals with management, recording, and music publishing contracts; copyright protection and administration; and licensing of intellectual and artistic property, chances are he or she won't sufficiently understand or appreciate the entertainment industry and its particular legal challenges.

❑ ***Get a Referral***. A referral from a satisfied client is a good start but...

❑ ***Get References.*** Always ask the attorney for at least two client-references you can call. This is a perfectly reasonable request and any lawyer who has a problem with this should be your cue to exit. Be sure the work the lawyer did for the client is similar to what you need and be sure also that the work was performed in the last 6 months to a year (this business changes too fast for sporadic legal excursions).

❑ ***Get the Dirt*** (if there is some). You can make two important phone calls to find out if there have been any complaints logged in your city or state against this attorney. They're calls worth making: Secretary of State's office (look for the phone number in the "Government" section of your phone book), and The Better Business Bureau (http://www.bbb.org/). The Better Business Bureau Directory lists the addresses and phone numbers of Better Business Bureaus in the U.S. and Canada.

❑ ***Have a Meeting***. Most attorneys will waive their usual hourly fee for the first consultation. At this consultation meeting you'll want to:
Ask the attorney about her basic business philosophy - even her philosophy of life. Why? Because this will help you understand her world view, a significant relationship component. If your world view turns out to be diametrically opposed to the attorney's, it probably means you're not a good match for each other. Feel the vibe - Trust your instincts.
Inquire about the extent and quality of the attorney's pertinent industry contacts.
Find out how the fee structure would work to avoid any misunderstandings.
A note on legal fees: Sometimes you'll need legal counsel for short-term projects like putting together the appropriate performance and partnership agreements, trademark searches of your business/band name, incorporating your business, or copyright registration. These kinds of projects are usually paid for as a "flat fee" based on the attorney's hourly rate.

Longer-term projects and legal representation to the music industry (to labels, publishers, merchandise companies, etc.) are often paid in "points" (percentage points) of contract advances and/or future royalties.

❑ ***Do-(some of)-it-Yourself***. You can handle a lot of the groundwork when it comes to short-term legal needs. For example, communication technologies like the Internet, allows you to do a national trademark search from your desktop. For tips on this and other do-it-yourself legal resources contact Nolo Press (http://www.nolo.com) or FindLaw.com (http://www.findlaw.com).

❑ ***Another first-stage option*** for longer-term legal projects is the VLA (**Volunteer Lawyers for the Arts**). Founded in 1969, VLA was "the first legal aid organization in the U.S. dedicated to providing free or low-cost arts-related legal assistance to artists and arts organizations in all creative fields who cannot afford private counsel." You must apply for assistance and there is a small application fee. The main VLA office is in NY (vlany@vlany.org) with satellite offices around the country.

Choosing an Accountant

You have several choices in who should maintain your accounting system. You can:

- Maintain the books your self.
- Hire an accountant on a full-time or part-time basis.
- Hire an accountant who can *set up* your books.

Most entrepreneurs set up a hybrid system in which they maintain the day-to-day reports, while an accountant does the period-end record preparation, summaries and reconciliations and the returns for sales tax, excise tax and payroll taxes.

In making the choice, you must decide whether you have the ability and time to set up and maintain good records or if you should engage an outside accounting service. Probably the best advice I can give you on the subject of taxes and your finances in general is this: *Hire an experienced accountant who specializes in small business*. You may not need to do this right away while your business is small and hasn't yet taken off. But eventually you will need help. Under ideal circumstances, your accountant is a trusted member of your close circle of advisors. This person should be a wise business counselor as well as a tax planner. You will want to retain someone you feel comfortable with. And do make sure she is a good listener! If your accountant is going to help you structure the financial future of your business, she had better understand your plans and believe in your vision.

Don't be afraid to shop around for the best person. Ask other business owners who they use and talk to your banker or attorney for recommendations. Sometimes your local college's accounting department can be a good source for referrals. Call the Society of Certified Public Accountants in your state. Many, though not all, have referral services.

Old Media/New Media Publicist

There is only one correct time to seek a media publicist: When you yourself have become thoroughly familiar with the publicity process, but because of manifold commitments and the lack of time fail to access all the publicity opportunities available to you. It's crucial for the do-it-yourselfer to have at least introductory experience working with the media. That way you're in a better position to evaluate a publicist's record and, once having done so, realistically evaluate just what is being done on your behalf.

A publicist helps create awareness of a person or business through the media.

A good publicist today will be expert in both *traditional* media (newspapers, radio, magazines, etc.) and *new* media (social networks, blogs, mobile apps, etc.). Traditional media has its rules and influencers, and new media has its rules and influencers. Where do you find this full-spectrum publicist? Start by asking for local recommendations. Also notice which bands and musicians are getting a lot of quality media coverage, both online and off.

Call or write to the publication and ask who the artist's publicist is. Shop around. Never take the first person who's available. You have nothing with which to compare his or her skills. Prices vary as does creativeness. What you are really purchasing when you hire a publicist is access to their network of relationships built up over many years.

Once you've found several possibilities use the following guidelines to be sure you get exactly what you need. Consider:

- ❑ Is the individual or firm *inventive*? Can they create distinction and dimension?
- ❑ Is the individual or firm *interested* in what you're doing?
- ❑ Is the individual or firm so *overwhelmed* by current clients that their ability to take on new work limited?
- ❑ Does the individual or firm now serve *clients with whom you compete*?
- ❑ What will it cost? Good publicists charge anywhere from $1500-3000/mo.

It is completely reasonable to request samples of their work and client references. After all, it is the musicians and music companies they've worked with who can give you the most relevant feedback about that publicist's work. As with most services, if they are reluctant to provide references, move on to someone else. Only hire those who are proud of their work.

Graphic Designer

For centuries human communication was limited by the distance that separated developed areas. In order to share a message with a neighboring town or village it was necessary to walk, set sail over a dangerous sea, ride a horse, beat a drum, or send a messenger to physically deliver it. Dispatch of a letter was an expensive process which often could take weeks — even months.

Fast forward to the dawn of the 21st century: The world is increasingly more media-oriented and we are surrounded by television, radio, print, the internet, and now personal media via wireless technologies.

Simple communication is not enough.

In days gone by there was little need for design services. It's hard to imagine Abraham Lincoln hiring a graphic artist to lay out his speeches. But in today's media-driven market, design is a crucial component of communication. A product or service surrounded by good design can mean the difference between failure or success. People *do* judge a book by its cover and so graphic design, both online and offline, will be an important ingredient in your success.

Working with Graphic Artists. Professionally designed materials create a successful image, but they don't come cheap. One way to make this more affordable is to seek out an art student whose style you like and see if you can work out a mutually profitable exchange. Some tips:

❑ ***Know your budget***. Request written estimates from designers you interview for a particular project (allowing a plus or minus 10% variation). Design and printing can be complicated and mistakes expensive.

❑ ***Screen artists carefully***. Ask around for referrals and check the Net for "Graphic Designers." Pick three and review their online portfolios. Call and discuss budget with them on the phone beforehand. Though this may feel awkward, it will save both of you time and frustration if your financial expectations are worlds apart. Ask to see samples relevant to your planned project and make sure the artist was responsible for these samples from concept to execution.

❑ ***Give the artist creative freedom***. Carefully describe the audience you want to reach and the message you want to impart. Show your artist design samples you like then let him or her create. Establish check points along the way so no one is running off in the wrong direction.

❑ **Perfect means professional**. When any text is part of the design, proofread! One proofreading tip that works: Hold a ruler under each line as you read. The ruler focuses your eyes on one line at a time and greatly improves your chances of catching errors.

❑ **Approve the design in the early stages**. Be sure to ask your designer for "comps" before a job is done. Comps are true-to-life renderings of a finished piece. They're usually not cheap but well worth the cost.

❑ **Observe deadlines**. Give you and your designer enough lead time. Never assign a job without a deadline.

❑ **Pay as you go**. Never pay an artist the entire amount up front. It's fair to pay one third at the start, one third midway through a job, and one third upon completion and delivery. Sometimes half down and half at completion is acceptable too. Your contract with an artist is a business agreement. Let mutual respect and fairness prevail.

Web Designers and Webmasters

Most businesses will greatly benefit from hiring a professional to design their Web site, but finding someone who is right for the job may not be easy. In hiring a designer, look for someone who has experience creating graphics for the Web, a style that appeals to your tastes, and who can provide all the services you need at a price you can afford. Creating graphics for the Web is different from designing print logos, business cards, and brochures. Having an eye for which kind of graphics looks good on a Web page is something learned with experience, and a good designer knows how to optimize a graphic for quick loading. If a designer can't create a graphic image for your site in GIF format at 15-25K size, then look for someone else.

The best way to source a web designer is to get a referral from someone you know. You can also see the name of the company that designed a web site you like somewhere towards the bottom of the site's home page. Examine the prospective designer's portfolio and visit Web sites that they've created. If you like what you see, hire them. Craig's List (craigslist.org) is a another good place to source freelance web designers, as is elance.com.

Webmasters are people who know and understand how the Web functions. They have the ability and knowledge of coding for HTML (HyperText Markup Language), Java Scripting, Flash animation and Applets. A "complete" Webmaster can also create the design you are looking for in a website, will listen to your ideas in order to incorporate them into the site, and be available for you when you need them.

On the other hand, HTML isn't rocket science. You can do some (or all) of this yourself and many do. The end product, however, has got to look professional because standards for a web presence have only gotten higher.

When hiring a Webmaster, ask a few questions before you make a final decision:

- ❑ ***Qualifications*** - How long have they been doing this work? Is webmastering their core business or just a part-time gig? Can they provide any client references? Make sure that they have been working on websites for at least 3 to 5 years; the longer they have been working with coding the more knowledge they will have on all the changes throughout the years. Speak to references and view sites that they have created in order to see if you like their style.
- ❑ ***Availability*** - You need to find out up-front how available the Webmaster is. How long will it take for them to make corrections or changes to your site when needed? Do they offer monthly maintenance? Can you opt for periodic updates? Do they fix technical difficulties as soon as they are informed? Ask these questions to their references as well as to the Webmaster.
- ❑ ***Coding*** - Some Webmasters do not actually use coding (HTML), instead they use ready-made software to fill in the blanks. Make sure that who you choose knows how to write code. This is imperative!
- ❑ ***Flexibility*** - Will the Webmaster work with you and use your ideas? Some Webmasters have their own way of doing things when it comes to creating sites. Be sure that they are willing to be creative and try new things. Ask their references about this too.
- ❑ ***Capabilities*** - Ask if they are capable or have the knowledge of using interactivity on your site. This may include forms, chat, and discussion boards. Do they offer services to maintain the interactivity for you? Can they add auto-responders for email? Will they be able to help you set up a blog or podcasts?

❑ ***Added Extras*** - If the Webmaster has extra services to offer, you will be better off. Find out if they offer or have their own web hosting company. How about 24/7 technical support?

❑ ***Charges*** - Webmasters charge for their services on either a monthly or hourly rate. Most charge at least $50–$100 per hour. Shop around and compare. Make sure there are no hidden fees.

Assembling Your Advisory Board

Advice is something the entrepreneur should always be seeking. "I started getting advice even before writing the business plan," says Nimbit co-founder Patrick Faucher, "and I'm always expanding my network of advisors and experts. It is a constant process that never stops at any stage." Advisors will compensate for your own blind spots and expand your view on many matters relevant to your business.

If you're not ready to take the plunge with a formal board of advisors, but need help with a particular problem, an advisory board (generally paid in stock and/or expenses) may be the answer. Here are six ways to work efficiently with an advisory board:

❑ ***Recruit noncompetitive advisors***. They'll bring a broader and more objective viewpoint to your group. Seek people outside your business rather than suppliers, customers and others who might have a conflict of interest.

❑ ***Don't be too informal***. Advisors aren't charged with fiduciary or regulatory responsibilities as boards of directors are. But professionalism and mutual respect should still be the hallmarks of your interactions.

❑ ***Schedule regular meetings***. Get the entire board together to brainstorm at least 2-3 times a year. In between meetings, consult with individual advisors whose areas of expertise can help solve a specific problem.

❑ ***Prepare for meetings***. Plan the agenda carefully. Even when meeting one on one, write down questions or issues. Give advisors a copy of the agenda at least one week in advance.

❑ ***Be open to coaching***. Encourage advisors to ask tough questions and challenge you. Breaking old patterns of thinking and operating will help you develop new strategies for growing your business.

❑ ***Be honest about your needs***. Acknowledge when you're "stuck" and need help negotiating the next phase of growth.

Building your team takes time and patience. Ideally, you want to achieve some measure success on your own before hiring so you can leverage that success when attracting others to join your company. Success begets success and strategic team building will help you multiply that success.

But *finding* your teammates is one thing; *managing* that team towards productive success is another. Beginning with the next chapter, we start exploring how to best manage the team you've put together as well as how to manage the manager.

CHAPTER SUMMARY

BUSINESS CONDUCTING: BUILDING YOUR TEAM

- **Defining Your Talent Requirements**
  A talent profile is a tool that can help you decide whether to hire or outsource, figure out the best ways to recruit candidates, and help you screen candidates. Here are several points to consider as you develop your own talent profile: Don't delegate this work to someone else, Always start by asking yourself, Consider what type of person will fit, and Think about your personal and team skill gaps.

- **Finding Talent**
  One of the biggest challenges in finding the appropriate candidate is deciding where to look. Whether you've decided to hire a full-time employee or pursue another option, there are many sources of talent available to you. Some tips: Use your own Network; Use online employment postings; and Consider hiring "Virtual Assistants".

- **Outsource or Hire?**
  You need to decide whether you should hire a full- or part-time employee, or outsource the work to an independent contractor on a temporary basis. Follow these steps to evaluate the benefits and costs of both options: Review your growth goals and operating budget, Determine the tangible and intangible benefits you could realize if you hire, Determine the costs of hiring, and Compare benefits with costs and decide whether to hire.

- **Co-Workers: Hiring Guidelines for the Entrepreneur-Employer**
  These are some strategies to help you create a recruiting program to suit your needs: Evaluate The Position, Profile Your Company, Design A Recruiting Strategy, Examine Candidates' Clues, Improve Your Interviewing, Perform 360-degree References, Adopt Flexibility, and Understand Your Legal Obligations.

- **Developing Your Internship Program**
  Internships can prove to be very rewarding for both the company and the intern. Once you've found the ideal intern, follow these nine rules of student hiring: Be prepared to teach; Let them do important work; Design specific projects; Be explicit about everything; Pay them (maybe); Check your liability; Invest in more equipment; If you want to hire your intern after the semester, speak up; When one intern leaves, ask her to help you find another.

- **If You Decide to Take on Partners.**
  In a partnership business, there are also the stresses and risks that can come with shared ownership. Money can be incendiary stuff, and when you share money, you're inevitably involved in an intimate relationship with your fellow partners. Some guidelines for developing and nurturing strong partnerships:
  - ❑ Find someone whose strengths complement your own.
  - ❑ Set up a trial period to see if you can work well together.
  - ❑ Make no promises or financial commitments until you are sure the chemistry is right.
  - ❑ Consider rotating positions and titles.
  - ❑ Communicate regularly to avoid power grabs and misunderstandings.
  - ❑ Define who will contribute the cash, property, or expertise.
  - ❑ Specify the percentage of ownership each person will have.
  - ❑ Prepare a business plan and financial forecast for the life of the partnership.
  - ❑ Figure out who will provide additional cash if it is needed.
  - ❑ Be sure the tax profit-and-loss allocations are consistent and fair for all the partners involved.
  - ❑ Provide a way to remove or buy out partners who fail to meet their obligations.
  - ❑ Define how, when, and in what order the profits will be distributed to partners.
  - ❑ Communicate openly and honestly with your partners.

- **Selecting an Attorney**
  When it is time to seek an attorney here are a few tips to help you with the screening process:

- ❑ Get Referrals from a reliable source.
- ❑ Get References from the attorney.
- ❑ Get the Dirt (if there is any).
- ❑ Have a Meeting.
- ❑ Do-(some of)-it-Yourself.
- ❑ Another first-stage option for longer-term legal projects is the VLA (Volunteer Lawyers for the Arts), though services vary greatly throughout the country.

- **Choosing an Accountant**
  You have several choices in who should maintain your accounting system. You can: Maintain the books yourself, Hire an accountant on a full-time or part-time basis, or Hire an accountant who can set up your books. It is recommended that you hire an accountant to help set up your books, do the final year-end preparations, and advise you as needed. There are several types of professionals you may consider: Certified Public Accountant (CPA), Enrolled Agent (EA) and Accredited Accountant.
  In addition to bookkeeping, an accountant can sometimes assist with cash flow requirements and budget forecasts, business borrowing, choosing a legal structure for your business and preparation and advice on tax matters.

- **Old Media/New Media Publicist**
  There is one correct time to seek a media publicist: When you yourself have become thoroughly familiar with the publicity process. A publicist helps create awareness of a person or business through the media. A good publicist today will be expert in both traditional media (newspapers, radio, magazines, etc.) and new media (social networks, blogs, mobile apps, etc.). What you are really purchasing when you hire a publicist is access to their network of media relationships built up over many years.

- **Graphic Designer**
  People *do* judge a book by its cover and so graphic design, both online and offline, will be an important ingredient in your success. Some tips on finding graphic artists: Know your budget, Screen artists carefully, Give the artist creative freedom, Perfect means professional, Approve the design in the early stages, Observe deadlines, and Pay as you go.

- **Web Designers & Webmasters**
  In hiring a designer, look for someone who has experience creating graphics for the Web, a style that appeals to your tastes, and who can provide all the services you need at a price you can afford. When hiring a Webmaster, ask a few questions before you make a final decision: Qualifications, Availability, Coding, Flexibility, Capabilities, Added Extras, and Charges.

- **Assembling Your Advisory Board**
  If you're not ready to take the plunge with a formal board of advisors, but need help with a particular problem, an advisory board (generally paid in stock and/or expenses) may be the answer. Here are six ways to work efficiently with an advisory board:
  - ❑ Recruit noncompetitive advisors.
  - ❑ Don't be too informal.
  - ❑ Schedule regular meetings.
  - ❑ Prepare for meetings.
  - ❑ Be open to coaching.
  - ❑ Be honest about your needs.

FURTHER RESOURCES

BOOKS

Collaboration: How Leaders Avoid the Traps, Build Common Ground, and Reap Big Results by Morten Hansen (2009, Harvard Business Review Press).

Hiring the Best: The Fast Track Guide to Win by Effective Interviewing, Recruiting, Hiring and Keeping the Best People by Nick White (2009, Emereo Pty Ltd).

The Idea-Driven Organization: Unlocking the Power in Bottom-Up Ideas by Alan G. Robinson (2014, Berrett-Koehler).

Creating Teams with an Edge by Harvard Business School Press (2004).

Leading Talents Leading Teams: Aligning People, Passions and Positions for Maximum Performance by Lee Ellis (2003, Northfield Publishing).

Optimizing Talent: What Every Leader and Manager Needs to Know to Sustain the Ultimate Workforce by Linda D. Sharkey (2011, Info Age Publishing).

Superbosses: How Exceptional Leaders Master the Flow of Talent by Sydney Finkelstein (2016, Portfolio).

Teaming Up by Paul & Sarah Edwards (1997, Jeremy Tarcher). An oldie, but a goodie!

Unlocking Potential: 7 Coaching Skills That Transform Individuals, Teams, and Organizations by Michael K. Simpson (2014, Grand Harbor Press)

12

BUSINESS CONDUCTING: MANAGING YOURSELF & OTHERS

The secret of getting ahead is getting started. The secret of getting started is breaking your complex overwhelming tasks into small manageable tasks, and then starting on the first one.

– Mark Twain

Good ol' Mark Twain. Sounds simple, huh? If it weren't for the fact that management incompetence is the number one reason for business failures, I'd think it was simple too. Management is the framework in which your entire business operates: planning, staffing, communicating, analyzing, producing, reporting, training, supervising, marketing, expediting and so on, takes place within this frame.

Imagine it's a year or two down the road. You've launched your music operation and here's a list of stuff you now have to deal with on a daily (or, at least, weekly) basis:

- *Writing web copy, sorting & mailing letters, flyers, promo kits, news releases, etc.;*
- *Answering, making, receiving, and returning phone calls;*
- *Writing, sending, sorting & deleting e-mails;*
- *Finding, contacting, assessing & convincing money sources;*
- *Finding, planning for and facilitating sales;*
- *Making rounds of weekly retail promo calls;*
- *Solving scheduling conflicts in the studio;*
- *Cleaning, purging and updating databases of outdated media contacts;*
- *Dealing with web server issues;*
- *Renewing registrations for company domain names;*
- *Taking time out to exercise;*
- *Dealing with an absentee staff member;*
- *Meeting with marketing director to go over promotional plans;*
- *Evaluating postage options for large shipments;*
- *Calling & facilitating general office meetings;*
- *Reviewing contract draft with an artist manager;*
- *Deciding about a permission to license a track to a compilation;*
- *Approving graphics for a special event flier;*
- *Holding a planning meeting for an upcoming release party;*
- *Doing some research on the video game market;*
- *Trying to fix the printer when it goes on the blink; giving up and spending time locating a technician who can service it;*
- *Reviewing album artwork for a release;*
- *Renewing subscription to* Billboard*; coming up with an extra $150!;*
- *Assigning tasks & motivating your street team leaders in other cities;*
- *Meeting with a top artist booking agent to discuss supporting a tour;*

- *Paying the ISP cable modem bill;*
- *Refilling stapler (where did I put those staples?!);*
- *Comparing rates and booking a flight to music conference across the country;*
- *Comparing rates and booking a flight to see your mom across the country;*
- *Timing it right to make those calls to the west coast before offices close;*

It's 9:30 pm – time to go catch a band at a local club!

One of the questions I asked music entrepreneurs interviewed for this book was: "If you were conducting this interview, what question would *you* ask?" Andreas Katsambas of The End Records came up with the following one and then answered it too: "If you have to divide your duties what's the ratio of doing things you like vs. tackling things that have to be done?" His answer? – 30/70. That's a telling answer and underlines a reality of entrepreneurial life.

Of all the challenges that entrepreneurs face, nothing matches in difficulty the everydayness of business ownership. It exists from the moment you wake up until the moment you collapse in exhaustion at the end of the day. It's exhilarating, terrifying.....and constant.

What keeps this relentless routine from taking undue toll on you is the management systems you put in place. Good management places you in the driver's seat rather than under the wheels. Studies show that businesses fail, not for a lack of a good product, and not for the lack of a market for that product.

Businesses fail primarily because of management incompetence.
The way you manage yourself, the approach you take to managing other people, and the ways you manage time, money and information will be the primary reasons you're company succeeds (or fails) in the long run.

The Many Faces of Management

The word "manager" itself is widely misunderstood and frequently misused in the business world. A manager is not the same as an executive, though "manager" is used to refer to both. As an entrepreneur you will be both – the manager and the chief executive, as well as the chief financial officer, VP of marketing, chief information officer, administrative assistant, and clean up crew all in one! To wear this many "hats" requires a strong set of managing skills.

But what is "management"? Here's a pretty good definition: It is making something planned happen within a specific time through the smart use of available resources. Catch that again:

Management is making something planned happen within a specific time through the smart use of available resources.

This definition encompasses planning, goals, intelligence and resourcefulness. Management is essentially "conducting" your business "orchestra" to "perform" the strategic "composition" magnificently. Your success as a manager comes down to the difference between managing your work and letting your work manage you. Therefore, like the maestro, the most important ingredient to your company's success (besides you) will be *smart, creative and resourceful conducting (i.e., management) of your business.*

The following chart illustrates the many dimensions of management you will be tackling. As you can readily see, management puts a lot on your plate:

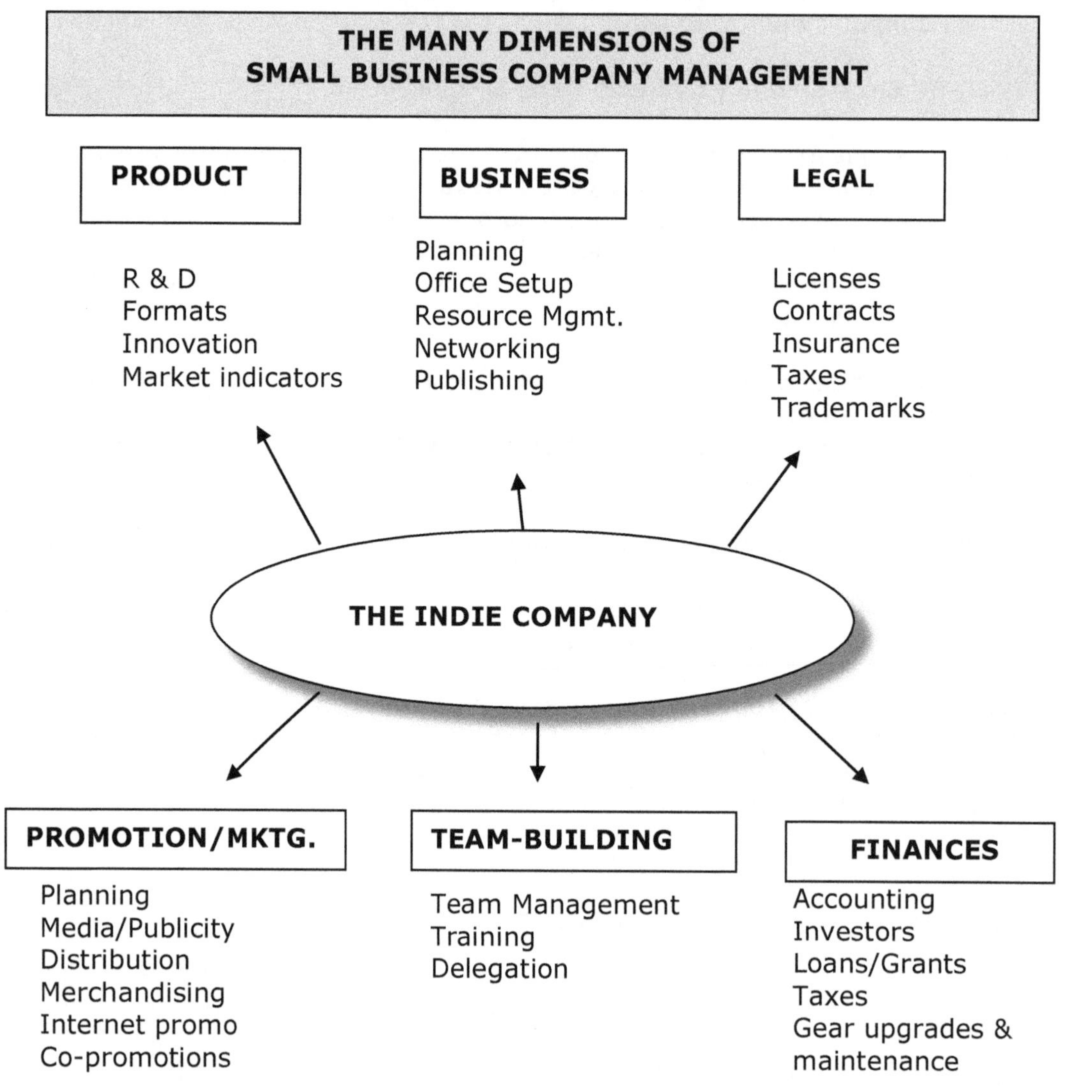

Managerial Functions

All businesses depend on effective management. Regardless of whether managers run a major international company like Sony Music or a small local or regional record label, they perform many of the same functions, are responsible for many of the same tasks, and have many of the same responsibilities. The work of managers can be broken down into the following categories: planning, organizing, staffing, supervising, controlling, coordinating and – always – innovating.

❑ ***Planning*** has to do with mapping out company direction and includes:

- Setting objectives.
- Establishing strategies to attain objectives.
- Setting benchmarks to measure progress.
- Choosing tactics to make the strategies effective; that is, making action plans.

- Determining resources needed: capital, equipment, facilities, personnel.
- Some basic questions to ask as a manager regarding planning:
- Where is my company going in the next three years?
- What challenges and opportunities do I face?
- What resources do I have—and what do I lack?

❑ ***Organizing*** has to do with arranging company resources and activities into a coherent structure. It is often helpful to work backwards from the organization's objectives and forward from the present. By doing so you determine:

- What tasks have been done?
- When?
- By whom?
- With what resources?
- Can this process be improved?

❑ ***Staffing*** involves building your team and includes:

- Assigning the right person to the right job.
- Making sure that someone is available for each necessary task.
- Projecting short-term needs (1-2 years) and long-term needs (2-4 years).

Managing staffing helps you avoid the ad-hoc staffing prevalent in small organizations — "This has to be done! Quick, get someone here to do it or I'll do it myself..."

❑ ***Supervising*** is the process of overseeing and supporting your teams' efforts so that maximum production is maintained and workplace culture is positive. It includes:

- Observing your workers and ensuring that they are performing their duties effectively.
- Training to make sure skills are up to the tasks.
- Upgrading the responsibilities of good employees whenever possible, in order to retain them.
- Building fun activities and fair incentives into workplace culture.

❑ ***Controlling*** means monitoring the company's performance to ensure the business is meeting its goals. For the basic control systems — operations, financial, accounting and book-keeping, personnel management – you will:

- Gather timely, factual information routinely.
- Analyze information for deviations from the norms set in your planning and managing efforts.

❑ ***Coordinating*** is the clearest example of the manager as music conductor. Making all the parts and people in an organization work in concert toward common goals is a task worthy of a maestro. Marketing and finance have to harmonize; fundraising and ongoing programs need to keep the same time. Think of the maestro conducting the orchestra: coordinating, timing, scheduling, prompting, and keeping all performers focused on the same score.

❑ ***Innovating*** is the never-ending attitude that keep a company on the leading edge and is ultimately motivated by the goal of ever-improving customer service. Allocate time to think about the future of your organization. Do not leave it to chance. What new products, new technologies, and new ideas will affect your organization in the next year? The next several years?

People who look for opportunities find opportunities. It's a management responsibility.

THE MANAGER'S DAILY TASK LIST

- **Accounting:** budgeting, paying bills, financial planning, credit, management, debt collection.
- **Administration:** purchasing, mailing, filing, correspondence, reception, invoicing.
- **Computer:** data entry, word processing, contract management, learning software, maintenance, upgrades, email, website.
- **Correspondence:** advertising copy, letters, press releases, articles.
- **Employees:** hiring and firing, training, motivation, payroll, arbitration.
- **Maintenance**: office and other equipment, tools, vehicles, building.
- **Problem-Solving:** troubleshooting, quality control, customer service.
- **Sales:** marketing, promotion, advertising, deliver, follow-up.
- **Warehousing:** inventory control, shipping, receiving, storage.
- **Your Job:** completing all the above in addition to generating income.

Managing a business is indeed like conducting an orchestra. You, as the conductor, have the whole score in mind as you lead the various parts of the orchestra in the process of unfolding the work. Managing is essentially organizing energy to get things done. We'll look at best practices for conducting/managing people, time, information and money. But the first order of business is managing the manager and that means *you*.

The Whole Manager

Everyone must row with the oars he has. - English Proverb

Entrepreneurs face lots of self-management challenges. First off, a one-person business has to rely on self-starting energy which usually is abundant, except when things go wrong on an emotional level. For example, the breakup of a relationship or a soured or mean-spirited customer can knock you out of your equilibrium. Too, only part of your business has immediate and direct rewards. A week's worth of work may not issue in anything substantial for a month of more. Entrepreneurs will also find that so much of their time is spent on "administrivia" which keeps them from focusing on their core mission. Entrepreneurial life, finally, can be lonely. Because the support that used to come from an extended family, clan or community isn't always present, and you yourself must figure out how to nurture your own support network.

All of this is daunting and can sap the life right out of you. All the more reason to tap into all the powers at your disposal, particularly your own *creative* energy. There's that word again.

Nothing speaks louder than something creative. No one can really define "creative" but we all know it when it's present. Unfortunately, most of us traffic with societies demanding little in the way of creativity. We can get by, and even be very successful with partial participation, re-cycling culture and conversation *ad infinitum*. Studies show that a child's creativity plummets at around age 5. What new activity usually begins at that age? Though the word "education" comes from the Latin *educare* (meaning, 'to draw out'), our systems betray a fear of human nature and instead *pour* in reams of information a committee somewhere decided we should know. In the process, the multidimensional child-artist is flattened and "de-programmed". To make room for all this intellectualizing art, music and drama are pushed to the margins of education and become the first casualties of budget cuts. As a result, a primary part of our nature, on a mass scale, is diminished. Subsequently, few of us get any training on how to tap our inner creative, neither from school and, sadly, nor from our homes. I believe the last few centuries were *outward*-oriented to the extreme and much of the ancient knowledge about *inner* human power went underground. As a result, we hear that humans use only 10% of their potential. Well, there are two responses to this: accept it as the "expert" opinion, *or push on to the other 90%!* Beginning in the 1950s and 60s a more inclusive consciousness began to spread, and people experimented more readily with new ways of thinking and acting. These "new ways" were, of course, old ways rediscovered and renamed. They included a more appreciative attitude about the body, the environment, and different lifestyles.

Another was a "turning inward" and a new emphasis on the power of thinking to affect reality. In its most basic form, it says, 'you are what you think you are.' Today we all have the chance to compose our own lives. It's a liberating prospect, but also daunting, because it requires a high degree of self-knowledge. If we don't start at the core – if we instead accept reflexive, inherited, or half-thought-out definitions of who we are and what we have to contribute – we run the risk of being overwhelmed by the possibilities that we face. Bear with me now. This might get a little strange...

We watch the Jedi and Siths push energy out of their palms and read thoughts; we marvel at the X-mens' and womens' strange powers; and we see these same powers expressed in TV shows like *Heroes* – all of them hinting at vast hidden powers in the human being. The more we study the human brain, in fact, the more fascinating the story becomes. For example, did you know that scientist's have recently discovered that humans have the same potential for echolocation as dolphins and bats?

We have to ask: What *more* lies beneath? Is the human being like that iceberg where 20% is manifest above the surface and 80% lies hidden?

It's been said that all of us are born with a grand piano inside us, but few of us learn how to play it. Another said it this way: Unlike the insect world, humans begin as butterflies but end up in cocoons. I personally believe we are born with a seed of selfhood that contains the spiritual DNA of our uniqueness – an encoded birthright knowledge of who we are, why we are here, and how we are related to others.

We may abandon that knowledge as the years go by and responsibilities crowd in, but it never abandons us. I find it fascinating that the elderly, who often forget a great deal, may recover vivid memories of childhood, of that time in their lives when they were most like themselves. They are brought back to their birthright nature by the abiding core of selfhood they carry within – a core made more visible, perhaps, by the way aging can strip away whatever is not truly us. Philosophers argue about what to call this core of our humanity: Thomas Merton called it "the true self". Buddhists call it "original nature". Quakers call it "the inner light". Hasidic Jews call it "a spark of the divine". Humanists call it identity and integrity. In popular parlance, people often call it *soul*.

What we name it matters little, but *that* we name it matters a great deal. For "it" is the objective, reality of selfhood that keeps us from reducing ourselves, or each other, to biological mechanisms, psychological projections, sociological constructs, or raw material to be manufactured into what society needs – diminishments of our humanity that constantly threaten the quality of our lives.

I think it can be argued that with our turning outward to conquer the world via machines we lost something precious in the process – a deeper sense of human power. Somewhere in the civilizing process mankind has separated the conscious mind from the deeper instinctive strata of the human psyche. With the meteoric rise of science and technology, the unconscious mind could not keep pace and fell far behind. Spiritual and moral traditions have disintegrated, causing worldwide disorientation, and our direct contact with Nature has diminished. The chart on the next page contrasts these two world views.

World View	Life Approach	Attitude	Outcome
Mechanical	Problem-solving	Defensiveness	Escape
Organic/Spiritual	Creativity	Openness	Creative Confrontation

In an effort to understand his world, modern man rejected all he could not understand through reason and experiment. In doing so, he denied the great Mystery of life and put his faith in *ratio*nality. A ratio is a portion, a part. In rationality, we divide life into parts. But in endless fragmentation, we miss the experience of the *whole.* Life is simultaneously the ratio (the part) and the whole – at once the same and different. A stream is the same stream, yet each moment the water is different. Starting from the ratio, life is an endless series of problems to be solved. Starting from the whole, life is a mystery to be revealed.

To break through to those other parts of ourselves sitting submerged beneath our everyday consciousness demands courage. To remind, there is nothing more brave than filtering out the chatter that tells you to be someone you're not. There is nothing more genuine than breaking away from the chorus to learn the sound of your own voice. In his 1994 inaugural address Nelson Mandela spoke these profound words: "Our deepest fear is not that we are inadequate. Our deepest fear is that we are powerful beyond measure. It is our light, not our darkness, that most frightens us."

That might seem counterintuitive. The poet Robert Frost similarly observed: "Something we were withholding made us weak, until we found out that it was ourselves." One of the qualities creative people share is the ability to identify issues others miss. Sometimes the issue lies inside, where obstacles prevent us from evolving toward the people we desire to become. To develop creatively sometimes means looking inward and addressing the hurdles that challenge our growth. The chart on page 249 suggests other ways to spark creativity. The journey of self-discovery is an important one to make and the early years of adulthood are probably the most crucial ones for this inner travel. College-age people, in particular, are deciding (whether they know it or not) what the threshold of their consciousness will be *for the rest of their lives*. It's a special time of discovery, review and decision.

Of course, adult wholeness is far more complex than the wholeness of infancy. It cannot be reduced to "embracing our inner child" as so many New Age mavens encourage. As adults we carry burdens and challenges children do not have – the burden of our failures, betrayals, and grief; the challenges of our gifts, our skills, and our visions – and we must carry all of it consciously as we travel the path.

Let's go even deeper.

Thinking for a Change

Mental is to physical what four is to one. – Two-time coach of the year, Bill McCartney

If I were to ask you to concentrate real hard and imagine yourself growing an inoperable brain tumor, would you do it? Most of us would probably hesitate. Would you? Why? Perhaps because you believe deep down that your mind, or the way you think, can actually have an affect on your body. And you would be right.

Modern brain research, as well as quantum physics, are discovering that the mind is a form of energy that cannot be reduced to measurable quanta or manipulated like samples in a test tube.

I've always been impressed that Greek philosophers five centuries before Christ, without a shred of physical evidence, came up with an atomic theory of matter that held up conceptually until just a century ago. As if drawing on some archetypal principles floating in space, they formulated the idea of particles and described atoms as indivisible units. Around 1900, someone discovered that an atom could in fact be subdivided into even smaller particles, electrons spinning around a tiny nucleus of protons and neutrons. For most scientists at the turn of the century, it seemed that nothing smaller than an atomic nucleus could possibly exist. But things would not be so simple. Even smaller atomic components continue to be discovered.

It is estimated that a person has about 40,000 thoughts per day. Thoughts are made up of electrons which are as real and solid as the desk I'm sitting at. In fact, this very same desk began as a thought inside the head of a designer somewhere. Eventually, the thought was externalized and made manifest as a metal and plastic desk. All human activities, from deciding what to have for dinner to designing a spaceship, begin as a vision in someone's mind. Artists use visualization everyday in their studios, transforming mental images into works of expressive beauty. Engineers visualize new bridges, architects imagine new buildings, musicians visualize or hear music in their minds. Everything we see is linked to thought. Thoughts become reality.

In 1820 it was discovered than an electric current produces magnetism. Did you know that there is electricity in almost everything, but it only flows when it is given energy or power? This energy can come from chemicals in a battery, from sunlight falling on a solar cell, or from moving magnets. If thoughts are electric energy then they also have magnetic properties. Can good thoughts inside magnetize good things outside? Likewise, can inner negative thoughts magnetize outer negative things in our lives? Seems so.

Becoming a better thinker is worth your effort because the way you think really impacts every aspect of your life. In his book, *Thinking for a Change*, author John Maxwell says that of the thousands of people he meets each year, a great many of them believe good thinking is so complicated that it lies beyond their reach. He observed that:

- Unsuccessful people focus their thinking on survival.
- Average people focus their thinking on maintenance.
- Successful people focus their thinking on progress.

Dr. Wayne Dyer, author of more than two dozen books, said, "If you change the way you look at things, the things you look at change." Strange, but true. Try it. The energy we put into our inner thoughts affects the outer life we see and achieve. Call it "intention", "visualization", "prayer" or "the law of attraction" – it all adds up to actively using your imagination to compose the kind of life you desire. Visualization is based on the understanding that the mind is a powerful engine that can trigger mental pictures that can affect us intensely. Kids do this naturally, imagining themselves as superheroes, doctors, or ballerinas.

On a more sophisticated level, world-class athletes have used this mental training technique for years in their quest for the Olympic gold. Because our subconscious does not differentiate between real and unreal, we can program our desired outcomes. Once the seed of an image is planted, our imagination provides abundant watering, and the idea grows on its own. Thinking *for a change*.

Many today are seeking a holistic approach to life and work, one that integrates the spiritual and material. Too often these seem separated by a wide chasm bounded by steep cliffs. Our lives take on a schizophrenic quality – spiritual here, practical there. We require a bridge or bridges – effective ways of uniting the spiritual and material, the sacred and the ordinary. To bridge the sacred and the ordinary, we must tap the spirit and emotional power of creative living and gain knowledge of how things are and how they work.

Understanding Your 'Value'

There is a lot of talk these days about "personal branding" – that is, figuring out what your unique contribution or "value add" is to an organization. Every now and then it's a good idea to pause and reflect on what your value is to the company you've founded, to those you work with and to your larger market. What are the core qualities you bring that no one else can? By understanding the value you bring to the table (and, by extension, the value your company brings), you will not only have a deeper appreciation of yourself, but you'll gain further insight on how to market this value to your target fans, clients and customers.

Begin by looking at the following chart to get a sense of the personal value you bring to the areas of Skills, Attitude, Experience and Results. As you consider each area, write down all the ways you manifest these characteristics. Eventually, you want this to become a living statement of how you bring value to the lives of others.

Your Current Value Assessment
What Do You Bring to the Table?

Skills and Talents

Technical expertise	Communication skills	Organizing skills	Financial skills
Team-building skills	Marketing and selling	Presentation skills	Management skills
Creative skills	Systematizing skills	Leadership skills	Strategic thinking
Analytic skills	People skills	Problem-solving skills	

Attitude/Work Ethic

Availability	Flexibility	Reliability
Commitment to completion	Stability	Cooperation
Willingness to go	Upbeatness/optimism	Honesty
"above and beyond"	Supportiveness	Loyalty
Harmony with company	Discretion	Leadership qualities
mission	Ambition	

Experience/Contacts

Years in current job	Education	Contacts from personal/
Years in related job at a	Years in different position	community/schooling
different company	within company	Reputation in industry
Loyal clients/customers	Years as freelancer/	Contacts from work
business owner	Specialized training	Agents/reps
Results/Productivity Energy	Accuracy	Volume
Follow-up	Independent worker	Ability to take direction
Speed	Good listener	Attention to detail

"I like to study physical subjects," says Jay Andreozzi, founder of Amalgam Digital. "I study and engage in thought-provoking sports like boxing and weight training and apply concepts I learn there to my business. I study human behavior and the mind. I am a student of Neuro-Linguistic Programming and apply the ideas that I find useful to my business. I read a lot about psychology in general as I believe it's important to know your customer, know your business, know your partners, and know your self and have the ability to take on multiple perspectives".

Some useful ways for creative personal development are suggested in the following chart. Practice these things to keep yourself fresh and comfortable 'outside the box'.

NURTURING YOUR CREATIVE LIFE

At least once a month	At least once every three months	At least once every six months
Attend a networking event	Complete a piece of work for your personal or professional portfolio.	Go on a job interview, if for nothing more than to stay in practice.
Participate in an activity with peers who are not part of your company.	Get your name in front of people who can help you (whether inside the company or your industry group).	Update a list of the ten companies where you would most like to work.
Meet somebody new in a company that interests you.	Attend an event showing a peer's work.	Update a list of two dozen people to call when you want a new project.
Read all of the relevant trade magazines that were published that month.	Attend an event by a creative wizard or someone who inspires you.	Update your daydream.
Read a magazine you've never read before, on a topic you know nothing about.	Go to an art museum.	Either leave the country, or make plans to leave the country within the next six months (or if not possible, seek out the contrast in a place you *can* visit).

Creativity is a mandate for music entrepreneur and ultimately stems from an attitude of creative engagement with your world.: "When your business is art, it's very much your life," says LA-based Randy Tobin of Theta Media Group. "But it's only one part of many in the overall scheme of things. I make time to create across all parts of my life."

> The eye sees only what the mind is prepared to comprehend.
>
> – Henri Bergson

A well-managed business has a captain who's physically, spiritually and emotionally healthy. It's hard to run a business when you're exhausted all the time or allow the business to rob you of life's pleasures. When you neglect to manage the manager, you work against yourself, the dream and its survival. Having an inner life is crucial for balance and for using and storing creative energy for whatever you encounter. Having a well-managed company takes that same creative juice and applies it to your business environment.

Organizing Your Work for Maximum Success

So much of your business success will depend on how well you organize and manage the things around you. What does a well-run business look like? It figures out ways to maximize production through the conducting of various energies, whether it's people, time, information, money or outreach.

First off, use these general tips as foundation principles for bringing order to the normal chaos of business office life.

❑ ***Get Rid of "Stuff"*** – Paper, publications and possessions require maintenance – maintenance costs time, energy, space and money. How long do you really need to keep your old project files, seminar fliers, reference materials, conference materials, association or business journals? Dispose of seldom or never-used items. Ask yourself, "What will happen if I let this go?" If the answer is "Nothing," get rid of it! Keeping it requires the same decisions over and over. Remember: It's ok to make a few mistakes; that's a small price for the contentment of having less "stuff".

❑ ***Limit Your Reading Material*** – Realize that you can't read, know, or retain all the information you receive. That's why we have public libraries and hard disks! Set up a read folder or other limited space for holding unread information. Pitch the oldest material (read or not) when that space is full. If you haven't read it by now, you probably never will. If you're scared you'll need it someday, then file it under the appropriate category. Take the advice of C.S. Lewis and read *much*, not many.

❑ ***Touch It Once! (or, at least try to)***– Be decisive: If at all possible, handle mail only once and move on. If later action is needed, put it in an action file. Indecision is organizational death - yet most people aren't even aware of their inability to make decisions. Don't shuffle papers with the vague "I-don't-know-what-to-do-with-this-so-I'll-put-it-here-for-now" syndrome. Use the simple DRAFT technique - Delegate, Read, Act, File or Toss. DRAFT spells death to ever-growing, work-in-process clutter.

❑ ***Think Before Acquiring More*** – Evaluate before buying/accepting new items. Get off mailing lists which serve no purpose; drop subscriptions to periodicals you seldom read. Ask yourself if you really *need* this item - or are you simply acquiring it because it looks interesting; because someone passed it on to you; or because "it might come in handy sometime"? Where will you store it? Items must *do* something more than collect dust. Accept as few papers and possessions as possible. For each item you do acquire, purge two!

AS YOU PLAN EACH WEEK, MAKE TIME FOR LIFE'S IMPORTANT "FIVE Fs":

• ***Fitness:*** Exercise aids positive, creative, and clear thinking—and your health. It's amazing the benefits one feels from just a half-hour walk or work-out. Your weight will decrease and productivity increase.

• ***Food:*** Learn to make healthy choices and eat regularly. Ditch the junk food. Keep the machine fueled with good premium "gas." Don't skip meals and include a balance of food groups.

• ***Family:*** They are the most important people in your life yet often the ones who suffer. Plan to spend chunks of time with them and ensure that it is quality time.

• ***Friends:*** People who work long hours often complain of spending little time with friends. Make a point of scheduling in some much-needed time with them. Never be "too busy" and neglect your friends—you need them more than you think.

• ***Fun:*** Think positive and be positive. Let yourself go and have a little fun. It's one of life's most important yet often forgotten ingredients.

❑ ***Organize Before Increasing Space*** – Adding storage space is often a disservice to yourself. The more space you have, the more inclined you are to be a saver. Keep things as simple as possible by retaining as few items as you absolutely need. Stamp out redundancies. Return supplies to your central supply area. Get in the habit of purging file folders and storage space before adding more.

❑ ***Keep Frequently-Used Items Handy*** – Keep within easy reach your current working papers and items you'll need when you answer the phone. Don't waste "up front" storage space with infrequently used items - store those further away. Keep like items together so you don't have to take "trips" to gather materials for tasks.

❑ ***Don't Crowd*** – Individual file folders over 3/4" thick need to be first purged, then sub-divided if necessary. Consider box-bottomed files for thick materials. If file drawers are stuffed, papers become mutilated, labels become hidden, and access is difficult. Leave at least 3" of extra space in file drawers.

❑ ***Do The Best Task At The Best Time*** - After selecting the most productive task, do it at a time when you can accomplish it most effectively. Do tasks physically or mentally difficult for you at your own peak energy times; this includes making tough decisions. Do jobs you enjoy most (even if others consider them hard work) at low-ebb times. Don't try to do difficult work against all odds when you know you'll have lots of interruptions. Maximize your energy waves.

❑ ***Be Prepared*** - Like the Boy Scouts, plan ahead for everything you'll need. Gather data and plan an agenda for telephone calls. For a report, assemble all the files, books, forms, copies, special writing equipment, etc., you'll use. For cleaning out, collect extra folders, boxes, cleaning equipment, and trash containers in advance.

❑ ***Don't Leave Until You're Finished*** - If you find items to be delivered elsewhere, put them in a specific place and deliver them there only when you're finished with your present task.

❑ ***Do Only What You Set Out To Do*** - Focus on your specified project. Resist the urge to be distracted by what your eyes see. Instead, like a boomerang, let your brain keep guiding you back to achieving your immediate goal. Put other reminders in an action file and do them when you're finished with this task.

❑ ***Break Your Work Into Units*** - If a project seems overwhelming, "divide and conquer." Break it down into manageable units and schedule the steps to execute it.

❑ ***Empower Yourself Through Delegation*** - Many people are reluctant to delegate. They find it hard to let go - to make decisions to give up a task - or are embarrassed to have others see their disarray. Take heart! Empower yourself with these strategies to most effectively use your support team - peers, employees, interns, assistants, etc.:

- Know what you and they do best (but don't take on their work just because you're good at it).
- Never delegate tasks that are not essential and should not be done at all. Toss them.

We'll look at delegation and other management challenges in greater detail later in this chapter.

Avoiding Overwork

We seem to be workaholics by nature, at least in America. According to Harvard economist Juliet Schor, the average American works 163 additional hours, or one month a year, more today than in 1969 ("The Over-worked American"). The Employee Benefits Research Institute tells us that Americans work more hours per year than any other industrialized nation—putting in an average of 6.5 weeks longer than the French workforce, and 8 weeks longer than Germany's. Lest we forget, the United States is the only industrialized country without a government mandate on vacation time.

Overwork is epidemic among entrepreneurs mainly because there's always more to do, we make our own schedules, and have access to our data at all times of the day and night via hand held and desktop computers. "I worked myself to the bone," admits Ariel Hyatt of Cyber PR Music. "I got really, really dedicated and I worked really hard, and I actually made myself sick because I worked so hard. So, I think the challenge when you're beginning a company is the challenge of balance, and understanding that you need to take some time to smell the roses. There's always more work to be done, and it's good to understand when to quit and when to be good to yourself".

This is also a challenge for those who work out of their homes or apartments. Without the formal division of office and home life, work can encroach on the amount of time we leave for ourselves and our personal lives.

Self-employment doesn't have to lead to overwork. Even if you have an office at home, a phone and a computer in your car, a beeper and a cell phone, you can still restrict the amount of work you do. But the responsibility lies with you. A lot of people use technology as an excuse to give up control over their work life and simply say, " It's the information age; I simply can't be out of touch!"

There is an undeniable reality that technology has ratcheted up the pace at which we are expected to respond to business demands, but you still can, and should, set limits on your work life. Consider the following steps to help yourself control the amount of time you work.

- ***Learn to determine what is not urgent.*** There's a tendency in the technology-laden business world to believe that everything has to be done *immediately* because the technology exists to transmit things without delay. Because of this, people tend to treat everything as urgent rather than determining what is urgent and what can wait. To learn to do this, begin asking questions about projects before you agree to "get something right out." This applies to requests from partners and customers. As long as you are conscientious, people will respect you for setting limits on what you can accomplish in a given time frame.
- ***Have a set beginning and ending time for your day, as if you still work in the office full-time.*** Just because you *can* work 24/7 because of technology, doesn't mean you *should*. There is always more work to complete, but that does not mean you should exhaust yourself working just because you have all of your work tools at your fingertips. There will be times you will need to work long hours, but in general, you should set strict beginning and ending times for your work days to avoid burnout.
- ***Designate a time each day when you are not reachable***. If you are always wondering if the phone will ring in your house or car, you will never be able to relax completely. For that reason, get into the habit of choosing when you will allow the phone to intrude and when you will not. This means turning the ringer off sometimes. It will be difficult to do this the first few time you try, but eventually you will wonder why you haven't done it before. Start by turning it off for just an hour and work your way up to more time.
- ***Give your home and cell number to a very few business contacts***. It is confusing for people to have too many numbers for you, and stressful for you to be reachable everywhere you go. Provide the majority of people with only your voice mail number and check it frequently. Email may also be your preferable gateway.
- ***Get to know yourself***. By knowing your work tendencies, you can develop techniques for managing yourself. For example, if you know that you are an overachiever and usually do more than what is asked of you, you may be able to scale back the effort that you put into projects. If you acknowledge that you are not good at prioritizing, you can find someone to help you.
- ***Establish a clear idea of what is expected of you.*** A large portion of the energy that people expend in work is spent in the wrong tasks. When you take on a project, ask as many questions as are necessary to obtain a clear picture of what is expected. This will help you cut down on overwork by limiting the time you waste on unnecessary work.
- ***Learn to say no***. If you consistently say "yes" to things that you later wish you had declined, set up a mechanism for helping yourself to say "no". When you are faced with a request, ask people if you can call them back in a few minutes. Take that time to think carefully about how you should respond. If you decide not to, you can work up your resolve to say "no" before returning the call.
- ***Create goals and use these goals as a matrix for deciding what to take on***. If you know what you are trying to attain, it will be easier to prioritize and prevent overwork. For example, if one of your goals is to cut down on the amount of time you work and improve your health, then you may have to accept that a choice project may have to go to someone else or be put off indefinitely. We'll look more closely at this subject in the next chapter, Conducting Time & Information.

❑ ***Stop and think before you make a phone call, write a letter, send a fax, or have a conversation***, and evaluate whether you should be spending time on that activity. Ask yourself what would happen if you didn't do it. If you can live with the consequences, do not complete the task. This streamlining is essential to gaining control of your schedule.

❑ ***Take yourself away from your work environment***. People who work in virtual offices particularly need regular breaks from work. A break can be a day on the weekend spent hiking or driving in the country, or any change in your environment. Have at least one full day a week during which you do not check your messages or do any work.

Dealing with Rejection

I have become very familiar with rejection over the years. I've had editors tell me my writing is boring, booking agents tell me my music won't draw, and distributors tell me my product is too unusual. When you work by yourself, rejection can really take a toll on you if you're not careful, because there is no one around to laugh about it with you. After a while, it can stop being funny. I have learned some tricks over time for coping with rejection. The advice that follows may save you some anguish. It saves me anguish – daily.

- **Expect some rejection**. If you expect every pitch to be a sale, every person to be nice to you, and every proposal to win you business, you are going to take rejection really hard. Rejection is part of life; you have to accept that and expect to be rejected. Remember, every record company in Britain rejected the Beatles initially; same with the Rolling Stones. Thicken your skin and hang tough.
- **Celebrate rejection**. When I first moved to Boston, my mentor told me to think of every rejection as bringing me one step closer to success. She was talking about odds. If you have a failure or setback, it means you've gotten one setback out of the way and you are therefore closer to getting what you want.
- **Do not be upset by rejection**. Rejection is a fact, but how you feel about being rejected is not a fact. People automatically assume that because you are rejected, you have to feel terrible. But rejection is just rejection - nothing more, nothing less. People have all kinds of reasons for rejecting you. Sometimes it has to do with you; many times it doesn't.
- **Do not be at other people's mercy**. If you are always looking to other people for approval or to verify that you are worthy, your life will be a roller coaster. When you get a lot of acceptance, you'll feel great; when you get a lot of rejection, you'll feel terrible. When someone rejects you in a work situation, it doesn't mean you are no good; it means you (or your idea) got rejected. Period.
- **Don't globalize**. It is important to make sure rejection does not wreak havoc on your psyche. Therapists call this "globalizing". It means that when you fail at one thing, you think *everything* is terrible. To avoid globalizing, give yourself a reality check when you suffer a rejection. Make a list, mentally or on paper, of what is going well in your business or your life, to remind you of your successes and failures.
- **Read the following passage (a lot).** He failed in business in '31. He was defeated when he ran for the legislature in '32. He failed once again in business in '34. His fiancee' died in '35. He had a nervous breakdown in '36. He went back into politics and was defeated in the election of '38. He decided to run for Congress and was defeated in '43. He was defeated for Congress in '46. He was defeated for Congress in '48. He was defeated for the Senate in '55. He was defeated for vice president in '56. He was defeated for the Senate in '58.

After that, you'd say he was through, wouldn't you? He was, as they say, "all washed up," wasn't he? He had had it, had he not? No, he hadn't at all. He went on to be elected President in 1860! The man, of course, was Abraham Lincoln.

The Ongoing Challenge of Managing Others

"Management" happens when you're there; "Leadership" happens when you're not there.
– Anonymous

The biggest shift to make when moving beyond solo is to go from directing yourself to supervising others. Managing others is not a natural-born talent, although some individuals seem to be particularly adept at it. Rather, it is a skill that develops with practice – and like most skills, with trial and error.

What you may lack in skills or experience, you can make up for with a natural sense of enthusiasm and mutual respect.

❑ ***Be Your Advice.*** The most effective leaders are those who set a good example—timeliness, thoroughness, integrity, consistency in words and actions, unconditional respect for others' opinions and an openness to new ideas—including those that may be unworkable.

❑ ***Communicate.*** Be clear in your instructions, explanations, expectations and requests with others. If you're a person who has difficulty yourself verbally, don't be afraid to turn to drawings, diagrams, charts, three-dimensional constructions, and other aids to help you communicate your ideas.

Part of communicating is listening. Early jazz players praised a fellow musician by saying he or she had "big ears" – meaning the person actively listened to another's playing and built on rhythm, lyrics and tempo. Most people will not really listen or pay attention to your point of view until they become convinced you have heard and appreciate theirs. Have big ears when you're talking with others – whether with one person, two people or a team.

❑ ***Stay focused with Goals***. Keep your team on track by committing to goals and proceeding with an organized plan. Workers' energies can become scattered – and morale can plummet – if your business is continually in a reactive "crisis" mode. Goals also ensure that you'll receive full value from the investment you make in your workers. Make it pay off by charting a clear plan of action.

❑ ***Delegate.*** As already mentioned, delegation is an art. Difficult for anyone to do, but especially "micro managers" and control freaks. Mentally count to 10 before you jump in,
and remind yourself of the long-term benefits you're trying to achieve: to free up more of your time so you can focus on more productive tasks. We'll look at this topic in more detail in the next section of this chapter.

❑ ***Encourage teamwork***. What kinds of factors promote teamwork? Giving workers a chance to provide input and choice in how they do their work, encouraging responsibility and leadership opportunities, and being tolerant of learning errors are three. As the leader, you will set the tone for the group interaction with your energy and enthusiasm. You'll need to be aware of the impact of powerful or negative individuals. Healthy group dynamics can easily be overcome by a single dominant personality. Acknowledge individual contributions, but place primary focus on the achievements resulting from cooperative efforts.

❑ **Stimulate creativity.** "Our office is full of dry erase boards," says Amalgam Digital CEO Jay Andreozzi. "I encourage everyone to use them. I am constantly drawing the company's plans on these boards and creating images that we turn into reality". Encourage some of the practices suggested on the chart from page 242.

❑ ***Choose & use workers wisely***. The best way to ensure management success is to screen potential workers carefully before they become part of your business. Be clear on exactly what you need before you try matching people to tasks. Seek a balance between *similarity* (those like you) and *complementarity* (those with skills and experience different from your own).

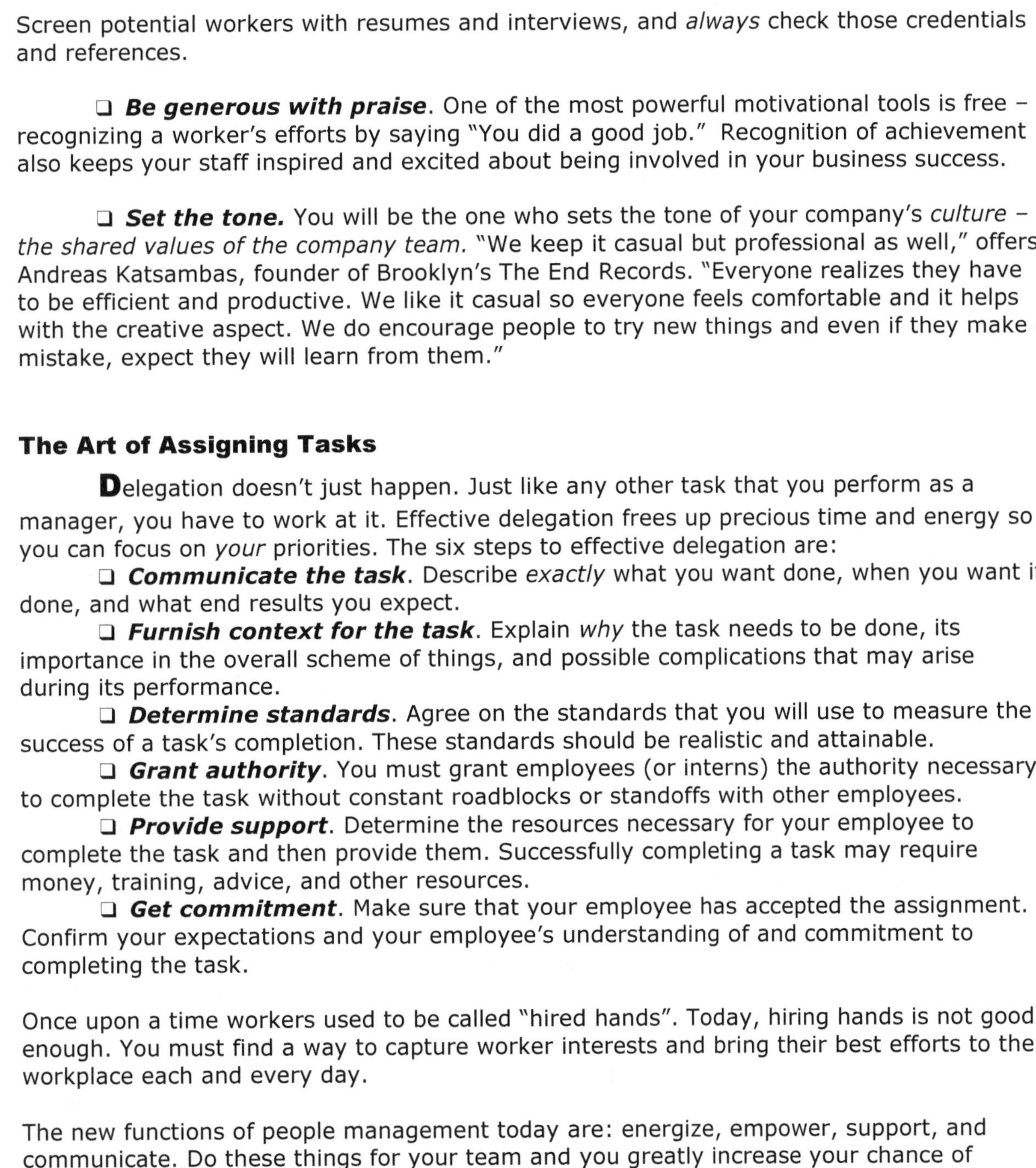

Screen potential workers with resumes and interviews, and *always* check those credentials and references.

❑ ***Be generous with praise***. One of the most powerful motivational tools is free – recognizing a worker's efforts by saying "You did a good job." Recognition of achievement also keeps your staff inspired and excited about being involved in your business success.

❑ ***Set the tone.*** You will be the one who sets the tone of your company's *culture – the shared values of the company team.* "We keep it casual but professional as well," offers Andreas Katsambas, founder of Brooklyn's The End Records. "Everyone realizes they have to be efficient and productive. We like it casual so everyone feels comfortable and it helps with the creative aspect. We do encourage people to try new things and even if they make a mistake, expect they will learn from them."

The Art of Assigning Tasks

Delegation doesn't just happen. Just like any other task that you perform as a manager, you have to work at it. Effective delegation frees up precious time and energy so you can focus on *your* priorities. The six steps to effective delegation are:

❑ ***Communicate the task***. Describe *exactly* what you want done, when you want it done, and what end results you expect.

❑ ***Furnish context for the task***. Explain *why* the task needs to be done, its importance in the overall scheme of things, and possible complications that may arise during its performance.

❑ ***Determine standards***. Agree on the standards that you will use to measure the success of a task's completion. These standards should be realistic and attainable.

❑ ***Grant authority***. You must grant employees (or interns) the authority necessary to complete the task without constant roadblocks or standoffs with other employees.

❑ ***Provide support***. Determine the resources necessary for your employee to complete the task and then provide them. Successfully completing a task may require money, training, advice, and other resources.

❑ ***Get commitment***. Make sure that your employee has accepted the assignment. Confirm your expectations and your employee's understanding of and commitment to completing the task.

Once upon a time workers used to be called "hired hands". Today, hiring hands is not good enough. You must find a way to capture worker interests and bring their best efforts to the workplace each and every day.

The new functions of people management today are: energize, empower, support, and communicate. Do these things for your team and you greatly increase your chance of retaining productive, loyal workers for a long time.

There is also such a thing as *over-delegating*. From 2002 Derek Sivers admits he gradually lost interest in the day-to-day operations of his company, CDBaby. The company was based in Portland, Oregon but Derek hadn't lived there in years. By 2007 Derek sold his car and moved to London, hardly ever talking with the managers at his company. By then, Sivers says, it was "a company run by eighty five 22-year-old stoners hired by friends while the owner was away for six years saying, 'Don't bother me'." While business hummed along and profits rose, communications became strained, feelings got hurt and the company moved in a direction he didn't support. Sivers admits he abdicated some important responsibilities and learned crucial lessons in the process, both about himself and others.

20 People Management Secrets of the World's Greatest Coaches

- Be available
- Build relationships
- Provide feedback
- Be a role model
- Have high expectations
- Share information
- Encourage teamwork
- Reward innovation
- Say 'thanks'
- Pick your issues carefully
- Promote participation
- Use delegation
- Allow mistakes
- Offer training
- Set goals
- Celebrate attempts
- Grow experts
- Have unannounced celebrations
- Show your emotions
- Be a team player

Source: Fred Pryor Seminar, "Coaching skills for Managers & Supervisors"

Negotiation Know-How: Guidelines for Negotiating Any Contract

If you're involved in the music business, sooner or later you'll sit down with someone you have to negotiate an agreement with. It may be a management or record contract, or perhaps a "work for hire" agreement where you provide music for some particular use.
My personal motto is – Enter all negotiations prepared to walk away from a bad deal. This mind-set can be quite liberating. It's part of my business filter, and I use it to scrutinize every client alliance and project that comes my way. There may be times when you're approached with opportunities for which the arrangements are more beneficial to the other party. You may be tempted to go along with the deal because you need the work or believe doing it one time won't hurt.

Consider this: You're setting a precedent that may be difficult to break away from. If you're in a contract-oriented profession (like so much music work is), you drag your industry down when you accept unattractive terms because it makes buyers believe that they can make any offer and someone is bound to accept it.

Bad deals come in various packages. First of all, avoid letting clients dictate payment terms to you. That practice is particularly common if your clients are larger entities. Scores of business people cringe as they agree to payment schedules they cannot afford for the sake of landing an account. Another scenario is taking on work that you won't make any money on. People confuse this with the "foot in the door" strategy. But introducing your business on a smaller scale means making less money initially, not giving your talents away.
Don't be afraid to negotiate. One reason many self-employed professionals agree to poor deal terms is that they haven't yet honed their negotiating skills. Your goal should be to arrive at a "win/win" outcome. Be prepared to offer some halfway solutions. For example, if a client tells you 60 days is its policy for making payments, you could counter by explaining that your normal terms are 30 days, but with a 50-percent deposit you'd be willing to carry the account for 45 days. Express to the other party that productive working relationships are built on win-win arrangements; this will set the tone for friendlier negotiations.

Use the following general guidelines to keep the communication on the best level possible:

- ❐ View every first-offer contract or agreement as only a draft requiring customization to the specific circumstances of the two parties. *Never* go with the first draft;
- ❐ Negotiate only with those in authority to agree to your requests;
- ❐ Have a prioritized agenda. Start with the most incontestable (i.e., agreeable) items and work downwards to the stickiest points;

- ❒ Put yourself in the other person's place and structure your arguments to address his or her concerns. Anticipate the other party's concerns;
- ❒ Never issue ultimatums. This is bad form and sets up a defense position;
- ❒ Never concede a point, however small, without winning a comparable concession in return;
- ❒ Take notes and verbally summarize each point agreed to before you move on to the next so that there's no misunderstanding;
- ❒ Follow up negotiations with a memo or letter summarizing what was agreed to, and ask for a written response within so many days or hours if any points are disputed;
- ❒ Make the other party feel good about the outcome.

A Note on 'Form Contracts'. There is no substitute for a complete contract between parties. However, I recognize that budget and time constraints may prevent some people from having a complete contract. There are many "form" books out there which contain "model" contracts in the music industry and you can find samples galore on the Internet. Some are better than others. There is, however, a danger in using such forms. Many people don't know how the forms work. They find a form which says, "Management Contract" or "Record Contract", they photocopy it, and have an artist sign the agreement.

It is crucial that you *understand* how the contract works before you use it. These are legal agreements and may not operate the way you expect. Before using any of these form agreements, learn how music contracts operate in general. Read about record, producer and management contracts, agency agreements, and work-for-hire agreements. Then compare your form with what you have read. I have never encountered a contract form which did not need some modification and customization.

When You Have to Fire Someone

One of the most difficult tasks you face as a manager or company owner is firing workers. Creative Director Claire Chase experienced this during the early years of the International Contemporary Ensemble: "I realized that some of the people I'd enlisted to work with me were not the right fit for the organization, and that disparate agendas created an unstable, competitive work environment that was antithetical to the work we needed to do and to the healthy, positive community we needed to create". The solution wasn't easy for Chase. "I had to let go of some people and that was very, very painful. But it's just another one of those things that you learn to do, and you don't think you're tough enough to do it until you just do it with clarity and courage."

As we have already seen, hiring the right people for your company is more art than science, one that will take experimentation. "Well, it just takes time and experience," says the always positive composer Norihiko Hibino, "but more likely, you can find the best staff member only through difficulties and troubles. Those trials will enhance and train the relationship between the staff. Good ones remain, inappropriate ones will leave, and you should not regret the staff member leaving, because in that way you can always get better ones next time around."

Employees who consistently break the rules, do not perform the functions of their job, or cause difficulties in the workplace can be a strain on the work environment and disrupt business from being performed. Here are a few steps and hints to help ease the nasty task of letting people go. These apply mainly to employees, not independent contractors, interns or temp workers, though it's not a bad idea to apply these points under those arrangements as well:

❑ ***Documentation.*** The first step in preparing to fire an employee is to make sure you have all the documentation you need. When you give verbal warnings, be sure to document them. In today's litigation-happy society, without the proper documentation, you may see yourself in a wrongful termination lawsuit.
Your company should have well documented procedures for what it expects from employees and anything that is considered grounds for immediate dismissal. Be sure to use these as guidelines.

❑ ***"I've been fired, but why?".*** Explain to the employee the performance you have expected, the steps you have taken to help them meet that performance, and that they have not met them. Do not say more than you have to, just state why they are being dismissed and fill out any exit paperwork. If you are upset, cool down before talking to them.

❑ ***Exit Procedures***. Make sure you backup any important files before firing the employee and take steps to lock them out of any computer systems. It is recommended you fire someone on a Monday versus a Friday. Employees fired on Fridays have the whole weekend to stew, while those fired on Mondays usually are more upbeat because they have the week ahead of them.

Be sure to explain when their last paycheck is coming, when benefits terminate, and any information regarding extending their health coverage or any other details.
Remember to keep the meeting short and to the point. Explain to the other team members that you fired the individual without going into too many details. When a new potential employer calls you for a reference, remember to just state the title and dates of employment; any further information about your former employee could draw a libel suit. Keep good records on employee mistakes, even when they're not firing offenses. Document your own actions and the reasons behind your employment decisions. You may also consider buying employment-practices liability insurance (EPLI), to cover additional "what-ifs".

CHAPTER SUMMARY

BUSINESS CONDUCTING: SELF & PEOPLE

- **The Many Faces of Management**
  Management is making something planned happen within a specific time through the smart use of available resources. This definition encompasses planning, goals, intelligence and resourcefulness. Management is essentially "conducting" your business "orchestra" to "perform" the strategic "composition" magnificently. Your success as a manager comes down to the difference between managing your work and letting your work manage you.

- **Managerial Functions**
  The work of managers can be broken down into the following categories: planning, organizing, staffing, supervising, controlling, coordinating and – always – innovating. Some of the manager's daily task list: Accounting, Administration, Computer, Correspondence, Employees, Maintenance, Problem-Solving, Sales, Warehousing, and Your Job.

- **The Whole Manager**
  Entrepreneurs face lots of self-management challenges. First off, a one-person business has to rely on self-starting energy which usually is abundant, except when things go wrong on an emotional level. One of the qualities creative people share is the ability to identify issues others miss. Sometimes the issue lies inside, where obstacles prevent us from evolving toward the people we desire to become. To develop creatively sometimes means looking inward and addressing the hurdles challenging our growth.

- **Thinking for a Change**
  Becoming a better thinker is worth your effort because the way you think really

impacts every aspect of your life. Because our subconscious does not differentiate between real and unreal, we can program our desired outcomes. Once the seed of an image is planted, our imagination provides abundant watering, and the idea grows on its own. Thinking for a change.

- **Understanding Your Value**

  Understanding your value is one thing. Nurturing and maintaining that value is another. Continual self-improvement should be a mantra for entrepreneurs. Avoid getting too comfortable with success by neglecting your own personal growth and development. Creativity is a mandate for music entrepreneurs and ultimately stems from an attitude of creative engagement with your world. Having an inner life is crucial for balance and for using and storing creative energy for whatever you encounter. Having a well-managed company takes that same creative juice and applies it to your business enterprise.

- **Organizing Your Workspace for Maximum Success**

  A well-run business figures out ways to maximize production through the conducting of various energies, whether it's people, time, information, money or outreach. Some general tips as foundation principles for bringing order to the normal chaos of business office life:
  - Get Rid of "Stuff"
  - Limit Your Reading Material
  - Touch It Once! (or, at least try to)
  - Think Before Acquiring More
  - Organize Before Increasing Space
  - Keep Frequently-Used Items Handy
  - Don't Crowd
  - Do The Best Task At The Best Time
  - Be Prepared
  - Don't Leave Until You're Finished
  - Do Only What You Set Out To Do
  - Break Your Work Into Units
  - Empower Yourself Through Delegation

- **Avoiding Overwork**

  Overwork is epidemic among entrepreneurs mainly because there's always more to do, we make our own schedules, and have access to our data at all times of the day and night via desktop and mobile computers. Self-employment doesn't have to lead to overwork. You can still restrict the amount of work you do. Consider the following steps to help yourself control the amount of time you work:
  - Learn to determine what is not urgent.
  - Have a set beginning and ending time for your day, as if you still work in the office full-time.
  - Designate a time each day when you are not reachable.
  - Give your home and cell number to a very few business contacts.
  - Get to know yourself.
  - Establish a clear idea of what is expected of you.
  - Learn to say no.
  - Create goals and use these goals as a matrix for deciding what to take on.
  - Stop and think before you make a phone call, write an email, send a fax, or have a conversation.
  - Take yourself away from your work environment.

- **The Ongoing Challenge of Managing Others**

  Managing others is not a natural-born talent, although some individuals seem to be particularly adept at it. Rather, it is a skill that develops with practice - and like most skills, with trial and error.
  - Be Your Advice
  - Communicate
  - Stay focused with Goals
  - Delegate
  - Encourage teamwork
  - Stimulate creativity

- Choose & use workers wisely
- Be generous with praise
- Set the tone

- **The Art of Assigning Tasks**
  Effective delegation frees up precious time and energy so you can focus on your priorities. The six steps to effective delegation are: Communicate the task, Furnish context for the task, Determine standards, Grant authority, Provide support, and Get commitment.

- **Negotiation Know-How: Guidelines for Negotiating Any Contract**
  First of all, avoid letting clients dictate payment terms to you. That practice is particularly common if your client is a larger entity. Don't be afraid to negotiate. Be prepared to offer some halfway solutions. Express to the other party that productive working relationships are built on mutually beneficial arrangements; this will set the tone for friendlier negotiations.

- **When You Have to Fire Someone**
  One of the most difficult tasks you face as a manager or company owner is firing workers. Employees who consistently break the rules, do not perform the functions of their job, or cause difficulties in the workplace can be a strain on the work environment and disrupt business from being performed. Here are a few steps and hints to help ease the nasty task of letting people go:
  - Make sure you have all the documentation you need.
  - Explain to the employee the performance you have expected, the steps you have taken to help them meet that performance, and that they have not met them.
  - Make sure you backup any important files before firing the employee and take steps to lock them out of any computer systems.

FURTHER RESOURCES

ONLINE RESOURCES

The Best Self-Improvement Links
http://superperformance.com/selftopicdirectory.html

BOOKS

***The First Time Manager*, 6th ed.** by Loren Belker, 5th ed. (2012, AMACOM).

Learned Optimism: How to Change Your Mind and Your Life by Martin Seligman (2006, Vintage).

Making Teams Work by Michael Maginn (2003, McGraw-Hill).

Managing Your Mind: The Mental Fitness Guide by Gillian Butler (2007, Oxford University Press).

Out of Our Minds: Learning to be Creative by Ken Robinson (2011, Capstone).

Project Management for Musicians: Recordings, Concerts, Tours, Studios, and More by Jonathan Feist (2013, Berklee Press).

The New Manager's Toolkit by Morey Stettner (2008, AMACOM).

The Seven Habits of Highly Successful People, 25th ed. by Stephen Covey (2013, Free Press).

13

BUSINESS CONDUCTING: MANAGING TIME & INFORMATION

Time is nature's way of making sure everything doesn't happen at once.
– Anonymous

Be passionate about your business because it will consume all your time!
– Sara Wheeler, Little Groove LLC

We work and live in a staccato environment. Emails, faxes, tweets, alerts, meetings, crises and constant pressure create a naturally frenetic cadence to the workday. Tasks that require short bursts of attentiveness (five-minute calls, emails, spontaneous conversations with clients and co-workers) are easy to get done, but responsibilities requiring more time and deliberation, like writing and analysis, are harder to tend to.

When managers feel overwhelmed they react by leaving many tasks untouched or unfinished. They fail to communicate that the jobs are undone and then they do the low-priority items first. The root of the problem very often is that they have no master plan for sorting out their tasks and, as a result, their work lacks direction.

It's worth repeating that the essence of management is the arrangement and conducting of energy. Effective time management involves an internal and external component. The *internal* aspect requires heavy doses of self-discipline. The *external* involves putting tools and resources to work that help you track how time is spent and how plans to spend it actually work out.

How Entrepreneurs Divide Their Time

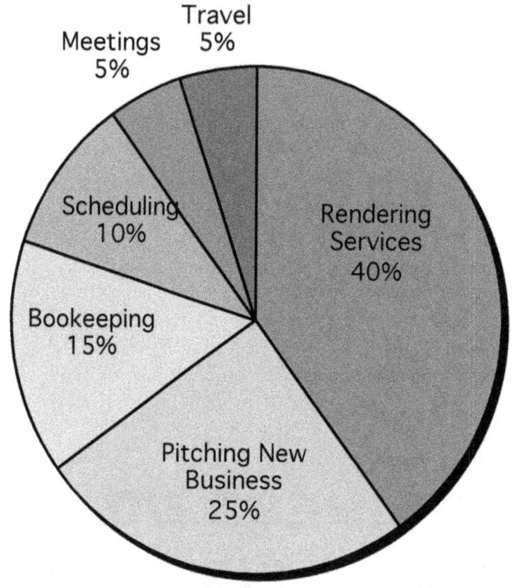

Working From Goals

Success is often defined as the progressive realization of a worthwhile goal. I like that. If you are doing the things that are moving you toward the attainment of your goal today, then you are "successful" even if you are not there yet. It's the goal that starts the whole journey. An illuminating study on goal setting sponsored by the Ford Foundation found that,

- 23% of the population has no idea what they want from life and as a result they don't have much;
- 67% of the population has a general idea of what they want but they don't have any plans for how to get it;
- Only 10% of the population has specific, well-defined goals, but even then, 7 out of the 10 of those people reach their goals only half the time;
- The top 3%, however, achieved their goals 89% of the time – an .890 batting average!

What accounts for the dramatic difference between that top 3% and the others? Are you ready? – the top 3% *wrote down their goals*. Are you laughing yet? It can't be that simple! Or can it? Dreams and wishes are not goals until they are written as specific end results on paper. In some very real sense, writing them down materializes them. Goals have been described as "dreams with a deadline". Written, specific goals provide direction and focus to our activities. They become a road map to follow. And the mind tends to follow what's in front of it.

Once you've set your long-range goals the key is to now *reflect them in your days*. You do this by working backward from the goal. For example, if your goal is to have 500 fans on your mailing list in one year, you will set short-range goals like: book thirty gigs in the next twelve months, increase subscriptions to my newsletter, etc. Jandro Cisneros of The Pillar Productions says it elegantly: " I believe that if what I'm doing right now is in harmony with my long term goals, then I will make them happen."

Reflecting your goals in your day means developing good time-use habits and setting the right order for tasks that need to get done. Here are some guidelines for getting the most out of your work time:

❑ ***Set priorities***. Begin by deciding what tasks must be done today, this week, or this month. If a project seems overwhelming or complex, break it down into manageable steps that can be handled one at a time. Write up a "Things To Do" list. One way to organize your list is with the most important item at the top, the next most important beneath that, and so on.

❑ ***Don't procrastinate***. Putting off unpleasant, routine, or difficult chores is human nature. But those who discipline themselves to tackle the things they dislike or fear will gain self-confidence and make better use of their time. Think about how great you'll feel when the chore is completed. Thinking positively about its outcome will supply you with extra energy to tackle it.

If the project is complex or overwhelming, break it down into a series of steps to be entered on your "Things To Do" list. Then set up a specific time and date to begin working on the first step, and follow through as if it were an appointment. Promise to spend just 15 minutes a day on the task until it's done, and schedule these daily segments at the same time - preferably for a quiet period when there will be no interruptions.

Create an incentive by promising yourself a special reward for getting the job done. Pick something that will give you genuine satisfaction and joy.
Realize that the task doesn't have to be done perfectly. Some attempt is better than no attempt. Maybe you can get away with doing only part of the job and then passing it along to someone else for completion.

❑ ***Delegate***. Speaking of delegation, are you spending time on tasks that could be handled by someone else? Gain precious hours by passing along mundane, peripheral, or partly finished work to assistants, and you will have more time for higher level work. Review the recommendations for delegating tasks from chapter 12.

❑ ***Avoid distractions***. Outside distractions can be a major time-waster - if you let them be. The key is to physically block out disturbances as much as possible, whether by shutting your door, turning your desk away from passersby, or by asking people to be quiet. Your mind can successfully tune out a great many signals if you tell it to.

If interruptions are a real problem, try setting aside a period every day during which you will meet with people and take phone calls; the rest of the time is "private time" in which you work, uninterrupted. Most people say they accomplish more when they work for a long period of time instead of many smaller, disconnected periods.

❑ ***Adjust your schedule to your energy levels.*** Most of us have certain times during the day when we're more alert and perform better. Once you've determined your pattern of physical and mental energy levels, try to adjust your daily schedule to mesh with it. By handling mentally demanding jobs during your peak energy periods, you can get more done in less time. Fit your schedule to your moods and energy levels, and you'll find that you'll save time and be more effective in your job.

❑ ***Handle each piece of paper only once.*** Paperwork is a necessary evil. To gain greater control over it, decide what to do with each piece of paper as it comes into your office. Then, get rid of it. Whether you pass it along, file it, sign it, revise it, or throw it out: The key is to take action on it right away. An ongoing challenge for me!

❑ ***Use the 80-20 Rule.*** Vilfredo Pareto, an Italian economist, observed in 1906 that 20% of the Italian people owned 80% of their country's accumulated wealth. Over time this analytic has come to be termed "The Pareto Principle", the 80/20 Rule, or the "Vital Few and the Trivial Many Rule". For example, you probably wear 20% of your clothes 80% of the time; and you probably listen to 20% of your song catalog 80% of the time.

The 80-20 Rule suggests that 80 percent of your accomplishments come from only 20 percent of your efforts. In a business context, the 80/20 rule reminds us that the relationship between input and output is not balanced.

"THE PARETO PRINCIPLE", aka 80/20 RULE

One fifth of everything in your life produces four-fifths of the results.

Here are some further examples of the Pareto Principle:

- **Time:** 20 percent of our time produces 80 percent of the results.
- **Products:** 20 percent of the products bring in 80 percent of the profit.
- **Job:** 20 percent of our work gives us 80 percent of our satisfaction.
- **Speech:** 20 percent of the presentation produces 80 percent of the impact.
- **Funds:** 20 percent of the people will donate 80 percent of the money.
- **Leadership:** 20 percent of the people will make 80 percent of the decisions.

It's an interesting concept. The trick, of course, is to figure out what makes that 20 percent so productive. Then, devote more of your time to these productive activities, and reduce the time spent on unproductive work. To analyze how you spend your time, keep a log of your daily activities for about two weeks.

The next step is to find solutions to these time wasters. Can you create form letters for replying to correspondence, or have your assistant draft replies? Can you or an assistant clean up and organize the filing system? How about combining business trips, or scheduling travel time for off-hours?

In sum, 20 percent of your priorities will give you 80 percent of your production if you spend your time, energy, money, and personnel on the top 20 percent of your priorities.

Smart Time Management

The key is in not spending time, but in investing it.
– Stephen Covey

In her book, *Working Solo,* Teri Lonier likens the entrepreneur's time challenge to that of a circus plate spinner: "With a single flick of the wrist, this performer keeps one, then two, then up to a dozen plates spinning on slender poles at the same time. If one starts to wobble, the plate spinner scurries to give it a slight adjustment to keep it centered and turning. Plate spinners are masters of timing and balance. They know how to pay attention to each individual plate while never losing sight of the group's performance as a whole. If attention wavers or too much time is spent with a single plate, chances are high that other plates will come crashing to the ground".

I think this is an apt metaphor. As entrepreneurs we are all plate-spinners. Always endeavoring to do many things simultaneously with both steadiness and quality. However, in spite of 21st-century progress, with time-saving devices in the home and office, it seems that 24 hours – minus eight or so for sleep – just aren't enough. This is why effective time management tactics will be one of your best friends. Try the following time-management techniques and see how much more you accomplish each day.

> **Did You Know?**
>
> The invention of the minute hand is often attributed to the great Swiss clock maker Joost Bürgi,whose work in the late 16th century coincided with a burst of technical innovation in clock making that would eventually bring whole new opportunities for guilt and shame.
>
> Along with all your other problems, you could now also be "late".

❑ ***Activity vs. Achievement.*** Effective time management begins with an awareness of how you spend your days. Do you squander them on the busyness of business? Are you focusing on activity instead of achievement?

Successful entrepreneurs guard their time like hawks, and devote their energies to specific short- and long-term goals. When deciding how to spend your time, choose with *intent*. Focus on actions that will advance your goals, not merely fill up your days.

❑ ***List of Seven.*** To get the most out of each day, create an agenda the night before. At the close of each day, jot down a list of the top seven things you'd like to accomplish the next day. When you come into the office the next morning, you'll be focused and ready to go, instead of wasting the fist hour struggling to ramp up and begin.

Creating a list of seven is also a great way to bring closure to a day. The moments you spend reviewing and planning bring perspective, and keep you on target toward your goals.

Why seven? It seems to be the maximum number of things we humans can keep straight in our head. Any more, we become overwhelmed. Any less, we aren't productive enough.

❑ ***Overlapping Plans.*** Use overlapping daily, weekly, monthly, and yearly plans for your business. This approach gives you a micro and macro perspective. Set aside time each week to review your master plan for changes, and to see if you've overestimated or underestimated the time needed to reach your objectives.

❑ ***Ease into Your Day.*** Get to work 15 minutes early, and use the time to relax. Running in the door and "jumping into the fire" sets the wrong tone for the day. You'll be more effective if you launch your day with a sense of ease and control.

❑ ***Measure Twice, Cut Once.*** Taking the time to plan and do things right is always cheaper and quicker than doing things in a hurry now to buy some time in order to do things right later. Remember the carpenter's maxim: measure twice, cut once.

Game composer Norihiko Hibino has some very simple advice for entrepreneurs when it comes to time management. "Wake up early, eat three times a day, and sleep well! Then you can maximize your time." Hibino divides his day according to the activity that will best be served at particular times. "I compose music very early in the morning when nobody is around to disturb me, and then when my staff arrives I do more business-oriented stuff. Corporate level people are usually morning people. In the afternoon I have a lot of appointments, and at night I meet creative people."

While the entrepreneur is indeed the 'conductor' of the business, this doesn't mean the 'score' won't change unexpectedly. Intrusions and interruptions happen despite our best-laid plans, entrepreneurial conductors must also be ready to improvise the score, flex with new developments, and adapt as needed.

Managing Information

To operate successfully, you also need a system for moving information through your office and an office design that reinforces that system. I'm not talking about the "touch it only once" kind of rules that sound sensible, but which most of us have never been able to apply. I mean you need to develop a system for placing things in your office in their various incarnations. You need a place for incoming and outgoing mail, and projects in their various stages of completion. This system will obviously vary greatly from one office to another; the important thing is that your system works for *you*.

Managers today are bombarded with a flood of info that can easily overwhelm even the most organized and diligent people. Not only will you get good, old-fashioned letters, memos, and other correspondence by the truckload through the standard distribution channels, but now you also have a whole new world of information sources to deal with. They've got your email address and you're going to know about them whether you prefer to or not.

Fax machines, pagers, cell phones, FedEx packages, and the like conspire to rob you of the time you need to think, plan or just relax. Instead of acting, you find yourself reacting to the deluge of info that threatens to swallow you whole and then spit you out.
These new sources of information - and the increased speed and frequency with which they find their way to your desk - have made sorting out what's important from what's not more difficult than ever. The activity trap - keeping busy without achieving much - just got deadlier.

You can avoid many legal problems associated with your business simply by keeping accurate records. This section helps you set up your business records the right way, so you can accurately - and legally - track your business activities from your first day in business and avoid problems down the road.

Must-Have Hard-Copy Records

Electronic documents are easy to store and take up much less space. But as of this writing, there are still some things that should be kept on paper. Technically, you can scan every scrap of paper you might keep and store it electronically. However, you might prefer, instead, to keep the paper version for a while, and only go the scanning route if you are certain the document is likely to be kept for archival purposes only.

Also, some legal documents can fall into a gray area. If you signed a contract with a client, keep the paper copy. It's much easier to prove the contract was actually signed. Here is a list of other paper records commonly retained by most businesses:

❑ ***Client contracts***. These are the contracts you and your clients sign when you agree to perform services. If the agreements are email/letter exchanges only, be sure to print those out and keep them in the same place as your other contracts. Get any verbal agreements confirmed in writing, even if it is only an email or letter reiterating your conversation.

❑ ***Working papers*** of current and past projects. These are the notes, research, drafts, and other items from each project. If you have a database of your work, these files would have the inventory number of the appropriate work.

❑ ***All business-related receipts*** (even if only part of the expense is business-related). Credit card slips should be saved, even though you will also have a monthly statement. Expenses in which only part is a business expense (e.g.,, your electric bill) should also be saved.

BASIC CONTACT/LOG

Name ______________________________

Company ______________________________

Title/Position ______________________________

Address ______________________________

Phone (w) ______________ **(h)** ______________

Email ______________________________

Referred By: ______________________________

Follow-up: ______________________________

Notes: ______________________________

____

Date	**Time**	**Action/Outcome**

❑ ***Informational files***. These are files about groups you belong to, issues affecting your services or subject matter, and copies of all marketing materials.

❑ ***Copies of tax returns***, beginning with the year you start your business. (you should probably keep your returns from prior years, too, although for non-business reasons. Check with your accountant or with the IRS website, www.irs.gov.) The same goes for state and local taxes.

❑ ***Previous versions of your business plan***. As your business plan changes and grows, you will want to keep past copies. Print your business plan and file a hard copy once every six months, or just before and after making broad changes to it.

Depending on the size and complexity of your company, important documents may also include the following:

- Legal entity papers: proprietorship, partnership, limited partnership, corporation, etc. documents.
- A time line for the company's goals and objectives during its first three years, including the amounts of capital needed at each stage of development.
- Sources and plans for raising capital.
- Complete list of equipment and furnishings with photos.
- Requirements for office and storage space, furnishing and equipment, etc.
- Sales and cash flow forecasting procedures.
- Accounts payable, billing, and collection policies.
- Personnel policies and financial security controls.

- Promotion, distribution, and sales policies including how these functions should be structured and/or pursued (i.e., to what degree should independents and subcontractors be utilized vs. in-house personnel).
- Departmental organization charts, reporting relationships, and management control techniques.
- Departmental budgetary controls.
- Incentive systems for founders, management, key employees, and non-key employees.
- By-laws, corporate formation, and corporate goals for the next three years and beyond, including possible exit strategies for investors.
- Timeline for product acquisition and releases, with decision tree scenarios to determine number of acquisitions and releases in years two and three.
- Parameters of authority for negotiating deals.
- Milestone budget allocations for acquisition and product development during the first three years.
- While some of this may seem excessive, a good part of a successful business will be having your company information well-managed. Much of the above will be part of your company's operational manual – a document you will use again and again for training new workers. While tedious in the short run, attention to these details will save you tons of time (and money) in the long run.

ASSUME THE WORST WHEN IT COMES TO INFORMATION

When you do deliver, be sure you make copies of ever single deliverable. Assume that the client will lose, break, or otherwise mishandle anything and everything. When you package the project, be sure to label every piece: you will not remember specifics in a year or two. Also, be sure to provide all backup documentation, and keep copies of these materials on file, too.

– Howard Blumenthal, *The Creative Professional*

Creating a System for Information Flow

Think about what kind of information, materials, and other items you regularly encounter. Presumably your list will include basics such as incoming and outgoing mail, phone numbers, current projects, and materials you want to keep but cannot focus on right now. Once you have created your list, visit an office supply store to find solutions for organizing all of your information. The perfect product to meet your needs is probably out there, though you may have to combine two products from the store, or buy one item and modify it to suit your purposes.

In general, you need to remove the burden of day-to-day decision making over what to keep and what to purge. Use the following eight questions to make decisions easier:

- Does it tie in with the core activities of your work?
- Will it help you complete a current project?
- Does it relate to a viable opportunity?
- Will it help you make money?
- Do you refer to it on a regular basis?
- Do you have time to do anything with this information?
- Would your work be affected if you threw this away?
- Are there any tax or legal reasons to keep it?

No matter how great your office setup is, information can easily overwhelm your space and so some "gardening" will be required to keep the information in your office organized and useful. Below are some tips for uncluttering your paper and electronic files.

❑ ***Paper Files***. Everyone knows what it is like to waste time looking for something in a file drawer. Periodic cleansing of junk from your files will cut down on this time-wasting activity. Weed out and recycle the following as you go:

- Old manuals and reports that have since been updated.
- Anything that someone else has the original of, and which you can replace if necessary.
- Hard copies of documents and reports, if the original is kept on the computer.
- Duplicates: Keep original document in a plastic sleeve for protection, keep one copy on hand, and toss the rest.
- Early drafts of letters, proposals, and reports: Keep the best (the final) and toss the rest.
- Unsorted mail over three months old.
- Product solicitations (Don't worry, they'll send you new ones whether or not you want them).
- Literature and promotional materials from companies you aren't interested in. And even those you are. If they have a Web site, and you have their number, why keep the hard copy?
- Invitations/conference brochures: Decide if you want to attend the event. If so, mark the date in your planner and toss the invite.
- Dated, unread reading material (newspapers over one week old, journals over three months, books you've had for years but ever read).
- Literature from past conferences containing information you already know.
- Internet printouts: Toss the paper but keep the Web site address on file.

If Your Data is Secure – Your Company's Metaphorical Butt is Covered

Backing up crucial data on a regular basis ensures it remains secure in the event of a technological breakdown.

The most basic method of backup uses software that will copy specified information to a different part of the hard drive for safekeeping. Unfortunately, if this hard drive fails, both copies of the data may be lost.

More advanced software will transfer requested data to a separate type of media (ex. CD/DVD, external hard drive, USB flash drive, or Mirra).

For even great security, store this backup media in a different room or building. A different planet would be ideal, but hose capabilities don't exist, yet.

Online backup securely copies data through the internet to be kept in secure storage areas. With authentication (username and password), this data can be retrieved through web at any time, from anywhere.

These services are growing in popularity as the cost of data storage plummets.

❑ ***Clean regularly***. Sort through your file cabinets at least once a quarter and throw things away you no longer need.

❑ ***Rename your files***. If you have trouble finding paper in your file cabinets create file names based on the first related word that comes to your mind when you create the file. Chances are, if this word comes to you when you are filing, it will be easier to remember when you are looking for it.

❑ ***Create sub folders in each hanging folder***. This will also increase the ease with which you can locate things.

❑ ***Group related hanging files together***. Keep client folders in one drawer or part of a drawer, articles you save and contracts in another. Keep your personal files in a drawer separated from all business material.

❑ ***Have sufficient filing space***. Organization is only feasible if you have enough space in your file cabinets. Invest in high-quality, large file cabinets that provide enough space for the material you need to store.

❑ ***Computer Files***. Your computer hard drive – the electronic equivalent to your file cabinet – also needs periodic house cleaning. Here are some organizing suggestions for your computer information.

• *Free up disk space by backing-up*. Delete or burn on disk anything older than two years that has not been used. Weed out early drafts and versions of documents that are now finalized. Keep only the final. Old or seldom used files can easily be transferred from the hard drive onto CDs or an external drive. Purge games or programs that you never use. This will increase the overall computer's speed.

• *Create subdirectories on the hard drive*. Broad subdirectories will allow for all related files on the root directory to be saved together in a group. Subdirectories are easy to create.

• *Give files sensible names*. Use general, comprehensive file names that can be easily identified, such as "payroll.2017." This can be particularly helpful when working with a large number of small files simultaneously, and will reduce the search time required to find specific files in a directory.

• *Compress your data.* If space on your hard drive is always an issue, there are programs that will shrink or compress your files, greatly increasing available storage space. Several data compression software programs are available.

❑ ***E-mail.*** Weed out:

- All junk mail
- Simple niceties and chatty e-mails.
- E-mail related to scheduling meetings and lunches.
- General announcements (meetings, events) that you've already accounted for.
- Early strings (save the final string only, which includes all correspondence).

Official Security Tips for Business

❑ ***Proactive software protection*** – Without antivirus and anti-spyware software, these malicious intruders can creep in to your computer and easily degrade its performance and corrupt or even destroy data.

❑ ***Use firewalls*** – Firewalls assist in blocking dangerous programs, viruses or spyware before they enter your system. Various software companies offer firewall protection, but hardware-based firewalls, like those frequently built into network routers, provide a better level of security.

❑ ***Be cautious of unknown or suspicious e-mails*** – Unfriendly (and we use that term loosely) emails can infect your computer **with** spyware and viruses.

❑ ***Manage and assess risk*** - Ask yourself, "What do we have to protect? And, what would impact our business the most?" Cyber-criminals often use lesser-protected small businesses as a bridge to attack larger firms with which they have a relationship.

❑ ***Password protection*** – Using good password practices and changing passwords at regular intervals are crucial to keeping your business' data safe.

Source: *Quickbooks.com*, 1/16

Developing Your Contact Management System

Few people can keep all their business contacts and relationships straight in their head. In fact, the difficulties of managing business contacts and relationships are so draining that they prevent many people from finding time to tackle new, exciting opportunities. This is why special software for "contact management" has become so popular. Once you off load the chore of remembering the who, what, where, when, how, and why of business relationships to software, you're likely to find your level of business success accelerating sharply.

I introduced contact management software in chapter 10. Now let's apply some of its features to running your business. To review, contact management software combines important functions from a word processor, a calendar/scheduling program, a communications package, and a database manager to manage the myriad of details woven into the typical business day.

For example, a database allows you to store your complete Rolodex file (an artifact that adorned most desks just fifteen years ago). Once entered by keyboard or scanner, you can search it at computer speeds for the person or company you want, and then have the software print an envelope or use the computer's modem to dial the telephone for you.

Good contact management software (like *ACT!* and *Now Up to Date*) makes it easy to store, search, and retrieve as much information as you need and want - everything from complete forms in blank you can fill in and then print, to complete reference information or notes on people, projects, appointments and events. It can also work like an automatic "tickler" file, reminding you on a "need -to-know" basis about what you have coming up on your schedule.

The software will also print an appointment list for a day or a week, a list of people to call, or customized versions of standard letters to new prospects, recent purchasers, or any other business contact.

For people who work away from an office, contact manager software loaded on a laptop or handheld can be priceless. In a sense, contact management software can automate your memory. Instead of writing on the back of an envelope or balancing paperwork on top of a pile, you enter it into your contact manager software. Having the information on-line let's you realize tremendous savings every time you want to see it.

For example, let your contact manager store your "To Do" list. You can easily edit each item, and reshuffle or prioritize them to reflect changes and delays. You can also add a note file to each item with background information, related tasks, memos, reports, and correspondence you've written and/or received on the item.

Still defining themselves, there are several different types and styles of contact management software. Before you buy any one of them, therefore, you should consider how you want to manage and use your information. As already mentioned, *ACT!* (for PCs) and *Calendar* (Macs) are two you should definitely check out.

Running a business in this Information Age is detail-oriented to the extreme. One lost contract, misplaced invoice or misspelled word can cost you in time, money, energy - and in lost customers. As the saying goes, haste makes waste, and skips every detail in between. Effective management of time and information is another effective way to get you out from under the wheels and put you in the driver's seat.

CHAPTER SUMMARY

BUSINESS CONDUCTING: TIME & INFORMATION

- **Working From Goals**

  Success is often defined as the progressive realization of a worthwhile goal. Here are some guidelines for getting the most out of your work time: Set priorities, Don't procrastinate, Delegate, Avoid distractions, Adjust your schedule to your energy levels, Handle each piece of paper only once, Follow the 80-20 Rule.

- **Smart Time Management**

  Try the following time-management techniques and see how much more you accomplish each day:
  - Activity vs. Achievement. Focus on actions that will advance your goals, not merely fill up your days.
  - List of Seven. At the close of each day, jot down a list of the top seven things you'd like to accomplish the next day.
  - Overlapping Plans. Use overlapping daily, weekly, monthly, and yearly plans for your business.
  - Ease into Your Day.
  - Measure Twice, Cut Once. Taking the time to plan and do things right is always cheaper and quicker than doing things in a hurry now to buy some time in order to do things right later.

- **Managing Information**

  To operate successfully, you also need a system for moving information through your office and an office design that reinforces that system. You need a place for incoming and outgoing mail, and projects in their various stages of completion. You can avoid many legal problems associated with your business simply by keeping accurate records. This section helps you set up your business records the right way, so you can accurately - and legally - track your business activities from your first day in business and avoid problems down the road.

- **Must-Have Hard-Copy Records**

  Electronic documents are easy to store and take up much less space. But as of this writing, there are still some things that should be kept on paper. Here is a list of other paper records commonly retained by most businesses: Client contracts, Working papers of current and past projects, All business-related receipts, Informational files, Copies of tax returns, and Previous versions of your business plan.

- **Creating a System for Information Flow**

  Think about what kind of information, materials, and other items you regularly encounter. Presumably your list will include basics such as incoming and outgoing mail, phone numbers, current projects, and materials you want to keep but cannot focus on right now. Below are some tips for uncluttering your paper and electronic files.
  - Paper Files. Periodic cleansing of junk from your files will cut down on this time-wasting activity.
  - Rename your files.
  - Create sub folders in each hanging folder.
  - Group related hanging files together.
  - Have sufficient filing space.
  - Computer Files.
  - E-mail. Weed out: All junk mail, Anything received as a CC or FWD, Simple niceties and chatty e-mail, E-mail related to scheduling meetings and lunches, general announcements and early message strings.

- **Developing Your Contact Management System**

  Few people can keep all their business contacts and relationships straight in their head. In fact, the difficulties of managing business contacts and relationships are so draining that they prevent many people from finding time to tackle new, exciting opportunities. This is why special software for "contact management" has become so popular. Good contact management software makes it easy to store, search, and retrieve as much information as you need and want – everything from complete forms in blank you can fill in and then print, to complete reference information or notes on people, projects, appointments and events.

FURTHER RESOURCES

BOOKS

The 25 Best Time Management Tools & Techniques by Pamela Dodd (2005, Peak Performance Press).

Getting Things Done: The Art of Stress-Free Productivity by David Allen (2015, Penguin).

Lifehacker: 88 Tech Tricks to Turbocharge Your Day by Gina Trapani (2011, Wiley).

Life Hacks: Any Procedure or Action That Solves a Problem, Simplifies a Task, Reduces Frustration in One's Everyday Life by Keith Bradford (2014, Adams Media).

The Office Clutter Cure by Don Aslett, 2nd ed. (2008, Marsh Creek Press).

Organize Your Office in No Time by Monica Ricci (2005, Que).

14

BUSINESS ORCHESTRATION: MANAGING MONEY

Beware of little expenses; a small leak will sink a great ship.
–Benjamin Franklin

From one perspective, the biggest challenge facing you as a new entrepreneur will be to graduate from a *cash*-dependent to a *wit*-dependent business person. It's the only way startups make it on their budget. When you listen to stories about how people came up with creative alternatives to their money problems, it's because there were no boundaries for believing an option was possible. It is that practice of tapping into your creative juices that will help you most as you learn to 'conduct' the money dimensions of your business.

> "A dollar spent in development is worth ten dollars in pre-production one hundred dollars in production, and one thousand dollars in post-production."
>
> – Howard Blumenthal, *The Creative Professional*

Books on entrepreneurship, especially those written by MBAs, put a tremendous emphasis on the financial aspects of new companies. Of course, money *is* crucial to keeping the business a float. But too much emphasis on financials can blind one to the simplicity of small business money management.

"Business is very simple," exclaims ultra-successful new media composer Norihiko Hibino. "Cash in and cash out. Between those two will be profit. People sometimes get confused by too many parameters in the balance sheet. But remember, you can only make money between those differences."

As we saw in the last chapter, keeping good records and staying on top of things is a key in good business management, and this is perhaps most crucial in the area of money. An appropriate record-keeping system can determine the survival or failure of a new business. For those already in business, good record-keeping systems can increase the chances of staying in business and the opportunity to earn larger profits. Complete records will keep you in touch with your business's operations and obligations and help you see problems before they occur.

In general, this is one area of business most people tend to ignore or avoid altogether. I find that very few people read contracts and financials, the grueling details of which most of us would prefer to leave in that pile on the floor. It all seems so complex and dry. However, the ability to concentrate on the details, even though we hate to do them, is essential for staying afloat. For example, if you must pay workers each week and your bills each month, but your customers (e.g., distributors) don't pay you for 60 or 90 days, the business has a cash flow lapse that you must plan for. What do you do?

Another scenario. Cash forecasting is a record of known expenses in future months. That record helps the new business owner avoid overspending whenever a big check arrives, only to starve a month later when the annual insurance premium is due. What do you do? Consistent financial planning and understanding will give you the tools to manage these common money challenges in your business.

"Financial management is the key to running the company successfully," says Andreas Katsambas of Brooklyn's The End Records. "Money shouldn't be the driving force, but is essential in keeping the wheel turning." Sean Hagon of Music Media Solutions agrees: "Financial management and taking ownership of it is crucial. As a sole proprietor, there are many tax issues to consider and you need to constantly educate yourself or seek help when the financial piece is out of your level of expertise."

This chapter explains the basic things you need for establishing a good record-keeping system and managing your cash flow.

Bean Counting in One Easy Lesson

Financial management goes a lot smoother when certain components are in place. These include: knowing basic accounting terms, understanding the purposes of accounting, learning to read financial statements (Balance Sheet, Income Statement, etc.), creating a budget, and forecasting income and expenses. Let's look at each in turn.

❑ ***Know the Lingo.*** In any area of life, if you do not understand the associated vocabulary you will not be able to succeed in it. If you plan to be a business owner be sure you are familiar with all of these accounting terms:

Revenue – what you earn.

Expenses – what you spend.

Net Profit – total revenue minus total expenses.

Net Income – same as net profit.

COGS – the cost of goods sold. What you pay for what you sell.

Gross Income – total revenue minus COGS.

Gross Margin – same as gross income.

Depreciation – reduction in value over time.

Appreciation – increase in value over time.

EBITDA – earnings before interest, taxes, depreciation, and amortization.

Amortization – the reduction of principal or debt at regular intervals.

Bond – debt instrument through with companies and governments can raise money.

Accounts Payable – money you owe for products and services already received.

Accounts Receivable – money owed to you for products/services already delivered.

Cash Flow – the in and out of money to/from your business.

Equity – ownership in a company.

Vesting – earning equity over time instead of all at once.

Option pool – a percentage ownership in your company set aside at founding for those who may come aboard later.

Asset – something you own that has value.

Liability – something you owe for.

Owners' Equity – The value of what the shareholders/owners have put into a company.

Appreciating Asset – something you own that is going up in value.

Depreciating Asset – something you own that is going down in value.

Balance Sheet – a financial statement that keeps track of assets, liabilities, and owners' equity.

Balance Sheet Formula – assets minus liabilities equal owners' equity.

Income Statement – a financial statement that keeps track of revenue, expenses, and profit.

Income Statement Formula – revenue minus expenses equals net profit.

Cash Flow Statement – a financial statement that keeps track of all the money that goes in and out of your business.

IPO – initial public offering, selling part of your company on the stock market in exchange for investment capital in your business.

❑ ***Understand What Accounting Tells You.*** Mention the words "accounting, bookkeeping, and taxes," and the average entrepreneur shudders. *Oh! To be left alone to run their business without this time-wasting, hateful chore!* Those who are not diligent in monitoring their business's financial records often experience an ultimately financial demise. Astute entrepreneurs who utilize their financial information to monitor progress and make decisions are usually more successful.

Accounting records act as a financial barometer for your business. An accurate set of accounting records transferred into financial statement formats and carefully analyzed can tell you the following:

- whether projected margins are being met
- where expenses are contributing to losses

- whether actual results are meeting projected results
- what percentage each overhead expense is costing in relation to sales
- which products or services are selling the most
- which products or services are profitable or losing money
- how much is collectively owing in accounts receivable and payable
- how much each customer owes and how much you owe each supplier
- the dollar cost of asset purchases from start-up
- the accumulated depreciation of assets and their book value
- how much the business owns in assets
- how much the business owes in liabilities
- your working capital
- your current tax situation, personal and corporate
- whether you are financially ready for growth
- whether wages and management salaries are too high (or too low)
- how to make future projections based on past history,

...and more. Quite simply, accounting tells you if you are making money. If you create a profit and loss statement each month, you can ascertain your position quickly. If you are losing money, you can make changes in your operations, such as increasing prices or reducing expenses, to correct the situation long before the year's end and ensure that your overall year will still be profitable.

❑ ***Understand Basic Financial Statements***. Numbers can be very instructive in business. An income statement, for example, breaks out every type of revenue and expense so the business owner can see trends. So, for example, if telephone charges are running higher than budgeted, the owner can investigate why and either take steps to control spending or adjust to reflect the needed additional spending.

Financial documents probably are foreign to someone who has never owned a business, and unfortunately, to some who have. Here is where you can benefit from the knowledge of a SCORE or SBDC advisor (see Chapter 4, "Knowing Your Resources"). Once you've learned the basics from this chapter, you can then create your own draft financial documents and take them to any Small Business Development Center, or send them to an online SCORE advisor to get feedback and suggestions. Seasoned business counselors will provide you with guidance and support as you work out your company numbers.

The main types of financial statements are the *balance sheet* and the *income statement*, also known as the *profit and loss statement*. The balance sheet is a report of a business's financial condition (assets, liabilities and capital) at a specific moment in time, and the income statement is a summary of profit and loss for a specific *period* of time, generally a month, quarter or year. Another, the *schedule of operating expenses*, details those costs associated with sales and administrative activities of the company. Samples of each document follow, designed for a fictitious music production company.

THE BALANCE SHEET
A **balance sheet** details a company's "assets" (cash, inventory, equipment), "liabilities" (accounts payable, loans) and "capital" (equity in the business). The bottom line on a balance sheet is *the company's net worth.*

Bones & Tones Recordings, Inc.

	Year 1	**Year 2**
Assets:		
Current Assets:		
Cash	$10,000	$20,000
Accounts Receivable	82,000	144,000
Inventory	185,000	230,000
Prepaid Expenses	5,000	5,000
Total Current Assets	282,000	399,000
Fixed Assets:		
Land	0	0
Buildings	0	0
Equipment	150,000	120,000
Accumulated Depreciation	- 30,000	30,000
Total Fixed Assets	120,000	90,000
Other Assets	10,000	11,000
Total Assets	$412,000	$500,000
Liabilities & Equity:		
Current Liabilities:		
Notes Payable—Short Term	60,000	42,400
Current Maturities of Long-Term Debt	30,000	30,000
Accounts Payable	82,000	86,000
Accrued Expenses	7,900	13,500
Taxes Payable	0	0
Stockholder Loans	0	0
Total Current Liabilities	179,900	171,900
Long-Term Liabilities	120,000	90,000
Total Liabilities	$ 299,900	$ 261,900
Owner's Equity:		
Common Stock	75,000	75,000
Paid-in-capital	0	0
Retained Earnings	37,100	163,100
Total Owner's Equity	112,100	238,100
Total Liabilities & Equity	$412,000	$500,000

THE INCOME STATEMENT

An **income statement**, often called a "profit-and-loss statement," shows a company's financial performance over a period of time.

Bones & Tones Recordings, Inc.

	Year 1	**Year 2**
Sales	$1,000,000	$ 1,500,000
Cost of Goods Sold	- 750,000	- 1,050,000
Gross Profit	250,000	450,000
Operating Expenses	- 200,000	- 275,000
Operating Profit	50,000	175,000
Other Income and Expenses	3,000	5,000
Net Profit Before Taxes	53,000	180,000
Income Taxes	- 15,900	- 54,000
Net Profit After Taxes	$37,100	$126,000

THE SCHEDULE OF OPERATING EXPENSES
A **schedule of operating expenses** details the day-to-day expense such as sales and administration, or research & development, as opposed to production, costs, and pricing.

Bones & Tones Recordings, Inc.

	Year 1	Year 2
Advertising	$5,000	$15,000
Auto Expenses	3,000	7,500
Bank Charges	750	1,200
Depreciation	30,000	30,000
Dues & Subscriptions	500	750
Employee Benefits	5,000	10,000
Insurance	6,000	10,000
Interest	17,800	15,000
Office Expenses	2,500	4,000
Officers' Salaries	40,000	60,000
Payroll Taxes	6,000	9,000
Professional Fees	4,000	7,500
Rent	24,000	24,000
Repairs & Maintenance	2,000	2,500
Salaries & Wages	40,000	60,000
Security	2,250	2,250
Supplies	2,000	3,000
Taxes & Licenses	1,000	1,500
Telephone	4,800	6,000
Utilities	2,400	2,400
Other	1,000	3,400
Total Operating Expenses	$200,000	$275,000

❑ ***Keeping Good Budget & Accounting Records***. For many small-business owners, the process of budgeting is limited to figuring out where to get the cash to meet next week's payroll. There are so many financial fires to put out in a given week that it's hard to find the time to do any short- or long-range financial planning. But failing to plan financially might mean that you are unknowingly planning to fail. Accounting records furnish substantial information about your volume of business, such as how present and prior years compare, the amount of cash versus credit sales, and the level and status of accounts receivable. But don't let all this financial mumbo-jumbo blind you to the essential function of a budget: *to help you pinpoint opportunities (and threats) for the company and direct the use of its resources most effectively.*

The most effective financial budget includes both a short-range, month-to-month plan for at least a calendar year and a long-range quarter-to-quarter plan you use for financial reporting. The long-range plan should cover a period of at least three years (some go up to five) on a quarterly basis, or even an annual basis. The long-term budget should be updated when the short-range plan is prepared.

When planning your budget be sure to allocate funds only for what you actually need at the time. It's easy to overspend at the beginning. "Question every dollar," says CDBaby founder Derek Sivers. "You don't need a nice desk, nice chair, and probably don't even need an office. People can work from home." On the other hand, you must spend in order to keep your business appearance up. "Be as cautious as possible with all expenditures," advises Kristin Samit of eMajor Marketing. "Shop around and be frugal, but don't cut corners on important items that represent your company: website, business cards, stationery, and money for convention travel (to meet people face-to-face)".

SOME ESSENTIAL DOS AND DON'TS OF FINANCIAL MANAGEMENT

Do Not:

1. Throw away any business-related receipt.
2. Pay bills until they are due - unless you receive a discount for early payment.

Do:

1. Have separate business checking & savings accounts.
2. Keep records for at least seven years, including:
    A. Receipts
    B. Bank statements
    C. Copies of tax return
    D. Ledger sheets
        - Income Received: Record all pertinent information on checks received: clients name, check number, amount, date, and type of income.
        - Check, Cash, and Credit Card Disbursements
        - Accounts Receivable
        - Profit & Loss Statements
        - Balance Sheets

Many financial budgets provide a plan only for the income statement; however, it is important to budget both the income statement and balance sheet. This enables you to consider potential cash-flow needs for your entire operation, not just as they pertain to income and expenses. For instance, if you had already been in business for a couple of years and were adding a new product line, you would need to consider the impact of inventory purchases on cash flow.

Budgeting only the income statement also doesn't allow a full analysis of the effect of potential capital expenditures on your financial picture. For instance, if you are planning to purchase real estate for your operation, you need to budget the effect the debt service will have on cash flow. In terms of the future, a budget can also help you determine the potential effects of expanding your facilities and the resulting higher rent payments or debt service. See how many important things numbers can tell you?

How Do You Budget? In the startup phase, you will have to make reasonable assumptions about your business in establishing your budget. You will need to ask and answer questions such as:

- How much can be sold in year one?
- How much will sales grow in the following years?
- How will the products and/or services you are selling be priced?
- How much will it cost you to produce your product? How much inventory will you need?
- What will your operating expenses be?
- How many employees will you need? How much will you pay them? How much will you pay yourself? What benefits will you offer? What will your payroll and unemployment taxes be?
- What will the income tax rate be? Will your business be an S corporation or a C corporation?
- What will your facilities needs be? How much will it cost you in rent or debt service for these facilities?
- What equipment will be needed to start the business? How much will it cost? Will there be additional equipment needs in subsequent years?
- What payment terms will you offer customers if you sell on credit? What payment terms will your suppliers give you?
- How much will you need to borrow?
- What will the interest rate be?

As for the actual preparation of the budget, you can create it manually (yes, many still do this) or you can go with the budgeting function that comes with most bookkeeping software packages. You can also purchase separate budgeting software such as *Quicken, M.Y.O.B.* or *Microsoft Money*. While it may seem like a lot of information to forecast, it's not as cumbersome as it looks.

❑ ***Create a Basic Budget Forecast***. The first step is to set up a plan for the following year on a month-to-month basis. Starting with the first month, establish specific budgeted dollar levels for each category of the budget. The sales numbers will be critical since they will be used to compute *gross profit margin* (that is, profit *before* expenses are figured in) and will help determine operating expenses, as well as the *accounts receivable* (that is, money owed to you) and inventory levels necessary to support the business. In determining how much of your product or service you can sell, study the market in which you will operate, your competition, potential demand that you might already have seen, and economic conditions.

For *cost of goods sold* (COGS), you will need to calculate the actual cost associated with producing each item on a percentage basis. For your operating expenses, consider items such as advertising, travel, depreciation, insurance, etc. Then factor in a tax rate based on actual business tax rates that you can obtain from your accountant.

On the balance sheet, break down inventory by category. For instance, a guitar manufacturer, has raw materials, work-in-progress and finished goods. For inventory, accounts receivable and accounts payable, you will figure the total amounts based on projected number of days on hand.

Once you have a written financial plan, staying within your business budget can be challenging. Unexpected circumstances such as changes in tax laws, changes in the business climate, and changes in income can affect your financial situation. But aside from issues that you can't control, you can control your spending habits. Purchasing certain luxuries for your business, such as new office equipment, when your old equipment would suffice is an unnecessary expense, especially if you're working on a shoestring budget. So when the urge to purchase an unnecessary item haunts you, remember that frugality has saved more businesses from going under than extravagance.

Guidelines for Setting Your Price & Your Fee

Setting your price can be tricky thing. The determination must be based on a broad, thoughtful basis and requires a basic understanding of both your financial and business goals. In calculating profits, managers weigh sales revenues against costs for materials and labor. However, they also consider the capital resources (people, plant and equipment) that the company must tie up to generate a given level of profit. The costs of marketing can also be substantial. To use these resources efficiently, many companies set prices to achieve a targeted level of return on sales or capital investment.

Follow these six tips for setting your price:

- ***Keep your prices realistic.*** Set your prices based on your own financial goals not those of your competitors' alone.

- ***Cover all your costs.*** A successful pricing strategy is one that results in the most dollars after all your costs are met.

- ***Check your price against inflation.*** If you maintain your prices despite inflation, you will erode your profit margin.

- ***Include in your pricing the value of your time***, as well as the other benefits your business brings to customers. Avoid committing the mistake of not including a salary for yourself, particularly if you are operating a service business. See chapter 16 for ideas on how you can adjust your pricing up by *adding value* to your products and services.

- ***Price low, but smart.*** Pricing low is a common strategy, especially for startups. But be careful! Low price can also signal low quality, and it becomes difficult to raise prices later once customers are accustomed to your low prices.

- ***Use discounts with care.*** Discounts are good for encouraging repeat/bulk orders, bundling sales, and early payment of customers. Discounts are also used to clear out merchandise that has become outdated.

Related to price, of course, is your fee. The following table illustrates how to determine your fees if you are a service-oriented business (that is, the bulk of your sales come as a result of providing a service – like music instruction – rather than through selling a product – like a CD).

The chart is based on a 40-hour work week, which leaves a maximum of 25 billable hours per week. Since overhead varies greatly from one business to another, it isn't included in this breakdown.

DETERMINING YOUR FEE: Time/Income Factor Analysis				
One Year	= 365 days - 104 days (weekends) = 261 days - 8 days (holidays) = 253 days - 10 days (health) = 243 days - 10 days (vacation) = 233 days x 8 hours per day = 1864 hours per year - 30% (promotion, operations, professional development) = approximately 1300 hours = approximately 25 billable hours per week			
Annual Income*	50% 12.5 hrs./week (650 hrs.)	70% 17.5 hrs./week (910 hrs.)	90% 22.5 hrs./week (1170 hrs.)	100% 25 hrs./week (1300 hrs.)
$25,000	38.50	27.50	21.50	19.25
$30,000	46.00	33.00	25.75	23.00
$35,000	54.00	38.50	30.00	27.00
$40,000	61.50	44.00	34.00	31.00
$50,000	77.00	55.00	42.75	38.50
$60,000	92.00	66.00	51.25	46.00
$75,000	115.50	82.50	64.00	58.00
$100,000	154.00	110.00	85.50	77.00
** Does not include allowance for overhead and taxes*				

Here's how to understand the chart: Let's say that you want to earn $35,000 this year before taxes. If you plan on working 50 percent (billing 12.5 hours per week), then you need to charge $54 per hour. If you think you will be able to work 90 percent (bill 22.5 hours per week), then you only need to charge $30 per hour. BUT, you also must include the costs in running your business.

Imagine that your fixed costs are $10,000 per year plus $6 per session. So, at a 50 percent workload, you need to cover $35,000 income, $10,000 fixed expenses, and $3900 per session cost (650 sessions), which equals $48,900. Look at the chart and you will find that to bring in gross revenues of $50,000, you need to charge approximately $76 per hour. Yet, if you plan on billing 90 percent, then you need to cover $35,000 income, $10,000 fixed expenses, and $7020 per session cost (1170 sessions), which equals $52,020. Check the chart and you will discover that you will only need to charge about $39 per hour. Use the chart as a guide for determining the best way to price your service.

With a grasp of basic accounting vocabulary, a familiarity with essential financial documents and budgeting, as well as a sense of your fee structure, you're ready for setting up your bookkeeping.

The Basics Small Business Bookkeeping

The following criteria are essential to a good financial record-keeping system:

- Simplicity
- Accuracy
- Timeliness
- Consistency
- Understandability
- Reliability and completeness

❑ ***Get the Software.*** There are several accounting systems that can be purchased and adapted to the individual business, or you may find it is better to use a system specifically designed for your business and one that meets the above-mentioned criteria. The two top-rated financial management programs for small business are *Quickbooks* and *M.Y.O.B.* Both of these programs interview you on the front end and then automatically adapt themselves to the particulars of your business structure. Very cool.

A good general ledger software program can offer you substantial assistance in recording business transactions and summarizing the information into appropriate accounting presentations. The programs also allow automatic posting of transactions directly to the general ledger.

Currently available software allows you to enter transactions individually; these transactions are posted directly to the general ledger (the 'grand central' of your company accounting). A printout at the end of a given period shows the individual account activity, and also includes a balance and total of the accounts and provides a trial balance presentation. If the software is designed properly, it will provide appropriately prepared financial statements (balance sheet, income statements, etc.) as well. Nice.

A SIMPLE BOOKKEEPING RECORD

In order to keep small business records of all the transactions in your business, you may use the "single entry" bookkeeping method, which is simple and efficient, as shown below:

Date	**Description**	**Revenue**	**Expenses**
4-Jan	Paid phone bill	-	$250.00
4-Jan	Performed repair service	$700.00	-
5-Jan	Paid rent	-	$500.00
5-Jan	Performed repair service	$1150.00	-
7-Jan	Paid all employees	-	$800.00
8-Jan	Paid Electricity bill	-	$150.00
	January totals	$1,850.00	$1,700.00

❑ ***Understand the Two Methods Of Accounting.*** There are two basic methods of accounting: ***cash*** **basis** and ***accrual*** **basis.** The method you choose will depend on your type of business. Cash basis is the simpler method. It is mainly used by service businesses that do not maintain inventory or startup businesses that do not offer credit. The accrual method is most commonly used by businesses that provide for longer-range sales or maintain an inventory.

- **Cash Basis Method.** In cash basis accounting, you record sales when cash is received and expenses when they are actually paid. Using the cash basis method is like maintaining a checkbook. Under this method, accounts receivable are not recorded as sales until they are collected. Accounts payable are not recorded as expenses until the account is paid. Bad debt, accruals and deferrals are not appropriately recorded under cash basis because they are examples of outstanding credit (business notes). The cash basis method is not appropriate for businesses that extend credit.

- **Accrual Basis Method.** In accrual basis accounting, you report income or expenses as they are earned or incurred rather than when they are collected or paid. The accrual basis also provides a method for recording expenditures paid in a single installment but covering more than one period. For example, interest may be paid semiannually or annually, but it is recorded on a monthly basis.

The accrual method satisfies the matching concept, i.e., matching income with related expenditures. Consequently, it can provide a clear and accurate view of business operations for a given period.

Other Important Financial Records

In addition to basic accounting records, you will need to keep separate records for accounts receivable, payroll and taxes, petty cash, insurance, business equipment and perhaps other items.

❑ ***Accounts Receivable.*** A good record-keeping system should provide you with a detailed report of accounts receivable (money owed your business), including current information on customers and a running balance of their accounts. To maintain a good accounts receivable system, record credit charges on a regular basis. It is essential that you follow up on all late paying and delinquent customers.

Accounts receivable should be 'aged' at the end of each month. This means organizing the accounts into those that are current, 30-, 60-, and 90-days old and older. This arrangement helps you to take appropriate, timely actions. An additional timely action to decrease the number of bad accounts and avoid the effort of collecting payments from slow-paying customers is to issue a formal complaint with your local credit bureau.

What is ('Negative Income')?

In accounting, subtraction and negative numbers are indicated by parentheses.
For example, ($2,000) means negative $2,000 or subtract $2,000, or a $2,000 loss.

Therefore, the above example may be written as follows:

	$ 1,000	Gross income
	(3,000)	Expenses
equals	$ (2,000)	Net profit (loss)

❑ ***Payroll and Taxes.*** As discussed in chapter 9, current Internal Revenue Service (IRS) regulations require that you withhold federal income tax and social security (FICA) from each employee. You must remit the amount for taxes to the IRS on a quarterly, monthly, or more frequent basis. A detailed reporting system for payroll will help you make timely tax payments and, fortunately, this reporting is built into the software programs already mentioned.

Gather specific information about each employee on individual employee record cards. All employees should fill out federal Form W-4, which indicates their filing status and the number of exemptions they claim. Use this information to compute the federal withholding and social security (FICA) deductions for each payroll check.
Prepare "Employees Quarterly Federal Tax Return" (Form 941) by totaling each employee's withholding for federal taxes and social security. File Form 941 with the IRS. Each payroll period, total the accumulated withholdings of both federal taxes and social security for all employees. If this total exceeds $500 for any month, you must deposit this amount by the fifteenth day of the following month in a depository bank (an authorized financial institution or a federal reserve bank).

Generally, when the total exceeds $3,000, you must deposit this amount within three business days. Any overpayment in taxes is paid back to you quarterly.
At the year's end, you are required to prepare not only the information normally required for that quarter, but also summaries of each employee's total earnings and withholdings for the year (Form W-2). Provide this form to each employee and the IRS.

A Word of Caution

It is very easy to fall behind in making tax payments. If you find yourself short of cash, do not be tempted to delay payment of taxes. The IRS will not bill your business for taxes due nor will it notify you of late payments. Delayed payments can easily add up to a large sum; the debt may impede the growth of your business and may even force you to close your business, to say nothing of the federal penalties incurred for late payments.

With a good record-keeping system, you can simplify the process of filing taxes to the point where the information needed to complete the forms is automatically generated. Setting up such a system is a rather technical task and you may need to seek guidance. This, again, is a good project to undertake with a SCORE or SBDC advisor.

❑ ***Petty Cash.*** Sometimes a petty cash fund is needed to purchase small items required on a day-to-day basis. If this is necessary, draw a check to petty cash for a nominal amount.
Problems often arise when cash is easily available; therefore, if possible, try to avoid a petty cash fund. However, very often the convenience of having a small amount of cash available will facilitate the smooth operation of your business. Be sure to balance this fund monthly, based on the cash balance plus receipts for all expenditures.

❑ ***Business Equipment.*** Keep an accurate list of permanent business equipment used on both a regular and stand-by basis. The list should describe the equipment and provide serial numbers, date of purchase and original cost. Keep the list available for insurance or other purposes. You will also need this information to prepare accurate depreciation schedules, if this applies.

Special Tax Guidelines for the Small Music Company

❑ ***The "Anti Hobby" Rule:*** The IRS keeps a watchful eye out for individuals who consistently run businesses at a loss just to amass valuable deductions. Their guidelines state that a business must make a profit three years out of five, or else the enterprise is considered a hobby, which lowers or eliminates possible deductions. There have been exceptions to this, however. By showing good records and a business plan, small enterprises *have* convinced the IRS that they at least are *intending* to be profitable.
The following list will help you determine if you're doing whatever you're doing to make a buck. No single item on the list settles or resolves the issue, nor is this a complete list used

by the IRS in making a decision, but these are the items normally taken into account. The IRS considers all the facts surrounding an activity in determining if the activity is engaged in for profit.

1. Carrying on the activity in a businesslike manner.

- Are your books and records kept completely and accurately?
- Is your activity carried on like similar businesses that operate at a profit?
- If methods you used proved unprofitable, did you change your methods or adopt new techniques in an attempt to improve profitability?

2. Expertise of the taxpayer or his advisors.

- Have you prepared to enter this business by studying the accepted managerial and technological practices of those already in the field?
- Are your business practices similar to others in your profession? If not, are you attempting to develop new or superior techniques that may result in future profits?

3. Time and effort expended.

- Do you put more time into marketing your business than you put into fly-fishing?
- Do you employ someone with the expertise you may not have or who puts in the time you are not able to?
- Did you leave another job to devote more time to this activity?

4. Expectation that assets used in the activity may appreciate in value.

- The term "profit" encompasses appreciation of assets. Will the land, equipment, or instruments used in your endeavor increase in value so that your future profit may be realized from the appreciation of your assets as well as from income?

5. Success in carrying on similar or dissimilar activities.

- Have you taken a similar activity and converted it from an unprofitable to a profitable enterprise?
- Have you had general success in running other kinds of businesses?

6. History of income or losses with respect to the activity.

Getting Paid in the Parking Lot: Cheating by Hiding Income

Under the table. In the parking lot. Off the books. Of course, it's income. And yes, you must report it on your tax return.

Miles Mingus plays a regular gig at Jazzy Jack's Pub. Jazzy Jack has a cash business; all his barflies pay for their drinks with hard currency- no plastic or checks, thank you. And Jack pays Miles the same way- in cash, which he takes from an envelope in his desk in the back office. Nobody's claiming a lot of the income and nobody's paying a lot of the taxes- until Jack gets audited.

The IRS is not a morality agency, it is a monetary agency. It doesn't care what you do for a living as long as you pay taxes on the income you make doing it. If you make your living as a hit man or a lady of the night or a drug dealer, be sure to pay the IRS its fair share. Remember the Chicago mobster Al Capone? He wasn't sent to prison for murder, bootlegging, or racketeering; he was convicted of tax evasion for not reporting the money he earned in his self-employed endeavors.

When the IRS calls for an audit, its only purpose is to collect more tax money with some interest and penalty to boot. Criminal activity is not suspected. But if you are caught in outright cheating- particularly in deliberately failing to report a significant amount of income- the IRS will not hesitate to prosecute you.

- Losses early in the history of a business are common. Are your losses due to heavy early expenses or have they extended beyond the normal time for this kind of activity to begin making a profit?

7. Amount of occasional profits.

- There may be a disparity in the amount of profits that you make in relation to the losses you incur or in the amount of money spent on assets used in your activity. The purchase of a $3,000 Gibson guitar, but not one paid gig, may tell the IRS it's a hobby. Do you have an opportunity to make a substantial ultimate profit in a highly speculative activity?
- A software developer may work on a project for years before it is viable. Is your business the type that will have an occasional large profit but small operating losses over many years?

Note: Be extra careful of the next two.

8. Financial status of the taxpayer.

- If this is your only source of income, then you must be in it to make a profit.
- If, on the other hand, you've got large income from other sources and this activity generates substantial tax benefits, this could indicate to the IRS that the activity is not carried on for profit but as a homemade tax shelter.

9. Elements of personal pleasure or recreation.

- The IRS says "elements of personal pleasure or recreation" may indicate the lack of profit motive. Does this mean your business can't be pleasurable too?

TAX "DEDUCTIONS" VS. TAX "CREDITS"

There is a big difference between a tax deduction and a tax credit

A tax deduction is subtracted from your income, a benefit to you because your tax is calculated on the amount of your income. A $1,000 deduction reduces your income by $1,000 and, depending upon your tax bracket and state taxes, could save you from zero up to $500 in taxes.

A tax credit on the other hand is an amount subtracted directly from your tax. A $300 tax credit reduces your tax by $300; a $1,000 tax credit saves you $1,000 in taxes. Credits are dollar for dollar reductions, and are much better than deductions. Here's why:

Let's say your taxable income is $40,000 and you get a $5,000 Tax Deduction. Now your taxable income is $35,000. You owe taxes on $35,000 instead of $40,000. With a 20% tax rate you owe $7,000 ($35,000 x 20%) in taxes. Without the Tax Deduction you would owe $8,000 ($40,000 x 20%) in taxes.

A tax credit on the other hand will reduce your tax...not your taxable amount. Let's keep your taxable income at $40,000. Your tax is $8,000. If we apply a $5,000 Tax Credit you now only pay $3,000 ($8,000 - $5,000) in taxes. Enjoy those credits!

❑ **Deductions:** To be deductible, a business expense must be both ordinary and necessary. An ***ordinary expense*** is one that is common and accepted in your field of business. A ***necessary expense*** is one that is appropriate and helpful for your business. An expense does not have to be indispensable to be considered necessary.

Section 179 of the tax code states that up to $18,000 in expenses for capital assets (like a computer or PA system) may be deducted per year. However, that deduction is limited by item cost and taxable income. This means that if you earned only $2000 you can take only a $2000 deduction even if the item costs more.

In order to qualify for a 179 deduction, you must fill out Form 4562 and attach it to your tax return. Of course, you want to also take a deduction if your business is run from your home or apartment. Three rules apply to the *Home Office Deduction*:

• *Rule 1: Exclusive Use* - The part of your home used for business must be used exclusively for business.

• *Rule 2: Used on a Regular Basis* - The part of your home used for business must be used on a regular basis for business.

• *Rule 3: Principal Place of Business* - Your home office or studio or workshop must be your principal place of business.

❑ **Write-off "dead" Inventory for Tax savings**: Do you have boxes of unsold merchandise lying around. No need to take a loss on it when you have the option of donating them.

Here's what's so cool about this write off: Regular C corporations can deduct the full cost of the inventory donated, plus half the difference between cost and fair market value, up to twice the cost. S corporations, partnerships, and sole proprietorships earn a straight cost deduction. Four nonprofit organizations that can handle your donations are the National Association for the Exchange of Industrial Resources (800-562-0955), the National Cristina Foundation (203-863-9100), and Educational Assistance Limited (630-690-0010). Donated items are redistributed to thousands of qualified schools and charities across the United States.

How might this apply to you? Have any unsold CDs, instruments or gear lying around?

❑ **Sales Tax Issues**: If you close your business or never get it off the ground after you have already procured a tax ID number, make sure you notify the department of taxation. If you don't, you will continue to get computer-generated estimated bills and fines! Also, if you buy a home-based business from someone else, make sure you have a bulk "Sales Tax Clearance Dome," which is an okay from the tax people that there are no liens on the business.

RETAINING RECORDS MADE EASY

• Keep tax returns (not records, but actual returns) forever. Label a box "My Tax Returns" and put them in there.

• Keep every year-end summary of your pension forever. Label a box "Pensions" and make a folder for each year you have. Put that plan's year-end statement in the folder and close the box.

• Keep everything else for seven years from the last time it had any impact on your financial life. Label a box "2016 Tax Records: OK to throw out 12/31/2023."

Year-End Tax Preparation

In the middle of December, right when you are running around trying to finish your holiday shopping and get all of your holiday cards written to your clients, you need to make time to do one more thing.

Take a look at your income and expenses for the year. Why look at your income and expenses in December? Because if you wait until January or February, and then discover you owe a lot of taxes for this year, it will be too late to do anything about it.

Here's how to do it right:

1. **Tabulate your income for the year** by looking through your pay stubs, bank statements, or whatever records you use for your business. Be sure you don't count loans to your company as income.

2. **Tally up your expenses** by looking at your receipts, credit card bills, and checkbook. Don't forget cash expenses.
Throughout the year, you should have been writing expense checks to yourself every week or month from your business account to keep track of your cash expenses. If you didn't, try to remember what you've spent cash on (and have receipts for,) and resolve to reimburse yourself by check next year. Throughout the year, staple these checks to the receipts they cover to keep your records straight. The software programs already mentioned are designed for personal income tracking and will help keep your business organized.

INCOME TAX & BUSINESS TAX DEDUCTION

For most people this will amount to about 35% of your income. So for every $100 you earn, $35 goes to pay taxes. The more you earn the more you pay. For example:

Since you pay about 35% of your income in taxes, when you take a business tax deduction, you're essentially saving 35% of the cost of the expenses you incurred.

So if I buy a desk, chair, filing cabinet, computer, printer and software for $3000 to set up my office, how much will it ultimately cost me?

$3000 x .35 = 1050. (3000 - 1050 = 1950)

The $1050 comes right off your taxable income, reducing the amount that can be taxed.

But ONLY if you save EVERY receipt and keep good records (write down what the exact item is on every receipt)

3. **Send all of this information to your accountant**. You could get a tax book and figure out what percentage of your expenses are deductible, but I don't recommend it. First of all, all tax laws are complex and are constantly changing. Second, even if you could calculate everything properly, you should be using your time for your business and delegating your tax responsibilities to someone who does taxes for a living.

By examining the financial condition of your business now, instead of next year, you can take action that may save you on taxes. If you haven't paid all the taxes you owe from this year, you may avoid some penalties by paying them before the year is out.

4. **If you find yourself with a large tax liability**, you can do the following before the end of the year to help defray what you owe:

- ❒ If applicable, open a *Keough account*, a retirement plan for the self-employed that must be funded before the end of the year (see page 297 for more on Keoughs).
- ❒ *Take advantage of the equipment-expense deduction*. If you face a large tax liability you can purchase equipment this year that you were planning to buy next year, thereby generating another deduction.
- ❒ *Pay business expenses for next year early*. Bills for electricity, legal fees, or business expense can be paid ahead of time to reduce your income. Ask suppliers if you can prepay their invoices.

- ❒ *Take advantage of tax deductions* available to businesses that employ family members. If your kids legitimately work for your home business, this is a way of moving money to someone who is taxed at a lower level. But don't try to fool the IRS by saying you employ your child if you don't. The IRS requires a lot of verification when you claim to employ a child, and it doesn't look too kindly on things like three-month-old employees!

- ❒ *Hire your spouse while you're at it.* If your husband or wife does the books or maintains your online connections and computer maintenance, call it a job and pay out a regular salary – *and* provide health benefits!

With a proper employee benefit plan, you can deduct all of your family's health insurance and health costs by providing them as a business perk. Check out AgriPlan/Biz Plan (800-298-2923, http://www.tasconline.com) for details about making this legal and expect to save about 50% on a $6,000 annual medical budget.

INCOME TAX + SELF EMPLOYMENT TAX = A LOT OF TAXES!

Here's an eye-opener about a solo entrepreneur's self-employment (SE) tax liabilities:

A $10,000 net profit for a self-employed at a 15% tax bracket means that $1,500 must go for federal income tax and another approximately $1,500 for SE tax. Add them up: 15% plus 15% equals 30%. Depending upon state and city, the indie owner may owe another 5% to 10%, or $500 to $1,000, for state and city income taxes. That could bring the figure up to 40% of net profit going toward taxes, or approximately $4,000 of every $10,000 net income. And remember, 15% is one of the lower tax brackets. For some, the government takes an even bigger bite - how about at a 35% federal rate! That would change the above total income going for taxes to 60% (35% plus 15% plus 10%).

5. **Use some Creative Tax Strategies**. No one is required to pay more tax than the law demands. Some of the more common tax-cutting strategies are:

- *Splitting income among several family members* (age 14 and older) or between legal entities in order to get more of the income taxed at lower brackets.
- *Shifting income from one year to another* in order to have it fall where it will be taxed at lower rates.
- *Shifting deductions from one year to another* in order to place them where the tax benefit will be greater.
- *Deferring tax liability* through certain investments and pension plan contributions.
- *Structuring your business* to obtain a tax deduction for some expenses paid for things that you enjoy (e.g., travel).
- *Investing your money* to produce income that is exempt from either (or both) federal and state income tax.

Options for Retirement Planning

Retirement at age sixty-five was always an arbitrary concept, based on an artificial concept of a "finishing line" to one's life's work. But there is no finishing line – life's activities do not come in neat, finite bundles of work followed by play. The future will see a much less sharply defined transition, one that better reflects people's interests and needs.

Moreover, the financial reasons for continuing to work may be compelling. Indeed, many Americans believe that they are more likely to see a UFO than to collect social security. Too, government pension plans in both the United States and Canada are undergoing radical restructuring to avoid massive deficits. That makes it all the more important that individuals save for their retirement. Financial planners recommend people save 10 percent of their gross income for every year that they work in order to enjoy a secure retirement. Here are several savings options to consider in your own retirement planning. All percentages and amounts are current as of early 2016:

❑ ***Annuities***

If you're working as an employee in addition to being self-employed, you may have a 401(k) or 403(b) tax-sheltered annuity (TSA) or tax-deferred annuity (TDA) retirement plan available to you at your job. These plans allow you to put a portion of your paycheck away for retirement while deferring tax on that income. These plans can also be set up for you as the employee of your own corporation.

❑ ***IRAs***

Individual Retirement Arrangements (IRAs) are available to anyone with earned income (i.e., wages or self-employment income). The maximum allowable contribution to an IRA account is the lesser of your compensation or $6,000 per year (If you are over 50, you may contribute a total of $7,000). If you have a loss from your business and no other earned income for the year, your compensation amount is less than zero so you're not eligible for an IRA. The ability to put money into an IRA doesn't necessarily mean that you'll be able to deduct the contribution. Deductibility depends on your total income and whether you have a retirement plan at work.

The Roth IRA is a newer plan that allows you to put money away for retirement. There is no tax owed on the money when it's distributed to you (a great deal). However, your IRA contribution is not deductible.

❑ ***SEP-IRA Accounts***

Similar rules for covering employees apply to the other type of retirement plan available to self-employed people: the Simplified Employee Pension, or SEP-IRA. All employees over age 20 must be covered as long as they worked for you three of the last five years and make at least $400 a year.

The contribution to your SEP-IRA is limited to the same 20 percent contribution as the money purchase Keogh (up to $53,000 or 25 percent of your profit, whichever is less.).

❑ ***SIMPLE Accounts***

The SIMPLE (Savings Incentive Match Plan for Employees) is designed for small businesses with employees that want to set up a retirement plan for their employees that is easier and less expensive to administer than a 401(k). Under SIMPLE rules, employers can choose from two different contribution methods: a Matching Option where the employer is required to match employee contributions or contribute 3 percent a year to the account of any employee who earns $5,000 or more during the year; or a Non-Elective Contribution Option where the employer contributes 2% of each eligible employee's compensation each year regardless of whether the participant contributes or not.

Since these programs change year to year, it is smart to speak to a fee-based retirement planning advisor to get the latest information for your own retirement plan. Tap into The National Association of Personal Financial Advisors to find one (napfa.org).

Maintaining Business in a Soft Economy

Many in the music industry are experiencing the same things right now as we all seek to grapple with the new world *dis*order. The economic downturn has pounded already weak sales in a music industry grappling with rampant piracy and slowing CD replacements. Gigs are drying up, distributors are 120 days out, customers are staying home, and your bills are piling up. Music groups are under pressure to make deep-seated changes to survive the times ahead and the "ripple effects" will be profound.

Despite a gloomy money picture for the recording industry, it is crucial to keep your head out of the sand. "Adjust accordingly and look for trends within your own company," recommends Amalgam Entertainment's Jay Andreozzi. "The statements will help you to better understand the cash flow of your company and allocate cash in an efficient way."

Times like these force us to reevaluate out deepest values and desires. We have before us a golden opportunity to take a fresh look at our businesses, streamline and strengthen our operations, and put ourselves on steadier economic ground.

Here are several management tips to help guide you and your company through economically turbulent times:

1. Play Doctor. An accurate diagnosis of the cause of your business problems is essential to resolving and preventing their recurrence. Though external factors play a big role in business dynamics, in most cases, the real cause of business troubles is often internal. So the first thing you should do is take your internal pulse.

Although every small business is unique, here are the most common causes of financial difficulty:

- Expenses that exceed revenues.
- Improper or inadequate financing.
- Overly rapid growth funded by debt rather than by business profit (watch those "free" credit card offers!).
- Poor management skills and business know-how among business owners (the #1 cause of business failures in the U.S.!).
- Ineffective mechanisms for decision-making and problem-solving.
- Inadequate attention to marketing or an ineffective marketing program.
- Key customer groups experiencing a financial downturn.
- A poor or faulty product or service.
- Lack of an adequate market for a product or service.
- An unwillingness to look objectively at business difficulties.

2. Choose Your Medicine. The specific actions you take to stabilize your business and resolve its problems will depend on your diagnosis. Following are some possible actions to consider:

- Evaluate all expenses including business-related travel or entertainment, subscriptions, the purchase of supplies, raw materials or equipment, insurance, the use of outside professionals, postage, phone services, etc. to determine which can be reduced, delayed or eliminated.
- Eliminate or shelve products or services that are not making money.
- Evaluate the effectiveness of your marketing activities and modify as needed.

- ❒ Assess current staffing levels to determine if there are positions that could be eliminated or consolidated without damage to your company's effectiveness and efficiency.
- ❒ Reduce staff salaries and/or benefits.
- ❒ Reduce your own salary.
- ❒ Cut prices. This action alone can sometimes provide the cash a business needs to turn itself around.
- ❒ Defer maintenance activities as long as possible.
- ❒ Increase efforts to collect your accounts receivables. Call those who owe you money, and press them for it. When necessary, use the services of a collection agency.
- ❒ Delay paying your accounts payable as long as possible but without incurring additional charges or jeopardizing your standing with suppliers, creditors, your bank, etc.
- ❒ Increase the productivity of your sales staff through special incentives, bonuses, training, etc.
- ❒ Sell assets that are not needed, including equipment, gear and office furniture.
- ❒ Consider moving to less expensive space or reducing the amount of space you are renting.
- ❒ Identify new sources of cash.
- ❒ Meet with your creditors, bankers and suppliers about lowering your monthly payments, restructuring or consolidating debt, obtaining additional credit, etc.
- ❒ Talk to the IRS about working out a payment plan for any back taxes.
- ❒ Improve your managerial skills and business know-how by taking classes or attending seminars (lots of great stuff online!).

3. Take Your Medicine. When a business is in crisis it is not a time to be secretive and protective, but a time to actually open up your situation to the people who are in effect your financial partners, and to ask them for their help. When necessary, provide your creditors with cash flow and sales projections, fact sheets and documentation that will help support your case.

If you are funded by angel investors or family, be ruthlessly honest about your situation and what you're planning to do about it.

Here are some additional cash-generating possibilities to consider:

- ❒ Cut expenses to the bone.
- ❒ Rent out office, studio, or plant space that you do not need.
- ❒ When not using it, offer others the use of your equipment or gear on a contract basis -evenings, weekends, slow times, etc.
- ❒ Keep less inventory on hand.
- ❒ Identify other ways to use your assets when they are not being used by your primary business.
- ❒ Barter for services (see next section for bartering ideas).
- ❒ Make greater use of freelancers, independent contractors, and interns.
- ❒ Take advantage of your recognized expertise or skill in a certain area, and develop a new product or service based on it that requires little or no additional expenditure of money, additional marketing, etc.
- ❒ Explore the possibility of a joint venture with a company in a similar or complimentary business to yours. For example, combine your products or services together with another business into one big package. You could split the profits. For example, a general business band can team up with a catering company to offer a package of services for corporate party and event planners. The possibilities here are endless.

- ❒ If you have not already done so, consult with outside professionals, such as representatives of SCORE or your local SCDC (Small Business Development Center as well as with your accountant, attorney or another reputable professional who may be able to provide you with ideas and advice.

Some of these guidelines may seem excessive or harsh; some are simply common sense reminders. But a key ingredient to successful business management is the ability to be ruthlessly objective: to clearly see what needs to be done and to respond intelligently and creatively to the challenge.

The Art of Bartering

Have you ever had trouble scraping together enough cash for a marketing campaign you really wanted to execute? How about the holiday party you wanted to throw for your staff?

Bartering may be the answer for you. In earlier times, barter was used more often than money, but the practice fell into obscurity over the years. Then, as now, businesses tended to have more services and products than cash on hand. Few companies have a budget that can accommodate all the unexpected expenses, sudden opportunities, or dreams of expansion that are part of a successful business. One cost effective way to obtain the services or products that accommodate those needs is to barter. Bartering involves trading one commodity or service for another of comparable value.

Opportunities to barter are limited only by the imagination and creativity of the business owner who wants to try a new way of financing business projects. For example, a club owner might offer to cater a holiday party for a local cleaning company in exchange for laundry services. Sara Wheeler's company, Little Groove, uses several spaces in Boston where it donates lessons in exchange for rent. The possible applications for barter are as varied as the products and services that make up the business community.

When cash is short, bartering may be your ticket. I've seen people trade music lessons for the use of a touring van, performances for a computer, and a commercial jingle for CD duplication. There are some rules that govern how successful a bartering venture will be. Here are some of the basics to keep in mind:

❑ ***Use a marketing approach to initiate barter agreements***. Show the potential partner how the arrangement is a boost for the company's market presence. Treat a barter agreement the way you would treat a valued customer. "You treat it just like an agreement where money changes hands," suggests Panos Panay, formerly of Sonicbids. "Time and services are sometimes even more precious than money. You spell it out, outline the expectations, and ensure that both parties are committed to a successful relationship."

❑ ***Barter with an intent to obtain equal value***, not an advantage. Voice training expert Jeannie Deva learned some bartering lessons the hard way. "Barters only work when the exchange being offered is *of value to both* parties. If not, the one who considers he's not getting something of value will tend to sidestep his end of the bargain. And if you're in the short-changed receiving side, you could find yourself in the distressing situation of not having received in kind what you have already given."

Typical Barter Offerings Barter arrangements can include a wide spectrum of services and products. These are some common offerings:	
Accountants Acupuncturists Advertising Alarm systems Alterations Answering services Appliance repair Architects Artists, artwork and supplies Athletic trainers Attorneys Automotive: dealers, repair and services Beauty salons Bed & breakfast Brokers Bulk mailing Business equipment: sales, services Carpet sales and cleaning Caterers Child care Chiropractors Cleaning service and products Clothing Computer: classes, consulting, sales service	Construction Dentists Education Electricians Entertainment Estheticians Furniture Gifts Graphic artists Health clubs Hotels Massage therapists Office supplies Painters Pets: boarding, care, grooming, supplies Photographers Physicians Plumbers Printers Psychotherapists Real estate Restaurants Salons Spas Travel Typesetting

❑ ***Finalize your agreement in writing***. Always a good idea. Deva continues: "It keeps things straight and avoids confusions on what has been agreed to – memories are not always accurate recorders."

❑ ***Set a timeline*** for completion of services or delivery of products.

❑ ***Consider using bartering collectives***. It is common practice to barter individually, but a cooperative barter venture offers more flexibility and opportunity. Members of these networks or clubs typically agree to a fixed value for their service or product at the time they join. Records of credits are recorded centrally, and can be earned by providing a service or product to any member. Members may then use their credits at any participating member's business. Careful records are important and staff to keep those records can be voluntary, or paid through a membership fee – or with barter credits! The number of online barter networks continues to grow. Some of the most well known include: Biz Exchange (bizx.com) and Joe Barter (joebarter.com).

Whether an individual or a group arrangement is used to set up a barter, the end result is a cash-free benefit for your business.

Bankruptcy & Other Issues Surrounding Financial Failure

Setbacks are often red flags, flashing signals that you're traveling in the wrong direction. It's tempting to ignore the signs if you have a predetermined picture of what your business should look like. Rather than considering a directional change, you will probably want to clamp down and persist in handling the setbacks the way you always have.

But a business that never seems to sustain its momentum is a candidate for directional scrutiny. The problem may be that you're trying to gain entry into the wrong market, courting the wrong customer, or marketing the wrong message. Perhaps you've become entrenched in a cash crunch and credit obligations are overwhelming your ability to manage your business.

At one time, individuals who could not pay their debt were jailed. Today, however, both organizations and individuals can seek relief by filing for *bankruptcy* – the court-granted permission not to pay some or all the debts. In recent years, large enterprises such as Continental Airlines, Muzak and R.H. Macy have sought the protection of bankruptcy laws as part of strategies to streamline operations, cut costs, and regain profitability.

In some cases, creditors force an individual or company into *involuntary bankruptcy* and press the courts to award them payment or at least part of what they are owed. Far more often, however, a person or business chooses to file for court protection against creditors.

A business bankruptcy may be resolved by one of three plans:

- Under a ***liquidation plan***, the business ceases to exist. Its assets are sold and the proceeds used to pay creditors.

- Under a ***repayment plan***, the bankrupt company simply works out a new payment schedule to meet its obligations. The time frame is usually decided by a court-appointed trustee.

- ***Reorganization*** is the most complex from of business bankruptcy. The company must explain the sources of it financial difficulties and propose a new plan for remaining in business. Reorganization may include a new slate of managers and a new financial strategy. A judge may also reduce the firm's debts to ensure its survival. Although creditors naturally dislike debt reduction, they may agree to the proposal, since 50 percent of one's due is better than nothing at all.

You should be aware that new bankruptcy laws are making it harder for individuals and businesses to declare bankruptcy. One of the changes is that a person must first acquire the services of debt counseling. Furthermore, a bankruptcy filing will stay on your credit report for up to ten years. You will also pay much higher interest rates when you try to rebuild your credit in the future. The best thing to do if you are considering this option is to call the Bar Association in your state to find an attorney who specializes in bankruptcy. In some cases you may find an attorney who offers a free consultation.

Much more can be written about small biz financial management, but hopefully you have the essentials needed to carry on this part of your business successfully. Again, use the free help available (like SCORE and SBDCs) to shore up those areas that are still shaky. Only by giving these matters your thoughtful attention *now* will you avoid bigger financial headaches down the road.

Now let's turn to the art and science of conducting your marketing program – the process of successfully making yourself visible to your intended market and making it want what you have to offer.

CHAPTER SUMMARY
BUSINESS CONDUCTING: MONEY

- **Bean Counting in One Easy Lesson**
  Financial management goes a lot smoother when certain components are in place. These include:
  - Know the Lingo (*Revenue, Expenses, Net Profit, Net Income*, etc.)
  - Understand What Accounting Tells You.
  - Understand Basic Financial Statements.
  - Keep Good Budget & Accounting Record
  - Create a Basic Budget Forecast

- **Guidelines for Setting Your Price & Your Fee**
  Follow these six tips for setting your price:
  - Keep your prices realistic. Set your prices based on your own financial goals not those of your competitors' alone.
  - Cover all your costs. A successful pricing strategy is one that results in the most dollars after all your costs are met.
  - Check your price against inflation. If you maintain your prices despite inflation, you will erode your profit margin.
  - Include in your pricing the value of your time, as well as the other benefits your business brings to customers. Avoid committing the mistake of not including a salary for yourself, particularly if you are operating a service business. See chapter 16 for ideas on how you can adjust your pricing up by adding value to your products and services.
  - Price low, but smart. Pricing low is a common strategy, especially for startups. But be careful! Low price can also signal low quality, and it becomes difficult to raise prices later once customers are accustomed to your low prices.
  - Use discounts with care.

- **The Basics of Small Business Bookkeeping**
  The following criteria are essential to a good financial record-keeping system: Simplicity, Consistency, Accuracy, Understandability, Timeliness, Reliability and completeness.
  - Get the Software to help manage your books.
  - Understand the Two Methods Of Accounting (Cash Basis Method & Accrual Basis method).
  - Understand the Accounting Cycle.

  The summary and totals from all journals are entered into the general ledger. A general ledger is a summary book that records transactions and balances of individual accounts, and is organized into five classes of individual accounts, as follows: Assets, Liabilities, Capital, Sales, and Expenses.

- **Other Important Financial Records**
  In addition to basic accounting records, you will need to keep separate records for accounts receivable, payroll and taxes, petty cash, insurance, business equipment and perhaps other items.

- **Special Tax Guidelines for the Small Music Company**
  - The Anti Hobby Rule: The IRS keeps a watchful eye out for individuals who consistently run businesses at a loss just to amass valuable deductions. Their guidelines state that a business must make a profit three years out of five, or else the enterprise is considered a hobby, which lowers or eliminates possible deductions.
  - Deductions: To be deductible, a business expense must be both "ordinary" and "necessary."
  - Write-off "dead" Inventory for Tax savings: Do you have boxes of unsold merchandise lying around. No need to take a loss on it when you have the option of donating them.
  - Sales Tax Issues: If you close your business or never get it off the ground after you have already procured a tax ID number, make sure you notify the department of taxation.

- **Year End Tax Preparation**
  Take a look at your income and expenses for the year. Here's how to do it right:
  - Tabulate your income for the year by looking through your pay stubs, bank statements, or whatever records you use for your business. Be sure you don't count loans to your company as income.
  - Tally up your expenses by looking at your receipts, credit card bills, and checkbook.
  - Send all of this information to your accountant.
  - If you find yourself with a large tax liability: If applicable, open a Keough account, a retirement plan for the self-employed; Take advantage of the equipment-expense deduction; Pay business expenses for next year early; Take advantage of tax deductions available to businesses that employ family members; Hire your spouse while you're at it.
  - Use some Creative Tax Strategies.

- **Options for Retirement Planning**
  Financial planners recommend people save 10 percent of their gross income for every year that they work in order to enjoy a secure retirement. Here are several savings options to consider in your own retirement planning. All percentages and amounts are current as of early 2016:
  - Annuities: These plans allow you to put a portion of your paycheck away for retirement while deferring tax on that income.
  - IRAs: Individual Retirement Arrangements (IRAs) are available to anyone with earned income (i.e., wages or self-employment income).
  - SEP-IRA Accounts: The Simplified Employee Pension, all employees over age 20 must be covered as long as they worked for you three of the last five years and make at least $400 a year.
  - SIMPLE Accounts: (Savings Incentive Match Plan for Employees) is designed for small businesses with employees that want to set up a retirement plan for their employees that is easier and less expensive to administer than a 401(k).

- **Maintaining Business in a Soft Economy**
  Despite a gloomy money picture for the recording industry, it is crucial to keep your head out of the sand. Here are several management tips to help guide you and your company through economically turbulent times:
  - Play Doctor. An accurate diagnosis of the cause of your business problems is essential to resolving and preventing their recurrence.
  - Choose Your Medicine. The specific actions you take to stabilize your business and resolve its problems will depend on your diagnosis.
  - Take Your Medicine. When a business is in crisis it is not a time to be secretive and protective, but a time to actually open up your situation to the people who are in effect your financial partners, and to ask them for their help. If you are funded by angel investors or family members, be ruthlessly honest about your situation and what you're planning to do about it.

- **The Art of Bartering**
  When cash is short, bartering may be your ticket. There are some rules that govern how successful a bartering venture will be. Here are some of the basics to keep in mind:
  - Use a marketing approach to initiate barter agreements.
  - Barter with an intent to obtain equal value
  - Finalize your agreement in writing
  - Set a timeline for completion of services or delivery of products
  - Consider using bartering collectives

- **Bankruptcy & Other Issues Surrounding Financial Failure**
  A business bankruptcy may be resolved by one of three plans:
  - Under a liquidation plan, the business ceases to exist. Its assets are sold and the proceeds used to pay creditors.
  - Under a repayment plan, the bankrupt company simply works out a new payment schedule to meet its obligations. The time frame is usually decided by a court-appointed trustee.

- Reorganization is the most complex from of business bankruptcy. The company must explain the sources of it financial difficulties and propose a new plan for remaining in business.

FURTHER RESOURCES

ONLINE RESOURCES

• Financial Reporting Resources:

Dun & Bradstreet
provides business credit-reporting services
(866) 879-4528
http://www.dnb.com/

Equifax Credit Information Services Inc.
provides credit-reporting services
(888) 202-4025
www.equifax.com

Experian
Provides credit-reporting services
(888) 397-3742
www.experian.com

First Data
Provides check-guarantee services
+1 800 735-3362
https://www.firstdata.com

TransUnion
Provides credit-reporting services
(800) 888-4213
wwww.transunion.com

• Bartering

barternetworkinc.com

Barternews.com

Biz Exchange
Bizx.com

Joe Barter
joebarter.com

u-exchange.com

BOOKS

How to Manage Your Money When You Don't Have Any by Erik Wecks (2012, CreateSpace).

Simple Money: A No-Nonsense Guide to Personal Finance by Tim Maurer (2015, Baker Books).

Small Business Cash Flow: Strategies for Making Your Business a Financial Success by Denise O-Berry (2006, Wiley).

Small Business Financial Management by Tage C. Tracy (2007, For Dummies).

Stop the Cash Flow Roller Coaster by Caroline Grim Jordan (2007, iUniverse).

The Power of Broke: How Empty Pockets, a Tight Budget, and a Hunger for Success Can Become Your Greatest Competitive Advantage *by Daymond John (2016, Crown Business).*

Why Didn't They Teach Me This in School?: 99 Personal Money Management Principles to Live by Cary Siegel (2013, CreateSpace).

15

BUSINESS CONDUCTING: MANAGING YOUR MARKETING

To me, marketing is one of the largest riddles there is in this business of music-making-for-public-consumption! –Ember Swift, Singer-Songwriter

Marketing is an attitude, not a department.
- Phil Wexler

How many times have you thought this: "I'm just not cut out to be a salesman," "I don't like promoting myself," and, "I'm too busy to spend my time marketing?"

At one time or another we've all shared these concerns. They are real. Fortunately, to get the business you need, you don't have to have a sales personality, or try to become someone you're not, or grit your teeth to do things that you find offensive.

However, until you become known and sought after, you *will* need to find ways to "toot your own horn" that you're comfortable with, ways that will produce the results you want.

The way you *think* about the fact that you'll on1ly have as much business as you can generate will have a great deal to do with how much business you get and how easy, or difficult, it is for you to get it. If marketing feels like a burden or toil you'd rather not do, it will be difficult, if not impossible, for you to communicate the kind of enthusiasm and excitement that will draw clients and customers to you.

Or, if marketing is something you only think about when you're desperately in need of business, and you must force yourself to do it begrudgingly, you'll have a hard time developing a creative and effective plan for getting the business you want and need.

Developing a Positive Marketing Mindset

I've found that people who have plenty of business don't think about marketing as a drag. Whether they're shy and retiring or outgoing and effervescent, they're so excited about what they have to offer that they want to make sure people know about it. In fact, they feel eager, almost compelled, to reach out and make contact in whatever ways come naturally to them so people will know about their products and services.

Even if you have no marketing or business background, even if you're starting out in a brand-new community without any existing relationships, even if you're competent but not yet outstanding at your work, you can develop a positive marketing mindset that will enable you to create effective and affordable ways to attract business. By making the following three mental shifts in *how you think about getting business*, you, too, can project a positive mindset and make getting business easier and infinitely more enjoyable.

❑ ***Think opportunity, not obligation***. Instead of thinking about what a drag it is to have to get business or how difficult, unpleasant, time-consuming, and costly it is to market yourself, shift your attention instead to how eager you are to let others know about what you offer. If you've chosen the right niche for yourself, you obviously like your work and think it's important. You know it's needed and that it improves the lives or the businesses of your customers. Your work is more than a good idea or a way to make some money; it's a benefit to those you serve.

Without the funds to pay for elaborate marketing efforts and the ability to hire top-notch professionals, your own compelling sense of passion for your work will be the most essential element in attracting business to you. This kind of passion is contagious. It will come through in all your spoken and written communication whether you're introducing yourself at a conference or created a classified ad. So, start to think about marketing as a way to share your enthusiasm for what you do.

❑ ***Think contact, not activity***. Marketing is about making contact with people who need what you offer. It's not about keeping busy. If you're offering a product or service that addresses an unmet need or solves a problem, you probably have a pool of potential customers who need what you have to offer right at this very minute. But chances are they all don't know about you and you don't know about all of them. Somehow you need to find each other. And that's what marketing is about.

Often people ask, "What's the best way for me to market what I do?" They're looking for *the one* steady, reliable way they can count on for making contact with clients and customers. But there is no single business-getting route that's guaranteed to reach everyone. As you'll learn later in this chapter, there is probably a wealth of activities that will work well for you and your business. Finding the ones that work best is an experiment. In fact, *marketing is an experiment*. People who are motivated to make contact with those who need them are always experimenting with new possibilities to get their message out.

❑ ***Think communication, not manipulation***. Often people think marketing is about being cute and clever, creating a lot of hype or sizzle, especially in the entertainment business. Worse, they fear it's about being manipulative. Sizzling, cute and clever hype may attract attention, but it doesn't build trust, respect, or value.

Instead of worrying about being cute and clever or manipulative, think about getting your message across. Shift your attention to what it is about that you do that's important to your customers. Think about how you can communicate your message to them in terms they'll understand. Think about how you can help them see the benefits of what you offer.

According to Laurence Boldt, in his book *Zen and the Art of Making a Living*, 'circulation' is the name of the game in marketing. He explains: "Our word circulation comes from a Latin root meaning 'to form a circle.' View your marketing strength in terms of the circles you have formed and the circles you intend to form: circles of friends, circles of acquaintances, circles of contacts, circles of leads, circles of clients and fans, circles of investors, circles of likeminded individuals...Remember, the wealth of the universe comes to you through people. No matter what kind of work you do, you are in the people business."

Managing Your Marketing Programs

Having an organized system in place will make all your marketing and promotional efforts flow more smoothly. Information is your ally as a marketer but if it's not organized it will quickly become your enemy.

The first thing to do is to come up with a list of topical areas or categories of marketing activity you will be engaged in. This may seem like more detail than you need, but information has a way of getting out of control very quickly and the key in business is to keep yourself in the driver's seat, not under the wheels, with all your information at your fingertips. Here's a list of business marketing categories to get you started. Use only those with most relevance to your particular business:

1. General Business Info - Under this broad area you create subdirectories for: Planning, Correspondence, Contracts & Agreements, Mail & Postage, Budgets & Financial records, Recording records, Royalty records, Copyright forms, Bar codes, ISRCs (see chapter 9), Licenses, Trademark info, Web site info, Manufacturers & packagers, Letterhead, Business support resources, Tax info, Insurance info, Inventory records, Organization memberships, Subscriptions and Idea file.

2. General Marketing Info - Subdirectories: Marketing plans, Marketing trends, Market research, Marketing resources, Logos & graphics, Media kit, Mailing lists (fans, media, industry - *see p. 101 on building your databases*), and Idea file.

3. Specific Market Info - Subdirectories: Direct to consumer, Film/TV, Terrestrial Radio, Satellite Radio, Online Radio, Distributors, Retail, Record Pools, Catalogs, Print media, Online media, Online retailers, Commercial music users, Touring & venues, Publishers & Licensors, Premiums & incentives, Foreign markets, Video outlets, and Idea file.

4. Graphics & Design - Design ideas, Graphic designers, Photos, Bios, Web site design, CD art, Packaging ideas, Display ideas, Advertising design, Printing vendors.

5. Publishing - Songs & compositions (lyrics, versions, in process), Copyright administration forms, Performing rights, Mechanical licenses, Sampling licenses, Promo & placement strategies, Infringements, Sub-publishers (foreign markets), and Idea file.

6. Sales - Formats & pricing, Distribution accounts, Retailer accounts, Consignments, POP (point of purchase strategies & materials), Listening stations, Co-op deals, Direct sales, International sales, Mail order & catalog sales, Idea file.

7. Promotion - Release campaigns, Release parties, Street teams, Giveaways, Co-promotion ventures, Sponsorship ventures, Promo novelties, Idea file, etc.

You will most likely have some additional topics that are specifically relevant to your project that aren't included here. Also, some topics can easily be telescoped out further. For example, under "Web site" you can have subdirectories for Domain names, Artist web sites, Label web sites, Design ideas, etc. Likewise, under "Print media" you'll probably want to include General newspapers, College newspapers, Weekly newspapers, General entertainment magazines, Music magazines, Specific writers & editors, Electronic newswires, Music publicists, etc.

Once you have your list of topical areas, create *both* a digital folder on your computer *and* a physical folder in your file cabinet for each one. One will complement the other and provide you with a way to save important documents to help all your marketing efforts have the best information backing them up and keep you from going crazy trying to find that design idea you cut out of a magazine two months ago.

Launching Your "Brand"

The first thing you hope will come to someone's mind when they need what you offer is *your* name or the name of *your* service, product or company. Major mass-market manufacturers spend millions of dollars on developing what is called "brand identity" for their products. As a small or home business, your business name is your brand identity, but of course you probably can't spend millions to make sure it comes to mind. So choose your brand name wisely (review chapter 6 for guidelines on this topic).

The word "brand", when used as a noun, can refer to a company name, a product name, or a unique identifier such as a logo or trademark. But branding today is much more than just a company name. In a time before fences were used in ranching to keep one's cattle separate from other people's cattle, ranch owners branded, or marked, their cattle so they could later identify their herd as their own.

The concept of branding also developed through the practices of craftsmen who wanted to place a mark or identifier on their work without detracting from the beauty of the piece. These craftsmen used their initials, a symbol, or another unique mark to identify their work and they usually put these marks in a low visibility place on the product.

Not too long afterwards, high quality cattle and art became identifiable in consumers' minds by particular symbols and marks. Consumers would actually seek out certain marks because they had associated those marks in their minds with tastier beef, higher quality pottery or furniture, sophisticated artwork, and overall better products. *If the producer differentiated their product as superior in the mind of the consumer, then that producer's mark or brand came to represent superiority.*

Today's modern concept of branding grew out of the consumer packaged goods industry and the process of branding has come to include much, much more than just creating a way to identify a product or company. Branding today is used to create emotional attachment to products and companies. Branding efforts create a feeling of involvement, a sense of higher quality, and an aura of intangible qualities that surround the brand name, mark, or symbol.

So what exactly is the definition of "brand"? If you ask ten marketing professionals or brand managers to define the word "brand", you'll probably get ten different answers. Most of the answers you receive, hopefully, will at least have some commonalities.

What is a Brand? In my own experience and in my study of brands and branding, there is one definition of "brand" that seems to most succinctly define exactly what a brand is:

A brand is an identifiable entity that makes specific promises of value.

In its simplest form, a brand is nothing more and nothing less than the promise of value you or your product make. This promise can be implied or explicitly stated, but nonetheless, value of some type is promised.

Perception is (almost) everything. Many people think that the logo is the brand, but, in fact, the logo is just one representation of the brand. Your brand isn't how you look or what you say or even what you sell. Your brand is what people believe you stand for. For example:

- ❑ Starbucks sells coffee, but *it stands for daily inspiration*.
- ❑ Apple sells computers, but *it stands for thinking differently*.
- ❑ Disney sells animated films and amusement park family entertainment, but *it stands for making dreams come true.*

What do you want your brand to stand for? Remember, your brand lives in consumer minds, so branding is the process of developing consumer beliefs and perceptions that are accurate and in alignment with what you want your brand to represent.

There are some additional elements that go along with branding:

❑ ***Brand image*** is defined as consumers' perceptions *as reflected by the associations they hold in their minds* when they think of your brand.

❑ ***Brand awareness*** is when people recognize your brand as yours.

❑ Brand awareness consists of both ***brand recognition***, which is the ability of consumers to confirm that they have previously been exposed to your brand, and ***brand recall***, which reflects the ability of consumers to name your brand when given the product category, category need, or some other similar cue.

❑ ***Top-of-mind awareness*** occurs when you ask a person to name brands within a product category and your brand pops up first on the list.

Today (mainly because of the Web), branding is *everything*—and I mean everything. Brands are not simply products or services. *Brands are the sum total of all the images that people have in their heads about a particular company and a particular mark.*

Your goal as a company should be "top of the mind" awareness based on the delivery of superior and unique service or products. When you hear the marketing term "positioning" think in terms of positioning your business in *peoples' minds*, not in some external marketplace.

Setting Your Marketing Goals and Objectives

Your goal is what you want your marketing to achieve; your objectives define how you'll achieve your goal. For example:

❑ ***If your goal is to win awareness for your company and its distinctions,*** your objectives may include gaining name recognition and knowledge of your unique point of difference among a defined segment of consumers in your target market within a certain length of time.

❑ ***If your goal is to enhance credibility and trust,*** your objectives may be to achieve awareness of and belief in your point of difference and your company promise

among a defined segment of consumers in your target market within a certain length of time. This becomes a similar though slightly different goal.

❑ ***If your goal is to motivate sales,*** your objective may be to add at least one new distribution channel and to realize a specified sales increase without sacrificing unit sale price within a certain length of time from the start of your brand launch.

Other marketing goals can include acquiring new customers, retaining current customers, driving more web site traffic, improving search engine rankings, or increasing the "stickiness" of your web site.

Commit your goals and objectives to writing in order to keep your efforts focused only on the marketing strategies and tactics that contribute to your success. Then each time a new marketing opportunity arises, you can put it to this easy litmus test: *Will this opportunity help me meet my goal? Does it support one or more of my objectives?* If the answer is "no", you can quickly decline the offer and turn your attention back to your plan.

❑ ***Creating your marketing budget.*** Most small businesses estimate their sales revenue, cost-of-goods, overhead and salaries, and then gross profit. Anything left is considered available funds for marketing. That may not be the best way. A more rational approach for setting your marketing budget is to estimate what your direct competitors spend in marketing support and then try to at least match that amount.

The secret to creating a high-impact marketing plan is to optimize your limited budget. A one-time radio ad blitz, glossy brochure, or flash-enabled website will quickly erode your budget and derail your marketing plans. Use low-budget marketing to get your message out to your customers on a regular basis, and watch sales revenue grow.

What follows is a sample 4-month marketing budget for an urban music production house. 5% of sales is allocated for marketing costs. Use it as a guide for creating your own:

SAMPLE MARKETING BUDGET

Four-Month Marketing Plan
Big Tone Music Services
January 2017 to April 2017

	Jan.	**Feb.**	**March**	**April**
Projected sales	$10,000	$12,500	$15,000	$16,000
5% marketing budget	**500**	**625**	**750**	**800**
Marketing methods:				
Spring music trade show	__	385	__	__
Chamber networking events	__	__	70	__
Conferences	80	__	__	130
Community newspaper, weekly small display ad	120	120	120	120
New Media Conference	__	__	__	200
Networking luncheon	15	15	15	15
Chamber monthly dinner	25	25	25	25
Press releases on new product	0	0	0	0
Publicity consult	180	__	180	__
Web site hosting	30	30	30	30
Newsletter to customers and prospects	__	__	250	__
Coupons, cards, gifts, promotional aids	50	50	50	50
Google AdWords	__	__	__	230
Total cost:	**$500**	**$625**	**$740**	**$800**

A five percent marketing allocation is on the low side, but it's a frugal approach. The key is spending your money on tactics that will deliver the best results. A good marketing plan interconnects advertising, promotions, and public relations as the means of getting the message out to your target market (identified way back in chapter 3). Marketing is something that you will consistently be doing throughout the life of your business.

From Push to Pull: Building Permission Marketing Networks

One of the biggest shifts in the advertising world over the past twenty years has been the one from a "push" strategy (cramming messages down our throats whether we like it or not) to a "pull" strategy (drawing us in with valuable information). Under the TV-industrial complex, ad agencies practiced the push approach (also called, "interruption marketing"), intruding their messages into whatever we were enjoying at the moment (music on the radio, a movie on TV, or a story in a magazine). Amazingly, it's estimated that the today's average consumer sees about one million marketing messages a year – that's about 3,000 a day.

But now, instead of causing a one-way interruption, marketing strategies are shifting to delivering content at just the precise moment your audience needs it. People prefer participation, not propaganda. They prefer to be pulled in, not pushed to.

Related to this shift is a phrase coined by best-selling author Seth Godin – ***permission marketing***. He clarifies the difference between these two approaches with the following illustration: "A book publisher who uses interruption marketing sells children's books by shipping them to bookstores, hoping that the right audience will stumble across them. A Permission Marketer builds book clubs at every school in the country."

The internet, of course, has accelerated this trend by providing a "bi-directional" channel as opposed to TV's and radio's "uni-directional" channels. Networked markets are not passive spectators waiting to receive the next marketing message. Networked markets are conversations. Godin goes on: "Permission Marketing is the tool that unlocks the power of the internet. The leverage it brings to this new medium, combined with the pervasive clutter that infects the internet and virtually every other medium, makes Permission Marketing the most powerful trend in marketing for the next decade."

So how might you apply permission marketing to your business? Here are some guidelines as applied to your email communication with clients and customers. Before sending email messages, be double sure that the people on your email list will welcome your message by seeing that they match at least one of the following descriptions (in other words, that you have their permission):

- They've opted into your email list by providing your organization with their email addresses. Most well managed email programs include a double opt-in system that accompanies a first emailing with a response request so that the recipient either reconfirms interest or opts out of future mailings.

- They're friends, colleagues, suppliers, customers, or prospects who have requested similar information in the recent past.

- They were referred to you by a trusted resource.

After you create an opt-in mailing list, manage it well by taking these precautions:

- Never publish your email list on your website, even in a well-meaning way that provides contact information for organization members or clients.

• Never enter recipient addresses in the "To" section of your blast email. Protect addresses by entering your own address in the "To" area and then entering all recipient addresses as blind carbon copies, using the "BCC" address option in your email program.

• Include an 'Unsubscribe' link in all emails so that people can opt out of your mailings.

• If you haven't used your opt-in email list for three or more months, send a pre-mailing before sending your blast email. In the pre-mailing, briefly announce that you've got a new e-newsletter or brand mailing, and ask recipients to "Click here" to receive your mailing. The pre-mailing helps you determine which email addresses are no longer valid and also helps you steer clear of the spam complaints you're bound to get by sending emails to people with whom you haven't been in touch for months on end.

Organizing Your Brand Introduction Tactics

Review the marketing tactics you came up with in chapter 5 as well as the "Time/Money Marketing Continuum" (page 129). In marketing jargon, this is called deciding on your "marketing mix" – that combination of tools and tactics designed to get your message across to your target market. As you plan the tactics you'll use to deliver your marketing message, keep the following options in mind:

❑ ***Public relations* activities are the backbone of most business introductions.** The field of public relations includes employee or member relations, community relations, industry relations, government relations, and media relations that result in news coverage of your brand introduction message. Events, meetings, newsletters, exhibitions, and publicity all fall under the category of public relations. All spread your news and generate understanding without involving paid advertising.

❑ ***Promotions* are marketing activities that aim to trigger a desired consumer action over a short period of time.** Marketers launching consumer brands use promotions to win support from distributors and retailers and to prompt customers to a first-time trial of the new product. Providing *samples* of your product or service is a promotional tactic.

❑ ***Advertising* creates awareness in audiences reached by newspapers, magazines, radio, and television.** Most consumer brands, as well as most brands being introduced over large market areas, use advertising to convey their brand messages to broadly dispersed markets.

When using advertising as a brand launch tactic, time your ad schedules so that ads break after your brand is released via news stories. After your message runs in ad form, editorial contacts may not view it as news, and you forego the chance to gain the credible third-party voice of a reporter or newscaster.

❑ ***Advertising Specialties* help brand your name and give it some mobility as well.** These include items imprinted with the company name given to customers, e.g., calendars, caps, desk sets, and gifts (premiums).

❑ ***Direct mail*** is advertising that's delivered on a one-to-one basis to mailboxes or email inboxes rather than through mass media. It's a great way to provide invitations, detailed information, or publicity reinforcement to individuals who are targeted because they precisely match your customer profile.

❑ ***Personal presentations and sales efforts*** are especially important to brand launches that depend on personal relationships, referrals, or support from established contacts and customers. Most business and service brands include launch events and personal presentations as essential introduction tactics.

❑ ***Sales materials,*** packaging, and point-of-sale displays are essential for consumer brands and for brands that involve complex features, high prices, or considerable deliberation prior to the purchase decision. For all but the smallest local market brands, sales and packaging materials require the design talents of established professionals. Never skimp on company aesthetics. Hire a designer, branding, or packaging specialist to create your materials. Chapter 11 can help you through the selection and hiring process.

❑ ***Online communications* play an increasingly important role in brand introduction tactical plans, as described in Chapter 7.** Banner ads, blogging, email marketing, link strategies, affiliate marketing and search engine optimization can all be used to effectively get your message out to your target market.

As we will see, dollar for dollar and hour for hour, publicity and public relations are the most cost effective marketing strategies you can employ in building your brand. In order to get your marketing juices flowing, here is a bunch of marketing ideas you can consider for your own business. Check off those you think might work for you:

100 Marketing Ideas

Graphical Marketing Tools

❑ Create a Logo that graphically represents your company
❑ Design Stationary including letterhead, envelops, etc.
❑ Design Business cards that communicate your niche
❑ Use Inside signs if your business has a physical location
❑ Use Outside signs if your business has a physical location
❑ Come up with creative Packaging and labels for mailings
❑ Design and display Electronic Press Kits (EPKs) for digital environments
❑ Develop a general Advertising approach
❑ Use Reprints of favorable media mentions for further promotion
❑ Design Flip charts for instructing clients about your products and services
❑ Take out a Yellow pages ad if appropriate for your company
❑ Conceive a Newsletter that provides useful information while selling your products and services
❑ Design Printed brochures as takeaways or mailings
❑ Write Classified ads for appropriate print or digital media outlets
❑ Design Newspaper display ads for targeted media outlets
❑ Design Magazine display ads for targeted media outlets
❑ Write and send Direct mail letters to your targeted market
❑ Write and send Direct mail postcards to your targeted market
❑ Design a Postcard for postcard deck
❑ Use Outdoor billboards when appropriate
❑ Develop a Fax-on-demand service for inquiries
❑ Show off displays that sell your products and services
❑ Create Audio-visual aids for special presentations
❑ Design Posters

Internal
Marketing Tools

- ❑ Write a Marketing plan to act as a map that will help you arrive at your business goals
- ❑ Schedule your goals on a Marketing calendar
- ❑ Own a Niche and Position your niche in the marketplace
- ❑ Come up with a catchy, memorable Name for your company
- ❑ Articulate a unique Identity for your company
- ❑ Think of a Theme for particular promotions
- ❑ Provide Hours of operation that meet your customers' needs
- ❑ Plan Days of operation most serviceable to your clients and customers
- ❑ Provide Flexibility (e.g. 24 hour service) for maximum customer satisfaction
- ❑ Develop a Referral program for cross-business promotion
- ❑ Write Telemarketing scripts for more effective cold calling
- ❑ Provide Gift certificates
- ❑ Encourage Word-of-mouth marketing
- ❑ Develop Community involvement activities to enhance public relations
- ❑ Show Neatness in both yours and your company's appearance
- ❑ Provide Guarantees or warranties to alleviate customer reluctance to purchase
- ❑ Pick a Location that provides easy access to all your customers
- ❑ Offer Sales training to all staff that need it
- ❑ Dress in appropriate Attire
- ❑ Encourage exemplary Service ("going the extra mile")
- ❑ Follow-up religiously with all initial marketing communications
- ❑ Empower all staff to be marketers
- ❑ Provide a Toll-free phone number
- ❑ Give free gifts that also promote your company (e.g., calendars, pens, etc.)
- ❑ Provide the option of Catalog ordering for your customers
- ❑ Let Speed of delivery, returned phone calls, etc. characterize your company

External
Marketing Tools

- ❑ Become involved with a Cause you believe in (e.g. environment, women's issues)
- ❑ Offer free seminars
- ❑ Cross-promote with other businesses (fusion marketing)
- ❑ Write a Column in a publication to position yourself as an expert in your field
- ❑ Write an Article in a publication to further your expert reputation
- ❑ Be a Speaker at a club or organization
- ❑ Mobilize your customers to become a sales force for you
- ❑ Practice good Public relations
- ❑ Develop your Publicity contacts
- ❑ Develop online marketing strategies
- ❑ Conceive and produce a Radio commercial
- ❑ Conceive and produce a TV spot (don't forget inexpensive cable TV)
- ❑ Produce an Infomercial
- ❑ Develop a film commercial
- ❑ Produce a Special event
- ❑ Rent or buy targeted mailing lists
- ❑ Develop and nurture your Customer mailing list
- ❑ Put together a Designated street team

Subtle
Marketing Tools

- ❑ Practice Sharing with others
- ❑ Make ongoing networking a priority
- ❑ Bring Quality to all you do and offer
- ❑ Provide Opportunities to upgrade your product or service
- ❑ Institute Contests and sweepstakes
- ❑ Conceive and provide Barter options
- ❑ Start a Club with memberships
- ❑ Provide Partial payment plans
- ❑ Practice and maintain a professional Phone demeanor
- ❑ Offer free consultations
- ❑ Offer free demos or tours
- ❑ Offer free samples
- ❑ Use phone on-hold time to communicate your service or product
- ❑ Share past success stories
- ❑ Stress the Benefits of your offering
- ❑ Provide as wide a Selection as possible
- ❑ Give ample Contact time with customers
- ❑ Pay attention to how you say hello and goodbye
- ❑ Emphasize your Competitive advantages
- ❑ Uphold your Reputation
- ❑ Show Enthusiasm (it's contagious)
- ❑ Communicate Credibility
- ❑ Make it easy to do business with you
- ❑ Show Competitiveness
- ❑ Increase your Satisfied customers
- ❑ Use Research studies to support the value of your offerings
- ❑ Seek Marketing insight
- ❑ Gather and use Testimonials
- ❑ Expand Brand name awareness
- ❑ Monitor and assess yourself and those who work for you relentlessly

Creating Media Awareness

M*edia* is the collective term for the agencies of public communication. Its individual participants - editors, reporters, critics, columnists, and commentators - are often described as the "tastemakers" of public opinion. Their job is to monitor the constant worldwide flood of new data and report only the information deemed most appropriate for targeted readers, viewers, and listeners.

Media exposure has many advantages. However, through the years of working with the media, I've narrowed its advantages down to two: 1) Media exposure is effective in helping you be first in people's minds even when you're not first in the marketplace, and, 2) it sows credibility seeds that can't be planted through paid advertising.

One thing all businesses have in their favor as far as publicity goes is this: *The media has space to fill and depends on us to provide the filler.* Did you know that 75% of what you read in blogs and magazines is "planted?" This means it came to the media vehicle from *outside,* from people like you and me. Publicity, therefore, provides an open door for new company promotion. Wooing the media is simpler than you think. When you approach them in the right way and with the right information, they'll be receptive to your message. This will mean:

• ***Speak their language*** - A large percentage of stories you see, hear and read in the media are generated from hundreds of news releases received each month. Unfortunately, most news releases (also called, press releases) are thrown in the trash because they're ineffective and not written in the proper format. I've included a number of publicity resources in the Further Resources section of this book. For now, you can visit Bill Stoller's publicityinsider.com for some lucid advice on how to speak 'media'.

• ***Build a targeted media list*** - Again, this is the lifeblood of all your marketing efforts. See chapter 5 ("Building Your Database of Connections").

• ***Make "waves"*** - The Public has an attention span of miniscule duration and a memory which is even shorter. This is why your publicity objectives can only be realized through successive "waves" of media exposure, each wave being linked to a significant action or event related to your company. Successive waves "coat" your market, raising the consciousness of your audience about your brand. These waves can include such things as a high-profile performance, record release party, important contract signing, endorsement, contest award, etc. The more of these you have the more waves you can organize.

• ***Sending timely, useful information*** - Releases that include startling facts or statistics, announce a deal between you and a known brand company, offer a free workshop or seminar, introduce a new product or service to an unusual niche market, etc. can be considered "newsworthy".

• ***Make yourself findable*** - Be sure your full contact information is included with your release. At the top *and* bottom say, "For further information please contact:".

• ***Prepare to ride the media roller coaster*** - Sometimes a placement will produce wonderful results and other times it may not yield a single phone call. As you become a seasoned publicity-seeker, you'll learn to stay focused and move on to the next opportunity, continually sending messages out to your list. It's the nature of the business, but it's an investment worth your time.

Dollar for dollar publicity may very well be the best investment you can make for you marketing program. For example, if you were to purchase space for a one-time "6 x 8" display ad in *The Boston Globe* newspaper, you would pay about $2000 for it (*on top of* the costs to design the ad). But say you get a story written about you and your music in the same publication, and it takes up the same amount of space. You're now $2000 ahead of the game!

Plus, publicity is more credible than a paid advertisements. You can make any product claim you want when you place an ad, and consumers know this. A journalist or reporter, however, doesn't *have to* feature you in their publication and, by doing so, lends more credibility to what you're about. Of course, the downside is you don't control the message when you don't pay for it.

Use the chart on the following page to map out your publicity plan based on the objectives you would like to achieve.

PLANNING PUBLICITY OBJECTIVES AND APPROACHES		
Publicity Objective	Media Channel	Nature of Story
Heighten awareness among business leaders and the financial industry	Business and financial publications, business sections of daily newspapers, business segments of broadcast outlets, business websites	Tie brand introduction to the announcement of a new business, product, or strategic direction, including forecasts for market opportunity, new jobs, and business growth
Heighten awareness in local or regional market area	Local and regional news outlets, including daily and weekly newspapers, radio and TV stations, alternative press, and websites distributing local/regional information	Tie brand introduction to the announcement of new products, services, or opportunities of interest to customers, prospective customers, and local/regional residents
Heighten awareness in the national/global market	Network radio and television channels, national and major metro newspapers, news wire services, consumer and lifestyle magazines, major websites and news portals	Tie brand introduction to a major announcement of a new product or service, new business direction, or other news of impact and interest to national and international consumers
Heighten awareness within your industry or trade group	Trade, technical, and professional publications and websites	Tie brand introduction to the announcement of a new product, service, production, distribution, or marketing campaign of interest to customers, suppliers, wholesalers, and retailers in your industry.

Distribute your news release. To distribute hard copy news releases, use one of these three approaches:

• Handle the task on your own by mailing, faxing, or delivering releases to your target media contact list. This will be most cost-effective.
• Contract with a public relations professional or public relations agency to write and distribute your new releases. This can be expensive.
• Use a news distribution service such as PR Newswire (www.prnewswire.com) or Business Wire (www.businesswire.com) to achieve simultaneous distribution of important news to national, international, or business media. (For more examples of email news distribution services, visit www.ereleases.com, www.prweb.com, and www.internetnews.com).

How to Craft an Email News Releases. Increasingly, journalists prefer to receive news via email. Before assuming that your news is welcomed by online delivery, however, do the following:

• *Confirm* with your target media outlet or editorial contact that your release will be accepted if it's transmitted via email.
• *Obtain* the correct email address.

• *Ask* whether to send the release as an email message or email attachment.

Staff at most media outlets don't open unsolicited attachments, so don't send your release as an attachment unless you're specifically told to do so.
Finally, when emailing releases, use plain text rather than HTML or other markup language. Prepare a traditional hard copy version of the release as well to enclose in media kits, to post within your company to distribute to clients and key contacts, and to provide as follow-up information to editors.

Integrating Your Marketing Program

Marketing is all the exhilarating big things and all the troublesome little things that have to be done in every nook and cranny of the entire corporate organization in order to achieve the purpose of attracting and holding a customer. - Theodore Levitt

Effective marketing strategies always work double time – feeding off of each other and creating a ripple effect. Just like your multifunction cell phone, your marketing tools should have multiple purposes. Rather than investing in a tactic that's used to communicate your message in one way, explore the potential for it to be integrated with other media as well for even better results. The payoff is that you'll get more bang for your buck.
Here are some examples:

• A music instrument store owner attaches her business card to a bunch of music magazines she then distributes freely to doctors' and dentist's waiting rooms. She does this while simultaneously running ads in the local paper and participating in a local business street fair;

• To create awareness for a festival, a promoter sends a notice to his whole email list that includes a "free ticket" contest that gets free ads in local newspapers and radio shows, as well as redistribution of his message to all their emailing;

• A music publicist uses her voice mail message for announcing specials or other appealing information about her company, instead of simply for managing her calls.

Integrated marketing is the approach of Amalgam Entertainment's Jay Andreozzi, which works to synergize its retail and artist development components. "We use newsletters, social networking sites, promotional items, and digital promotion but we have created a unique hybrid company that works off itself symbiotically. It's segmented into part digital store part record label and the established artists on the label help direct traffic to the store so that consumers may find lesser known independent artists by way of discovery. At the same time the store helps serve as a powerful platform for the label (advertising, profile, direct source of income/lower expenses)."

Look for ways to repackage your work and use the previous list of "100 Marketing Tools" to get some ideas for the best kinds of vehicles to integrate and repackage with. A case study about how you solved a client's problem can be printed in a promotional newsletter or work as a supplement to your brochure or proposals. Newsletters, ezines and blogs are mileage maximizers, too. They provide an outlet to share useful information while indirectly promoting your expertise, products and services. At least 50% of my Music Business Solutions clients come directly from reading my newsletter, *Music Biz Insight*, which I've been publishing now for ten years.

Strategies with a multiplying effect give you more value for your initial efforts and free you to concentrate on other ways to build your business.

Measuring Marketing Effectiveness

Just as important as creating a strong marketing plan is following through on the results. How will you know which tactics are working if you don't analyze the results? Check the effectiveness of your advertising programs regularly by conducting one or more of the following tests:

• Run the same ad in two different publications with a different identifying mark on each one. Ask customers to clip the ad and bring it in for a discount or a free sample. Or, if you are running an ad that asks customers to order by mail, put a code in your company address such as "Dept. SI." By looking at the marks on the clipped ads or the addresses on the mail-in (or emailed) orders, you'll be able to tell which and pulled better.

• Train everyone in your company who answers the phone to ask customers *where they heard about you.* Create a one-page form with checkboxes so this process is simple to follow and the results are easy to evaluate. Just bear in mind that customers will sometimes get it wrong, they may say they saw you on TV when you don't run a TV campaign. But overall, asking for this information will be valuable.

• Advertise an item in one and only outlet. Don't have any signs or otherwise promote the item in your store or business. Then count the calls, sales or special requests for that item. If you get calls you'll know the ad is working.

• Stop running an ad that you regularly run. See if dropping the ad affects sales.

• Always check sales results. This is especially important when you place an ad for the first time.

Checks like these will give you some idea of how your advertising and marketing program is working. Be aware, however, that you can't expect immediate results from an ad. Advertising consistently is important, especially if you run small-space ads, which are less likely to be seen and remembered than larger ads.

One study showed that attention to an ad is significantly impacted by its size - in fact, a 1 percent increase in ad size leads to the same percentage increase in attention. You must also run your ad in multiple issues (at least six) before readers will notice your ad and buy what your selling. Of course, an ad can be everything from a flier and a newspaper display ad, to a banner and a Google text ad.

Working the Sales Machine:
How To Handle the Most Common Objections

"Making the sale" is always a challenging activity. A recession calls for additional effort from your side to attract new customers, hold on to existing ones and increase the dollar amount that those customers spend. But if you know your potential customer's complaint or still unanswered question about what you are offering, you'll have a much easier time providing a resolution and closing the sale.

Most objections stem from one of the three following areas of concern.

❑ ***Lack of trust in your brand:*** Here's where testimonials and endorsements can come to the rescue. Be gathering these every step of your business life.

❑ ***Preference for a competing brand:*** Arm your sales force with a clear recap of the benefits and value your product or service delivers so that they can present a positive response that favorably compares your offering to like products without taking any digs at competitors.

❑ ***Concern over your offer:*** Prepare your sales force to probe the concern and to avoid jumping to the conclusion that price is the issue. Often concerns have as much to do with questions about ease of use, appropriateness of the offering, perceived risk in dealing with a new product or brand, or even lack of authority to make the purchase. For each form of concern, provide sales materials and scripts to address the issue.

There may also be:

❑ ***Price concerns:*** Provide ways to demonstrate worth, present product value,

show cost/value ratios, and show money- or time-saving potential. Also provide salespeople with a range of purchase options—from trial offers to bulk discounts to special terms of installment plans—to address price barriers.

❑ ***Time concerns:*** Provide ways that salespeople can demonstrate ease of use, installation, product adoption, training, or other time concerns.

❑ ***Risk concerns:*** Demonstrations, trial offers, no-risk guarantees, or service assurances minimize the risk customers associate with a purchase. Also present testimonials, endorsements, and case studies that replace risk concerns with product assurances.

Here are some ways to respond to customers with these types of objections.

Your price is too high.
- "What are you comparing it with?"
- "Is it what you really need (or want)?"
- "Let's consider how this will improve your situation."
- "What we offer differs from what others offer in the following ways.
- Which of these differences might be important to you or your company?"

We can't afford such a product or service.
- "Let me show you how we can actually save you money."
- "What is your budget? Let me find something in that range."

We can't afford it right now.
- "We can make special billing arrangements for you."
- "With references we would be happy to open an account for you."
- "Can you afford not to?"
- "Will you regret not passing this up?"

It won't work for us.
- "Let me show you how it could."
- "We will be happy to tailor it for your specifications."
- "Let me show you how it has worked for others in your situation."

We need it in another form.
- "Exactly what changes do you need?"
- "We will be happy to work with you to meet your needs."

I don't have time to discuss it right now.

- "Your time is very valuable. I promise to be brief. Just answer this one question."
- " Of course, you are busy. When would be a time to show you how we meet your needs."
- "I know your time is pressing, but I don't want you to lose an opportunity."

I'll think about it.

- " Do so. I know you will find it a great advantage to you. I will contact you early next week to see if you need any further information."
- " Are there other questions in the back of your mind right now?"
- "What additional information would be of help to you in making a decision?"

Thanks. We'll call you.

- "I will give you a call next week to see if you need any further information."
- "Let me ask you honestly: does this interest you?"

As you've discovered in this chapter, marketing and sales are ongoing processes that require continual refinements as you try to reach potential buyers in new ways. When I asked the entrepreneurs what percentage of their work and time they devote to marketing their business, most said between 30 and 40%. Even when you seem to have plenty of business it is crucial to always be planting seeds for the future. Keeping your marketing creative, consistent and well-managed will ensure you are maximizing your chances of getting the business you need to thrive.

While some entrepreneurs find marketing a chore, many feel that it's one of the most creative parts of their ventures. Each message you present about your business - whether in person, in print, on a web site, or on the telephone - reflects your unique style and vision. It's an outlet for personal creative expression that never ends.

CHAPTER SUMMARY

BUSINESS CONDUCTING: MARKETING

- **Developing a Marketing Mindset**
  Develop a positive marketing mindset enables you to create effective and affordable ways to attract business. By making the following three mental shifts in how you think about getting business, you can project a positive mindset and make getting business easier and infinitely more enjoyable.
    - ❑ Think opportunity, not obligation.
    - ❑ Think contact, not activity.
    - ❑ Think communication, not manipulation

- **Managing Your Marketing Programs**
  Having an organized system in place will make all your marketing and promotional efforts flow more smoothly. Information is your ally as a marketer but if it's not organized it will quickly become your enemy. The first thing to do is to come up with a list of topical areas or categories of marketing activity you will be engaged in. Here's a list of business marketing categories to get you started. Use only those with most relevance to your particular business: General Business Info, General Marketing Info, Specific Market Info, Graphics & Design, Publishing, Sales, and Promotion.

- **The Meaning of Launching a "Brand"**
  A brand is an identifiable entity that makes specific promises of value. Brands are the sum total of all the images that people have in their heads about a particular company and a particular mark. Perception is everything. Many people think that the logo is the brand, but, in fact, the logo is just one representation of the brand. Your brand isn't how you look or what you say or even what you sell. Your brand is what people believe you stand for.

- **Setting Your Marketing Goals & Objectives**
  Your goal is what you want your marketing to achieve; your objectives define how you'll achieve your goal. For example:
  - If your goal is to win awareness for your company and its distinctions, your objectives may include gaining name recognition and knowledge of your unique point of difference among a defined segment of consumers in your target market within a certain length of time.
  - If your goal is to enhance credibility and trust, your objectives may be to achieve awareness of and belief in your point of difference and your company promise among a defined segment of consumers in your target market within a certain length of time.
  - If your goal is to motivate sales, your objective may be to add at least one new distribution channel and to realize a specified sales increase without sacrificing unit sale price within a certain length of time from the start of your brand launch.

- **From Push to Pull: Building Permission Marketing Networks**
  One of the biggest shifts in the advertising world over the past twenty years has been the one from a "push" strategy (cramming messages down our throats whether we like it or not) to a "pull" strategy (drawing us in with valuable information). Permission Marketing is the tool that unlocks the power of the internet. The leverage it brings to this new medium, combined with the pervasive clutter that infects the internet and virtually every other medium, makes Permission Marketing the most powerful trend in marketing for the next decade. Before sending email messages, be double sure that the people on your email list will welcome your message.

- **Organizing Your Brand Introduction Tactics**
  As you plan the tactics you'll use to deliver your marketing message, keep the following options in mind:
  - Public relations activities are the backbone of most business introductions.
  - Promotions are marketing activities that aim to trigger a desired consumer action over a short period of time.
  - Advertising creates awareness in audiences reached by newspapers, magazines, radio, and television.
  - Advertising Specialties help brand your name and give it some mobility as well.
  - Direct mail is advertising that's delivered on a one-to-one basis to mailboxes or email inboxes rather than through mass media.
  - Personal presentations and sales efforts are especially important to brand launches that depend on personal relationships, referrals, or support from established contacts and customers.
  - Sales materials, packaging, and point-of-sale displays are essential for consumer brands and for brands that involve complex features.
  - Online communications play an increasingly important role in brand introduction tactical plans.

- **Creating Media Awareness**
  Media exposure has many advantages: Media exposure is effective in helping you be first in people's minds even when you're not first in the marketplace, and, it sows credibility seeds that can't be planted through paid advertising. When you approach them in the right way and with the right information, they'll be receptive to your message. You need to:
  - Speak their language
  - Build a targeted media list
  - Make "waves"
  - Send timely, useful information
  - Make yourself findable
  - Prepare to ride the media roller coaster

- **Integrating Your Marketing Program**
  Effective marketing strategies always work double time – feeding off of each other and creating a ripple effect. Just like your multifunction cell phone, your marketing tools should have multiple purposes. Rather than investing in a tactic that's used to communicate your message in one way, explore the potential for it to be integrated with other media as well for even better results. Look for ways to repackage your work and use the list of "100 Marketing Tools" (p. ____) to get some ideas for the best kinds of vehicles to integrate and repackage with.

- **Measuring Marketing Effectiveness**
  Check the effectiveness of your advertising programs regularly by conducting one or more of the following tests:
  - ❑ Run the same ad in two different publications with a different identifying mark on each one. Ask customers to clip the ad and bring it in for a discount or a free sample.
  - ❑ Train everyone in your company who answers the phone to ask customers where they heard about you.
  - ❑ Stop running an ad that you regularly run. See if dropping the ad affects sales.
  - ❑ Always check sales results.

- **Working the Sales Machine**
  Most objections stem from these following areas of concern:
  - ❑ Lack of trust in your brand
  - ❑ Preference for a competing brand
  - ❑ Concern over your offer
  - ❑ Price concerns
  - ❑ Time concerns
  - ❑ Risk concerns

FURTHER RESOURCES

ONLINE RESOURCES

Chris Brogan
chrisbrogan.com

Hubspot
hubspot.com

Learn Local Marketing
moz.com/learn/local

Seth Godin
sethgodin.com

Social Marketing Success Kit
marketo.com

The Essential List of Startup Marketing Resources
ryangum.com

BOOKS

How to Get a Meeting with Anyone: The Untapped Selling Power of Contact Marketing by Stu Heinecke (2016, BenBella Books).

Music Distribution: Selling Music in the New Entertainment Marketplace by C. Michael Brae (2014, Hitman Records).

Music Marketing: Press, Promotion, Distribution, and Retail by Mike King (2009, Berklee Press).

The Self-Promoting Musician: Strategies for Independent Music Success by Peter Spellman (2014, Berklee Press).

Steal Like an Artist: 10 Things Nobody Told You About Being Creative by Austin Kleon (2012, Workman Publishing).

Sticky Branding: 12.5 Principles to Stand Out, Attract Customers, and Grow an Incredible Brand by Jeremy Miller (2015, Dundurn).

What Great Brands Do: The Seven Brand-Building Principles that Separate the Best from the Rest by Denise Lee Yohn (2014, Jossey-Bass).

16

ENRICHING & ENLARGING THE SCORE

Most people would succeed in small things if they were not troubled with great ambitions.
– Longfellow

The larger the island of knowledge, the longer the shoreline of wonder.
– Ralph Sockman

Growth presents its own management challenges. When a business grows gaps begin to appear – These are the needs in your business processes that are not being met. The key is learning "how to develop new procedures an d create a flexible environment that enables growth," says indie label head Andreas Katsambas. He goes on, "When we had a small amount of [CD] releases it was easy to recall the available stock for each one. But eventually we had so many titles we needed to automate the process. We had no idea how to do it and it took a lot of research to eventually figure it out."

Wave after wave of technological improvement also drives the entrepreneur to explore new ways of doing business and creative ways to nurture the business he has. When asked what he has planned for making the Sonicbids' web site even more effective, founder Panos Panay ticked off a list to make any manager's head spin: "Updating marketing message; improving user experience; redesigning all our online tours; updating customer interaction and pricing choices offered through the site; offering many more collaborative tools." Keeping up with the latest technology is a herculean task, but essential for staying relevant to an ever-changing market.

S.W.O.T. Your Business (and Your Career!)

Before considering any expansion of your business you should perform a SWOT Analysis. SWOT is a powerful technique for understanding your **S**trengths and **W**eaknesses, and for looking at the **O**pportunities and **T**hreats you face. The essence of the SWOT Analysis is to discover what you do well, how you could improve, whether you are making the most of the opportunities around you, and whether there are any changes in your market – such as technological developments, mergers of businesses, or changes in suppliers – that may require corresponding changes in your company, or career.

Used in a business context, it helps you carve a sustainable niche in your market. Used in a personal context, it helps you develop your career in a way that takes best advantage of your talents, abilities and opportunities. What makes SWOT particularly powerful is that, with a little thought, it can help you uncover opportunities that you are well placed to exploit. And by understanding the weaknesses of your business, you can manage and eliminate threats that would otherwise catch you unawares. So look objectively at your company and use the chart on the following page to assess your business before making any decisions to expand it.

STRENGTHS What advantages does your company have? What unique or lowest-cost resources do you have access to? What do people in your market see as your strengths?	**WEAKNESSES** What could you improve? What are people in your market likely to see as weaknesses? What factors lose you sales?
OPPORTUNITIES Where are the good opportunities facing you? What are the interesting trends you are aware of? How can you turn your strengths into opportunities?	**THREATS** What obstacles do you face? What is your competition doing that you should be worried about? Is changing technology threatening your position?

Once you have done your SWOT Analysis you will have a much clearer idea of your assets and value, as well as what you still need before taking your next steps. Complimentary to the SWOT are seven key areas of your business that should work intrinsically together to make it successful. If you fall down in one of these, it can directly affect the others and your overall progress. Check this list periodically to see how you are progressing.

	Yes
1. **I am administratively active:** Your paper flow, accounting, inventory and computer systems are incredibly efficient. Your employees are happy, motivated company ambassadors.	❑
2. **I am constantly creative:** You are always looking for new and exciting ideas and methods to grow your business. You don't fear change and change with the times, and you practice tapping your inner creative energy.	❑
3. **I am customer conscious:** Every customer is important to you. They refer you, are loyal, and you give them the red carpet treatment before, during, and after the sale.	❑
4. **I am fiscally fit:** You monitor the financial figures regularly, work to a business plan and have a monthly budget. You plan for taxes and future growth, and confer regularly with your accountant.	❑
5. **I am positively positioned:** You have a good sense of humor, keep educated, and stay up with competitors. You have built a positive work environment and can be flexible.	❑

6. **I am technologically terrific:** You have harnessed technology to your advantage and streamlined systems. You have a strong web presence and use your database for increasingly effective marketing. ❑

7. **I am a trend-tracker:** You attend industry conferences and trade shows and read industry magazines, e-zines and reports. You keep up with global, consumer, local, and national news and trends, and let this inform your planning. ❑

Both the SWOT analysis and the above questions will help you get the necessary read on where you are at *currently* before considering any vertical or horizontal movement for your business. With this in mind you can now assess which of the following expansion strategies may make sense for you. We won't look at all of these growth strategies, but will consider several in this chapter.

Ten Ways to Expand Your Business

Consider these suggestions:

- Expanding your line of products
- Expanding the services you offer
- Offering consulting services
- Exporting your product or service
- Buying an existing business to expand
- Importing products
- Franchising your business
- Partnering with another business
- Opening a second location
- Offering seminars, workshops, or training services.

Growing Your Business Vertically & Horizontally

Even if you plan to always work from home, you'll probably eventually need to expand. You might want or need more money. You might need to diversify your offerings, just to keep up with your competition. If nothing else, you know that some of your customers will eventually disappear, and the cost of doing business will continue to rise. So expansion isn't just an ambitious dream—it's a real-world necessity.

Business expansion usually follows a "vertical" path, meaning the business will try to sell more of its current product or service. It makes sense because the effort usually requires few major adjustments or risks. For example, a retailer who sells drums will always try to sell more drums. If the market is hot, that's all he needs to do.

But the market is probably not hot enough for him to sell *only* drums. So the shop owner expands "horizontally" by adding DVDs, accessories, cases, instructional materials, or any other complementary item that his customers might want. In this way, he not only gains more sales from customers who buy drums, but also from those who might only want a road case or a cowbell.

The principle is no different for a home-based business. A self-employed performing musician might decide to also market music lessons or other services, as well. A festival organizer might branch out into special events planning, awards' ceremonies, or even office parties.

When Horizontal Expansion Makes Sense. Horizontal expansion makes sense when your "vertical growth" has reached its limit, but you still want to expand. Even when more

vertical growth is possible, a point of diminishing returns can be reached when further expenditures of time or money are not justified.

David Frey, author of, *The Small Business Marketing Bible*, suggests that horizontal expansion is best for home businesses whose products or services can be added with little cash outlay and risk. "If you have a large and growing customer following and much of your business is brought in through referrals, then offering more products and services might be a good idea since you can expand without all the associated marketing costs. Another good example would be businesses whose vendors can drop ship most of the products to customer, since they won't need to tie up money in inventory or extra personnel."
With some exceptions, it's usually easier to expand *product* rather than *service* offerings since product selling tends to require less preparation and involvement than service selling. To add a service, for instance, you might need to learn new skills. Even if you already possess the requisite knowledge, your level of experience in the new area won't be equal to that associated with your traditional service.

It can also be difficult to frequently shift from one skill to another. Most freelance film composers, for instance, won't find it easy to shift from writing original scores to radio jingles. Highly skillful people who can quickly shift mental gears are the exception; most others do best by more narrowly focusing on highly specialized tasks.

Making the Move. You'll be ready to make your move once you've gotten your basic business down to a science. Still, there will be more preparation than you might think. For example, you'll need to specifically identify new target markets, and devise a strategy for reaching them.

Your company literature and web site will also need to be updated to include the new product or service offerings. If relevant, vendors, suppliers, distributors, salespeople, and clients will also need to be updated.

The most important first step is to work out potential conflicts between new and traditional offerings. For example, if the new initiative will take time or money away from your normal work, that should be addressed before you expand. You should also have concrete solutions for a number of other important details. A new product, for example, demands you address questions like:

- ❑ How do you determine the potential of a new product?
- ❑ Who will be your supplier? Will there be more than one?
- ❑ Will you sell your new product to the same customers, other customers, or both?
- ❑ Can you accurately estimate demand for the new product? How?
- ❑ Is the product subject to damage or other risks?
- ❑ Where will you store inventory, and how much will that cost?
- ❑ What will be your full spectrum of costs?
- ❑ Are there any legal risks associated with your new product?
- ❑ How will you handle returns?

A smart planning mantra is this: *The unforeseeable is usually seeable to those who bother to look.*

Blueprint for Horizontal Expansion

Before you launch your horizontal expansion, consider these guidelines:

❑ ***Do first things first.*** Before you expand, be sure you are well established in one main line of business. Be sure the core of your business is sound. Even if you've planned from the outset to offer multiple products or services, it's always easier to advance one step at a time and to work through initial problems before you move into another area. If you are a new entrepreneur, you also need to get to discover your own strengths and weaknesses — something that only experience can teach you. You also need to learn the tastes and idiosyncrasies of your market before you can gauge its wants.

❑ ***Prepare a blueprint***. Because expansion requires very careful thought, it should — like a business plan — be plotted in a written plan. Be sure to address such considerations as:

- What you plan to offer.
- Where you will obtain the product, materials, or skills.
- Whose help you will need.
- How much you will budget.
- What markets you will target.
- The timetable you will follow.
- Current and likely competitors.
- Amount of income needed to justify the expansion.
- Potential conflicts between old and new offerings.
- How the new offering might boost your current offerings.

❑ ***Master the details.*** Learn everything you can about any new product or service before you market it. Not only will your customers expect your expertise, but you will also need to know how well you will work with it. If it's a product, examine it closely and try it for yourself. If useful, seek the input of friends, relatives, or business associates. Give away some for free, if you can. It can be a very worthwhile investment in order to learn how much people will value your new product.

❑ ***Study competitors.*** What are they offering? How widely have they expanded? Take special note of those that have narrowed their range of offerings. You can be sure there's a reason for that.

❑ ***Test market.*** Another good way to test the waters is through test marketing your new product or service to a limited number of prospects. You might begin with a small circle of close acquaintances of familiar customers from whom you can get honest feedback. This will also enable you to discover the costs and demands the expansion will place on you before you have taken it too far.

Adding Value to Existing Products & Services

Another form of growing your business is by adding value. *Price* is just one component of your company's offerings. *Value*, however, can encompass much more. You add value when you develop a product or service and then add materials, processing or services to create a more valuable end product. You then sell the product in its *value-*

enhanced form.

Value may be added by:

- ❑ putting the product through an additional process;
- ❑ combining the product with other products;
- ❑ offering the product as part of a larger package of services;
- ❑ removing something to change the use of the product; or
- ❑ increasing levels of service.

Some examples of adding value include:

1. A student who operated a demo recording business expanded the operation by offering half-day recording seminars and special discounts to clients.

2. A businessman bought large plastic cup lids, licensed CDs, attached them to the lids and marketed them as "LidRocks" at concerts.

3. Three bands put together a triple-bill package for a local club, give it a theme and build a contest into it, then present the package to the club owner.

4. A record company creates an appropriate recording or compilation for a tie-in with an environmental organization's benefit project.

5. Here's one from the recent music press: The Marlin Hotel in Miami's South Beach combines a luxury hotel with a state-of-the-art recording studio.

ADDING VALUE – THE DISNEY WAY

"With the movie *Beauty and the Beast,* the creative people at Walt Disney Studios took a well-known story (the "information" in this case) and added value to it in many different ways. Writers developed the story and wrote a screenplay; cartoonists created and animated characters; actors and actresses provided voices; artists designed backgrounds and special effects; composers and lyricists wrote an original score; instrumental musicians and singers performed the songs; directors and editors brought it all together into a pleasing whole."

– Carol Eikleberry, *The Career Guide for Creative & Unconventional People*

How to Add Value to What You Offer:

❑ **Pick an existing product or service and think of an additional process**, material or service that could be added to create a new product. For example, a product or service may be more successful if an additional element such as packaging or special delivery is added.

❑ **Identify a process or service which you could provide**, then look for types of existing products or services which could be used as a base for your desired operation. For example, provide a compilation CD to an auto dealer to include with all new car sales in a certain month.

❑ **Find an existing product which could be changed** into a different or improved product by adding or subtracting one or more elements. If additional elements are required, locate a source for these and develop a method of adding them. Conversely, if elements must be subtracted, find a workable way of doing so.

❑ **Find a customer group which has needs that are not being met** by existing products and services. For example, providing iPod owners with a service that loads their CD collections into their players so they don't have to spend the time doing it themselves.

❑ **Find a product which does not work well**, or is not well-accepted by a customer group because of its inadequacies. Then improve it by adding or altering elements. For example, adding contact directories to a regional monthly music magazine.

The Power of Linking Up: Discovering Creative Partnerships

Affinity partnerships, joint ventures and other types of creative alliances are keys to career and business success, and another method of business expansion. The idea is to take advantage of business alliances that provide additional revenue, while minimizing your effort or risk. An affinity partnership is when two or more businesses come together to work on a project for a set period of time. Well-orchestrated joint ventures like these can further your chances of increasing sales and profits, save time and money, provide valuable referrals, and increase your market visibility.

There are several ways to work such partnerships. You might, for example, take referral fees for business you pass to others, while also enjoying business they send your way. Your associates might also be able to provide complementary goods or services that will make your offerings all the more appealing to your customers. For example, an event planner would be wise to be associated with various types of entertainers, or companies that provide amusements.

Even just having access to those who might be useful to your customers can be surprisingly advantageous to your business. For instance, a home-based guitar instructor — though she only teaches guitar — might do well to work with local schools or with any other persons associated with music instruction in the area. In this way, she can expand from guitar instructor to a one-stop service center for those in need of music instruction.

Partnering, of course, is nothing new for musical artists. Songwriters collaborate with each other, musicians form "bands" of like-minded players, performers team up with producers, and recording artists sign up with record companies - all in the hope of creating "synergy" where the sum result is greater than the singular parts.

Strategic partners come in all forms and can be found just about anywhere. A surprising number, in fact, are found accidentally or through casual contacts. But if you prefer to find them now rather than waiting to chance upon them, begin by asking yourself what sorts of partners would be most helpful to you. Those who can complement your services would be obvious choices. A jingle writer, for example, would do well to hook up with radio professionals, new media mavens or music libraries.

The online space, in particular, offers numerous possibilities. Creative alliances can cover anything from trading links to selling one another's products. There are literally thousands of possibilities. Think in terms of what kind of affinity your company's offerings have with others. Here are some suggestions:

❑ The simplest joint venture would be exchanging links or banners with other related web sites.

❑ Sharing a web site with another business with the same target market. You both will be marketing and advertising the same web site, which means double the traffic. For example, a jazz guitarist can share a web site with a t-shirt company specializing in "jazzy" designs.

❑ Combine your products or services together with another business into one big package. You could split the profits. For example, a reggae band can team up with a promoter to offer special entertainment packages for local cruise lines.

❑ Do you have a product or service that that you can offer as a free bonus ("freemium") for another business's product or service? Jandro Cisneros of The Pillar Productions established a strong collaboration with a local recoding studio in Boston. "I earned the trust of the owner by doing in the past free high quality job for him, and by being always on time and very reliable." Cisneros goes on. "I built the relationship for almost one year, and after a while he started sending me clients, and we partnered for recording and mixing sessions. One of the clients he sent me was for example was Dwayne Johnson "The Rock" actor's girlfriend Lauren Hashian, we built a great relationship with them and also we earned credibility and improved our portfolio."

You may also want to do a straight trade or barter with a company if it allows you to expand into other markets. "We actually do a lot of trades," says Andreas Katsambas of The End Records. "We generally trade our releases with other releases. This was how were able to get our titles to places like South America, Asia, Eastern Europe, etc."

Here are some guidelines for developing strong teams and creative partnerships:

❑ Find someone whose strengths complement your weaknesses and set up a trial period to see if you can work well together. The key is chemistry and chemistry involves experimentation with different combinations of elements until the right formula is found.

❑ Define who will contribute the cash, property, service or expertise. Each can be exchanged and each has a value.

❑ Communicate regularly to avoid power grabs and misunderstandings. Talk openly, honestly and relentlessly with your partners. Never let things build up to the point of explosion.

❑ Specify the percentage of ownership each person will have and define how, when, and in what order the profits will be distributed to partners.

❑ Prepare a business plan and financial forecast for the life of the partnership. This provides a map and an agreed-upon route to your goals.

❑ Provide a way to remove or buy out partners who fail to meet their obligations. Disagreements inevitably happen. People fall in love and leave town, another band snatches your drummer, a job with a steady paycheck becomes just too irresistible – in essence, people change. Prepare for this scenario beforehand and you'll save countless hours of heartache and stress later.

❑ Never forget you're dealing with friends (when this is the case). Don't let the stupid biz stuff and tedium get to you. Stand back from the petty conflicts that inevitably crop up and keep the "big picture" in sight.

You don't, however, want to be linked to disreputable or unreliable people. So before you enter into any business relationship, do some background checking. One way is to talk to business leaders who are familiar with the person you're thinking of teaming with. The best way is by talking to a number of the prospective associate's clients.

CO-BRANDING CHECKLIST

Before joining up with another brand, be sure you can answer a strong "yes" to each of these questions:

❑ Are your brands compatible without directly competing with each other?

❑ Do your brands appeal to the same or very similar customers?

❑ Will both brands enhance their reputations through the co-branding partnership?

❑ Do customers, media, investors, and other members of the public equally respect both brands?

❑ Are the management and marketing styles of both brand owners compatible?

❑ Do you trust each other?

❑ Are all the details down on paper and signed by both parties, including the co-branding marketing plan, budget, timeline, and responsibilities?

❑ Can you explain the co-branded product or promotion in a sentence that will make sense to your employees, customers, and others? Are both brands explaining it in exactly the same way?

Diversifying Your Activities & Revenue Streams

As your company grows in one area, you may want to consider diversifying into other areas. I've seen this time and again with small recording studios. Typical expansions for recording studios and production houses are: record label services, distribution, music publishing, promotional services, even venue development.

This kind of business expansion is illustrated in the development of New Jersey's Silk City Recordings (http://www.silkcitycd.com/services.html)

Silk City Recordings prides itself in offering "End to End Capabilities" for music clients. The company's staff has been offering a wide spectrum of services to the musical community since 1980.

The idea at Silk City is to provide clients with a "soup-to-nuts" solution for their music

recording needs. This is Silk City's niche. While many service providers in the industry are very good at producing *individual pieces* of this solution, Silk City differentiates itself in taking clients "End to End" with one team effort, as seen in the following chart.

Diversifying Your Revenue Streams

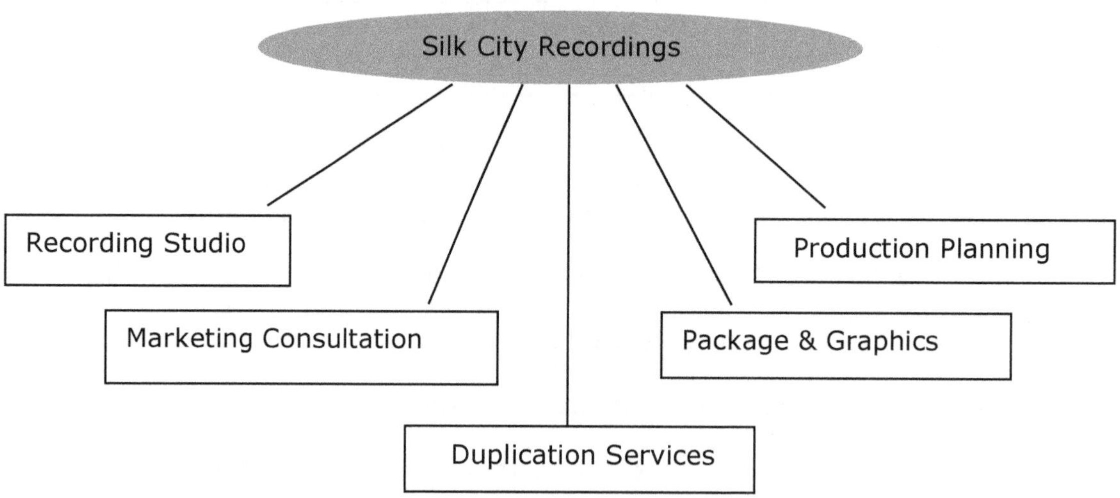

Silk City's services include:

- **Consultation** - An initial team conference where they scope out the direction and make sure their goals are set with the client's end in mind.
- **Development** - They can assign an experienced Executive Producer to a client's project who can work up the Development Plan and define all of the required activities and milestones.
- **Production** - The Recording Producer then makes sure the proper recording technologies are at the client's disposal to insure the best possible physical and emotional environment available to enhance client creativity in the recording process.
- **Recording** - They offer a wide range of Studio and Remote Recording solutions that can be custom configured around client goals (and project budget). Their capabilities include both Digital and Analog Multi-Tracking Recording in their in house studio facility. They can also provide various other technologies for any Special Projects that may arise.
- **Mixing** - Silk City's experienced engineering and production professionals will provide top notch analog or digital mixing with the artist present (if you desire) in their in house studio. Mix Down can be done to Digital Audio Tape (DAT) or CD-R.
- **Mastering**- Their strategic alliance with Luna Sound gives clients access to a state of the art Digital Mastering Lab, just minutes from their Recording Facility. For artists desiring to stay in the "analog domain", they offer Analog Mastering at their Sound Over Sound studio by master engineer and producer Jonathan Bross.
- **Graphics and Graphic Design**- Designing something to look great in a 4.25" x 4.25" space (CD tray size) can be a challenge. Bernard Doyle, who heads up their Graphics Department, has designed and implemented magnificent CD designs, as can be evidenced on their releases "Standing Room Only: Songs from the Last Roadhouse", "Dance, You Sinners", and "Hobo Jungle: Independent Blues Artists". Silk City offers complete layout and design for client projects in a Mac/Quark ready format, templated for Compact Disc manufacturing, complete with Bar Code (UPC). They also offer Photography sessions as part of their Graphics Design Services.
- **Manufacturing** - Using state of the art Duplication/Packaging facilities, Silk City can deliver a "retail ready" product in any format.
- **Distribution** - Silk City can provide On-Line Retail Store Distribution for select products and artists. In addition, they are in constant contact with Physical Distribution

companies that service chains and independent retailers. In addition, they can offer to design and host web pages for selected artists using their services.
Of course, each stop on the pipeline is another revenue stream for Silk City Recordings. Many other music companies are offering similar "service packages" to music clients. With smart management, these extra services can grow and develop, and even be spun off or sold as separate businesses as the "mother" company desires.

Developing Additional Profit Centers. If you rely on only one main product or service, especially in this economy, you are like the investor who has just one stock. That stock may go up, but it also may go down. It's risky. You need to diversify your business portfolio. Here's how:

❑ **Look for compatibility.** Whatever new profit center you choose, be sure that it complements what you are already doing. You need to choose a new endeavor that does not confuse your customers.

❑ **Look at line extensions.** Offering extra products or services — creating line extensions — often is the best way to create additional profit centers. The key to extending your line is to correctly assess what products or services you can add that complement and expand your current offerings.

❑ **Start with baby steps.** Whatever additional profit center you offer, be sure to start small. Do not just jump in without first really testing the waters. Start small, and test, test, test. See what works. Project how much money you can make. See what it will cost. Once you are certain that the plan will work, you can then devote more time, money and effort to the project.

Going International: Exporting and Licensing

If your ship doesn't come in, swim out to it. - Jonathan Winters, Comedian

As international markets expand, they are, collectively, becoming larger players in the potential profits for music entrepreneurs. Even the more remote regions of Latin America and Eastern Europe are developing at record paces. The sleeping giant China is poised to bring over a billion potential consumers to the music market. "New markets bring new challenges," says singer-songwriter Ember Swift. "I am currently working in Asia in an attempt to build my Asian profile and expand my learning of this market. The cultural differences are extreme, but the steeper the hill the more I seem to want to climb it!" More and more media opportunities are being created in the foreign markets as well.

The more opportunities to expose an artist to the public, the greater potential there is for sales (and income). As technology grows, the world continues to move towards one global culture. A label and an artist who work together to commit effort to development outside of the artist's own borders, will have the opportunity to become part of this global culture. Marshall McLuhan coined the phrase "global village" to describe a world created by the homogenizing effects of the universal availability of electronic media. Since his time the world has shrunk even further and our horizons have grown wider through the new media technologies of computers, satellite broadcasting, cable TV, cellular technology and wireless Internet.

The evolution of these communication technologies have had many effects, not the least of which is the fact that the "stars" of the contemporary entertainment industry are increasingly catering to an international audience that is constantly growing. In fact, it's probably fair to say that popular music is now the *lingua franca* for a large segment of the world's youth population. Amalgam Entertainment president, Jay Andreozzi took a niche interest in hip hop and turned it into a growing $2 million+/year music label and distribution service, covering all of Europe, Japan, as well as the U.S. Music seems to be the most universal means of communication we now have, instantly traversing language and other cultural barriers in a way few of us fully appreciate. *In fact, one could argue that music is perhaps the essential component linking the different sectors of the global entertainment industry.*

Of course, recorded music sales are just one *part* of the picture. Licensing tracks and concert tours by both superstars and indie upstarts continue to make their mark in the global music village. For example, I recently heard of a blues harp player from Massachusetts who's been in Southeast Asia for the past five years playing the Blues six nights a week with a Thai back up band! And he's just one of *many*.

International Touring. Gigging overseas presents exciting opportunities for North American bands and artists, *if* your are ready for it *and if it is ready for you.*
In general, European and Japanese venues are more professionally run than those in the U.S. People have more experience arranging tours, sound systems are better quality, and bands are often provided food and drink (and even sleeping accommodations!) routinely. There is also a more organized DIY network, especially for punk and metal bands. For jazz, classical and world music acts there are other kinds of support infrastructures that allow international acts to set up performances fairly easily (see my book *Indie Marketing Power* for more detailed information on touring overseas).

The first and biggest concern is knowing *when* you are ready to tour overseas. Currently Europe is full of U.S. and Canadian touring acts, both small, grassroots efforts as well as larger, "reunion" bands that are all the rage. This doesn't mean there isn't room for *your* act; it just means you need to be more resourceful and have personal contacts in the places you wish to tour.

!!! SECURITY ALERT !!!

I have heard some bizarre tales of shady promoters making arrangements with local mafia to steal bands' gear and bands having to pay the local mafia to get their stolen van and gear back. Overseas you should probably stay security conscious at all times, keep a person with your van, and think proactively.

It's recommended that a band wait until they have several releases in the overseas music market they're targeting before attempting to tour there. Too many acts take advantage of the ease of European travel before they really have an audience in those regions, and the result is less than satisfying both for your morale and your bank account.

Entertaining Soldiers Overseas. If you are looking to expand your fan base internationally and carry out a truly unique, memorable tour, the branch of the military known as Armed Forces Entertainment (AFE) may be looking for you. Charged by the Department of Defense to help entertain the troops overseas, the AFE is actively seeking talented U.S. musicians to perform at military bases around the world. Unlike the affiliate organization, the U.SO. (think Bob Hope) who coordinate celebrity tours for the troops, the AFE focuses on booking up-and-coming talent and have helped hundreds of indie acts reach new and receptive audiences. The booking process may be a little more involved than the average stateside gig – this is the government after all – but the rewards are innumerable. Learn more about the AFE at http://afe.afsv.af.mil.

If at all possible, team up with a label in the country you're going to tour. Ideally, you want to have a licensing or distribution deal with a company that knows the scene and is plugged into the channels that will help the tour go smoothly. This could be an exclusive release or a European pressing of a U.S. record.

Sometimes a "trade partnership" can be set up between the touring band and a label: they'll help sell your records in exchange for you taking some of their releases back to the States to sell. However, the DIY labels in the U.S. who are trading often find that there is a limit to the amount of European stuff they can reasonably get sold in the U.S.

I would recommend finding a European label you like and trust, and work closely with them to do a European release in advance of the tour, help you with booking, transportation, and backline and also to do a new release for the tour.

One caveat: European distributors are shameless when it comes to selling your records at *your shows*. This can be a problem when you're also trying to sell your records and only making wholesale off of *their* sales, but this is "standard industry practice" over there.

Licensing. Your distributor may take care of export sales for you but you may not be contractually obliged to go through them. If this is the case, you are free to sell your product to exporters or direct to shops around the world.

Foreign territory licensing can be an easy way to make money with neither additional investment nor effort beyond actually securing the deal. In a good licensing agreement, both parties benefit. The licensor gains the benefit of a brand extension and related marketplace presence and sales revenue (via royalties) without any investment in product development, production, or marketing. To the brand owner and licensor, licensing is a no-cost form of brand value leverage.

The licensee gains the benefit of the licensor's brand name, which lends immediate awareness, distinction, and trust to the manufacturer's product rollout. Without the need for any brand development investment, the licensor is able to achieve marketplace dominance and command a premium sales price thanks to the lease of the licensor's name. You need to find a licensee who does the job efficiently, so check their performance by speaking with some of their client-labels. Your licensee will probably want to start with one release to test their market. If that does well, then expect to be offered a blanket license for your whole catalog.

One simple way to make contact with the world's record industry is to attend international trade shows. The two biggest in Europe are Midem in Cannes France every January (http://www.midem.com) and Popkomm in Cologne Germany every August (www.popkomm.de), though this year's Popkomm struggled to stay afloat. Midem has recently spawned Midem Net, a one day conference about on-line developments, which takes place on the day preceding the 5-day exhibition. Another biggie for international dance music is the Miami Winter Music Conference every March (http://www.wmcon.com). Indie record labels flock to these conventions, seeking licensing deals for their catalogs. If successful, licensees will take on all the legwork in their licensed territories, remitting royalties for sales generated, often starting with an advance on future sales.

Of course, if you have an online presence you are already international. I fondly remember that within one day of putting up my web site back in 1997, I had a book order from Taiwan. In fact, any business that traffics in information (e.g., music, books, films, reports, software, etc.) will have the easiest time selling internationally. This becomes even more attractive because there are no special tax laws governing internet sales. However, just having a web site won't necessarily bring in the level of international business you seek. You should decide on potential allies in the countries you're seeking to do business in, using the guidelines provided earlier in this chapter to build the necessary bridges, slow but sure.

Exiting: Four Ways to Leave Your Business

There may come a time when you feel you've taken your company as far as you want it to go, or as far as you want to go with it, and it is time to sell. Trying to decide on the best price to put on your business will be a combination of company assets, the state of your industry and the current economic climate. The four most common ways to leave your business are: transfer ownership to a family member; sell your interest to a co-worker, key employee or all employees; sell to a third party, such as a competitor or someone interested in entering your field; and liquidate by selling off your assets, usually at "fire sale" prices.

❑ ***Transfer ownership to a family member:*** The down side to this method is that it simply might not be an option, it could increase family tension, and it might stir resentment from the non-family members in your business. The benefits include being able to exercise more control, particularly in terms of setting a monetary value on the business and the repayment schedule.

❑ ***Sell to a co-worker, key employee or all employees:*** The down side is that you will not have control of the quality of services provided once you are gone. Yet this method significantly reduces your risks and you can increase the likelihood of retaining the same quality and degree of success if you have a staff person buy into your business while you are still active. In effect you are pre-qualifying your buyer through on-the-job training and observation. You can even establish a fund within the operation of the business to go toward the eventual purchase price.

❑ ***Sell to a third party:*** Selling to a third party (e.g., a competitor or someone interested in entering your field) is the preferred method when the business is too valuable to be purchased by anyone other than someone with access to a lot of capital. This is most likely to be your best avenue if you have a sole-proprietorship.

The down side is that the buying party inherently has more bargaining power (compared to other options), you can't be certain if the buyer's style and abilities will fit well with your current clientele and staff, and you will be required to carry some (or even most) of the purchase price – which means you will still be involved in the business for one to three years. The benefits are that you will most likely get a good price and if you have any staff at all, you will be giving them the opportunity for continued employment.

❑ ***Liquidation:*** Liquidation or simply closing down your practice should be the last resort – although sadly it's the most common method chosen by many failed businesses today.

❑ ***Business Valuation Guidelines***. Always consult with an attorney and accountant familiar with these matters. It is also advisable to hire a business broker or agent. A good agent will cost you nothing. He or she will more than make up the commission you pay by getting a higher price for your business and effecting a smooth and legal transaction. There are six common methods for pricing a business. Price Based On –

- Assets
- Capitalized Earnings
- Integrating assets and cash flow
- Duplication cost

- Carry back
- Net present value of future earnings

Price based on ***assets*** is done by determining the market value of the assets being sold and deducting the cost of liabilities to be assumed by the buyer. Assets include furniture, fixtures, equipment, supplies, inventory, client lists, accounts receivable, real estate (this isn't limited to owning property, it could include possessing a lease in a prime location) and existing contracts. This is a fairly straightforward method.

Most service businesses are mainly based on ***capitalized earnings***. To obtain this figure first calculate the adjusted cash flow and deduct a fair wage for the new owner. This is the base figure for the method. Next determine a fair return that a buyer should receive for investing in this business. Most buyers use a 15-20 percent figure for a low risk business and a 25 percent or higher for a risky business. Convert this percentage into a multiple by dividing it by 100. To get a selling price, multiply the base figure by the multiple. The formula would look like this: *Projected Earnings x Capitalization Rate = Price.*

If the business has both ***assets and cash flow***, the first step is to determine the value of the hard assets. Then calculate the adjusted cash flow. Add those two figures together. If, as the seller, you want a full cash sale, this number is your selling price. If the business is in excellent condition or your selling terms include payments over several years, the amount you can ask for is the hard assets plus up to twice the adjusted cash flow.

Pricing your business on the ***duplication cost*** is done by taking the market value of assets and combining it with the cost for the number of years it would take a beginning entrepreneur to reach the same profit level. It can be rather tricky to determine the latter figure, particularly if you didn't market and build your business on a consistent basis. Also, since the potential buyer is an unknown quantity, he may be excellent or abysmal at marketing. Try to avoid this approach.

Carry back is generally appropriate for small business. Calculate the adjusted cash flow of the business. Deduct the anticipated wages the buyer would need and the expenses required to run the business for one year. This figure gives you the cash available on which to set the sales amount. If you assume the loan to be a five-year payoff, simply multiply the cash available by five. You can add a reasonable down payment amount to this figure to get a total selling price.

The ***net present value*** method is wise to consider if you have built a very strong, diversified company which includes other subcontractors, corporate contracts, creative alliances or product sales. The technique involves the following steps: Adjust the company statements to show true present profit; develop your business plan and project the growth for the next five years; calculate the profit, investments and returns for the next five years; and then discount the figures to present using a discount rate which reflects the degree of risk as well as projected inflation. The major problems with this method are that the projections are purely speculative and the discount rate is totally arbitrary.

I recommend you get together with your accountant and a Small Business Development Center advisor and calculate your selling price using all the above methods and see what the results show you. Inherent in all of these methods is the problem that they don't take into account that many people will buy an existing business simply to ensure themselves of a "job." Also, your business may include intangible assets on which it's difficult to put a price tag. These include your credibility, reputation, goodwill and presence in the community.

Another idea to consider is incorporating a ***contingency clause***. As a result, you can ask for a higher price since you are minimizing the buyer's risk. Two techniques for contingent payment (after the down payment) are: the buyer makes the additional payments only if the business meets certain expectations (e.g., at least 50 percent of the clients stay), or the buyer only has to pay you a set percentage of the fees received from your current customers.

Selling a company can, of course, be bittersweet but it can also be a disaster. Note what recently happened to Festival Productions (the producer of the JVC Jazz Festival, the jazz and folk festivals in Newport, RI, and many others). In 2007 impresario George Wein sold Festival Productions to Festival Network, which continued to employ him as producer-emeritus. Things quickly soured, however, when the Festival Network began dropping the ball on a number of important benchmarks, leading to uncertainty whether the key festivals would even go on in 2009. Mr. Wein watched the babies he nurtured for almost 40 years face possible extinction, eventually stepping out of retirement (at 83!) in order to steady the sinking ship through a new company and creative sponsorships.

Buyers will test the desirability of purchasing your business. The first test in buying a small business is how the cost returns and effort required in running the practice measure against investing their money elsewhere. The biggest test is the "justification test". The buyer must be convinced that the business will be able to provide sufficient cash flow to repay the loan, support the business operational expenses, give a reasonable return on the down payment and allow for reasonable wages.

What a buyer can afford and what they are willing to pay will more often depend on the cash required than the selling price. The more favorable the terms of sale (such as no cash down, no security deposit, minimal interest, a lengthy repayment schedule or contingency terms) the easier it will be for you to find a buyer.

Finally, don't underestimate the psychological ramifications of letting go; many entrepreneurs slide into a deep depression after they sell their "babies." To soften the blow, write down all the things you never seemed to have time to do – and try to start luxuriating in your new-found freedom!

Commencement:
Continual Self Improvement and Company Strengthening

The truth must dazzle gradually or every man be blind. –Emily Dickenson

As we look to the future, the possibilities for entrepreneurs are indeed bright. Technological advances are bringing us greater power and mobility, giving us the freedom to reach customers and work with associates in all parts of the world. Major corporations, while continuing their downsizing, will turn to independent professionals to complete the work formerly done by employees. The rising number of virtual workers will lead to new partnerships and to exciting opportunities for individuals interested in working in these new relationships. Perhaps most important – the world desperately needs a good dose of creative solutions and entrepreneurs, as always, will lead the way.

Staying sharp and relevant is a chronic challenge for today's music entrepreneur, especially

those engaged with the world of music technology. "As various digital formats unfold, we'll continue to stay abreast of the technologies," says Randy Tobin of music media outfit Theta Media Group. "Music production is still basically the same as it was 30 years ago. The main difference is digits instead of tape. Having a good ear, knowing your art and craft, knowing what communicates and how to achieve emotional impact through audio, video, packaging and web sites, are the keys to being successful and helping clients achieve their visions."

Continual self-improvement is the antidote to the inevitable trials that come your way as a business owner. "Business can be very soulless or take on a spirit of it's own," acknowledges Jay Andreozzi, head of Amalgam Digital. "A company is an entity which you created and in which you have an obligation to fulfill. Corporate protocol and the systems required to run a successful business can sometimes take the enjoyment out of it. But I try to operate my business as an art. I look at business as an art form...I create, innovate, plan, and execute. The same way I design my company is the same way I write a verse or produce a piece of music. Get inspired, think about what I want to create/build and put the pieces in place and abstract on it from that point."

Maintaining that curious attitude is key in growing both as a person and as a professional. "Once a student, always a student," Canadian singer-songwriter Ember Swift adds. She goes on: "The changing market realities keep me entertained, on a business side...I'll always *do my art*, but I also hope to conduct my business in way that enables me to *do my art justice*."

May all music entrepreneurs find creative forms to hold their passions, manage it all towards success, and make a lasting difference in the world. Forward!

CHAPTER SUMMARY

ENRICHING & ENLARGING THE SCORE

- **SWOT Your Business**
  SWOT is a powerful technique for understanding your Strengths and Weaknesses, and for looking at the Opportunities and Threats you face. The essence of the SWOT Analysis is to discover what you do well, how you could improve, whether you are making the most of the opportunities around you, and whether there are any changes in your market - such as technological developments, mergers of businesses, or changes in suppliers - that may require corresponding changes in your company.

- **Growing Your Business Vertically & Horizontally**
  Business expansion usually follows a "vertical" path, meaning the business will try to sell more of its current product or service. It makes sense because the effort usually requires few major adjustments or risks. Horizontal expansion makes sense when your "vertical growth" has reached its limit, but you still want to expand. Even when more vertical growth is possible, a point of diminishing returns can be reached when further expenditures of time or money are not justified.

- **Blueprint for Horizontal Expansion**
  Before you launch your horizontal expansion, consider these guidelines:
  - ❑ Do first things first
  - ❑ Prepare a blueprint
  - ❑ Master the details.
  - ❑ Study competitors
  - ❑ Test market

- **Adding Value to Existing Products & Services**
  You add value when you develop a product or service and then add materials, processing or services to create a more valuable end product. You then sell the product in its value-enhanced form. How to Add Value to What You Offer:
  - ❑ Pick an existing product or service and think of an additional process, material or service that could be added to create a new product.
  - ❑ Identify a process or service which you could provide, then look for types of existing products or services which could be used as a base for your desired operation.

- Find an existing product which could be changed into a different or improved product by adding or subtracting one or more elements.
- Find a customer group which has needs that are not being met by existing products and services.
- Find a product which does not work well, or is not well-accepted by a customer group because of its inadequacies. Then improve it by adding or altering elements.

- **The Power of Linking Up: Discovering Creative Partnerships**

  Affinity partnerships, joint ventures and other types of creative alliances are keys to career and business success, and another method of business expansion. An affinity partnership is when two or more businesses come together to work on a project for a set period of time. Well-orchestrated joint ventures like these can further your chances of increasing sales and profits, save time and money, provide valuable referrals, and increase your market visibility.

- **Diversifying Your Activities & Revenue Streams**

  If you rely on only one main product or service, especially in this economy, you are like the investor who has just one stock. That stock may go up, but it also may go down. You need to diversify your business portfolio. Here's how:
  - Look for compatibility. Be sure that it complements what you are already doing.
  - Look at line extensions. The key to extending your line is to correctly assess what products or services you can add that complement and expand your current offerings.
  - Start with baby steps. Start small, test, see what works.

- **Going International: Exporting and Licensing**

  More and more media opportunities are being created in the foreign markets as well. For example, the more opportunities to expose an artist to the public, the greater potential there is for sales (and income). As technology grows, the world continues to move towards one global market. Gigging overseas presents exciting opportunities for North American bands and artists. Ideally, you want to have a licensing or distribution deal with a company that knows the scene and is plugged into the channels that will help the tour go smoothly. Of course, if you have an online presence, you are already international.

- **Exiting: Four Ways to Leave Your Business**

  The four most common ways to leave your business are: transfer ownership to a family member; sell your interest to a co-worker, key employee or all employees; sell to a third party, such as a competitor or someone interested in entering your field; and liquidate by selling off your assets, usually at "fire sale" prices. There are six common methods for pricing a business, price based on Assets, Capitalized Earnings, Integrating assets and cash flow, Duplication cost, Carry back, and Net present value of future earnings.

- **Continual Self Improvement and Company Strengthening**

  Technological advances are bringing us greater power and mobility, giving us the freedom to reach customers and work with associates in all parts of the world. Staying sharp and relevant is a chronic challenge for today's music entrepreneur, especially those engaged with the world of music technology. Continual self-improvement is the antidote to the inevitable trials that come your way as a business owner. Maintaining that curious attitude is key in growing both as a person and as a professional.

FURTHER RESOURCES

ONLINE RESOURCES

• General Resources for Doing Business Overseas

Cheap Tickets
www.cheaptickets.com
Want a bargain flight? Cheap Tickets sells airlines' empty seats at huge discounts. And it now offers discounts on hotel rooms, too.

ExecutivePlanet.com
Has detailed information about 45 countries. Learn about appropriate business attire, gift-giving, entertaining, public behavior, and negotiations.

GoogleMaps
google.com

International Business Forum
www.ibf.com
Here you'll find extensive information on opportunities in foreign markets.

LonelyPlanet.com
Provides maps, pictures, and essential facts for many countries around the world.

MapQuest
www.mapquest.com

Trade Information Center
http://export.gov/
This site form the U.S. Department of Commerce brims with links, tips, how-tos and details on federal help for exporters.

Worldtravelguide.com
Includes general and statistical information, business profiles and business etiquette, and detailed travel guidelines.

• Overseas Gigging

Passports. 3 Months before you leave make sure all band members have a current passport. If a band member needs to obtain or renew his/her passport application and renewal forms can be downloaded from the Internet at http://travel.state.gov/content/passports/en/passports/forms.html or mailed from your passport office.

Visas. Make sure you have passport size photos on file for all band members in case they need a visa. Visas are not required for Canada, Mexico, the Caribbean Islands and most Western European countries. For those European countries where visas are required you can contact the embassy of that country for a visa application form, and apply at least two months before the gig. The U.S> government publishes a pamphlet that is updated yearly entitled "Foreign Entry Requirements" which is available for .50 from the consumer information center department 363F, Pueblo, Colorado 81009. OR you can call 1-719 948-3334.

Eurail. Traveling by train in Europe is cost efficient and extremely comfortable. The Eurailpass is the least expensive way to travel by train in Europe. For information, contact Rail Europe, B mail at 2100 Central Avenue, Suite 200, Boulder, Colorado 80301, by phone @ 1-800-438-7245 or on the internet @ www.raileurope.com
http://www.raileurope.com

• Tour Directories

AustralAsian Music Industry Directory
industry.themusic.com.au

International Showcase, The Music Business Guide
www.showcase-music.com
Covering all of Great Britain, it also includes sections on Europe, South America, South Africa, Australia, and Japan. Listings include: record companies, music publishers, artist managers, producers, venues, promoters, booking agents, tour support services, recording studios, festival organizers, and much more. *Available in the U.S. through The Music Business Registry (musicregistry.com)*

The North American Folk Business Directory
Folk Alliance International
www.folk.org
Listing U.S. and foreign folk venues, folk press, radio stations, newsletters, publications, record companies, agents, managers, performers, publicists.

Musical America
musicalamerica.com
Listing of presenters and festivals for ethnic, folk, children's dance, Jazz, theater, classical, opera.

Music Directory of Canada
musicdirectoryofcanada.com
Listings of artists, agents, managers, labels, festivals, presenters, and other music related resources.

• Websites for
Touring and Career Assistance

Folkmusic.org
http://www.folkmusic.org
Folk music venues, shows, house concerts, business databases, folk radio list, and more.

Globetrade.com
http://www.globetrade.com
Helps entrepreneurs and small businesses expand internationally.

Gig Swap
http://www.gigswap.org/
Gig swapping has existed for decades and is constantly pursued on an informal basis throughout the United States and beyond. GigSwap.com was invented to streamline and support this empowering method of artist development.

Kompass
http://www.kompass.com
Supplies global business information on more than 2.2 million companies in 70 countries. Buyers can pinpoint suppliers and send them requests for quotes.

Gigmor
www.gigmor.com

BOOKS

The Art of Opportunity: How to Build Growth and Ventures Through Strategic Innovation and Visual Thinking by Marc Sniukas (2016, Wiley).

Mapping Experiences: A Complete Guide to Creating Value through Journeys, Blueprints, and Diagrams by James Kalbach (2016, O'Reilly Media).

The 7 Irrefutable Rules of Small Business Growth by Steven Little (2005, Wiley).

Multiple Streams of Internet Income by Robert Allen (2006, Wiley).

Six Disciplines for Excellence: Building Small Businesses That Learn, Lead & Last by Gary Harpst (2007, Synergy).

General Resources to Fuel Your Business

GENERAL

Online Reference & News Resources
American Information Directory
http://www.itypeusa.com/news/
Links to newspapers and media around the world.

BizJournals
http://bizjournals.com
A grand central of local business journals (weekly newspapers). Searchable.

Business Research Site
www.brint.com/interest.html
Links to almost everything your need business-wise. Scroll down and be amazed.

Information Please Almanac
www.infoplease.com
Simply amazing in its organization and detail.

OneLook Dictionaries
www.onelook.com
Some 75 dictionaries -from slang to physics and accounting- are online and searchable.

Reference Desk
www.refdesk.com
Provides everything from links to the major search engines, newspapers and magazines, government data, facts on every conceivable demographic or special interest, statistical resources, writing/style guides, people and business finders and hundreds of reference tools, to vast libraries of data. One click on "vital public records," for example, takes you to the largest directory of links to free public record databases on the Internet.

Wikipedia
www.wikipedia.org
A user-generated online encyclopedia.

PERSONALIZED NEWS

Personalized news services let you select a topic and then deliver a daily feed of relevant news stories to your desktop. They're free and easy to set up. Try them! Here are three:

News is Free
www.newsisfree.com
This is an excellent site that allows you to select news from a wide variety of newspapers from around the world.

News to You
www.newstoyou.com
This is a small Java-based program. It gives you the option to set a time relevancy for news items starting from 5 minutes to 24 hours ago. The program is still in development but it is worth exploring.

Crayon
www.crayon.net
Crayon.net is an interesting site and an excellent educational tool. Like other personalized news services, crayon.net lets you create your own newspaper. It provides two nice features: your own URL allowing you to share your newspaper with others, and the creation process takes you through the different sections of a newspaper.

GENERAL MUSIC INDUSTRY
News & Reference

All Music Guide
www.allmusic.com
The online "grand central" of all things musical

Arts Journal
www.artsjournal.com
Filters arts-related articles into an easy-to-use directory (classical & pop music mainly).

Billboard
www.billboard.com
Core industry news

CMJ New Music Report
www.cmj.com
College radio and alternative music tip sheet.

The Daily Chord
sxsw.com/music/daily_chord/

Hollywood Reporter
www.hollywoodreporter.com
Covers news regarding U.S. and international developments in the entertainment industry. Often prints special supplements on events or topics of special interest including periodic features on film and television music. The Tuesday edition features a list of film and television projects currently in production.

MusicDish
musicdish.com
Music-related news and other content categories. Indie music-oriented.

The Music Business Registry
www.musicregistry.com
Great informational resource for the music

entertainment industry.

Variety
www.variety.com

Wired & Wired News
www.wired.com
News from the tech corners of the entertainment world.

MUSIC BIZ BLOGS

Hypebot
hypebot.com

Mesa Sand
mesasand.com/

Music Biz Blogs
musicbizblogs.com/

Music Ally
musically.com

Music Career Juice
mcareerjuice.com

Music Think Tank
musicthinktank.com/

INDEX

ABOUT THE AUTHOR

Peter Spellman is an artist development specialist, helping musicians apply their entrepreneurial instincts to create success. He is Director of The Career Development Center at Berklee College of Music, and founder of Music Business Solutions, a training resource for music entrepreneurs. In addition, he teaches music career development at Berklee Online (berkleeonline.com).

Peter has over thirty years' experience as a performing and recording musician, and has worked as a booking agent, label director, music editor, artist manager, producer and writer.

His books include:

- *The Self-Promoting Musician: Strategies for Independent Music Success*, 3rd ed. (Berklee Press, 2013)
- *The Musician's Internet: Online Strategies for Success in the Music Industry* (Berklee Press, 2003)
- *Indie Power: A Business-Building Guide for Record Labels, Music Production Houses and Merchant Musicians*, 2nd ed. (2006)
- *Indie Marketing Power: The Resource Guide for Maximizing Your Music Marketing*, 3rd ed. (2006/2008/2011)
- *Your Successful CD Release: Market Planning for Singer-Songwriters* (with Dave Cool, 2007)
- *Plan Your Band!: Sample Band Business Plan and Investor Agreement All-in-One* (2008)

Most of the above books can be found at: mbsbooks.rock

Peter also performs and records as percussionist with improvisational ensemble, Underwater Airport.

You can find out more about Peter, his services, and his career-building books at **mcareerjuice.com**

NOTES

NOTES

CPSIA information can be obtained
at www.ICGtesting.com
Printed in the USA
LVHW060112031218
598984LV00001BA/13/P